English as a Lingua Franca

English as a Lingua Franca: Studies and Findings

Edited by

Anna Mauranen and Elina Ranta

CAMBRIDGE SCHOLARS

PUBLISHING

English as a Lingua Franca: Studies and Findings,
Edited by Anna Mauranen and Elina Ranta

This book first published 2009. The present binding first published 2010.

Cambridge Scholars Publishing

12 Back Chapman Street, Newcastle upon Tyne, NE6 2XX, UK

British Library Cataloguing in Publication Data
A catalogue record for this book is available from the British Library

ISBN (10): 1-4438-1726-0, ISBN (13): 978-1-4438-1726-4

TABLE OF CONTENTS

Part III: Features of ELF in Interactive Discourse

INTRODUCTION

ANNA MAURANEN

English has established its position as the global *lingua franca* beyond any doubt; along with this status, it has become one of the symbols of our time, together with globalisation, networking, economic integration, and the Internet. Like other *zeitgeist* symbols, it has been subject to much debate and has raised many fears. English has been seen as a threat to local languages and cultures, or alternatively, its global uses have been seen as a threat to Standard English. Such negative attitudes, even hostility, towards English are nevertheless comparatively recent and intertwined with the current wave of globalisation, more complete than anything hitherto experienced and more closely associated with just one language. At the same time, English has been welcomed as a vehicle of efficiency in for example business and science, or as a new means of communication for globally emergent localities in a variety of non-mainstream subcultures.

The spread of English from the British Isles has taken place over a long period, starting from the early 17th century, and it has taken different forms in different parts of the world. In some cases new native varieties developed, like those spoken in North America and Australia; they now enjoy the prestige of 'core varieties' or 'inner circle varieties' along with British English. In other cases, again, English was adopted as a second language in mainly Africa and Asia, and the resulting varieties are often spoken of as 'outer circle' varieties, 'New Englishes' or 'World Englishes'. The latter have not gained equal prestige to the 'core' varieties, but there has been fairly extensive descriptive research carried out on their specific as well as shared features. Kachru's work since the 1980s (e.g. Kachru 1982, 1985) has raised awareness of the issues relating to World Englishes, and important research has been done towards the description of these varieties, notably for instance brought together in Platt, Weber and Ho (1984) and Kortmann and Schneider (2004).

In contrast to the native and the established second language varieties, the use of English as a lingua franca (ELF) has been hotly debated but relatively little studied. English as a language of communication between speakers for whom it is an additional language is assuming an increasingly vital role outside countries where English has an official status. The consequences of this to the development of English and our understanding of the language are surely worth attention in English Studies. A good deal of the debate around ELF has been carried out in Applied Linguistics and English Language Teaching. Important eye-openers have been contributions by people like Widdowson (e.g. 1994), Seidlhofer (e.g. 2001), and Jenkins (e.g. 2000, 2007), who have pointed out that the use of English as a lingua franca has become the fastest-growing and at the same time the least recognised function of English in the world. Research into English as a lingua franca has been slower to take off, despite pioneering work by a handful of scholars, such as Firth (1996), House (2002), Knapp (1987), Meierkord (1998), as well as Seidlhofer and Jenkins with their research groups. The ELFA project started in the early years of this decade (see e.g. Mauranen 2003, 2005, 2006; Mauranen and Ranta 2008), but it is only very recently that substantial research interest has been expended on ELF. The sea change in the research community has nevertheless been fast, and currently ELF is a vibrant field of study. A sign of the scale and determination of researchers in the field is that two million-word corpora of spoken ELF have recently been completed: in Helsinki the ELFA corpus of academic ELF in 2008 (www.eng.helsinki.fi/elfa) and in Vienna the VOICE corpus in 2009 (www.univie.ac.at/voice). These large databases allow the study of ELF on a new scale, along the lines of ENL varieties (cf. COBUILD, BNC), native and Outer Circle Englishes (cf. ICE) and learner English (cf. ICLE). The mere existence of the ELF corpora ushers in a new era in ELF research. The size of the corpora equals that of the first, pioneering ENL corpora from the 1960s (Brown and LOB, both one million words of written English), and they are in fact twice as large as the much-studied London-Lund Corpus of Spoken English.

Shortly before the completion of the first ELF corpora, the first international conference of English as a Lingua Franca was held at the University of Helsinki (see www.eng.helsinki.fi/elfa/elfforum08.htm). The conference clearly met a demand that was already there: it was attended well beyond initial, rather hazy expectations, by about 150 participants from all over the world. The conference papers spanned theoretical analyses, empirical studies, pedagogical questions and ideological issues around ELF, and delved into local and regional situations of using ELF in different institutional and educational settings in a variety of countries.

The present volume grew out of the presentations at that conference. However, although the conference welcomed ELF-related papers of a wide variety, this book represents a clearly focused selection: the emphasis here is on empirical research into ELF. The volume does not address pedagogical issues or the ideological controversies surrounding ELF and the teaching of English. We felt very strongly as editors that it would be important to provide a forum for presenting ongoing and recent studies on English as a lingua franca, since the current surge of research activity is expanding our understanding of ELF in use—its processes, practices, and linguistic features. At the same time, this new and incipient research gives rise to new questions, and inspires further explorations into the complex phenomenon of ELF. English is the lingua franca of an enormous variety of social and cultural contexts, of which only a fraction has been investigated. Looking into new contexts calls for new ways of seeing context and situated language use. Contexts of ELF use typically involve different social formations from the speech communities of traditional analyses, and therefore norms, identities, and practices get negotiated on new grounds as well. We need new conceptual and methodological tools for making sense of these often transient, frequently multilingual and always complex social and linguistic configurations that typify ELF-using situations.

The book opens with five papers that address fundamental issues in ELF: attitudes, approaches, conceptualisation, universality and comprehensibility. In the first paper, **Jennifer Jenkins** gives a brief overview of the phonological features that contribute to intelligibility in ELF communication (in "(Un)pleasant? (In)correct? (Un)intelligible? ELF Speakers' Perceptions of Their Accents"), and goes on to illuminate the conflicting, changing, and often self-contradictory attitudes that particularly teachers of EFL hold of ELF accents. **Barbara Seidlhofer** ("Orientations in ELF Research: Form and Function") contrasts two research approaches to ELF, one that focuses entirely on formal features uncovered in a corpus, and another that takes a functional view of language in use. The situationality involved in the latter type is able to open new kinds of explanatory insights compared to the more traditional categories of the former. **Martin Dewey** continues the discussion of methodological approaches in "English as a Lingua Franca: Heightened Variability and Theoretical Implications". He looks into the conceptualisation of ELF, calling for a new approach to ELF with creative dynamism, locality and performativity as key concepts. **Elina Ranta**'s paper "Syntactic Features in Spoken ELF—Learner Language or Spoken Grammar?" turns the attention to ELF as language, addressing objections to ELF as a valid object of research in its own right, often raised on the basis that it is merely learner language. She then goes on to show that ELF manifests many syntactic features that are parallel to other non-standard varieties of English, whether native or not. This, in turn raises the question of universal features in ELF. In the final article in this section, **Jagdish Kaur** ("Pre-Empting Problems of Understanding in English as a Lingua Franca") explores comprehensibility in ELF communication, focusing on participants' use of repetition and paraphrase in interaction. Her findings support earlier observations that communication breakdowns do not occur with notable frequency in ELF discourse, largely because speakers resort to pre-emptive strategies to ensure mutual comprehensibility.

The second section of the book focuses on ELF interaction in institutional settings, particularly in business and education. Both are important sites of global ELF use and consequently also where a substantial proportion of the research hitherto has been carried out. **Susanne Ehrenreich** sets the scene by looking into a business community from an 'emic' perspective (in "English as a Lingua Franca in Multinational Corporations—Exploring Business Communities of Practice"), and reflecting upon her discoveries, explores the concept of Community of Practice. As many other ELF researchers, she finds the concept highly relevant for the analysis of ELF speaking business communities, and she calls for further development of the concept in the context of ethnographic studies of ELF communities. **Patricia Pullin Stark**'s paper continues in the business world, and looks into the use of humour in ELF from the perspective of power balance in the context of business meetings (in "No Joke—This is Serious! Power, Solidarity and Humour in Business English as a Lingua Franca (BELF)"). She sees humour as an interactional achievement among ELF speakers, who make use of its many roles, above all for establishing common ground. Like business, higher education has been a major domain of using ELF in multilingual settings. **Philip Shaw**, **Tim Caudery** and **Margrethe Petersen** investigate exchange students in Denmark and Sweden (in "Students on Exchange in Scandinavia: Motivation, Interaction, ELF Development"), gauging their expectations and experiences in using English as well as the local languages and the development of their English. Students adapted quickly to each others' English, improved their fluency, but did not necessarily shift to a predominantly endonormative perception of ELF. **Ute Smit**'s article "Emic Evaluations and Interactive Processes in a Classroom Community of Practice" reports on her study, combining an etic perspective with an emic one, of an international hotel management programme in Austria. The longitudinal perspective, rarely employed in ELF studies, enables change to be shown, for instance in decreasing discussion of (un)intelligibility. The findings also show a growing preference for direct and explicit illocutionary acts. With **Beyza Björkman**'s paper "From

Code to Discourse in Spoken ELF" the focus moves back to a Scandinavian university environment. She looks at several non-standard features of spoken ELF among engineering students and lecturers, observing that although they do not cause communication breakdown, they nevertheless give rise to some irritation. Important pragmatic strategies seem to be those relating to clarification.

Part Three of the volume looks into different facets of ELF as it is successfully used in interactive dialogues. Each paper is based on a sample of authentic transcribed recordings of ELF speech. **Alessia Cogo** (in "Accommodating Difference in ELF Conversations: A Study of Pragmatic Strategies") first discusses some of her extensive work on accommodation as a key to successful accomplishment of ELF communication. Her subjects are language teachers engaging in small talk. The focus is on repetition and code-switching, both of which are found to manifest creativity and play important roles in communicative success. **Julia Hüttner**'s paper "Fluent Speakers—Fluent Interactions: On the Creation of (Co)-Fluency in English as a Lingua Franca" continues the theme of communication as a co-constructed achievement. Hüttner assumes a strongly dialogic perspective on fluency, arguing that a reconceptualisation of fluency is warranted by studying ELF interaction closely, and that in this area much research is needed which combines emic and etic perspectives. **Marie-Luise Pitzl** approaches the tricky relations of idiomaticity and metaphor in her paper "'We should not wake up any dogs': Idiom and Metaphor in ELF", arguing that the "re-metaphorisation" of sleeping idioms, likely to be accessible to ELF users, and indeed manifest in some VOICE corpus examples, is an important resource for communicative success in ELF. Irrespective of formal dissimilarities to ENL idioms, metaphors fulfil several important functions. **Cornelia Hülmbauer** explores the relationships of correct form and communicative effectiveness (in "We don't take the right way. We just take the way that we think you will understand"—The Shifting Relationship between Correctness and Effectiveness in ELF"), arguing that if effective, successful communication is the goal, 'incorrectness' may not just be something that can be overlooked, but actually an integral part of the success. Lexicogrammatically 'erroneous' forms may work better for both production and comprehension. In the final article, **Theresa Klimpfinger** addresses a phenomenon that has been touched upon in some of the other papers as well, namely the role of code-switching as an ELF strategy (in "She's mixing the two languages together"—Forms and Functions of Code-Switching in English as a Lingua Franca"). As in other contexts, code-switching in ELF serves many interactionally relevant purposes.

With several examples, she shows how code-switching serves to construct identity, fluency and communicative success, and specifically, brings speakers' plurilngual resources to play. Since ELF is typically used in situations where many language backgrounds come together, code-switching is a particularly appropriate resource to be drawn on.

Some of the papers in this book have been written by native speakers of English, others not, but all have been written by expert users of English. No policy of having the L2 authors' texts checked by native speakers for linguistic correctness has been applied, because this was regarded as an irrelevant practice in a book presenting international English scholarship. Whether English has been the first or an additional language to the writers, they have been addressing an international audience, not primarily ENL communities. Their contributions thus reflect the kind of language use they discuss: effective English as an international lingua franca.

Bibliography

ELFA. A corpus of English as a Lingua Franca in Academic Settings. http://www.eng.helsinki.fi/elfa/elfacorpus.htm

Firth, A. 1996. "The Discursive Accomplishment of Normality: On 'Lingua Franca' English and Conversation Analysis." *Journal of Pragmatics* 26 (2), 237-59.

House, J. 2002. "Developing Pragmatic Competence in English as a Lingua Franca." In *Lingua Franca Communication*, ed. K. Knapp & C. Meierkord, 245-67. Frankfurt: Peter Lang.

Jenkins, J. 2007. *English as a Lingua Franca: Attitude and Identity*. Oxford: Oxford University Press.

—. 2000. *The Phonology of English as an International Language*. Oxford: Oxford University Press.

Kachru, B. B. 1985. "Standards, Codification and Sociolinguistic Realism: The English Language in the Outer Circle." In *English in the World. Teaching and Learning the Languages and Literatures*, ed. R. Quirk & H. G. Widdowson, 11-30. Cambridge: Cambridge University Press.

—. 1982, ed. *The Other Tongue. English Across Cultures*. Urbana: University of Illinois Press.

Knapp, K. 1987. "English as an International Lingua Franca and the Teaching of Intercultural Communication." In *Perspectives on Language in Performance*, ed. W. Lörsche & R. Schulze, 1022-39. Tübingen: Narr.

Kortmann, B. and E. W. Schneider, eds. 2004. *A Handbook of Varieties of English*. Berlin: Mouton de Gruyter.

Mauranen, A. 2006. "A Rich Domain of ELF: The ELFA Corpus of Academic Discourse." *Nordic Journal of English Studies* 5 (2), 145-59.

—. 2005. "English as Lingua Franca: An Unknown Language?" In *Identity, Community, Discourse. English in Intercultural Settings*, ed. G. Cortese & A. Duszak, 269-93. Bern: Peter Lang.

—. 2003. "The Corpus of English as Lingua Franca in Academic Settings." *TESOL Quarterly* 37 (3), 513-27.

Mauranen, A. and E. Ranta 2008. "English as an Academic Lingua Franca—The ELFA Project." *Nordic Journal of English Studies* 7 (3), 199-202.

Meierkord, C. 1998. "Lingua Franca English: Characteristics of Successful Non-Native—Non-Native Speaker Discourse." *Erfurt Electronic Studies in English* 1998. http://webdoc.sub.gwdg.de/edoc/ia/eese/eese.html.

Platt, J., H. Weber and L. Ho 1984. *The New Englishes*. London: Routledge and Kegan Paul.

Seidlhofer, B. 2001. "Closing a Conceptual Gap: The Case for a Description of English as a Lingua Franca." *International Journal of Applied Linguistics* 11 (2), 133-58.

VOICE. Vienna-Oxford International Corpus of English. http://www.univie.ac.at/voice.

Widdowson, H. 1994. "The Ownership of English." *TESOL Quarterly* 28 (2), 377-89.

PART I:

BASIC ISSUES OF ELF

(UN)PLEASANT? (IN)CORRECT? (UN)INTELLIGIBLE? ELF SPEAKERS' PERCEPTIONS OF THEIR ACCENTS

JENNIFER JENKINS

1. Background

Anyone working in the field of English as a Lingua Franca (henceforth ELF) has to face sooner rather than later a serious contradiction: that despite the widespread acceptance of the extensive role of English as an international lingua franca and its increasing number of functions in this respect, there is still an almost equally widespread resistance to this lingua franca's forms. Given the well-established sociolinguistic fact that languages are shaped by their users, and that nowadays "native speakers are in a minority for [English] language use" (Brumfit 2001, 116), it would make sense for English language teaching to move away from its almost exclusive focus on native varieties of English. This suggestion always meets, however, with strong resistance from many quarters, and this is particularly so in the case of accent. The result is that two particular native speaker English accents, Received Pronunciation (RP) and General American (GA), continue to command special status around the English-speaking world including international/lingua franca communication contexts where sociolinguistic common sense indicates that they are inappropriate and irrelevant.

In the case of RP, the continued promotion of native speaker (NS) English accents has become even more untenable over the past few decades, during which the use of this already minority British accent, has declined even further, especially among younger British people. As Trudgill points out:

> This raises the interesting question: if RP is so very much a minority accent, why do we spend so much effort teaching it to non-native speakers, especially since, as David Abercrombie (1956) pointed out, it would make

> much more sense on purely phonetic grounds to teach, for example, Scottish pronunciation? (Trudgill 2002, 172)

In addition, as Macaulay argues, there are other reasons why RP does not make good sense as the target accent for non-native learners of English:

> Since RP is not necessarily the easiest or most appropriate accent of British English for foreigners to learn, the choice of RP as a model is difficult to justify. It would be better for everyone if linguists, phoneticians, and teachers overcame their fascination with the accent of an élite minority and concerned themselves more with the speech of the majority of the population. (Macaulay 1988, 115)

Yet the "fascination" with RP continues to this day, and the accent continues to be aspired to even in ELF contexts, where much of the communication does not involve NSs of English at all. Materials for learners of English especially in Europe, but also in parts of Asia and Latin America, still promote RP as being superior. In fact it is often the *only* accent presented as a model for production, even if other NS accents and occasionally NNS accents may be presented for receptive training purposes. And because of this, and because of the spurious links still often made in the English language teaching literature between RP, original/authentic English, and the ownership of English, it seems that RP has a place that it does not merit in the psyche of English speakers, both native and non-native, regardless of whether they have an RP accent themselves, or even wish to have one.

The situation is further exacerbated by sociolinguists, who might be expected to treat non-native English accents with the same objectivity and respect that they treat non-standard native English accents, but do not necessarily do so. For example, in a slightly later article on English accents than that quoted above, Trudgill argues forcefully for RP and against ELF accents, justifying his position as follows:

> ...it seems to me that even if native speakers do not 'own' English, there is an important sense in which it stems from them, especially historically, and resides in them. (Trudgill 2005, 87)

And because many NNS learners and teachers of English link British English with RP, this is exactly the sort of claim that convinces them that RP is somehow superior and non-native English accents inferior. Indeed, this argument, that NS English is 'real', 'authentic', and 'original' English was mentioned time and again by the participants in my recent interview study (see Jenkins 2007 and below) when they explained why they felt RP should be their personal goal, even if they were not necessarily happy about this. And the argument in turn convinces many NNSs that NS English with an RP accent is essential even when English is used as an international lingua franca and no NS of English is present in the interaction. For example in an article promoting RP, Scheuer, a Polish phonetician, echoes Trudgill in arguing that:

> ...native speakers [of English] will always remain, if not the owners of the language itself, at least the keepers of the key to what is irritating and what is acceptable in interactional exchanges all round the globe, whether they actively participate in them or not. (Scheuer 2005, 127-128)

The problem goes beyond RP, however, and beyond the issue of inappropriateness: intelligibility is also implicated. For both RP and GA, the two most widely taught English accents, have been found empirically to be less intelligible to NNSs than other NNS accents (see e.g. Smith 1992). Because of this, I carried out a large-scale empirical research project with the aim of identifying which features of RP/GA were necessary for intelligibility in ELF communication, and which were unnecessary or even damaging to intelligibility (see Jenkins 2000). The data was drawn from NNSs of English with a large number of first languages interacting with each other in a wide range of contexts, both educational and social, and was analysed to identify which intelligibility problems could be traced directly back to pronunciation. The items that emerged as necessary for intelligibility I labelled the Lingua Franca Core (although the term has unfortunately been frequently misinterpreted to refer to *all* linguistic levels of ELF). The following is a summary of the main features of the Lingua Franca Core (LFC):

1. Consonant sounds except voiced/voiceless *th* and dark *l*
2. Vowel length contrasts (e.g. the difference between the vowels in 'pitch' and 'p**ea**ch')
3. Restrictions on consonant deletion (in particular, not omitting sounds at the beginning and in the middle of words)
4. Nuclear (or tonic) stress production/placement

In addition to these core features, accommodation also emerged from the research as crucial to ELF pronunciation. One of several misinterpretations of the LFC is that its advocates are claiming that these core features are always necessary in ELF communication, regardless of who is speaking with whom. However, when interlocutors share alternative variants for core features (e.g. they might prefer to use /v/ rather than /w/) then there would be no advantage, intelligibility-wise, for each of them to replace their mutually preferred use simply because /w/ would be correct in NS English pronunciation. On the other hand, it would be important for them to have /w/ in their phonetic repertoires so that it was available for use with ELF interlocutors for whom /v/ might cause intelligibility problems.

The other typical features of NS English pronunciation were shown in the research to be unnecessary for pronunciation intelligibility in ELF (as opposed to NNS–NS) communication. The non-core features can be summarised as follows:

- Vowel quality except for the vowel sound in RP 'fur'
- Consonants in (NS English) clusters separated by the addition of vowels (e.g. Japanese English 'product' as *peroducuto*), as well as vowels added to consonants at the ends of words (e.g. Korean English 'luggage' as *luggagi*)
- Features of connected speech such as elision, assimilation, weak forms
- Consonant sounds *th* (e.g. German English 'think' as *sink*), and dark *l* (e.g. in French English, the 'l' in 'hotel' pronounced by raising the tip rather than the back of the tongue)
- Word stress placement
- Pitch direction

I went on to argue that in these non-core areas, speakers engaging in ELF communication should be free to pronounce English with their own first language regional accent influence instead of the NS way, without being seen as making pronunciation errors. Another way of thinking about these non-core areas, and especially items such as 'th' is in terms of NS shibboleths. As Barbara Seidlhofer points out about ELF in general:

> A very clear tendency emerging from empirical ELF work is that successful ELF communicators avoid, consciously or unconsciously, precisely those native-speaker 'shibboleths' that indicate membership of a very specific, confined native-speaker community, and of which some accomplished *EFL* learners exhibit impressive mastery. (Seidlhofer 2005, 71)

2. Responses to ELF and the LFC

While the notion of ELF in general and the LFC in particular were welcomed in some quarters, in the main they were seen at best as controversial, and more often than not they provoked considerable hostility. One reason for this appears to be that neither ELF nor the LFC have been well understood. These are the most prominent misinterpretations of the LFC with, in each case, the correction in parentheses:

- The LFC is a model for imitation. (This is not so. The 'model', in so far as we can still speak of a model, is the bilingual teacher who has the core and local features in his/her repertoire; but as accommodation plays such a critical role in ELF, it is not viable to present learners with a single all-purpose model—they need to develop their accommodation skills as well.)
- The LFC is a single accent variety. (Again this is not so. There are as many ELF accent varieties as there are second language groups of English speakers.)
- The LFC promotes errors. (This misinterpretation results from an inability to separate ELF from EFL, where pronunciation errors are determined entirely by comparison with NS accent norms.)
- The intention is to prescribe ELF/the LFC for all learners. (Once again this is not so. ELF researchers believe that learners should be free to choose which kind of English they want. It is supporters of the *EFL* status quo who believe in prescription, and prescribe NS English with RP or GA accents for learners. Unlike these traditionalists, ELF researchers argue that learners should be made aware of the sociolinguistic facts relating to the spread of English, which will enable them to make informed choices about which kinds of English they want to aim for.)
- The aim of the LFC was to make learning easier. (This is completely wrong: the LFC was based on intelligibility. The fact that for many learners it lessens the number of pronunciation features to be learnt is a fortuitous side effect, but this was never its guiding principle.)
- The LFC is an artificial language rather than the result of empirical research. For example, citing a study by Bryła (2006), Siek-Piskozub, Wach and Raulinajtys (2008, 71) say the following:

> 70 non-native speakers of English expressed their opinion on the importance of native-like pronunciation and accent preferences [...]

> Their responses questioned the very idea of creating an artificial accent and under mining (*sic)* the position of native speakers in international communication. (Siek-Piskozub, Wach & Raulinajtys 2008, 71)

These 3 Polish authors also seem to imply that the LFC intentionally set out to undermine the position of NSs in international communication. This may ultimately be an outcome for NSs who continue (as many do) communicating internationally exactly as if they're talking to each other in London and Los Angeles, but it was not an aim.

But it was not simply a question of misinterpretation. Responses to the LFC (and to ELF in general) from both NNSs and NSs often seemed to involve strong attitudes towards NNS English. And it was not at all clear to me whether the negative attitudes were themselves the result or cause of the misinterpretations. In particular, the kinds of language being used by people who responded negatively implied the existence of deep-seated attitudes towards issues such as 'good' and 'bad' English, and especially English accents, a belief that NNS English accents are innately inferior, and a conviction—whether conscious or not—that in some sense, NSs of English had special rights over the language, even when it was being used in international contexts, simply because they spoke it first.

3. Exploring ELF Accent Attitudes

It seemed to me that it was essential to find out more about these accent attitudes and beliefs, and I therefore embarked on a second project in which I explored English teachers' responses to my work on ELF phonology. The new project involved three main studies:

1. An analysis of written texts (articles published in academic journals) and spoken discussions (at MA seminars and conference workshops) about ELF (see Jenkins 2007 Chapter 5 for full details)
2. A questionnaire drawing on folk linguistics research methods and administered to (predominantly NNS) English teachers
3. Semi-structured interviews with non-native English teachers

In the remainder of this section of the paper, I provide some examples from each of these three parts of the research.

3.1. Analysis of Written Texts and Spoken Discussions

3.1.1. Written Texts

In the written texts I looked at both the overtly stated arguments and the ways in which they were expressed, including their use of metaphor, repetition, lexical choices and the like. The following extract is typical of one of the texts:

> Giving up on this *high* objective [i.e. RP]—and the LFC *boils down* to this exactly—will easily bring the ideal *down into the gutter* with no checkpoint along the way. (Sobkowiak 2005, 141; emphasis added)

Earlier in his article (p.136), Sobkowiak had said in reference to an article by Henry Widdowson (1994) from which he had quoted: "Most readers will probably agree that this text is highly emotional, even hysterical". His reason for this was Widdowson's argument that how English develops internationally is no business of its NSs. And yet Sobkowiak's use of language shows that it is he who is "highly emotional" in his concern about threat to RP from ELF and the LFC. His article abounds with this kind of metaphorical and emotive language: "boil down", "down into the gutter", and so on. Meanwhile, his metaphors are sometimes used in contradictory ways suggesting a conflict between his hopes and fears.

For example, he claims at one point that proposals such as the LFC are always "still born", but a couple of pages later warns that the LFC is dangerous because proposals of this kind "spread like wild fire". A writer of another of the texts that I analysed argues that we need to "protect" the English language, and a third that ELF "sets the bar too low". And intriguingly, all the authors quote and heavily criticise *exactly* the same well-known passage from Widdowson (op.cit.) about how English develops internationally being no business of NSs of English. Given the fact that the writers come from very different linguacultural backgrounds, this suggests that the belief that NSs 'own' English may be a lot more widespread than is generally appreciated.

What emerged from my analysis of the written texts was, on the one hand, their authors' inability to think of ELF and the LFC outside of a framework of language errors and deficiency, and on the other hand, their fears that ELF and the LFC might actually succeed.

In other words, they seemed unable to conceive of English norms for international use being led by its NNSs because, in their view, when

NNSs' English differs from NS English, no matter what the context of use, it is simply *wrong*. By contrast, there is no attempt at any point to think about the language contact situations within which ELF's linguistic processes are taking place and from which ELF features are emerging.

3.1.2. MA Seminar Discussions

The same kinds of attachment to NS English norms occurred in the spoken data. For example at two MA seminars where the LFC was presented, the following were some of the reactions:

- "All English will *fragment* so that nobody understands each other" (NNS)
- Or, by contrast, "We'll all become *the same*" (NS)
- "Learners will *sound odd* if they don't use weak forms" (NS) in which the commentator appears to equate 'odd' simply with being 'unlike native speakers'.

However, there were occasional acknowledgements by some of the NNS participants of the links between accent and identity, and some of their comments foreshadowed what many of the interview participants were to say later. For example:

> It [the NNS accent]'s part of a person's identity—why should you try to *strip them* of that? You don't necessarily want to *strip them* of their accent. A person doesn't necessarily want you to *strip them* of their accent. (NNS)

Again, the strength of feeling is indicated by the choice of metaphorical language and emphasised by the repetition—which is almost poetic in a 'Deborah Tannen' kind of way.

On the other hand the following was sent to the lecturer by email the day after the first seminar:

> I feel I can't get my head round some of the issues you raised i.e. the *watering down* of the pronunciation system as it exists *to suit NNS* communicating with other NNS. I'm a *purist*. (NS)

This person clearly associates good pronunciation with NS pronunciation ("pure"), and NNS pronunciation with being "watered down" (and note how often the word 'down' and its synonyms occur with reference to the LFC/NNS pronunciation). There is also a suggestion in her use of the words "to suit NNSs", that she feels the LFC is wrong because NSs should take priority. This is similar to the point made by the authors I quoted earlier, who argue against any undermining of the position of NSs, and also to the point made by the writers above who are so critical of Widdowson's point about NSs of English.

And this is an email that was sent to the lecturer the day after the second seminar (the phonetics are the student's own):

> Some classmates said after knowing the idea, they felt a kind of relief and they won't correct their students' pronunciation any more. But I feel we should correct them at the beginning to let them know what the standard should be (either RP or GA). When my boyfriend asked me out at first, he's Korean, I'm Chinese, he said 'would you like /kopi/?' I was just struggling to try to understand what he meant, but I didn't make it. Now I understand everything he says. 'Let's go to see a /pilm/' or 'I'll meet you in /trapalgar Square/'.

Although this student finds the notion of the LFC a 'relief', there is once again an assumption that the standard is nevertheless NS English, and that non-native departures from this are fundamentally mistakes in need of correction. The student also completely misses the significance of her own point about familiarity and receptive accommodation, both of which are important elements in the LFC proposal.

3.1.3. Conference Workshops

The outcome was broadly similar in the conference workshops. In this first example, drawn from a seminar on ELF pronunciation, the speaker clearly distinguishes between a NS "ideal" accent for the stronger students and what he calls "the English as an international language kind" for the weaker ones (the capital letters indicate an extra level stress):

> I was just going to say I think there's probably two kinds of students. Erm one—er the kind of student who finds pronunciation very easy and natural and would sooner embrace erm the native speaker iDEAL, and another kind of student who has much more, much more problems understanding natives who would, who would much prefer to embrace er the English as an international language kind. (NS)

On the other hand, there were once again occasional examples of speakers realising that the LFC approach has benefits for them in terms of projecting their own identities:

> At last I've found some justification for my OWN exISTence. Well er it used to be that er a non-native teacher cannot really teach pronunciation and be a model, at least er if teaching non-native speakers means playing the tape as the right model. So it appears that if my Japanese students have a touch of Russian accent in their English, it won't do them too much harm on the whole. (NNS)

But it was 'business as usual' at another conference discussion, this time on ELF in general. One participant made a clear connection between NS English and 'real' English:

> ...is this possibility of this developing where the speakers of ENGlish as a lingua franca beLIEVE they are speaking the REAL English? (NS)

In other words, no matter how many ELF speakers there are, they do not speak 'real' English because 'real', by definition, means NS English regardless of how few people speak it.

Another participant argued that ELF is in fact the same as 'caretaker' speech—the kind of speech parents use to young children and language teachers to low level learners:

> ...no English teacher in the history of English language teaching has ever been anything but an ELFer, I mean obviously ALL teachers of language caretake ... and of course one NEVer speaks to one's students in the way that one speaks to one's mates down the PUB, I mean one is ELFing all the time, so teachers are skilled practitioners of lingua franca, at least the student exchanges they're using well correct models but they're ELFing if you like. (NS)

The final example is drawn from data collected at a workshop given in a British university. One of the participants argued that it was important for NNSs not to say 's' instead of 'th', because if they said, for instance, "I'm sinking", he, the lecturer, would assume they meant that they were drowning, not that they were thinking. This is reminiscent of an example Milroy and Milroy (1999) quote from the Oprah Winfrey Show, a TV chat show in US. An audience member complained about Black English, arguing that when Black people say "aks" instead of "ask", she does not understand what they mean. Obviously, in both cases the commentators *do* understand, otherwise they would not have been able to articulate the point in the first place. In other words, it seems that this is largely an attitudes issue rather than a linguistic one, and the result of the stigmatising of the ways of speaking (and particularly the pronunciation/accents) of certain English-speaking groups.

The spoken discussions and written texts revealed a number of common features:

1. how difficult most of these teachers of English find the concept of ELF in general and ELF accents (especially the notion of core/non-core) in particular;
2. how closely and instinctively they identify with a NS English norm, regardless of whether they themselves are NSs or NNSs;
3. how reluctant they are to disassociate notions of English correctness from English nativeness;
4. an inability to assess intelligibility and acceptability from anything but a NS standpoint;
5. how they intuitively regard NS English as being more widely understood regardless of its context of use.

3.2. The Questionnaire

Moving on to the questionnaire, this had four parts: accent ranking, accent rating, map labelling and a comment section. Responses were elicited from approximately 360 English teachers, mainly NNSs of English from 12 Expanding Circle countries.

3.2.1. Ranking of English Accents

In the ranking task, respondents were asked to select from all English accents around the world, including their own group's, the five they thought were the best, and rank them first best, second best and so on to fifth best. A few respondents queried the notion of 'best' accent, but most of these carried out the task regardless of any such reservations.

Taking the rankings in order, the respondents overwhelmingly placed NS English accents as 'best'. In the case of first best (see Figure 1), almost 170 named UK accents (by which they usually meant RP), and 100 chose US accents (by which they usually meant GA). Tiny numbers named others, but these were still NS accents in the main: Australian, Canadian, and Irish English. Interestingly, one Japanese respondent named Japanese, perhaps as an 'act of resistance' in Canagarajah's (1999) sense.

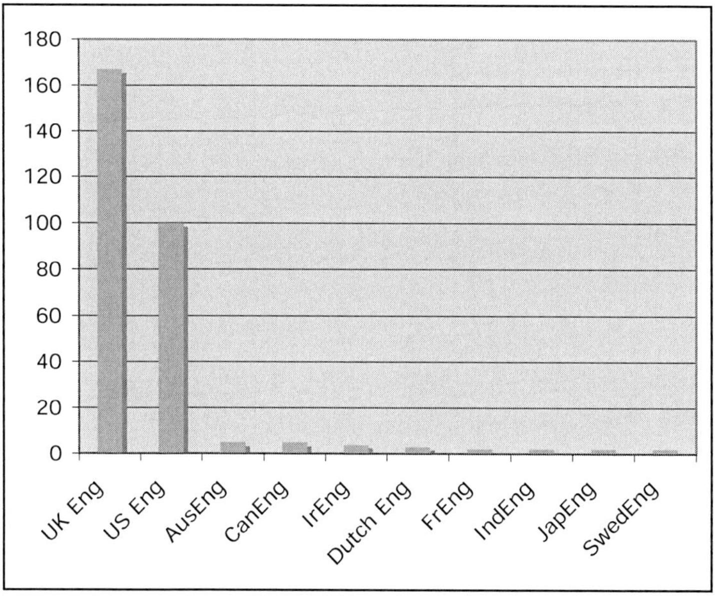

Figure 1. English accents ranked 1st
(Figures and table taken from Jenkins 2007)

In the case of second best (see Figure 2), the UK and US positions were simply reversed, with 98 selecting US accents and 92 UK. Again small numbers chose others, and again, these were mainly Canadian, Australian, and Irish English accents.

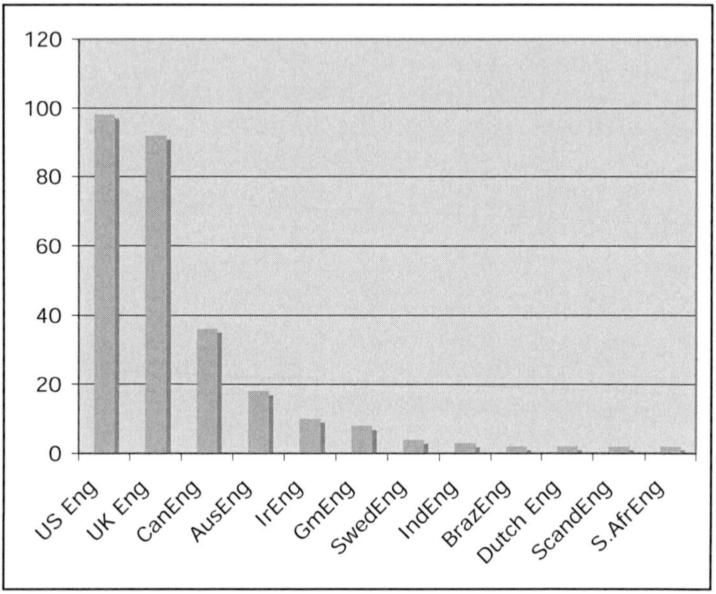

Figure 2. English accents ranked 2nd

Now that most respondents had already listed UK and US English, other NS accents were selected the most frequently for third best (see Figure 3): Canadian English accents, followed closely by Australian English, and then UK and US accents. Interestingly, China English accents also do fairly well, coming after the four NS accents and Swedish. In fact this turned out to be Chinese respondents naming their *own* accent—though from their comments, they did not seem to be engaging in 'acts of resistance' as in the case of the Japanese naming a Japanese accent as second best. In the Chinese case, it appeared to be more of an expression of confidence in their Chinese identity.

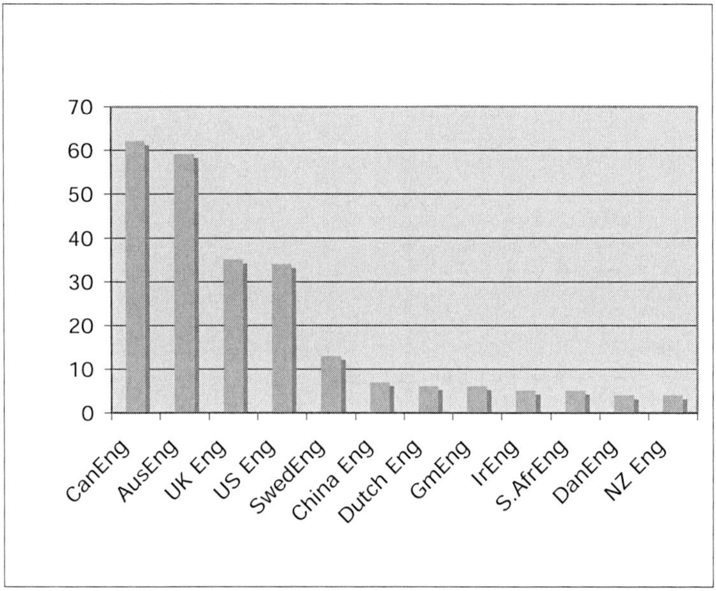

Figure 3. English accents ranked 3rd

Turning to fourth best (see Figure 4), for the first time a NNS English accent is near the top, i.e. Swedish English accents, coming second to Australian. However, the gap between the two is very large, and in any case, Swedish English is generally considered to be close to NS English accents, so it is not a 'typical' NNS accent.

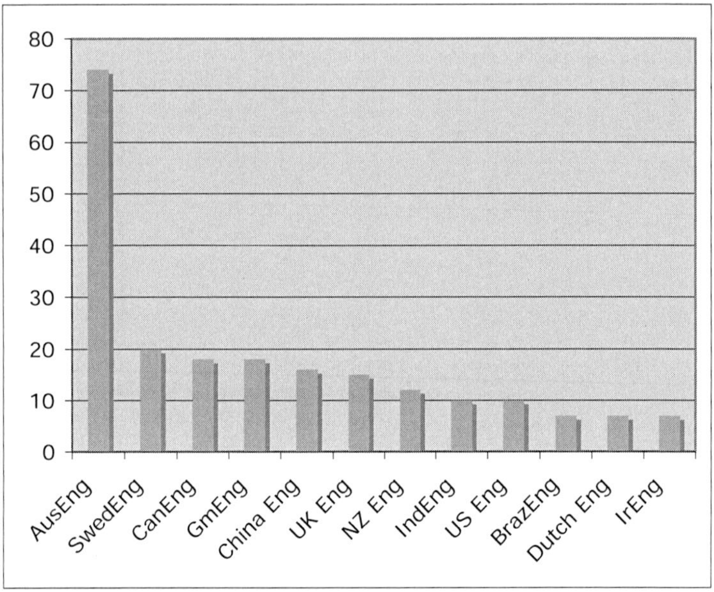

Figure 4. English accents ranked 4th

The pattern continues for fifth best (see Figure 5), with NS accents being selected the most frequently, followed by the near-native NNS accents, Swedish and German English, and then an interesting range of other NNS accents, Spanish, Brazilian–Portuguese, and China English—all of which were named to some extent by respondents from their own first language group.

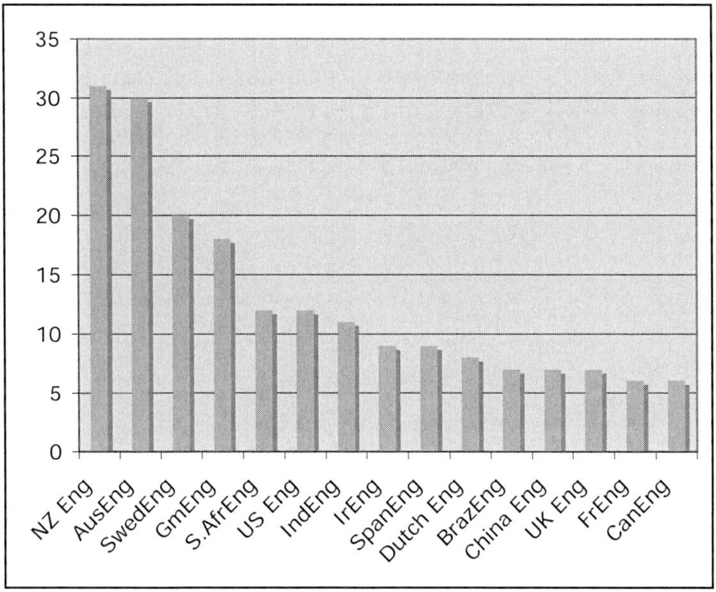

Figure 5. English accents ranked 5th

Overall, then, it is clear that 'best' accent is linked in these respondents' minds with NS accents, especially RP, then GA, then the others. On the other hand, it is also a promising sign that a number of respondents, albeit small, were willing to choose NNS accents that are not considered near-native, rather than leaving blank spaces (as many did) once they had exhausted their ideas for NS accents.

3.2.2. Accent Rating Task

In the rating task, the respondents were asked to rate (from 1 to 6, with 1 representing 'very correct, pleasant' etc, and 6 representing 'very incorrect, unpleasant' etc.) ten specific accents (specifically chosen to represent Inner and Outer Circle countries as well as (primarily) a selection from across the Expanding Circle), for correctness, international acceptability, pleasantness, and their own (i.e. the respondents') familiarity with the accents. The means for each accent on each variable are shown in Table 1 (from the highest rating to the lowest).

Table 1. Rank ordering of NNS respondents' accent rating means

Correctness	Acceptability	Pleasantness	Familiarity
UK Eng 1.471	US Eng 1.550	UK Eng 1.781	US Eng 1.548
US Eng 1.812	UK Eng 1.558	US Eng 2.086	UK Eng 1.762
AusEng 2.137	AusEng 2.161	AusEng 2.482	AusEng 2.789
SwedEng 2.698	SwedEng 2.620	SwedEng 2.854	China Eng 3.162
GmEng 3.188	GmEng 2.860	BrazEng 3.348	GmEng 3.286
IndEng 3.373	SpEng 3.311	GmEng 3.360	JapEng 3.508
SpEng 3.504	China Eng 3.342	SpEng 3.405	SpEng 3.526
China Eng 3.583	BrazEng 3.348	China Eng 3.719	SwedEng 3.650
BrazEng 3.594	IndEng 3.413	IndEng 3.797	IndEng 3.740
JapEng 4.055	JapEng 3.836	JapEng 4.110	BrazEng 3.917

The main findings that emerged from this task can be summarised as follows:

1. Once again UK and US English were rated most highly on all four variables, with the other NS accent, Australian English coming third. It is interesting, bearing in mind what was said above about RP, that UK English (by which the respondents usually meant RP) was rated higher than US English for correctness and pleasantness and similarly to US English for international acceptability. In other words, RP seems to elicit more positive evaluations even by those who have studied American English with a GA accent themselves—as had many of the respondents in my questionnaire study.
2. The concept of ELF and of the appropriateness of NNS accents in international contexts does not seem to have occurred to the majority of respondents.

3. Japanese English came out worst on all three evaluative variables (i.e. not on the familiarity scale).
4. The respondents were willing to rate certain accents very negatively or, conversely, very positively despite also stating that they were unfamiliar with these accents, thus demonstrating that stereotyping was in some way involved in their evaluations.

3.2.3. Map-Labelling Task

In the map labelling task, the respondents were asked to label English accents on a world map and comment on these accents. In the first part of the task, the same ten accents were specified as for the rating task, and in the second part, respondents were asked to label any accents with which they were familiar. Not surprisingly, their comments followed much the same pattern as their responses to the ranking and rating tasks. NS English accents were described in the most positive terms of all, with UK accents receiving uniformly positive terms and US accents receiving generally positive comments but also occasional references to sloppiness:

UK (RP) English accent, typical labels:
"normal, traditional, authentic, proper, classical, clear, very easy to understand, perfect, beautiful, elegant, lovely to listen to…"

US English accent, typical labels:
"pleasant, beautiful, relaxed, laid back, informal, clear, easy to understand, correct, comfortable" and less often "careless, sloppy" by those who preferred UK English

Accents perceived as 'nativelike', especially SwedishEnglish, were also described positively, and often in terms of their nativelike-ness:

Swedish English accent, typical labels:
"almost mother-tongue like, quite natural like native speakers, near-British, well-mastered, precise, clear, fluent, accurate, a very good accent, excellent pronunciation…"

On the other hand, NNS accents perceived as being more distant from NS accents were described negatively, and the more distant, generally the more negative the description:

Russian English accent, typical labels:
"harsh, unfriendly, heavy, sharp, aggressive..."

China English accent, typical labels:
"choppy, incomprehensible, short and abrupt (ping pong), broken, appalling, quarrel-like..."

Japanese English accent, typical labels:
"difficult to understand, funny, strange melody, flat, bad, menacing, torture..."

3.2.4. Respondents' Comments

In the final comment section, the respondents' comments fell into six clear categories:

- accent problems
- personal preferences
- familiarity
- intelligibility
- reservations (about the tasks they had been asked to complete)
- prejudice.

But the vast majority of comments related to problems—comments on why NNSs have problems with English accents, and always taking as a given the notion that NNSs' pronunciation goal should be a native-like accent:

> In my opinion, when a non-native English speaker speaks English, she/he does not pay attention to the correct way of how to pronounce a word or his/her mouth shape. And also the effect of their native accent. To be a good speaker in English, imitating is the first thing.
>
> Actually, most of the non-native English learners are trying to pronounce English like native speakers. But it's very difficult because the accents and pronunciation would relate to the movements of the tongue and lips, velum and so on. Korean people often pronounce /f/ sounds as /p/ sounds, and for Japanese learners, /r/ and /l/ sounds are very difficult.

Very occasionally respondents demonstrated an awareness that attitude is involved in their orientation to an accent 'problem'. For example, one respondent commented:

> I don't really know why, but the fact that Spanish speakers have a difficult time distinguishing between /s/ and /z/ in words like 'cosy', for example, really bothers me. What's interesting is that it doesn't hinder communication, usually.

Some of the respondents were even more overtly aware of their own accent attitudes and prejudices, as the next two comments reveal:

> I've tried to be honest when providing these answers but my honesty sometimes scares me. I am probably as biased towards certain accents of English as I encourage my students not to be.

> It was difficult to deal with the concept of 'correctness' as it is already filled with prejudice to say the least. Applying it to the ever-called 'native speakers' of English felt very odd and uncomfortable, which in my opinion, served to show me how much I'm still attached to the idea that the English spoken by its native-users still is the model to be followed.

In one sense, then, the patterns revealed throughout the responses to the questionnaire were entirely straightforward: NS English accents, especially UK and US, were preferred in all respects by this large group of (mainly) NNS English teachers, while NNS accents were non-preferred. And the more distant an NNS accent was from one of the two favoured NS accents, the more dispreferred it was. So it seems that for many of these respondents, there were really only two categories of English accents: positively evaluated NS and negatively evaluated NNS. This is reminiscent of a point made by Abercrombie more than half a century ago:

> The accent-bar is a little like a colour-bar—to many people, on the right side of the bar, it appears eminently reasonable. It is very difficult to believe, if you talk RP yourself, that it is not intrinsically superior to other accents. (Abercrombie 1965, 15; originally published in 1951)

If we substitute "NS accent" for RP, what Abercrombie said all those years ago seems to hold equally true for NNS and NS attitudes towards non-native English accents today. And the problem for ELF accents is not only the attitudes themselves but also attitudes towards those who do not share them. For, as Lynda Mugglestone points out:

> For all their weaknesses, such attitudes can prove remarkably pervasive as notions of 'standard' and 'non-standard', 'good' and 'bad', continue to be fostered in popular reactions to linguistic change or to *what is seen as the*

> *misguided liberalism which informs the tolerance of descriptive linguistics.* (Mugglestone 2003, 287; emphasis added)

3.3. The Interviews

The sense of ambivalence that had been hinted at in some of the questionnaire comments, especially those about prejudice, emerged a lot more forcefully in the interviews. The interview participants were all Expanding Circle teachers of English. Unlike the questionnaire respondents, all but two knew something about ELF in theory and all except those two expressed feelings of ambivalence and even conflict between the English accent they thought they needed to see themselves and be seen as successful English speakers and teachers, and the accent they felt would signal their identity in their English and that was validated by ELF research.

For the sake of comparison, this is an example taken from one of the two participants who knew nothing about ELF. A Spanish participant describes what kind of English accent she would like to have:

> I would really try to speak as close as I can to a NATive speaker, that's for sure. But er because I think that all of us tried to do things in a REAL way, get through to the REAL thing. I mean if you are learning English, I WANT to- or I'd like to speak English the way an English person would do.

In other words, for this participant, real English can only be NS English, and a real English accent only a NS English accent. The remaining examples shown here are typical of the comments made by the participants who did know about ELF. For example, this is one of the two Polish participants explaining whether she likes her Polish–English accent:

> I'm happy with my English ... I'm PROUD of my English.

But later in the interview she says this:

> I've still got this probably a little bit of linguistic schizophrenia ... erm ... the thing that... well I know that I don't need to speak like a British person... but because I've been taught for so many years that I SHOULD do it... when I hear let's say someone speaking erm British English like a nice RP pronunciation ... I LIKE it.

So on the one hand she is happy with her Polish–English accent, even proud of it. Yet on the other hand, she cannot help liking RP and feels that she suffers from what she herself describes as "linguistic schizophrenia".

The two Italian participants expressed similarly conflicting feelings about their accents. When asked whether she liked her English accent, one of them answered:

> Erm, mm, no, I think there are some problems that I have to solve

But later on, when asked which English accent she would most like to have, she immediately replied:

> Oh, mine, mine. Because I don't want to ... how do you say ... I don't want to be what I am not. I am ITALian. I have my own culture, my original- my roots are Italian so I like if people tell me yes ... my origin. I LIKE it.

Thus, on the one hand, she says she does not like her accent because of its "problems", which all turned out to involve Italian influences on her English accent. But on the other hand, she also says that her Italian accent is her identity and that she does like it. The same conflict occurred in the case of the Chinese participants. This is one of them explaining which English accent she would most like to have:

> [5 second pause] I think my OWN accent [laughter] yeah because er: because first of all I am Chinese. I don't have to speak like n- American or British … it's like identity, because I want to keep my identity [laughter] yeah.

But later in the interview, when I pointed out that she had said she would be "happy" if her accent was mistaken for that of a NS of English, this was her response:

> it's quite conflicted- conflict for me because I feel HAPpy when they say okay you have a native accent but erm if they cannot recognise from my pronunciation and if they think okay you are definitely American erm I don't feel that comfortable because I am inDEED a Chinese.

Overall, the interview participants made very similar points despite their differences in first language, teaching context, teaching experience, age and so on. There was a strong sense that they felt that their local ELF accent expressed their identity in English, but also that, at least in some ways, they wanted a NS accent. This pull in opposite directions led to a number of contradictory statements, or "linguistic schizophrenia" as one of the participants put it. But all except the two who did not know about ELF also said that they would be glad if ELF was accepted: that they would then feel relaxed and confident about their accents, and no longer under pressure to try to sound 'nativelike'. Meanwhile most of them also expressed some kind of sense of solidarity and community with other ELF speakers.

4. ELF and Developments in World Englishes

One thing that would probably have pleased the interview participants if it had been available at the time, is Graddol's modification to Kachru's three circle description of English. In Kachru's original model, Expanding Circle speakers were seen as *EFL* speakers and said to be dependent for their norms on NS English, unlike Outer Circle speakers, who were said to be 'norm developing'.

In the revised model (shown in Graddol 2006, 110), there is no distinction of any kind between NSs and NNSs, or between different kinds of NNS, and the description is, instead, entirely based on proficiency. The new Inner Circle consists of around 500 million highly proficient English speakers made up of both NSs and NNSs who have "functional nativeness". Around this new Inner Circle, speakers go from proficient to less proficient as they move towards the circumference (see Jenkins 2009, section A3, for further details of Graddol's revision of Kachru's model). This revised model thus fits in well with the concept of ELF, as proficiency no longer depends on nativeness in the traditional sense, and "highly proficient" must mean in today's world to be able to communicate well at an *international* level, not only at a *local* one, whether that local one is in Britain, Finland or wherever. And this would include having an internationally intelligible accent and good accommodation skills. So whereas all my interview participants would belong to the Expanding Circle according to the original model, all but two of them (the two who see NS English as their goal) would qualify for Kachru's revised Inner Circle—unlike the many NSs of English, who are not able to communicate successfully in international communication.

But the changes brought about by the spread of English have so far passed unnoticed by many British institutions. For instance, this is the Chairman of the British Council, Lord Kinnock, still promoting the notion that English belongs to the British, and implying that the British are the best at teaching the language:

> One of the reasons that the UK maintains its position [in ELT publishing] is because it's known as the home of English language teaching and the centre of innovative product and materials development. English Language Teaching is one of the UK's leading and most significant exports. (Speech given at the 2007 British Council Innovation Awards, London)

And this is the British Prime Minister, Gordon Brown, who has a similarly skewed view of the advantages of the spread of English for Britain:

> English is our heritage, but it is also becoming the future of human commerce and communication. This is a great opportunity for Britain [...] We will take up with vigour the bold task of making our language the world's common language of choice. (Gordon Brown, British Prime Minister, China, 17 January 2008)

Strangely, they both seem to be ignoring something that they must be aware of. A couple of years ago, the British government asked the think tank Demos to investigate what the spread of English would mean for British people. And the conclusions reached by Demos were completely different from the views expressed above by Kinnock and Brown:

> We [the UK] have retained ways of thinking about the English language that were more suited to empire than they are to a modern, globalised world and we are at risk of becoming outdated [...] Where once we directed the spread of English around the world, we are now just one of many shareholders in the asset that it represents. (Jones & Bradwell 2007, 12)

But it appears that the situation is still worse than this. Evidence is starting to suggest that far from being the most advantaged English speakers in the world, NSs are becoming the least advantaged in international communication. The majority are not only monolingual, but also (perhaps as a result of monolingualism) less skilled at accommodating their English to suit different communication contexts, as well as less quick to accommodate receptively so that they can understand English varieties different from their own. As Robert Phillipson has pointed out:

> In many international fora, competent speakers of English as a second language are more comprehensible than native speakers, because they can be better at adjusting their language for people from different cultural and linguistic backgrounds. (Phillipson 2003, 167)

And this already seems to be having an effect on commercial decisions. For example, according to a British newspaper:

> Korean Airlines "reportedly chose a French supplier for its flight simulators because its 'offshore' international English was more comprehensible and clearer than that of the UK competitor." (*Observer* Business Supplement, July 2005)

Meanwhile, Graddol has devoted an entire section of his new book to "The native speaker problem" (2006, 114-115). He points out that once the vast majority of educated people in the world speak English as their second language, there will not be any advantage to speaking it as a first language, and a considerable disadvantage to speaking *only* English.

What does all this mean for the future of ELF accents? Well, much will depend on whether publishers begin to realise that Britain is no longer "the home of English language teaching and the centre of innovative product and materials development", and start to produce more appropriate materials for the international market. As one of my interview participants put it:

> the materials they have, it's mainly videos or tapes, it's all native speakers' accents so that's the only model they have. Maybe if more materials around was with different accents and non-native speaker accents, then it's like recognising- it's like codifying, it's like accepting it worldwide

I sometimes discuss these issues with a North American colleague who specialises in pronunciation teaching and who sees her role as helping NNSs of English to acquire accents close to those of NSs. She justifies this endeavour on the grounds that it is to NNSs' benefit because they will, as a result, be more successful in their lives in a climate where attitudes towards NNS English accents the world over are generally negative. She argues that there is no point in approaching the issue from the opposite end and trying to change the attitudes themselves. I disagree. I believe that the more this situation is researched and discussed, and the more these attitudes are challenged, the more likely things are to change. As Jasmine Luk and Angel Lin put it:

> In light of the spread of English and what is known about the links between accent and identity, all English speakers need to (re)visit these issues and decide for themselves whether or not they truly believe that Anglo accent norms are the most appropriate for lingua franca English. (Luk & Lin 2006, 19)

Bibliography

Abercrombie, D. 1965/1951. "RP and Local Accent." In *Studies in Linguistics and Phonetics*, ed. D. Abercrombie. Oxford: Oxford University Press.

Brumfit, C. J. 2001. *Individual Freedom and Language Teaching: Helping Learners to Develop a Dialect of Their Own*. Oxford: Oxford University Press.

Bryła, A. 2006. "European Veto to the Ideological Assumptions of the LFC Voiced by Continental Learners of English (Survey Analysis)." In *Proceedings of the Mikorzyn Conference on Teaching Foreign Pronunciation, 8-10.5.2006*, ed. W. Sobkowiak & E. Waniek-Klimczak, 18-35. Konin: Państwowa Wyższa Szkoła Zawodowa.

Canagarajah, A. S. 1999. *Resisting Linguistic Imperialism in English Teaching*. Oxford: Oxford University Press.

Graddol, D. 2006. *English Next. Why Global English May Mean the End of 'English as a Foreign Language'*. London: British Council.

Jenkins, J. 2009. *World Englishes. A Resource Book for Students*, 2nd ed. London: Routledge.

—. 2007. *English as a Lingua Franca: Attitude and Identity*. Oxford: Oxford University Press.

—. 2000. *The Phonology of English as an International Language*. Oxford: Oxford University Press.

Jones, S. and P. Bradwell 2007. *As You Like It. Catching Up in an Age of Global English*. London: Demos.

Luk, J. and A. Lin 2006. "Uncovering the Sociopolitical Situatedness of Accents in the World Englishes Paradigm." In *Spoken English, TESOL and Applied Linguistics*, ed. R. Hughes, 3-22. Houndmills, Basingstoke: Palgrave Macmillan.

Macaulay, R. 1988. "RP R.I.P." *Applied Linguistics* 9 (2), 115-24.

Milroy, J. and L. Milroy 1999. *Authority in Language. Investigating Standard English*. London: Routledge.

Mugglestone, L. 2003. *'Talking Proper'. The Rise of Accent as Social Symbol*. Oxford: Oxford University Press.

Phillipson, R. 2003. *English-Only Europe? Challenging Language Policy*. London: Routledge.

Scheuer, S. 2005. "Why Native Speakers Are (Still) Relevant." In *English Pronunciation Models: A Changing Scene*, 1st ed., ed. K. Dziubalska-Kolaczyk and J. Przedlacka, 111-30. Frankfurt am Main: Peter Lang.

Seidlhofer, B. 2005. "Language Variation and Change: The Case of English as a Lingua Franca." In *English Pronunciation Models: A*

Changing Scene, 1st ed., ed. K. Dziubalska-Kolaczyk and J. Przedlacka, 59-75. Frankfurt am Main: Peter Lang.

Siek-Piskozub, T., A. Wach and A. Raulinajtys 2008. "Research on Foreign Language Teaching in Poland." *Language Teaching* 41 (1), 57-92.

Sobkowiak, W. 2005. "Why not LFC?" In *English Pronunciation Models: A Changing Scene*, 1st ed., ed. K. Dziubalska-Kolaczyk and J. Przedlacka, 131-76. Frankfurt am Main: Peter Lang.

Smith, L. 1992. "Spread of English and Issues of Intelligibility." In *The Other Tongue. English across Cultures*, ed. B.B. Kachru, 2nd ed. Urbana, IL: University of Illinois Press.

Trudgill, P. 2005. "Native-Speaker Phonological Models and Thee English Lingua Franca Core." In *English Pronunciation Models: A Changing Scene*, 1st ed., ed. K. Dziubalska-Kolaczyk and J. Przedlacka, 77-98. Frankfurt am Main: Peter Lang.

—. 2002. *Sociolinguistic Variation and Change*. Edinburgh: Edinburgh University Press.

Widdowson, H. 1994. "The Ownership of English." *TESOL Quarterly* 28 (2), 377-89.

ORIENTATIONS IN ELF RESEARCH: FORM AND FUNCTION

BARBARA SEIDLHOFER

1. Introduction

For me personally, it seems particularly appropriate that the first international ELF conference should have taken place in Helsinki: it was in Helsinki, at the ESSE (European Society for the Study of English) conference in the year 2000 that I first announced my intention to compile an ELF corpus. After I had presented my paper outlining the reasons why I thought that it was high time to provide a basis for description(s) of what was, after all, the most widespread use of English worldwide, there was much shaking of heads, shrugging of shoulders, even laughter. But also some very positive reactions—I remember for instance a group of Italian colleagues congratulating me on the idea after the session, saying that they felt that there was an urgent need for an ELF corpus. And during the discussion time Anna Mauranen got up and said that she thought an ELF corpus was such a good idea that she didn't understand why it wasn't being done already, and that she was also thinking of building a corpus, of academic ELF, i.e. what is now known as ELFA. Although explorations into the nature of ELF had of course already been started, notably in Jenkins (2000), the idea of making corpus-based descriptions of ELF possible was to be taken up for the first time. Tentative beginnings.

Since then, the study of ELF has changed beyond recognition, from an outlandish idea to a massive new research agenda. The best witness to this development is the large number of ELF researchers gathered at the first international ELF Forum in Helsinki in 2008—8 years after ESSE 2000 there it was, the assembled evidence of the dynamics of the field of ELF research in various guises. This very volume, based on a specialised conference, is testimony to the fact that ELF research is now reaching a 'critical mass'. From the early 1990's onwards we first saw a period when discussions of the phenomenon of global English, its advantages and (mainly) its dangers and drawbacks were essentially limited to the meta-level, without touching on implications of what the spread of English might mean for how we think of the language itself. It has only been over the last few years that the study of the actual use of ELF has gathered real momentum. Now there are a number of descriptive studies, often in the form of research theses, that have described and analyzed many different kinds of spoken ELF interactions from a wide variety of perspectives. The emphasis has been on qualitative studies situated in specific contexts. Overviews of such work can be found in Seidlhofer (2004) and, with examples of case studies and a special focus on Europe, in Seidlhofer, Breiteneder and Pitzl (2006).

2. Matters Arising

Most of this empirical work is based on usually fairly small corpora of spoken ELF that individual researchers 'purpose-built' for their studies. But whether large or small, all corpora first need to be compiled according to explicit criteria researchers have to decide on; and all electronic corpora make it possible to employ procedures of automatic text retrieval and analysis. But the value of corpora is not limited to helping us get results more quickly. Both the process of ELF corpus compilation as well as the findings that emerge, preliminary though they may be, bring out in quite stark relief various theoretical issues not only about ELF but about the nature of language variation and change in general. Nothing is more corrective of conceptual vagueness than being confronted with the need to be precise about language data and how it can be interpreted as evidence —and to decide what the findings are evidence *of*.

Certainly in Vienna, we have found that the very process of the compilation of VOICE, the Vienna-Oxford International Corpus of English, and all the factors that had to be taken into account when deciding on corpus design, have served to sharpen our perception, have brought to light new issues, and have made us see old issues in a new light.[1] So John Sinclair's observation from a quarter of a century ago, when he was pioneering the corpus linguistics of English as a native language (ENL), is now proving true for approaches to ELF. The following quotation comes from a book entitled *English in the World*. Although there is no mention of English as a lingua franca, it is difficult, 25 years on, to read what Sinclair says *without* seeing it as referring to ELF:

> The categories and methods we use to describe English are not appropriate to the new material. We shall need to overhaul our descriptive systems. (Sinclair 1985, 251)

The "new material" resulting from the global use of English as a lingua franca represents a particularly demanding challenge, of course. For the purposes of this paper, there is no need to rehearse the facts and figures of the unprecedented spread English has seen over the last few decades. 'Unprecedented' is the operative word here: we have witnessed the emergence of English as the world's first truly global language. In his aptly titled book *The Language Revolution*, Crystal characterizes the situation thus:

> The situation is unprecedented, with more people using English in more places than at any time in the language's history, and unpredictable, with the forces promoting linguistic identity and intelligibility competing with each other in unexpected ways. For those who have to work professionally with English, accordingly, it is a very difficult time. After all, there has never been such a period of rapid and fundamental change since the explosions of development that hit the language in the Middle Ages and the Renaissance. (Crystal 2004, 40)

Yes, it is a difficult time for English professionals, but also an exciting one, with new challenges appearing that indicate that previous thinking may no longer apply. The emergence of ELF holds the exciting, if uncomfortable, prospect of bringing up for reappraisal many of the self-evident truths that linguists have been relying on for the last 50 to 100 years.

As regards 'external factors', conditions of language use in the early 21st century have changed drastically compared to even the second half of the 20th. Countless interaction networks are now independent of physical proximity and are instantiated through interaction over vast distances, often without the participants ever meeting in the same physical space. Instead, virtual communities have achieved considerable significance in the sum of global interactions. Changes in communications brought about by technological advances have accelerated and forced changes in the nature of communication (see Seidlhofer 2007, Dewey this volume). Where communities are no longer characterized by shared primary socialisation nor by a common native language, the need for a lingua franca is paramount. And for the time being anyway, the only genuinely global lingua franca is ELF.[2]

Studying the nature and development of this lingua franca at a time of such rapid and drastic change is what ELF research is all about. Faced with a new phenomenon, the unprecedented global spread of a language, ELF researchers are breaking new ground by definition. And obviously when exploring uncharted territory, it does not make sense to try and find one's way by consulting existing maps of other places (and to complain that one doesn't find what is on the map). What is required is the drawing of new maps, perhaps the devising of new ways of describing features of landscapes not previously encountered. If such expeditions are to lead to genuinely new insights, they require that explorers make cautious use of, or even suspend, familiar concepts and categories in order to allow an understanding of new terrains to emerge. Forcing findings into preconceived categories is always likely to obstruct an understanding of new phenomena.

3. Form and Function

One central issue, and an old one, is the relative significance we attribute to forms and functions of the language under investigation. Corpus compilation necessarily detaches language from the context in which it was produced, and corpus analysis typically proceeds by accessing language forms, essentially as search strings and by extracting bits of text. The attraction for linguists is to know that the forms are there, captured in the corpus, and that a clever use of corpus tools will enable them to reliably identify and count specific forms and uncover all sorts of fascinating patterns.

There is no doubt that this process of form-identification and description has yielded reliable empirical evidence of actual patterns of textual occurrence that we would otherwise be unaware of. This of course is the advantage of the 3rd person observed data, particularly when it is done electronically. But the 'factuality' and visibility of forms can be a disadvantage by leading us to overlook or undervalue what is not immediately apparent and what cannot be directly read off from textual facts, namely what actually motivates the production of these forms, how they are being used by interlocutors to express their meanings and relate to each other—in other words, what these forms symbolize in terms of their underlying functions, what these forms are *symptomatic of*. These things are not of course immediately apparent and cannot be objectively stated as facts. They are, nevertheless, clearly of crucial importance—indeed one might argue that it is precisely the functional significance of forms that is of primary interest and should therefore be central to our enquiry into any kind of communication through language. Labov made a similar point many years ago when talking about the limitations of formal linguistics:

> ...it is difficult to avoid the common-sense conclusion that the object of linguistics must ultimately be the instrument of communication used by the

> speech community; and if we are not talking about that language, there is something trivial in our proceeding. (Labov 1972, 187)

One might suggest that in the same way, if in studies of ELF we do not concern ourselves with how it is used functionally as an "instrument of communication", there is "something trivial in our proceeding" also.

Of course Labov was not concerned with English as a lingua franca, but one could argue that the importance of this kind of functional perspective is even greater in the case of ELF, since unlike with native-speaker usage, where one can count on some conventional association of form and function, such an association cannot be assumed in ELF.

So linguistic systems do not appear from nowhere, they do not just happen but are motivated in some way or another. As Halliday suggests, forms are motivated by the social functions a language has evolved to serve, and so the organization of language needs to be explained in terms of a functional theory. The contexts utterances are produced in are crucial, and there is "a systematic relationship between the social environment on the one hand, and the functional organization of language on the other" (Halliday 1985, 11). In this view, the encoded systems of the language are a reflection of the way a language has developed in response to social requirement. Surface forms are symptomatic both of underlying ideational, 3rd person oriented concepts and of interpersonal, 2nd person oriented communicative strategies.

Perhaps the most obvious and familiar case of functional motivation is the process of pidginization/creolization. In the reduced forms of pidgin one can see the way speakers identify what is linguistically necessary to complement the context for the rudimentary transactions they are engaged in. There is no motivation for any further elaboration since this would be surplus to requirement. As creolization sets in, however, with increasing social demands on the language, especially the need to move beyond simple transactions to the interactional use of language to negotiate social meaning, linguistic forms will naturally elaborate in order to give expression to these extended functions. Pidgins and creoles thus illustrate with particular clarity a point that can be made about any naturally-occurring language, namely that the linguistic forms that are actually produced are really only explicable in terms of the functions they are designed to serve.

Another, and related, basic insight into the evolution of semiotic systems is that languages are unstable, always in flux; all living languages vary and change over time in reaction to circumstances and conditions of use, and this varying and changing never stops, there is never an end-point except when a language dies out. And when a language spreads particularly wide, and fast, it will also change fast. Massive language spread brings with it heightened language contact through speakers and therefore heightened variability and possibly accelerated change. But just what forms this heightened variability gives rise to will depend on what functions the language is called upon to fulfil (see also Cogo 2008).

Functions, then, are fundamental. But for the linguist they pose the problem that they are elusive and cannot be read off directly from linguistic forms. They have to be inferred by taking into account various contextual factors. Labov again becomes relevant here. As he points out in his work on variation in New York City speech, it is one thing to identify the existence of different forms and give a quantitative account of the frequency of occurrence of different variants. It is quite a different thing to investigate their social significance. The occurrence of postvocalic /r/ as distinct from its absence has, as he has famously shown, considerable functional significance in that it indicates social meaning (Labov 1966). It follows from this that it is not especially helpful to talk of distinct varieties of language defined by their formal characteristics particularly since such variety demarcations are notoriously difficult to make. It is more theoretically interesting to think in terms of what underlies variation. In other words, in thinking of function it would seem more relevant to think of variation as a process of use and not of varieties as states of usage.

So one cannot account for the occurrence of certain forms simply by assigning them to distinct varieties but they occur as motivated by different contextual circumstances, so that the same feature may occur in two supposedly different 'varieties' but function differently in different contexts.

This may seem obvious enough, but these insights do not seem to have always been carried over into research efforts concerned with language variation beyond that of native speakers. Here the old assumption that forms must be necessarily assigned to distinct varieties however they function sometimes still seems to be in place.

4. Focus on Form

In the course of the last decade, a number of commentators have repeatedly raised the question as to whether ELF constitutes a separate variety, or a set of varieties. While this question is not one that exercises the minds of many 'protagonists' of ELF research, it seems to be important to some people, linguists as well as linguistic laypersons, especially journalists and language teachers. This is not surprising, as it is a fundamental human urge to see oneself and others according to in-group and out-group markers of community membership.

For linguists interested in addressing the 'variety question', the usual procedure is to essentially follow in the footsteps of traditional dialectologists. This means checking out the occurrence and frequency of certain features and asking whether they together constitute a distinct system that can be recognized as a variety, or varieties of English. If so, that variety could then be identified/verified as existing, as having come about as a result of processes that are not themselves the object of the investigation. If not, no distinct/independent variety would be recognized, and the language of that group would then have to be subsumed under the language belonging to some other group, e.g. the native speakers in the 'homeland' of the language. In either case, the categorisation is decided on the basis of observed features, the forms the speakers in question have used.

When it comes to the issue as to what to call manifestations of ELF, the 'membershipping urge' dictates that the research question has to be whether these manifestations merit the label 'variety'. The categories available for thinking about different kinds of language are accepted as given. In the case of English in today's world, there are three categories of users: native speakers (in Kachru's Inner Circle), second-language speakers (in Kachru's Outer Circle), and foreign language learners (in Kachru's Expanding Circle) (cf. e.g. Kachru 1992). And there are three types of variety: the English of a particular group can either be a native language, a nativized/indigenized language, or a foreign/target language. Since these are the only three categories available, ELF will have to fit into one of them.

Given the relative scarcity of empirical work on ELF, any research effort in this area is to be welcomed, and obviously allowance should always be made for different ways of interpreting the data. But the danger of a fixation on form outlined above is a real one, and it is illustrated by a recent publication: Mollin (2006), *Euro-English. Assessing Variety Status.*[3] As the very title suggests, this book is particularly relevant to my theme, and so it is appropriate to pass it under critical review—not in any negative spirit, but positively to follow through on this major issue of forms and functions I have been discussing.

As her title indicates, Mollin is interested in English in Europe (the European Union, to be precise) and the way the language is used as a lingua franca among European citizens of different first languages. Her introduction offers a thumbnail sketch of her study. She explains her research question and the assumption that underlies it as follows:

> The research question that guides the present work is whether the label of 'Euro-English' has any legitimacy. It is assumed that such a term, analogous to other variety labels such as 'British English' and 'Indian English', is only rightfully used if it refers to a variety of English in Europe which is different from native speaker varieties and has developed its own norms of usage. ... The question of the legitimacy of the label 'Euro-English' will thus be answered in the present work by examining whether there is a variety of English in Europe that fulfils the criteria of an ESL-variety, which is non-native, but nevertheless endonormative. (Mollin 2006, 1)

Mollin also makes clear at the outset that she is working within the "tripartite model" which "divide[s] speakers into three categories: speakers of English as a native language (ENL), a second language (ESL), or a foreign language (EFL)" (p.1), and that this is "the general conceptual framework in which the present study is embedded" (p. 2). This means of course that as far as 'Euro-English' is concerned, the findings will have to fit into either the ESL or the EFL category. By accepting this model, which Mollin herself points out originated in the early 1970's, she thus rather limits the scope of the answers she can seek to her research question. Together with the fact that this research question, "whether the label of 'Euro-English' has any legitimacy" is a yes/no, i.e. closed, question, this signals that probing the suitability/adequacy of the conceptual framework is not on the agenda. So while the phenomenon under scrutiny may be unprecedented, the findings will have to fit earlier precedents. The world of English users here is thus divided into the native and nativized on the one hand and learners on the other. If ELF speakers in Europe do not belong to the native or nativized category, the only remaining option for them is to be (EFL) learners.

Within the limits set for the investigation, the study is thorough and extensive. The introduction announces that "criteria for ESL-status will be laid down", and this is what is then done. Mollin then seeks to establish to what extent these criteria are fulfilled: 'expansion', i.e. the spread and functions of English in Europe, 'nativization', i.e. the degree to which distinct 'Euro-English' forms can be discerned, and 'institutionalization', the attitudes Europeans have towards instances of 'Euro-English'.

With regard to the first criterion, expansion, the survey leads to the conclusion that "the role of English as the linking language of Europe is undisputed", but that "Europe is a special case that is not easy to grasp with the instrument of the distinction between ESL and EFL", that "Europe does not fit the definitions of either ESL or EFL" (p. 86). Mollin even goes on to say that

> the tripartite model of English has to some extent been overcome by the realities of the globalized world with English as the global language. A distinction between settings with typical postcolonial characteristics and settings with no historical connection to the English-speaking world may no longer hold. (Mollin 2006, 86)

So the model used to describe 'Euro-English' is recognized to be inadequate to the purpose. However, readers who expect the conceptual framework to be modified as a consequence of this recognition are disappointed. For the passage continues:

> Yet it is still useful to apply these strict 'traditional' criteria to a specific case in order to gauge the extent of its divergence from the ideal type. (ibid)

No explanation is given for just why it should be useful to persist with an inadequate model, why sticking to the traditional criteria should be preferable to pursuing the intriguing questions suggested by the uniqueness of Europe in this respect, which the author herself clearly recognizes.[4]

The investigation of the next criterion, nativization, constitutes the centrepiece of the book, with the longest chapter devoted to it. The title of the chapter itself clearly indicates the formalist orientation: "Evidence for the Formal Independence of Euro-English". For the purpose of her enquiry, the author compiled her own sizeable "Corpus of Euro-English" in order to check out certain hypothesized features of 'Euro-English'.

Such an undertaking brings with it a number of rather daunting conceptual and methodological challenges. The latter the author addresses with varying degrees of thoroughness, the former she does not address at all. It would go beyond the scope of the present paper to give a detailed summary of this chapter.[5]

The "Corpus of Euro-English" consists of just over 400 000 words of spoken and informally written, i.e. online text (cf. p. 92ff), carefully balanced in terms of numbers of first languages represented proportionally to numbers of inhabitants per EU country. The 240 000 words of spoken data are subdivided in "Dialogue: Public Discussions (160,000)" and "Monologue: Speeches / Briefings (80,000)". The 160 000 words of "Informally Written" data are subdivided into "Dialogue: Chat (70,000)" and "Monologue: Discussion Group (90,000)". This means that there is more spoken than written data; however, the nature of the spoken data in particular is noteworthy. Mollin states that

> The sampling of the corpus followed a scenario of the most likely case, i.e. the contexts sampled are those where a Euro-English is most likely to develop, namely among those Europeans who habitually use English in a large part of their daily professional routine, and possibly, also their personal social lives. (Mollin 2006, 155)

and that

> within the spoken subcorpus, the largest emphasis lies on public debate. Private conversations did not figure, which is due to the fact that they are not as easy to come by (p. 93)

The sampling process already reveals a formalist orientation which disregards sociolinguistic considerations. Thus there is no satisfactory explanation of how or why scenarios (i.e. contexts in which language functions) were identified as "the most likely case". Certainly it is surprising (to say the least) from a functional point of view that public debate, specifically press briefings by the European Commission, press conferences by EU officials and speeches, should be regarded as a "scenario of the most likely case". The speakers involved are doubly 'on record' as it were, speaking at a public event and knowingly being recorded for the EU audio archive. From all we know about sociolinguistics, this type of situation is one very likely to encourage 'attention paid to speech' (Labov 1972) and thus very unlikely to support a natural vernacular way of speaking. Mollin also seems to assume that if she had recorded the same speakers (or even younger people!) having casual conversations with family and friends she would have found them using the same forms, i.e. that the style of the talk captured in the corpus is irrelevant.

Mollin's corpus analysis can only be sketched very briefly. She starts off by identifying, from a striking variety of sources, a number of lexicogrammatical features that might be regarded as characteristic of 'Euro-English', as an indication of 'variety status' if their occurrence is systematic and communal. Mollin then checks her corpus for occurrences of these features and compares frequencies with the spoken component of the ICE corpus. The question, then, is whether there are significant differences, and the answer, *tout court*, is that there are not. But what is 'significant'? This question Mollin does recognize as a problem, and she discusses it:

> Since the question asked in the present chapter is whether Euro-English differs in its form from the native standard (and following that, whether these differences are systematic and communal), the decisive problem of

> operationalization is: how different does it have to be? Is a variety only different enough when it has a completely new realization in 100% of cases of a certain feature? Or does a different pattern of preferences for a variable suffice? In the absence of standard measures, we will here decide on a case by case basis whether there is a real difference between Euro-English and native English, yet other observers may come to other conclusions when they apply a different standard. It is, however, important to remember that those national varieties of English that are already accepted today actually do not differ from each other to a great extent… (Mollin 2006, 100)

Despite this last concession, Mollin then does set a cut-off point:

> The general thrust of the present study regarding the problem of 'how different does it have to be to be different?' will be to submit the potential variety of Euro-English to a rather strict test: it will only deserve the label if it differs considerably from native English, meaning that new features need to be used in at least 50% of cases. This is necessary foremost since smaller differences may easily be due to sampling differences... (Mollin 2006, 101)

This seems to be a surprisingly arbitrary decision that contrasts noticeably with the meticulous precision with which the corpus composition was undertaken. There is no discussion of the phenomena that are really at stake here, namely the relationship between language variation and change. The focus is on formal features and their frequencies, not on processes of variation. It is at this point in the book that we come across a striking passage which conveys a sense of the author being aware of these 'big questions', but she decides that they are "too large":

> Finally, what can we conclude if we do find characteristic patterns of usage among the speakers sampled in the corpus? These could be seen as Euro-English characteristics, but also as English learner universals, especially if they coincide with those features claimed as characteristic of other varieties of English. […] This is a question that should be kept in mind, but it is nevertheless too large to be addressed completely here. If the features of non-native varieties of English all come down to them being non-native, then the whole paradigm of non-native Englishes needs rethinking. We will, for the time being, confine ourselves to the question whether Euro-English has shared characteristics that make it systematically different from the native-speaker input. (Mollin 2006, 102f.)

This quotation is reminiscent of Mollin's earlier observation discussed above about the bad fit of the ESL/EFL labels for Europe. In both cases, there are glimpses offered of important questions, but they do not get pursued. From my own 'ELF perspective' indicated at the outset of this paper, the study sometimes briefly touches on issues that clearly call for exploration at a theoretical level and for consideration with reference to a sociolinguistic variationist framework, but this unfortunately remains 'the road not taken'.

The preoccupation with linguistic forms and disregard of their functional motivation become apparent in the following:

> …it is disturbing that she [Seidlhofer] does not even claim to describe Euro-English as it is used by her informants, but that she explicitly sets out to explore features that are unproblematic in conversation, i.e. which do not cause misunderstandings. […] Her emphasis is clearly not on the actual usage of certain structures by the speakers, but on the value of those structures in communication. […]
> …this approach needs to be kept well apart from descriptive research into emerging new standards (be they European or anything else). (Mollin 2006, 8ff.)

The two approaches *are* well apart from each other, pertaining to two quite different orientations as outlined above. As I see it, it is problematic to fix upon a number of formal features and an arbitrary frequency threshold as criteria for the existence or otherwise of an "independent variety". This is an insight of variationist sociolinguistics that has been recognised for a long time (cf. e.g. Bailey 1973), and it is especially important to bear it in mind with respect to ELF with its characteristic variability, hybridity and fluidity. This is not to say that descriptions of features are not of interest, but what is crucial is how they are interpreted. As Chambers (2002) comments:

> Before a change takes hold, there is a gradual, almost imperceptible, rise in frequency until the new form attains some kind of critical mass. At the earliest stage, the change apparently affects too small a population to serve as a model, but at some point it becomes perceptible, though usually beneath consciousness, and spreads through the community. No one has been able to establish the point of critical mass as an absolute value, and it appears to be different for each change, subject, as are all social developments, to countless possible influences. (Chambers 2002, 361)

It thus seems a pity to expend considerable time and effort to definitively answer a closed, yes/no question about a variety as a category rather than to engage with the many intriguing open questions that the processes of language variation so evident in today's Europe suggest. (See also Seidlhofer 2005.)

What I am interested in is delving into precisely the kind of 'complicating' aspects of research that Mollin briefly mentions in a couple of places but then abandons: the intriguing question of why the phenomenon of ELF in Europe does not seem to fit the traditional categories of ENL, ESL and EFL, and the hunch that we may need to rethink "the whole paradigm of non-native Englishes" in the light of processes of variation and possibly change that the sheer scale of English as a global lingua franca may be bringing about.

The problem is that answers to these difficult questions cannot be found by fixing on linguistic forms and counting them, however fascinating such 'feature-spotting' may be. In fact, quantitative approaches may be necessary but are certainly not sufficient in our attempts to achieve a better understanding of ELF, and they bring with them the danger that they may well deflect from what is really significant.

5. Focus on Function

An alternative to the formalist approach, then, would be to start from the assumption that ELF research throws up different questions from traditional dialectology and to ask what functions the features you observe are symptomatic of. This second procedure represents a shift from a categorization of the surface forms to an attempt to understand what motivates their occurrence. The focus is on communication processes and features as pointers to these processes.

In this view, the main question is what the variability of ELF tells us about the communicative and interpersonal functions the observed forms are being used to express. The focus is on developing an understanding of how ELF users exploit the resources of the language to achieve their communicative outcomes. The existing categories of ENL, ESL and EFL are not necessarily relevant, as ELF is seen as not fitting any of the three Circles but cutting across them—this is also why ELF has its own acronym.

The main difficulty here is that, as I have mentioned earlier, the functions the language serves are not visible as such in the corpus. They give rise to the observable forms, but they are not manifest themselves, they cannot be formulated as search strings and tracked down. Functions have to be inferred by engaging closely, and emically, with the contextual factors relevant in particular interactions, to particular speakers in an attempt, as the phrase goes in cultural anthropology, "to figure out what the devil they think they are up to" (Geertz 1983, 58).

Trying to understand what ELF speakers "are up to" through qualitative, emically oriented studies is now becoming 'ELF mainstream' (if that is not a contradiction in terms) and many contributions in this volume bear this out. This is not to say that these investigations are not interested in the forms observed in ELF interactions. They are, very much, but they see these forms as motivated by communicative functions and contextual factors, and it is indeed the interrelationship between functional and formal considerations that gives rise to new theorising. A good example of such exploration (and thus indicating the impossibility of getting at interesting insights by proceeding purely through linguistic forms) is Pitzl's study of idiom and metaphor in ELF (this volume)—how would one ask the computer to identify idiomatic creativity? How would a concordancing program recognize a metaphor?

What is of primary interest in these situated, exploratory studies is how ELF users, usually bi- or plurilingual, exploit the potential of the language in ways that result from the purpose of the talk and the interpersonal dynamics of the interaction.[6] There are now many examples of such descriptive work, including—to mention but a few—Björkman 2008; Böhringer 2007; Cogo 2007; Ehrenreich 2008; Hülmbauer 2007; Klimpfinger 2007; Lichtkoppler 2007; Pitzl, Breiteneder & Klimpfinger 2008; Ranta 2006; Thompson 2008; and Watterson 2008.

In order to illustrate empirical work on ELF that is conceived more along these 'exploratory' lines with reference to another monograph, I propose to look at Martin Dewey's (2007a) *English as a Lingua Franca: An Empirical Study of Innovation in Lexis and Grammar*, an (as yet unpublished) PhD thesis.[7] The first obvious difference between this study and Mollin's is that Dewey does not focus on ELF in Europe but is looking at ELF in general, i.e. including speakers from non-European first language backgrounds (but in specific settings). The research agenda signalled by the title is fairly open, but it is made clear that he also conducts an empirical study, of what he terms "innovation".

The thesis is actually broader in scope than its title suggests. The empirical study does form a substantial part, but the main thrust of the thesis is that the emergence of ELF needs to be approached through an enquiry into the more general processes of variation and change in English due to its role as an international lingua franca, and within the wider context of globalization. Dewey also devotes a chapter to the pedagogical implications of his research, in particular for course and materials design and teacher education.

Again, it is only possible to mention a few aspects here that are relevant for the point I wish to make in this paper—and of course I can refer to Dewey's contribution to the present volume.[8] What Dewey has in common with Mollin is that he also conducts a corpus study into lexicogrammatical features. But the corpus design, the approach and the questions he asks are very different.

Dewey's corpus consists of (transcriptions of) spoken data only, interactions which he recorded himself, in contexts he was familiar with. There are various types of speech event captured, but with the exception of five short presentations they are all conversations and discussions. The data run to about 8 hours of recordings and to some 60 000 words. There are 55 speakers from 17 different first languages. The corpus is thus very considerably smaller than Mollin's, but highly interactive.

Dewey's approach is a qualitative one, although he does provide quantitative results too to support his argumentation. While he does take into account previously hypothesized characteristics of ELF, the features he investigates are not primarily brought to the corpus from outside as it were but emerge from it. This is what he says about his research questions:

> The description of the corpus data will focus on emerging innovations in the lexis and grammar of lingua franca communication, after which the study will seek to explain how different types of ELF might in future be characterized. To this end the following research questions were posed to provide a framework for descriptions of ELF and thereby serve as a platform from which to begin to explain the linguistic nature of international lingua franca usage.
>
> [1] What grammatical constructions and lexical items are commonly used in successful ELF communication that would not usually be found in standard ENL varieties?
>
> [2] Can we identify systematic features common to successful NNS-NNS interaction that could then be considered characteristic of ELF varieties?
>
> [3] To what extent can speakers be said to accommodate towards a co-construction of emergent ELF forms?
>
> [4] Which items in 'non-standard' L1 English lexicogrammar lead to miscommunication, and what might thus constitute an error in lingua franca usage? (Dewey 2007a, 54)

It is obvious from these questions that Dewey too compares his ELF data with standard ENL, and homes in on those forms that differ. His interest, however, goes beyond ascertaining frequencies of occurrences of features in that he foregrounds discussions of processes of accommodation and communicative effectiveness. This he does by assuming "a micro-level perspective with the aim of giving a qualitative description of the most frequent lexicogrammatical forms" (p. 81).

It is of course particularly difficult to summarize detailed discussions of qualitative findings, but to offer an insight into how Dewey proceeds, let us look at an example: the famous/notorious 3rd person singular *–s* vs. zero marking. In the "Description of findings" chapter, Dewey dedicates nearly 10 pages to this feature. Purely quantitatively, his results can be stated very briefly: main verbs have the zero morpheme more often (52%) than the *–s* morpheme (48%), while only 4% of the auxiliary verbs have the zero morpheme. It is thus immediately obvious that the distinction between main verbs and auxiliaries is an absolutely crucial one that a mere counting of *–s* vs. zero occurrences would fail to reveal. Moreover, Dewey discovers a number of other facets of the usage of *–s* vs. zero: he establishes that zero is widespread across settings, domains and speakers of different first languages. He also notices that the interactions where there is a high occurrence of *–s* are fairly formal ones, with a 'socially salient' native speaker of English present. This latter observation Dewey finds so striking that he conducts a statistical analysis as to the correlation of occurrence of *–s* and presence of English native speakers, and he finds this to be clearly statistically significant. He then conducts a small discourse analytic study of a few extracts, looking at the probable role of accommodation in the usage of zero and *–s* respectively, which culminates in the claim that

> the more natural option for 3rd person singular verbs is the zero variant [...] This use of 'make' with zero marking is far more representative of the behaviour of 3rd person singular verbs in the data, and thus possibly more typical of informal ELF communication in general. That the form occurs here despite the semi-formality of the situation and the presence of a NS teacher indicates the strength of this naturalness. It is also worth noting that, perhaps ironically, the form occurs here despite the 3rd person –s being explicitly discussed previously in the conversation, with Lucy [a Russian speaker] insisting that it had always been important for her to have teachers who corrected her if she did not use the form. (Dewey 2007a, 90)

This example of the Russian speaker illustrates how the functional salience of this particular feature takes precedence over correctness in terms of Standard ENL, so that even a speaker who is striving to be correct in accordance with the norms she has been taught may not produce the prescribed form in contexts of use, presumably at least partly because the functional motivation is lacking so that zero seems "more natural". This account is in stark contrast with Mollin's treatment of 3rd person present singular zero. She introduces the topic thus:

> Naturally, this remarkable hypothesis [that zero marking may be a feature of 'Euro-English'] has been included in the catalogue of tests run on the Corpus of Euro-English. It is remarkable since omitting the third person –s is a beginner's error in learner English that English teachers will try to get rid of very early on, probably even in the very first year of English education. It would thus be surprising if a feature like this were to resurface as a common feature of those Europeans who use English with each other routinely. (Mollin 2006, 148)

Mollin (who of course worked with a much larger but untagged corpus, and so decided against 'manual' searches) then proceeds by limiting herself to a purely formal procedure, namely identifying "all instances of *he*, *she* and *it* and to extract all cases where present tense marking is obligatory (i.e. simple present, present progressive and present perfect)" (p. 148). Whatever the practical constraints, it is surprising that she finds it legitimate to limit her search to the third person singular pronouns as opposed to nouns, since these might be hypothesized to be strong triggers for using 3rd person *–s* marking. Personal pronouns are after all often presented and practised together and in opposition to each other: "I think, you think, he/she thinks", which is likely to associate the morphological marking of the verb particularly strongly with the 3rd person singular pronouns. What is even more surprising is that she also includes the present progressive with its fixed paradigm *he/she/it is* (*verbing*). The problem of course is that if in corpus work you fix on what is most readily identifiable and automatically retrievable, you are likely to neglect crucial distinctions, thereby making a functional link even more difficult to infer. Not surprisingly, the search returns "an absolutely tiny error rate of 0.58%" and leads Mollin to close the case of 3rd person singular marking with the verdict that

> It does in fact seem that European speakers, even though they may have initial problems with this particular morpheme, do not drop it to any considerable extent later on. Occurrences such as *it need to be done* must thus be considered individual learner's errors. (Mollin 2006, 148)

Returning to Dewey, he goes on to observe that while the range of different (main) verbs that take the zero morpheme is very broad, this is not the case with main verbs with *–s* marking: "Approximately half of all cases of 3rd person *–s* occurring in main verbs can be accounted for by only 4 verbs: *has*, *means*, *looks*, and *depends*" (Dewey 2007a, 86). These verbs tend to occur in prefabricated chunks such as *depends on* and *looks like*. The discussion of "[t]he pragmatics of 3rd person singular zero" in Cogo and Dewey (2006) also makes these points very clearly.

In his summary of empirical findings with reference to the four research questions quoted about, Dewey characterizes the features of "innovative language use" he investigated as frequent, widespread, and systematic (p. 131ff.) and concludes that "innovative language use most often leads to effective interaction, and in terms of lexis and grammar very seldom results in miscommunication" (p. 131). He emphasizes that accommodation (cf. research question [3] above) emerges as "one of the key processes by which ELF settings generate innovative use of English":

> It seems very much to be the case that in effective intercultural communication speakers are especially characterised by a willingness to interact co-operatively. ELF speakers use the language in mutually convergent ways, often resulting in the emergence of new patterns of lexis and grammar." (Dewey 2007a, 131)

In relation to research question [4], he summarizes that

> There are practically no cases in this corpus where innovations in lexis or grammar lead to a breakdown in communication, or which appear to result in a slowing down or even momentary miscommunication. There are occasions when speakers orient very carefully and attentively to an innovation in the lexis, overtly addressing the intelligibility of an item they are using. Where there were problems in the interactions, this is primarily either to do with auditory problems or was related to features of phonological difference, problems which were usually overcome by straightforward repetitions. There are, however, a number of non-standard items which tend to be closely monitored by speakers themselves. These primarily involve the tense system, with speakers often modifying the verb according to the temporal frame of reference, except in the case of the present perfect – past simple distinction, which tends to be far more invariant. (Dewey 2007a, 132)

Dewey's overall conclusion from his empirical findings is that there is

> a clear distinction to be made between those features that can be regarded as innovative, and those that are best regarded as more idiosyncratic (Dewey 2007a, 135).

What is particularly relevant to the present form-function discussion is that Dewey's findings chapter is followed by a chapter entitled "The underlying processes and motivations that effect change", which offers a discussion of the motivating forces that he discerns as giving rise to the features reported in his, as well as other ELF researchers', empirical findings. Here we can only consider briefly what is said here about the findings on the 3rd person singular zero as discussed above. These are treated under the heading "Exploiting redundancy", and Dewey comments that 3rd person singular zero is "indicative of several different factors motivating change" (p. 137). Drawing particularly on Trudgill (1986) and Trudgill's (2002) discussion of the development of this feature in 16th century Norwich, he points out that especially in language contact situations, it is not surprising that the zero option should prevail, given that it affords added systematicity and exploits communicative redundancy—especially since English, unlike e.g. highly inflected European languages, is a non-pro-drop language. It is interesting that Breiteneder (2005 and 2009), who focuses on European contexts in her qualitative ELF studies of 3rd person singular *–s* and zero, presents findings and a discussion that are very much in line with these observations.

The functional orientation which Dewey adopts in discussing the third person zero and *–s* also informs other processes of variation in ELF, including accommodation, reinforcement of proposition, added prominence and increased explicitness. All of these are concerned with the functions that bring about the occurrence of certain forms, and the forms are adduced not just as data for their own sake but as evidence of motivated variation. In other words, the approach is not a matter of spotting and counting discrete features but of looking for insights into variability and potential change that the increased use of English as a lingua franca makes possible.

6. Conclusion

Obviously, like all research, especially in the humanities, the insights one gains depend on what one is getting at, with what questions in mind one approaches one's subject. When faced with a new phenomenon, English used as a lingua franca for intercultural communication, one can decide to make use of existing frameworks and procedures, and choose well-established categories to work with, such as 'speech community' and 'variety'. Alternatively, one can decide that the frameworks and categories that were developed for different phenomena may not fit the new situation, and that we need to modify our frameworks or develop something new. Essentially this has to do with whether one wants to ask closed or open questions.

Obviously, I do not mean to argue against corpus-based studies that home in on certain features. We need to amass as much textual evidence of ELF interactions as possible. After all, the raw material linguists work with are manifestations of particular languages, and whatever research questions are being asked, the 'tangible' object of study is the actual language produced by speakers or writers. But it is important that both the data we work with and the interpretations that it is possible to derive from our analyses should be as supportive of situated, qualitative study as possible. This is what we have set great store by in our compilation of VOICE, the Vienna-Oxford International Corpus of English, and it seems that similar considerations have guided the building of ELFA (cf. e.g. Mauranen 2006). VOICE gives researchers access to complete speech events rather than decontextualized extracts. Whole speech events support work from an emic perspective since on the one hand, they are the frame for what the participants in the talk experience, on the other hand they are also meaningful units for the corpus user and can serve as analytic constructs for the researcher. VOICE also offers ample contextual information about domains, setting, speech event types and the purpose of the interaction, the speakers involved, and rich mark-up that fosters understanding of 'what is going on' in the interaction.

Early on in this paper I quoted David Crystal remarking that the "rapid and fundamental change" English is currently undergoing makes for difficult times for English professionals. One way of confronting the difficulty is to resort to the security of established categories and ways of thinking, and fit the new data into old categories. A much more rewarding alternative is to confront the difficulty and to welcome the "explosions of development" Crystal mentions as opportunities for gaining new insights, as a challenge to think in unprecedented ways about the unprecedented phenomenon of ELF.

Bibliography

Bailey, C.-J. N. 1973. *Variation and Linguistic Theory*. Washington, DC: Center for Applied Linguistics.

Björkman, B. 2008. "'So where we are?' Spoken Lingua Franca English at a Technical University in Sweden." *English Today* 24 (2), 35-41.

Böhringer, H. 2007. *The Sound of Silence: Silent and Filled Pauses in English as a Lingua Franca Business Interaction*. MA thesis, University of Vienna.

Breiteneder, A. 2009. "English as a Lingua Franca in Europe: An Empirical Perspective." *World Englishes* 28 (2), 256-69. A special issue *Symposium: 'Englishes in World Contexts'*, eds. M. Berns & B. Seidlhofer.

—. 2005. "The Naturalness of English as a European Lingua Franca: The Case of the 'Third Person –s.'" *VIenna English Working PaperS* 14 (2), 3-26. http://www.univie.ac.at/Anglistik/Views0502ALL.pdf

Breiteneder, A., M.-L. Pitzl, S. Majewski and T. Klimpfinger 2006. "VOICE Recording—Methodological Challenges in the Compilation of a Corpus of Spoken ELF." *Nordic Journal of English Studies* 5 (2), 161-88. http://hdl.handle.net/2077/3153.

Brutt-Griffler, J. 2002. *World English. A Study of Its Development.* Clevedon: Multilingual Matters.

Chambers, J. 2002. "Patterns of Variation Including Change." In *The Handbook of Language Variation and Change*, ed. J. Chambers, P. Trudgill & N. Schilling-Estes, 349-72. Oxford: Blackwell.

Cogo, A. 2008. "English as a Lingua Franca: Form Follows Function." *English Today* 24 (3), 58-61.

—. 2007. *Intercultural Communication in English as a Lingua Franca: A Case Study*. PhD diss., King's College London.

Cogo, A. and M. Dewey 2006. "Efficiency in ELF Communication: From Pragmatic Motives to Lexico-Grammatical Innovation." *Nordic Journal of English Studies* 5 (2), 59-94. http://hdl.handle.net/2077/3148.

Crystal, D. 2004. *The Language Revolution*. Cambridge: Polity Press.

Dewey, M. this volume. "English as a Lingua Franca: Heightened Variability and Theoretical Implications."

—. 2007a. *English as a Lingua Franca: An Empirical Study of Innovation in Lexis and Grammar*. PhD diss., King's College London.

—. 2007b. "English as a Lingua Franca and Globalization: An Interconnected Perspective." *International Journal of Applied Linguistics* 17 (3), 332-54.

DYLAN. Language Dynamics and Management of Diversity. http://www.dylan-project.org

Ehrenreich, S. 2008. "English as a Business Lingua Franca in Multinational Corporations—Contexts of Use and Attitudes." Paper presented at the *AILA World Congress*, Essen, August 24-29, 2008.

ELFA. Corpus of English as a Lingua Franca in Academic Settings. http://www.eng.helsinki.fi/elfa/elfacorpus.htm

Geertz, C. 1983. *Local Knowledge. Further Essays in Interpretive Anthropology*. New York: Basic Books.

Halliday, M. A. K. 1985. *Spoken and Written Language*. Oxford: Oxford University Press.

Hülmbauer, C. 2007. "'You moved, aren't?'—The Relationship between Lexicogrammatical Correctness and Communicative Effectiveness in English as a Lingua Franca." *VIenna English Working PaperS* 16 (2), 3-35. http://www.univie.ac.at/Anglistik/Views_0702.pdf.

Jenkins, J. 2000. *The Phonology of English as an International Language*. Oxford: Oxford University Press.

Klimpfinger, T. 2007. "'Mind you sometimes you have to mix'—The Role of Code-Switching in English as a Lingua Franca." *VIenna English Working PaperS* 16 (2), 36-61. http://www.univie.ac.at/Anglistik/Views_0702.pdf.

Kachru, B., ed. 1992. *The Other Tongue*. 2nd ed. Urbana and Chicago: University of Illinois Press.

Labov, W. 1972. *Sociolinguistic Patterns*. Philadelphia: University of Pennsylvania Press.

—. 1966. *The Social Stratification of English in New York City*. Washington, D.C.: Center for Applied Linguistics.

Lichtkoppler, J. 2007. "'Male. Male.'—'Male?'—'The sex is male.' The Role of Repetition in English as a Lingua Franca Conversations." *VIenna English Working PaperS* 16 (1), 39-65. http://www.univie.ac.at /Anglistik/Views_0701_pdf

Mauranen, A. 2006. "Signaling and Preventing Misunderstanding in English as Lingua Franca Communication." *International Journal of the Sociology of Language* 177, 123-50.

Modiano, M. 2007. "Euro-English from a 'Deficit Linguistics' Perspective?" Review of *Euro-English: Assessing Variety Status* by Sandra Mollin. *World Englishes* 26 (4), 525-33.

Mollin, S. 2007. "New Variety or Learner English? Criteria for Variety Status and the Case of Euro-English." *English World-Wide* 28 (2), 167-85.

—. 2006. *Euro-English. Assessing Variety Status*. Tübingen: Narr.

Pitzl, M.-L. this volume. "'We should not wake up any dogs': Idiom and Metaphor in ELF."

Pitzl, M.-L., A. Breiteneder and T. Klimpfinger 2008. "A World of Words: Processes of Lexical Innovation in VOICE. *Vienna English Working PaperS* 17 (2), 21-46. http://www.univie.ac.at/Anglistik/ views_0802.pdf

Prodromou, L. 2008. Review of *Euro-English: Assessing Variety Status* by Sandra Mollin and *English as a Lingua Franca: Attitude and Identity* by Jennifer Jenkins. *Applied Linguistics* 29 (4), 732-36.

Ranta, E. 2006. "The 'Attractive' Progressive—Why Use the *–ing* Form in English as a Lingua Franca?" *Nordic Journal of English Studies* 5 (2), 95-116. https://gupea.ub.gu.se/dspace/handle/2077/3150

Seidlhofer, B. 2007. "English as a Lingua Franca and Communities of Practice." In *Anglistentag 2006 Halle Proceedings*, ed. S. Volk-Birke & J. Lippert, 307-18. Trier: Wissenschaftlicher Verlag Trier.

—. 2005. "Language Variation and Change: The Case of English as Lingua Franca." In *English Pronunciation Models: A Changing Scene*, ed. K. Dziubalska-Kolaczyk & J. Przedlacka, 59-75. Bern: Peter Lang.

—. 2004. "Research Perspectives on Teaching English as a Lingua Franca." *Annual Review of Applied Linguistics* 24, 209-39.

Seidlhofer, B., A. Breiteneder and M.-L. Pitzl 2006. "English as a Lingua Franca in Europe." *Annual Review of Applied Linguistics* 26, 1-34.

Sinclair, J. M. 1985. "Selected Issues." In *English in the World*, ed. R. Quirk & H. G. Widdowson, 248-54. Cambridge: Cambridge University Press.

Thompson, A. 2008. "English for Ideational Exchange in International Workplaces." Paper presented at *GlobENG (International Conference on Global English)*, Verona, February 14-16, 2008.

Trudgill, P. 2002. *Sociolinguistic Variation and Change*. Edinburgh: Edinburgh University Press.

—. 1986. *Dialects in Contact*. Oxford: Blackwell Publishers.

VOICE. Vienna-Oxford International Corpus of English. http://www.univie.ac.at/voice.

Watterson, M. 2008. "Repair of Non-Understanding in English in International Communication." *World Englishes* 27 (3-4), 378-406

Notes

1 See also Breiteneder, Pitzl, Majewski and Klimpfinger (2006).

2 Of course, "genuinely global" does not mean "globally equitable" in respect to the actual access to the language.

3 This is the slightly adapted published version of Mollin's doctoral thesis completed at the University of Freiburg in 2005. For reviews of the book, see Modiano (2007) and Prodromou (2008).

4 One might have expected, for instance, a discussion of the two different types of what Brutt-Griffler (2002) calls 'macroacquisition' here, which might be helpful for thinking about Europe as a 'linguistic community'.

5 See chapter 5 of the book, and a journal article on the findings, Mollin (2007).

6 This is also what the Vienna research team of the EU project "Language Dynamics and Management of Diversity" (DYLAN) is investigating.

7 This thesis was completed at King's College London in 2006.

8 See also Cogo and Dewey (2006), Dewey (2007b).

ENGLISH AS A LINGUA FRANCA: HEIGHTENED VARIABILITY AND THEORETICAL IMPLICATIONS

MARTIN DEWEY

1. The Methodological and Ontological Positioning of ELF

On the one hand, ELF research shares significant common ground with variationist studies, in that part of its focus is the description and analysis of sociolinguistic variability for the purpose of identifying core features deemed to be characteristic of a particular variety. Although conceptually the conventional notion of *variety* needs some rethinking in the context of ELF, identifying typical or core features has been the focus of a good deal of empirical work. This is largely the case with Jenkins' (2000) Lingua Franca Core and her foundational ELF research into phonology, which explicitly aims to identify the set of key features necessary to guarantee international intelligibility. This is also to a certain extent the case, though conclusions have necessarily been more tentative, with some of the VOICE (Vienna Oxford International Corpus of English) findings that have so far been reported (e.g. Seidlhofer 2004) or with regard to other corpora such as the ELFA (English as a Lingua Franca in Academic Settings) project (e.g. Mauranen 2003). However, the variationist tradition has tended to be concerned with distinct groups of speakers (determined for example by class, gender, geography and so on) whose speech patterns serve as markers of membership and identity, thus demonstrating how language is tied to particular social groups. Although Heller (2008) highlights some important recent ideological shifts, commenting that variationist sociolinguistics is increasingly beginning to pay closer attention to ethnography and discourse analysis, it is still true to say that in variation studies, variables are mostly interpreted as a reflection of the speaker's membership in a social category (though see Eckert 2008 for a less static, 'indexical field' approach). By contrast, ELF interactions occur amid multiply varied socio/linguacultural networks, often of an especially transient nature, and usually operating more across conventional boundaries than within them.

This fluidity has become increasingly acknowledged by a number of scholars working in ELF, and notably to the extent that there has also been a subsequent and growing unease with the concept of *variety* in the context of the emerging empirical data. This trend is very much in evidence in several recent papers that report on ELF findings. In a research review paper published in *ARAL,* Seidlhofer (2004) discusses lexicogrammatical similarities and differences displayed across domains and first language backgrounds in light of whether or not we can justifiably describe ELF as an emerging variety in its own right (see p. 230, note 5). There is no definitive answer given as yet, but it seems indicative of the emerging mood that she concludes the paper by referring to ELF not as a variety, but as "a distinct manifestation of English" (2004, 230). In a subsequent, co-authored paper, (Seidlhofer, Breiteneder & Pitzl 2006) the terminological issue is addressed far more explicitly. Although the authors pose a similar question (but this time from the more specific context of ELF in Europe), regarding whether or not ELF can be referred to as a variety, they also observe the following:

> Uncoupling the language from its native speakers and probing the nature of ELF is a special methodological challenge because most of the descriptive and analytic categories and approaches available have evolved through work on fairly stable codes in native-speaker communities, so these cannot automatically be assumed to be appropriate. (Seidlhofer, Breiteneder & Pitzl 2006, 21)

In light of this challenge to customary analytical categories, the most appropriate answer to the question regarding whether ELF is a variety in its own right, is yes the evidence shows that it is emerging in its own right as distinctive, but that the term *variety* is too tied to stable, rather static notions of community to adequately capture the especially fluid nature of ELF.

As a consequence of this distinctiveness from conventional variationist studies, ELF research also therefore shares some common ground with scholars who are more concerned with the dynamics of an interaction, working within a tradition where ethnicity, gender and so on are not seen to be clearly defined, but rather enacted during the practice of discourse. ELF is similarly an interactional phenomenon, though ELF research has so far been far less interested in the finely-detailed analysis of micro moments than is the case in interactional sociolinguistics (cf. Rampton 2006). ELF is thus to a certain extent caught methodologically and theoretically some way between these two different approaches to language and discourse. The ELF findings discussed in this paper are presented in light of this uniqueness. Bearing this positioning in mind, ELF is then best understood as a dynamic, locally realized enactment of a global resource, best conceptualized not as a uniform set of norms or practices, but as a highly variable, creative expression of linguistic resources which warrants a distinct analytical framework. Research into naturally occurring ELF talk tends to reveal a heightened dynamics of spoken interaction, a phenomenon which is particularly characteristic of lingua franca communication. In the next section, I address this aspect of ELF with reference to recent empirical findings.

2. The Situated Nature of ELF Innovation

Elsewhere I have attempted to highlight some of the underlying processes at play in the emergence of innovative features in ELF lexicogrammar. In Dewey (2007) for example I describe some of the motivating forces that tend to give rise to the features reported in ELF research findings. I will return to these findings here, elaborating on some of their aspects in order to support my current arguments. If we take for the moment two such processes, *exploiting redundancy* and *enhancing prominence*, it becomes clear just how situated the analysis of an interaction needs to be in order that we can reliably identify any linguistic innovation. These two processes would appear in fact to be contradictory: that is, by exploiting grammatical redundancy, a speaker is opting to omit a linguistic item; whereas, to enhance the prominence of a referent, a speaker will invariably add an item. To illuminate how these competing motives manifest themselves in ELF talk we can look at this in terms of the surface level features that these processes give rise to. This can best be demonstrated by reference to a single language item, by identifying moments where it appears and does not appear and then tracing its deployment and non-deployment to the specific communicative needs of the surrounding interactional discourse.

This is certainly the case with speakers' use of the definite article. In a relatively small-scale corpus of ELF talk[1] I have found that this variable displays some very notable characteristics in the way it is being used in lingua franca interactions. At the outset it should be stated that, despite my own initial intuitions to the contrary, occurrence of *the* in the ELF corpus was statistically very close to its occurrence in a comparable ENL corpus. Initially during the data collection phase it seemed to be the case that definite and indefinite articles were frequently absent in contexts where they would be used in ENL varieties, as in examples such as *first time I went to London*, and *I'm university student*. Yet this proved not to be as straightforward as first appears, and analysis of the ELF corpus as a whole reveals that indefinite and definite articles tend to be no less significant in lingua franca spoken discourse than they are in L1 Englishes.

A comparison of the statistics of definite and indefinite articles in the ELF corpus and an ENL spoken corpus reveals that the frequency of these items is in fact very similar across both corpora. For this purpose word lists were produced for the current data and comparable ENL data using *Oxford WordSmith*—these lists were then organised according to the frequency of each item and the statistics were then compared. In the demographic component of the British National Corpus (BNC) for example, a spoken corpus of over 900,000 words, the indefinite article ranks sixth in the frequency list. The combined scores for *a* and *an* in the ELF word list give a ranking of the eighth most frequent item out of a total of 3,079 word types. The definite article has similarly close frequency rankings in the two sets of data. In the BNC demographic component and in the ELF data *the* is the third most frequent item in both corpora. The difference therefore seems not to lie in the overall importance of articles in ENL and ELF respectively but in the nature of their distribution. It is not the case that the indefinite or definite article is used less in ELF, but that the article system is being employed differently.

One particular aspect of article use that the findings reveal lies in a tendency for speakers in ELF to use zero article in contexts where an ENL variety would involve use of the definite article. This is especially evident in stretches of discourse in which the ENL pattern would entail an element of redundancy and/or idiomaticity. The combination of definite article *the* with certain high frequency adjectives, adjectival and adverbial phrases, in L1 Englishes is a case in point. This is certainly true in the following two extracts, both of which occur in a single conversation between a Korean speaker (S1) and a Japanese speaker (S2). In these extracts it is telling that both speakers (S2 in the first extract, S1 in the second) use the phrase *same as* with zero article rather than the definite article.

Extract 1

(S1: L1=Korean, S2: L1=Japanese)

S1: after holiday I I feel I I lost some English <xxx> vocabulary
S2: yeah yeah
S1: so now er I think a little bit panic (.) and how about you? @@@

S2: @@@ actually I'm **same as** you (.) yeah until last week I felt my English has improved (,) but (.) I don't know why (,) after holiday I feel something has stuck yeah my English has (,) stuck

Extract 2

(S1: L1=Korean, S2: L1=Japanese)

S2: so: when I went – came to london first er I I felt freedom something (,) freedom because people really don't care about other people so: and also there are lot of nationalities so I felt freedom
S1: hmm
S2: but er actually it's similar to tokyo
S1: yes
S2: er I think (.) and er: but tokyo is much more crowded and we have lots of people in tokyo (,) compared to London
S1: ah hmm (,) free time activities (,) interests? Ah usually I go to the cinema with my friends or go to the coffee shop and chat with my friend (.) shopping (,) cooking (,) **same as** another girl @@@

In the first extract S2 expresses agreement with S1 by reporting a shared experience "I'm same as you", where the speaker describes feeling that her proficiency in English had declined after a recent holiday in which she returned to her home country. In the second extract S1 describes how she tends to spend her free time, reporting that she does what she feels is typical behaviour "same as another girl". The nature of this feature can be further attested if we examine the following concordance sample for the word *same.*

In this corpus there are 23 occasions out of a total 72 tokens for *same* where the word is used with zero article, both in cases where it appears as an adjective, as in *I have same problem,* and as part of a phrase, as found in the numerous occurrences of *same as you.* The range of contexts in which this form appears is extensive, being produced by a wide range of speakers in a range of different situations. While the use of the zero article in this context is not exclusive—there is also a significant number of incidents and in a similarly wide range of contexts of the definite article forms *the same* and *the same as*—it does represent a relatively established alternative option. It is also similar in an important way to a number of other cases in the data where the zero article is used in contexts where L1 Englishes[2] would require use of the definite article. What seems especially significant here is the fact that this particular use of *the* in standard English varieties appears to be largely idiomatic and communicatively redundant. This is probably especially true of a particular category of words consisting of postdeterminers and adjectives where the meaning is intrinsically an expression of uniqueness, including for example ordinals such as *first, second, third,* superlative adjectives such as *best* and *worst,* sequence related words as in *next* and *last,* as well as other expressions of singularity, including *only, sole,* and of course *same.* It is thus evident that wherever ENL definite article patterns involve an element of redundancy, this can be exploited by ELF speakers opting for the zero article in its place, thus enhancing what is described in Cogo and Dewey (2006) as "efficiency in ELF communication".

To return to the second process mentioned above, *enhancing prominence*, we can also see how this may be traced in relation to the article system. In the corpus, there are in fact many occasions of definite article use in contexts for which the unmarked ENL pattern would favour either the use of zero or indefinite article. There is for example very widespread use of *the* for generic reference, both in conjunction with either uncountable or abstract nouns, and with singular and plural countable, as in the case of respectively *the life, the child, the people,* all of which are attested in the data with general rather than specific referents. The use of definite article with abstract concepts is particularly commonplace. A concordance for *the* organized according to the word immediately to the right of the search word reveals many such examples, including nouns such as *advice, democracy, euthanasia, industry, marriage, nature, pollution,* and *society,* all of which appear with some regularity in the data. In the following extract, in which the participants are discussing whether it is preferable for children to be brought up in a more urban or rural environment, there are two such instances. Here, the speaker refers to what she feels is the ease with which children can adapt to living "in the nature or in the society".

Extract 3

(S1: L1=Mandarin, S2: L1=Japanese, S3: L1=Korean)

S1: five years is too long
S2: @@@ hm, depends
S3: from two and five, it's not too: they are too young
S2: yeah (,) it's not so big deal for children
S3: yeah
S1: five years is too long
S2: @@@ hm, depends
S3: from two and five, it's not too: they are too young
S2: yeah (,) it's not so big deal for children
S3: yeah

S2: because they (,) they know how to play (,) they know how to survive in **the nature** or in **the society**, instinct – un – unconsciously because they're children
S3: yeah, they are very <xxx>
S2: flexible

In relation to this use of definite articles in contexts where ENL favours the zero article, one hypothesis is that the underlying motive in these cases often relates to the relative importance attached to the noun it determines. Where abstract and plural nouns occur with the definite article and reference is generic, in a number of cases the 'keyness' of the word in question appears to be a determining factor (see Dewey 2007 for a more detailed discussion). This becomes apparent on investigation of specific cases of abstract nouns used with a definite article, where close analysis of the contexts in which these cases occur reveals quite compellingly that one function of inserting the article is to make a referent more prominent in the interaction, in other words to serve as a kind of discourse highlighting feature.

There are therefore some notable innovative patterns of usage emerging in much of the data, part of which involves a shift in the article system away from a distinction between specific and generic reference. A more significant factor determining whether the zero or definite article is the preferred option in ELF often involves the relative level of importance attached to a noun or noun phrase in a given stretch of discourse. If an item is deemed to be of particular importance it will often be preceded by the definite article, while if the item is relatively unimportant it will often more likely be used with the zero article. Therefore, a primary function of the definite article seems to be to provide additional emphasis to a noun and thus signify its increased importance relative to the discourse. This suggests quite strongly that in ELF, patterns in the article system are far more context dependent and meaning driven than they tend to be in ENL. In particular, the formal rules handed down through (especially idiomatic) use in ENL have little or no value in lingua franca settings. It is simply not the case in ELF that the selection of an article will depend on the nature of a noun in terms of any inherent qualities it may hold, such as level of specificity, uniqueness and so on. Furthermore, what is most significant in the current discussion is the extent to which there is both inter and intra-speaker variability with regard to the definite and zero variants of the article. In other words, and in stark contrast to the way articles are in pedagogic grammars described according to predetermined sets of rules, the way ELF speakers deploy definite or zero realizations is entirely contingent on the specific communicative environment of a particular interaction. I turn now to a consideration of how these findings relate to the question of how we may or may not situate and rationalize ELF empirical data within the existing paradigmatic framework and with reference to existing terminology.

3. The 'Object' of Study in Applied Linguistics

Some of the current difficulties involved in applying conventional terminology to a study of ELF lie in a longstanding tendency towards an objectification of language. In much applied linguistic work, there has been a tradition for regarding language as an object of enquiry. As a result, language becomes held up for analysis as an autonomous and reified system, exteriorised from any of the speakers who might actually produce it. Indeed, as Holborow (1999) observes, the legacy of structuralist linguistics has involved a refocusing of attention on the study of language as an abstract, socially disconnected system. This has resulted in language systems being made primary at the expense of language users, thus "giving language an over-determining role by making its speakers mere conformers to its intricate rules" (Holborow 1999, 4). The tendency to reify the system has manifested itself in fairly deep rooted ways, with the result that language is most often defined and related to in terms of established rules of usage, as has been suggested above is the case for example in relation to the presentation of the article system in language reference texts.

This object of enquiry approach has created a culture of linguistic analysis that has tended to highlight individual surface level features, which in other words involves looking at language from a competence perspective. In the process this has also often meant that interest in the underlying communicative processes are confined to the margins of any study, with any divergence away from the normative pattern being characterized as 'merely' a property of performance, assigned to what has often been seen as a peripheral concern. Without doubt this is especially the case with early Second Language Acquisition (SLA) research, with studies focusing on discrete items, such as the morpheme studies provide, or with the route of acquisition displayed in specific subsystems (Ellis 1994, chapter 3, provides a detailed review of order and sequence studies in SLA). English Language Teaching (ELT) in essence continues to define language competence according to the 'command' a speaker has over particular discrete items or systems. Communicative strategies that language learners and speakers might use are thus seen as a compensatory device; in other words, strategies for communicating effectively are deemed to be simply what speakers do when they do not know the grammar or cannot find a lexical item. We define language proficiency in entirely normative terms, so much so that intelligibility is disproportionately equated with standard language norms.

The influence of this as a cultural practice in applied linguistics and ELT can also be seen in ELF studies, a point which Seidlhofer (this volume) draws our attention to when she warns against too much "feature spotting". It is of course inevitable that ELF research has begun in this fashion: as a newly emerging field of enquiry it has needed to engage with the current frames of reference, and inevitably much of our empirical work has so far needed to focus especially on surface level features in order to highlight the ways in which ELF speakers are actively involved in the creative use of linguistic resources. By investigating, say, the use of 3rd person *–s* (see e.g. Breiteneder 2005, Cogo & Dewey 2006), we have been able to further the argument that ELF is in fact "sui generis" (House 1999). More recently, as ELF research has continued to emerge, there have been a number of studies which have looked more specifically at the interactional properties of ELF talk, that have begun to pay closer attention to the kinds of strategies and processes at play in lingua franca communication, such as code switching (Klimpfinger 2007, and this volume), use of idioms (Pitzl, this volume), and the nature of communicative effectiveness (including what Hülmbauer 2007 describes as "canny moves"). A common theme running through a number of recent papers is an orientation more towards the processes of ELF communication, for example the way speakers often engage in a process of exploiting redundancy, rather than the resulting features, such as the use of 3rd person singular zero. This requires a methodological and theoretical reorientation that downplays the "language as object" metaphor, and 'up-plays' the performativity of language interaction.

The tradition of objectification is a theme which is taken up, and then developed still further, by Pennycook (2006) during a discussion in which he highlights the extent to which notions of performance have customarily been downplayed in much applied linguistics. Partly as a result of Saussure's distinction between *langue* and *parole*, though more notably as a result of the continuing influence of Chomsky's bisection of competence and performance, the predominant focus of linguistic enterprise has disproportionately been on abstraction rather than actualization of language (cf. Firth and Wagner's 1997 critique of mainstream SLA on similar grounds). And as Pennycook comments, despite several attempts to build on Hymes' notion of communicative competence, English language pedagogy has continued to maintain Chomsky's original division, thus regarding competence as an underlying capacity. This capacity is somehow seen as separate and entirely distinct from performance, and therefore of any actual realization of language. Importantly however, Leung (2005) has given a lot of attention to the manner in which communicative competence, a concept originally developed for ethnographic research, has tended to be interpreted in ELT in quite a narrow sense. Leung observes that the transfer of the concept from research to pedagogy brought with it an abstraction of context and an idealization of social rules of use, adding that recent work in World Englishes and ELF requires ELT to become more engaged with contemporary developments in language and socio-cultural realities. This would entail adopting what Leung refers to as "ethnographic sensitivities", which would enable the ELT practitioner to better accept the infinite diversity of language in use, and to thus move away from an assessment of all language difference as incorrect. Adopting the sensitivity he calls for also entails, among other things, a similar move away from the objectification of language that I am arguing for. Although in the following quote, Leung is referring explicitly to the curriculum, his arguments express a similar sentiment. Furthermore, the native speaker idealization he describes is entirely indicative of regarding the language system in reified terms, that is to say, as something which can be described in abstract terms and in the absence of particular speakers or context.

> The objectification and reification of curriculum knowledge largely based on native-speaker idealizations and the reduction of the social to mean classroom interaction have effectively insulated the concept of communicative competence from the developments in English and the myriad ways in which it is now understood and used in different contexts. Theoretically as well as pedagogically, there is every reason to reconnect with the social world if the concept of communicative competence is to mean anything more than a textbook simulacrum of Englishes in the world. (Leung 2005, 139)

Reconnecting with the social world particularly requires an engagement with the especially dynamic uses of English that the globalization of the language has brought about. ELF findings are beginning to provide evidence that lingua franca communication displays a heightened degree of dynamism, a reality that makes it evermore difficult to describe English within traditional frameworks that are accustomed to studying language as an object. For the most part, whether the focus of attention has been on ENL, or ESL studies of language variation have oriented towards a description of any particular version of 'E' as a determinable set of linguistic features. Similarly, and as Pennycook (2006) argues, the task of World Englishes scholars has tended to involve a study of the pluralization of English as an entity. Yet as Pennycook comments, "[l]anguages are not so much entities that pre-exist our linguistic performances as the sedimented products of repeated acts of identity" (2006, 13).

4. Objectifying the 'E' in ELT

It is clear, however, that the way in which we have become accustomed to regard language in ELT professional practice pretty much involves objectifying English. The English language is arguably rationalized in this way considerably more so than any other language, due to the extent to which it is mostly regarded by stakeholders in the industry as marketable, what Pennycook (1994) describes as a "Global Commodity". The extent to which this is the case is best illustrated in Neil Kinnock's foreword to Graddol (2006) in which, as Chair of the British Council, he comments that as a sector ELT generates some £1.3 billion in import revenue in the UK and an estimated £10 billion a year in education related exports. The language has also become, especially so in recent years, a very prominent part of the UK Home Office strategy for controlling immigration, as can be seen very explicitly in the following passage, which appears in the current annual report.

> Only those who demonstrate a commitment to Britain can stay in the country. All migrants who want to settle here need to pass a test of English language and knowledge of the British way of life. Under the Government's earned citizenship proposals, full access to benefits will be withheld until a migrant has earned the right to live here and become a British citizen or been granted permanent residence. (The Home Office Departmental Report 2008, 51)

English language tests are thus used as a powerful tool in the British Government's current policy of restricting access to citizenship and resources to those who are deemed most deserving under a newly introduced points-based system. Anyone outside the EU member states wishing to settle in the UK must "earn the right" to call him or herself a citizen by demonstrating a willingness to display the right kind of language and cultural knowledge. Needless to say the type of language and culture being implied here are essentialized versions, a point which is perhaps most poignantly attested by the significant number of outer-circle native speakers who are also required to sit language exams[3]. Increasingly, state funded ESOL providers in the UK are therefore having to focus much of their teaching efforts on what is for many students some pretty high stakes exam preparation.

The English language is in ELT methods and practices (even more so in the private sector) thus not usually seen as the sedimentation of performances of course, but rather as an entity in its own right. Again, this is arguably the result primarily of a disproportionate concern with competence, while the performance element of language is mostly seen to be of minor importance. In fact, when it is the focus of attention this has tended to be in terms of imperfect realizations of the system, which in educational contexts usually involves some kind of exercise in error spotting. There is quite substantial evidence to this effect to be found in several places. Firstly, research into language attitudes among language practitioners and non-specialists alike shows that it is commonplace for participants to predominantly express beliefs (see especially Jenkins 2007 for extensive empirical work in this area) about language by orienting towards it in reified terms, as if it were an object, something that exists outside of and separate from particular performances.

In addition, the tendency to orient towards language as an object is further evidenced in the way in which language assessment criteria are characteristically determined. For example, the *Common European Framework of Reference* (CEFR) (Council of Europe 2001) provides a common basis for describing the 'competences' which are deemed important for language learners to meet in order to communicate effectively in a second language. Taylor (2006) in fact cites the CEFR as an example of how language testing has in her view moved away from a deficit competence model where candidates are penalized for not adhering to a NS norm. In her defence of Jenkins' (2006) criticisms of ELT language testers, Taylor argues that the framework represents a shift in focus whereby emphasis on correctness is replaced with an emphasis on communication. Although intended as a 'framework' and thus a means of providing a common frame of reference for a wide range of different specific contexts for language learning and language assessment, much of what is contained in this document can be interpreted as prescriptive in tone. It is a centrally devised, hierarchical scheme, which ultimately treats learning and assessment in fairly universal decontextualized terms: the goal of which is measured in relation to a set of fairly fixed, predetermined, and thus objectified norms. Close inspection of the Council of Europe framework seems in fact to imply that language assessment is still largely characterised by a culture of correctness, which would support Jenkins' (2006) arguments that so far language testers have been slow to react to socio-cultural developments in the language. The CEFR, for instance, describes common reference levels for spoken language use, with descriptors provided under the following headings, *range, accuracy, fluency, interaction* and *coherence*. Although competence is therefore defined according to a range of communicative skills, reference to control of grammatical structure and avoidance of errors is particularly prominent. The following table shows the qualitative descriptors for the common reference levels as given under the column heading 'accuracy' in the CEFR document.

Table 1. Assessment of accuracy according to CEFR. (Extract from Council of Europe 2001, 28.)

	ACCURACY
C2	Maintains consistent grammatical control of complex language, even while attention is otherwise engaged (e.g. in forward planning, in monitoring others' reactions).
C1	Consistently maintains a high degree of grammatical accuracy; errors are rare, difficult to spot and generally corrected when they do occur.
B2+	
B2	Shows a relatively high degree of grammatical control. Does not make errors which cause misunderstanding, and can correct most of his/her mistakes.
B1+	
B1	Uses reasonably accurately a repertoire of frequently used 'routines' and patterns associated with more predictable situations.
A2+	
A2	Uses some simple structures correctly, but still systematically makes basic mistakes.
A1	Shows only limited control of a few simple grammatical structures and sentence patterns in a memorised repertoire.

There are several words and phrases in this particular extract which appear to be key to the way in which evaluation of language learners is approached in current ELT practice, and these especially include 'accuracy' and 'control', words which occur with particular frequency and prominence throughout the document. There are also a number of essential questions that the above text gives rise to: who for example is being implied as the judge of grammaticality in all of the above measures? Who exactly determines whether a 'mistake' causes misunderstanding or not? We can only assume that for the most part this will be interpreted to mean that grammaticality is measured according to the proximity of a speaker's use of English to the norms of standard NS usage, and that a NS interlocutor (or even NS judge who is in fact external to the interaction being assessed)[4] determines the level of understanding that has taken place.

Furthermore, the data presented by empirical ELF research (see especially Jenkins 2007, Seidlhofer, Breiteneder & Pitzl 2006) suggests quite strongly that there is a potential contradiction inherent in this type of framework. This is because interaction can most often be assessed to be effective when speakers accommodate towards their interlocutors, often doing so in ways that may involve variations on established norms. Thus, for a speaker to be communicating very successfully, this might involve the production of certain 'errors' that appear as the result of mutual convergence. An assessor could choose to reward this accommodative behaviour and value it as an important communicative skill, but research in language assessment suggests otherwise. McNamara (1996), for example, reports findings that suggest examiners are influenced more by grammatical accuracy (as determined by degree of adherence to the NS norm) than any other factor when assessing language use. There is therefore in the current frameworks used for language assessment little scope to incorporate what is probably the most distinctive characteristic of ELF interactions; namely the adeptness with which interlocutors estimate and thus select and adapt the shared linguistic resources available to them in order to best achieve communicability. ELF is, it seems, especially characterised by a heightened variability in the deployment of lexicogrammar. The growing body of ELF empirical research indicates very clearly that non-selection of NS norms, say by opting to use 3rd person zero as opposed to the NS standard 3rd person *–s*, (see e.g. Breiteneder 2005, Cogo & Dewey 2006) has little or no impact on interactive success.

Language assessment in ELT tends therefore to be very much concerned with prescription and proscription regarding ENL norms, and the goal of learning and teaching seems largely to be defined according to avoidance of difference (which is generally categorised as "deviation"). The general attitude to learner language and to 'errors' in language teaching is clearly encapsulated in the title of an influential book in the field, *Learner English: A Teacher's Guide to Interference and Other Problems* (Swan & Smith 2001). This text occupies a prominent place on reading lists for pre- and in-service teacher training programmes, and in my experience is a very popular source among trainers and trainee teachers. In the text there is no mention of the use of accommodation in spoken communication, and 'learner language' is cast only in a negative light. As well as having implications for the relative importance attached to the traditional items of the grammatical syllabus, the importance of flexibility and mutual convergence in ELF settings, suggests that there need to be significant changes in current language teaching approaches. This will also involve a considerable reconceptualization of language, one which will entail moving more towards an orientation to discourse as a phenomenon which is generated *in situ* during specific interactions through the enactment (or performance) of linguistic and extralinguistic resources. Thus, we need in pedagogy to look for ways in which we might encourage teachers and learners alike to regard language less in terms of something which pre-exists, as therefore less an entity which can be transmitted intact and unchanged. Effective communication seems to be most characterized by the transformative ways in which resources are adopted and adapted in particular communicative settings. Therefore, the language we use in our interactions is not so much a set of patterns and rules we select and apply, but rather a slightly more conceptual notion of communicative means that are transformed to suit the particular purposes of actual interactants as they engage in meaning making. To my mind, the only way ELT will be able to respond in any meaningful way to ELF research and discourse is if there is a cultural shift away from objectifying language and communication.

5. From Speech Community to Community of Practice

In addition to rethinking the way we orient ourselves to the notion of language itself, ELF research is also giving rise to some fairly fundamental questions about the way we understand the domains in which communication takes place. The site of study of ELF empirical work is especially complex, in the sense that it is not definable in conventional sociolinguistic terms. For the most part research in variation has tended to focus on one or other specific speech community. But if we consider for a moment some early definitions regarding this notion, it is not difficult to see ways in which the concept *community* as originally established in sociolinguistics has needed to be updated. Gumperz (1971, 101) in an influential early account defines the speech community thus:

> [It is] held together by frequency of social interaction patterns and set off from the surrounding areas by weaknesses in the lines of communication [… and] may consist of small groups bound together by face-to-face contact or may cover large regions, depending on the level of abstraction we wish to achieve.

Similarly, Hymes (1974, 51) describes a community as, "a local unit, characterised for its members by common locality and primary interaction". What is most significant in relation to both these classic descriptions is the extent to which, in the current epoch, the frequency of social interaction can be maintained over far larger distances and with more immediacy than ever before as the result of the many far reaching technological developments that have taken place in recent years. With the advent of the world wide web, and especially with the continued development of video conferencing, plus the growth in video linked internet calls made possible by software such as Skype, 'face-to-face' contact is no longer bound by geographic constraints. What is determined as local is no longer definable on the same kind of terms: we may have as much contact, or may often feel more connected with people outside our immediate surroundings than within them. With regard to my own day-to-day working life, for example, there are colleagues within my own department with whom I share fewer contacts than I do with colleagues in other universities, both in and outside the UK. This is, of course, far from unique in the contemporary world; it is probably in fact a very typical state of affairs in many academic and professional disciplines. The professional associations and networks to which we belong may well operate beyond the immediate confines of a particular university campus, and the interactions we enter into might very often take place as part of a network which is more virtual than physical.

Given the immense sociopolitical changes that have thus taken place with the passage of the past three decades or so, it is of course not at all surprising that substantial reconceptualization of the notion of speech community is necessary. There have indeed been numerous ways in which the concept has needed to be developed in order to address contemporary factors (see Patrick 2002 for a fairly thorough discussion of its history). Nevertheless, it is worth stating here that despite some considerable debate surrounding the nature of community as relevant to a consideration of language and communication, the conventional account of this concept remains influential in applied linguistics and ELT, and some notion of *community* remains key to any empirical work. Given the ongoing digitization of our media and discourse, the way we understand this notion and its relevance to studies of language variation is dramatically beginning to change. As Seidlhofer (2006) observes, the unprecedented speed with which the global spread of English has taken place in recent years has brought with it, as a corollary of that spread, a growth and acceleration in language variation and change. And as Seidlhofer adds, "[w]hereas change was previously regulated by factors of physical proximity, these constraints have now to a large extent been eliminated" (2006, 307).

The impetus behind Seidlhofer's argument is that the unprecedented extent to which English has become a lingua franca on a global scale, and the unparalleled sociolinguistic reality that ELF settings have become the predominant domain for English language use require the development of entirely new conceptual frameworks. Central to the reconceptualization required is a consideration of the relationship between the concepts of 'community' and 'variety', which as Seidlhofer suggests are inadequate and in need of substantial rethinking. Part of the problem lies in the way in which these concepts have to date been defined as interdependent. In other words, a variety emerges within a particular location as the result of the consistent use of language innovations that reach a (non-specified) threshold level of homogeneity, and which then come to represent the linguacultural identity of this group of speakers. Schneider (2003), for example, identifies and elaborates in detail on five distinct phases in the evolution of new Englishes. He describes at length the parameters involved in this evolutionary cycle, and what is vital at each stage in this trajectory is the pivotal importance of a notion of speech community. What makes the identification of a variety possible then is the identification of a particular community—within current Applied Linguistics paradigms you cannot have one without the other.

However, as Seidlhofer goes on to argue, our notion of what constitutes a community has in recent years been fundamentally altered. It has far less to do with proximity or geographic location, less to do with group cohesion or socialization into a particular set of values or beliefs, and far more to do with a more 'virtual' conceptualization:

> [...] in the post-modern world the metaphor of "international, or global, community" has turned into an everyday reality in a different literal sense. Countless interaction networks are independent of physical proximity and are instantiated through interaction over vast distances, often without the participants ever meeting "in the flesh". This means that virtual communities have achieved considerable significance in the sum of global interactions, giving rise to a very different meaning of 'community'. (Seidlhofer 2006, 313-314)

The significance and the pervasiveness of virtual communities continue to grow exponentially as new technologies emerge and develop at seemingly ever expanding rates. This is perhaps best illustrated in the rapidly growing, Second life, a virtual world where 'residents' via their online avatars meet, do business, go shopping, have affairs, get married, and even participate in organised crime. This is a world in which Linden dollars (the official Second Life currency) are traded on-line for real world currencies, and virtual land is bid for in actual dollars on e-bay. In his 'journey through virtual worlds', Guest (2007) describes how IBM use virtual worlds to train new staff in India; how IBM scientists, consultants and executives 'meet' to discuss strategies and experiment with the potential of virtual worlds (reportedly virtual worlds allow far more creativity and experimentation of ideas than meetings held via conference calls); how the US military use huge virtual worlds for training scenarios, and gaming simulations to test the suitability of new recruits; as well as how Reebok commissioned a virtual branding agency to help build brand value in virtual worlds, with the aim of marketing in the real world the best 'selling' shoe (Guest 2007).

Clearly, innovations of this kind are becoming more and more a part of the fabric of contemporary social structures. Virtual worlds do not simply any longer belong to the realm of gaming. They are beginning to have substantial impact on the way we communicate, relate to each other, and especially the way in which we see ourselves as belonging to a community. Seidlhofer (2006) also comments that in contrast to conventional notions of 'speech community', a concept which is locally determined, a global concept of community can be more appropriately described as a discourse community, or better still a 'community of practice' (Wenger 1998). She suggests that adopting this term enables a rethinking of the more established convention in such a way that would make our description of community more compatible with the changed circumstances of the postmodern world. By associating the concepts of 'community' and 'practice', Wenger (1998) points out that it is possible to characterize both of these in more manageable, and potentially more flexible terms. In lingua franca settings, however, Wenger's notion needs to be somewhat reappraised in order to better fit the fluidity of ELF settings. As the multiple influences of globalization, interconnection and contact become evermore important to our understanding of the world (see e.g. Dewey 2007), and with distances continually being compressed through communications technology, traditional boundaries become more fluid, and are more often transgressed. In this light, Wenger's notion is arguably a more conservative one than is required here, especially given the protean nature of ELF communities. To better reflect this characteristic, we can envisage a still more fluid concept of community of practice, where the practice itself is modified as it is enacted. Nevertheless, by borrowing this term, and perhaps only slightly modifying its earlier definitions, we are able to detach descriptions of language variation and change from geographically defined locations. And, again as Seidlhofer argues, we can move forward still further from a characterization of sociolinguistic work as "the description of dialects as reified entities" (2006, 314), and can thus better describe current changes in discourse and communication, especially in the use of English as the lingua franca of wider, globally diffuse interactions.

6. An ELF Paradigm

All of the matters arising in the above discussion reflect important issues regarding how we rationalize ELF research in relation to existing paradigmatic frameworks. The need for a reorientation towards the way we define key conceptual concerns, from the domains of use, communities of speakers and forms of the language, requires a very different way of looking at English from a theoretical and ideological perspective. In the following table (see Table 2), I have attempted to identify the key concerns that a paradigmatic shift would entail by drawing comparisons between current paradigmatic trends[5] and the way I see ELF emerging as a distinctive paradigm.

In the first shift, we see a move towards reversing the tendency to downplay the performance element of language use, especially necessary because of the heightened dynamism of ELF and the fact that ELF research is predominantly concerned with the realizations of language in specific interactions. Therefore, instead of conceptualizing English as an entity which can be tied to (especially nationally defined) speech communities, it is seen in a more virtual light as a set of resources that transgress conventional boundaries. This has a substantial impact on how we determine levels of language proficiency, whereby under the new framework expertise is regarded as more context dependent, with communicative effectiveness more relevant than linguistic heritage. As a result, intelligibility is not seen to reside in the language system itself, but rather as something that must be achieved through effective, accommodative use of resources. In other words, successful communication is not tied to any one set of ENL norms, and variation is not simply a deviation from those norms. Instead, the enhanced variability that is so characteristic of ELF is seen as a creative, enterprising and inevitable result of language interaction. In relation to the pedagogic implications of this perspective, language learning targets and teaching materials are thus more locally defined (compare a similar account of a "leveled" rather than "hierarchical" approach in Canagarajah 2005).

Table 2. ELF as an emerging paradigm.

Current ELT & SLA Paradigms	Emerging ELF Paradigm
Downplaying of language performance—system and competence are primary	Highlighting of performative nature of language—actualization of system is primary
Native and nativized Englishes closely tied to one or other speech community, within particular nation states	English as a global, 'virtual' set of linguistic resources, with transgression of nationally defined varieties
Level of 'nativeness' / linguistic heritage determines level of competence	Expertise context dependent, locally determined and interactionally relevant
Success thus depends on adherence to centralized, standardized norms. Imitative measures used for language assessment	Success depends on ability to accommodate / shift speech patterns to achieve communicative effectiveness
Variation seen as 'deviation' from ENL and linguistic deficiency	Heightened variability and linguistic diversity—variation seen as inevitable and necessary
Native norms as target / use of 'authentic' materials and methods	Norms, materials and methods of local relevance

To sum up, the above paradigmatic shift means that we can describe, analyse and discuss ELF in a way that is far more congruent with the current social, cultural, and linguistic consequences of globalization. In Pennycook's (2006) discussion of the global presence of English, he considers the role of the language in what he terms "transcultural flows", a useful term in making sense of the fluidity involved in the way English is currently being used. Pennycook presents a case study of the global phenomenon of hip-hop, and asks whether the global spread of hip-hop involves an overarching cultural form connecting different practices around the world, or whether it is the sum total of its many local appropriations. The same question may be posed in relation to the global spread of English: to what extent can we define an ontology of English that holds together its many different realizations, and to what extent is it the product of all its different uses? At least with regard to existing conventional frameworks, there is a risk that we apply categories that are too fixed and too narrowly defined, which thus places a 'stricture' on language use that is incompatible with the way in which communication is achieved in lingua franca settings. Just as the world of global hip-hop is one of language mixing and 'transidiomatic' (Jacquemet 2005) practices and refashioned identities, the use of E in ELF is an appropriation of the language which draws on multiple local influences—it transecends or 'transgresses' (Jenks 2003) the local and the global, occupying a space in-between. The notion of performativity is particularly helpful here (see e.g. Butler 1997), as this makes possible a way of thinking about language use that avoids essentialized categories of, inter alia, language, culture, and identity. It is certainly a notion which I have found relevant to the proposed paradigmatic shifts presented in Table 2. From this point of view, we are not as we are because of some inner being but because of what we do. Applying this to language involves seeing English not so much as an entity, but rather as a means of communication that is enacted in communicative practices. It is constituted in what it does, in the functions it performs and the interactions it serves. As ELF settings and interactions continue to become the most widespread, this very distinctive practice of lingua franca communication in English is especially constitutive of what this language currently is.

Bibliography

Butler, J. 1997. *Excitable Speech: A Politics of the Performative*. London: Routledge.

Breiteneder, A. 2005. "The Naturalness of English as a European Lingua Franca: The Case of the 'Third Person –s'." *VIenna English Working PaperS* 14 (2), 3-26.

Canagarajah, A. S. 2005. "Introduction." In *Reclaiming the Local in Language Policy and Practice*, ed. A. S. Canagarajah, xiii-xxx. Mahwah, NJ.: Lawrence Earlbaum Associates.

Cogo, A. and M. Dewey 2006. "Efficiency in ELF Communication: From Pragmatic Motives to Lexico-Grammatical Innovation." *Nordic Journal of English Studies* 5 (2), 59-94.

Council of Europe 2001. *Common European Framework of Reference for Languages: Learning, Teaching, Assessment*. Cambridge: Cambridge University Press.

Dewey, M. 2007. "English as a Lingua Franca and Globalization: An Interconnected Perspective." *International Journal of Applied Linguistics* 17 (3), 332-54.
Eckert, P. 2008. "Variation and the Lexical Field." *Journal of Sociolinguistics* 12 (4), 453-76.
Ellis, R. 1994. *The Study of Second Language Acquisition*. Oxford: Oxford University Press.
Firth, A. and J. Wagner 1997. "On Discourse, Communication, and (Some) Fundamental Concepts in SLA Research." *Modern Language Journal* 81 (3), 285-300.
Graddol, D. 2006. *English Next*. The British Council.
Guest, T. 2007. *Second Lives: A Journey through Virtual Worlds*. London: Hutchinson.
Gumperz, J. J. 1971. *Language in Social Groups*. Stanford, CA: Stanford University Press.
Heller, M. 2008. "Language and the Nation-State: Challenges to Sociolinguistic Theory." *Journal of Sociolinguistics* 12 (4), 504-24.
Holborow, M. 1999. *The Politics of English: A Marxist View of Language*. London: Sage.
Home Office 2008. *Departmental Report 2008*. London: The Stationery Office. Available online at www.tsoshop.co.uk
House, J. 1999. "Misunderstanding in Intercultural Communication: Interactions in English as a Lingua Franca and the Myth of Mutual Intelligibility." In *Teaching and Learning English as a Global Language. Native and Non-Native Perspectives*, ed. C. Gnutzmann, 73-89. Tübingen: Stauffenburg Verlag.
Hymes, D. 1974. *Foundations in Sociolinguistics: An Ethnographic Approach*. Philadelphia: Centre for Curriculum Development.
Hülmbauer, C. 2007. "'You Moved, Aren't?'—The Relationship Between Lexicogrammatical Correctness and Communicative Effectiveness in English as a Lingua Franca." *VIenna English Working PaperS* 16 (2), 3-35.
Jacquemet, M. 2005. "Transidiomatic Practices, Language and Power in the Age of Globalization." *Language and Communication* 25 (3), 257-77.
Jenkins, J. 2007. *English as a Lingua Franca: Attitude and Identity*. Oxford: Oxford University Press.
—. 2006. "The Spread of English as an International Language: A Testing Time for Testers." *ELT Journal* 60 (1), 42-50.
—. 2000. *The Phonology of English as an International Language*. Oxford: Oxford University Press.

Jenks, C. 2003. *Transgression*. London: Routledge.
Klimpfinger, T. 2007. "'Mind You Sometimes You Have to Mix'—The Role of Code-Switching in English as a Lingua Franca." *Vienna English Working Papers* 16 (2), 36-61.
Leung, C. 2005. "Convivial Communication: Recontextualizing Communicative Competence." *International Journal of Applied Linguistics* 15 (2), 119-44.
Mauranen, A. 2003. "The Corpus of English as Lingua Franca in Academic Settings." *TESOL Quarterly* 37 (3), 513-27.
McNamara, T. 1996. *Measuring Second Language Performance*. London: Longman.
Patrick, P. 2002. "The Speech Community." In *The Handbook of Language Variation and Change*, ed. J. K. Chambers, P. Trudgill & N. Schilling-Estes, 573-97. Oxford: Blackwells.
Pennycook, A. 2006. *Global Englishes and Transcultural Flows*. London: Routledge.
—. 1994. *The Cultural Politics of English as an International Language*. London: Longman.
Pitzl, M.-L. this volume. "'We Should Not Wake Up Any Dogs': Idiom and Metaphor in ELF."
Rampton, B. 2006. *Language in Late Modernity: Interaction in an Urban School*. Cambridge: Cambridge University Press.
Schneider, E. 2003. "The Dynamics of new Englishes: From Identity Construction to Dialect Birth." *Language* 79 (2), 235-81.
Seidlhofer, B. this volume. "Orientations in ELF Research: Form and Function."
—. 2006. "English as a Lingua Franca and Communities of Practice." In *Anglistentag 2006 Halle Proceedings*, ed. S. Volk-Birke & J. Lippert, 307-18. Trier: Wissenschaftlicher Verlag Trier.
—. 2004. "Research Perspectives on Teaching English as a Lingua Franca." *Annual Review of Applied Linguistics* 24, 209-39.
Seidlhofer, B., A. Breiteneder and M.-L. Pitzl 2006. "English as a Lingua Franca in Europe: Challenges for Applied Linguistics." *Annual Review of Applied Linguistics* 26, 3-34.
Swan, M. and B. Smith 2001. *Learner English: A Teacher's Guide to Interference and Other Problems*. 2nd ed. Cambridge: Cambridge University Press.
Taylor, T. 2006. "The Changing Landscape of English: Implications for Language Assessment." *ELT Journal* 60 (1), 51- 60.

Wenger, E. 1998. *Communities of Practice: Learning, Meaning and Identity. (Learning in Doing: Social, Cognitive & Computational Perspectives).* Cambridge: Cambridge University Press

Notes

[1] This corpus was originally gathered as part of a PhD thesis presented at King's College London. The corpus consists of approximately 60,000 words of fully transcribed primarily naturally occurring face-to-face ELF talk among international postgraduate students at a London university. The recordings were conducted predominantly in informal, non-classroom-based settings, with a small number of recordings conducted in more formal institutional settings (5 from a total of 42 communicative events) where participants were giving presentations and engaging in subsequent class discussion.

[2] With regard to my terms of reference for describing English, in this paper I use 'L1 Englishes' and 'ENL' as largely synonymous means of referring to what would be described in a Kachruvian sense as "inner circle" varieties. I also refer to 'Standard English' in places, and elsewhere to 'ENL norms', both of which are terms I have used when highlighting the distinctiveness of ELF features in a contrastive way, especially with regard to the way in which ENL tends to be understood in language pedagogy. In other words, with regard to how ENL/L1 English is largely understood to be a set of norms to be applied in all language learning settings.

[3] There are particular language tests which are sanctioned for this purpose, administered by various different examining bodies, but all of which would fit the largely conservative profile of ELT language testers provided in Jenkins' (2006) critique.

[4] The Cambridge ESOL main suite exams consist of spoken tests that take place in dyads of candidates, with the assessor sitting outside of the conversation as an external observer.

[5] I am not suggesting in any sense that there is a unified coherent framework in either ELT or SLA, and there are of course huge differences in approach across different subdisciplines. So at the risk of oversimplifying matters, what I am attempting to do here is provide a summary of typical characteristics in the way English is most usually conceptualized.

SYNTACTIC FEATURES IN SPOKEN ELF—LEARNER LANGUAGE OR SPOKEN GRAMMAR?

ELINA RANTA

1. Introduction

The critics of English as a lingua franca (ELF) research have challenged ELF from its early days by claiming that this new research field is nothing but a variant of Second Language Acquisition (SLA) research, and that all there is to say about ELF has already been said within the studies of learner language. Especially the grammatical features of ELF have merely been identified with learner errors that merit no further investigation.

The purpose of this paper is to take a closer look at these common claims to find out whether they are justified. This is of course nothing new in itself in the field of ELF, as many ELF researchers have patiently tried to make clear the differences between the concepts of English as a lingua franca and learner language many times before (cf. e.g. Jenkins 2006 and Seidlhofer 2004), but in this paper the discussion is approached from the standpoint of *spoken language* and *spoken language grammar*. The paper aims to show that we can adopt quite a different stance (from that of an SLA perspective) towards grammatical features of second language (L2) speech if we regard L2 speech as normal speech (as ELF does) instead of erroneous speech (as in SLA) and set it in a fair comparison with other varieties of *spoken* English. This is illustrated with the help of three verb-syntactic features that emerge as re-current features of spoken ELF in the ELFA corpus—the first 1-million-word spoken corpus of academic ELF, compiled at the University of Tampere and University of Helsinki.

The paper, however, begins with an overview of the discussion of the conceptual differences between learner language and English as a lingua franca in an attempt to summarize some of the main points. This is then followed by a discussion of spoken language and its grammar, after which the focus shifts to the three salient spoken ELF features and the comparison of these to those in other spoken varieties of English. Finally, the discussion will be drawn together and some ways forward suggested in the conclusion.

2. Learner Language vs. English as a Lingua Franca

The term "learner language" (or interlanguage) stems from the studies of second language acquisition. Thus, it is important to take a closer look at what kinds of premises this research field is built upon to be able to see what the concept of "learner language" holds, and how it differs from English as a lingua franca.

Given that SLA is a fairly young research field (with its origins usually dated in the late 1960's), it has seen a rapid expansion and proliferation in its methods and also in its field of inquiry especially in the recent decades (see for example the various methods of analysis described in Ellis and Barkhuizen 2005). However, at the same time debates have arisen in SLA regarding the scope and even the object of study. Some people are willing to welcome diversity in the field—as manifested, for instance, in Ellis and Barkhuizen (2005) who maintain that "SLA is multi-disciplinary" (p. 3). But it is still fairly easy to discern in the literature a kind of "hard core" of SLA research that seems to predominate the field. Following from this, studies carried out in this core framework are often termed "mainstream SLA". It is this mainstream SLA that concerns us here.

Both the fact that this kind of core still exists, as well as the premises of mainstream SLA research became evident in a *Modern Language Journal* debate which was ignited by Firth and Wagner's (1997) article suggesting a reconceptualization of SLA. Firth and Wagner criticized, among other things, SLA's core concepts of "learner" (usually seen as a deficient communicator in SLA and allowed only this reduced identity), the idealized concept of a "native speaker" (NS), as well as "interlanguage" (with native speaker competence as a goal). Further, the writers criticized the individual-cognitive orientation of SLA research with its focus on the second language speaker's underlying psycholinguistic competence as opposed to performance, and called for increased "emic" (i.e. participant-relevant) analyses of SLA data (as opposed to observer-relevant "etic" analyses). Moreover, they demanded an overall broadening of SLA database to include more naturally-occurring conversations (rather than data elicited in experimental settings) and conversations between non-native speakers (NNS) (and not just NS-NNS interactions). They also pointed out that mainstream SLA research tends to focus on difficulties and problems that learners are seen to struggle with rather than on their communicative success. On the whole, Firth and Wagner suggested SLA take more interest in the *use* of a second language in everyday communication rather than focussing on data from formal learning environments (i.e. classrooms).

Among the responses Firth and Wagner received there were both supporting and opposing ones (see the *Modern Language Journal* issues 81/3 and 82/1). But what concerns us here is that those opposing the reconceptualization of SLA as suggested by Firth and Wagner essentially confirmed that the aspects of SLA that the writers had criticized indeed were the key constructs of the field—and were so for a good reason. I will not go into the details of the debate but suffice it say that generally speaking, according to the opponents, the goal of SLA was to study *acquisition* (not everyday *use*) of L2 by primarily looking into the psycholinguistic processes of how a learner's interlanguage knowledge progresses from one stage to another (see Kasper 1997, Long 1997, Poulisse 1997, and Gass 1998). In her response, Gass (1998, note 3) even explicitly divided the study of L2 use and acquisition into different research fields. So even though the field of SLA may have seen a diversification in its methods and objects of study (as Ellis and Barkhuizen 2005 demonstrate), the kinds of changes that Firth and Wagner (1997) suggested have still stayed in the margins of so-called mainstream SLA.

Thus, the *Modern Language Journal* debate seemed to confirm that in SLA, second language speakers are seen primarily as *learners* of the L2 on their way to native (or near-native) proficiency in that language. And even though the so-called learner language or interlanguage they use is considered a system in its own right, not comparable to that of a native speaker (as Corder 1967 and Selinker 1972 originally suggested), native speaker proficiency is still the target that L2 speakers in SLA are regarded to be striving for (see e.g. Kasper 1997, 310). Moreover, the kind of proficiency that mainstream SLA is actually interested in, is the speaker's underlying competence (in Chomskyan terms) and not his or her overt performance *per se*. This has led mainstream SLA to occupy itself mainly with an individual's cognitive processes and the individual's mental representations of the L2, and relevant data for these kinds of studies most often come from elicited samples from clinical or experimental settings (see e.g. Ellis & Barkhuizen 2005, 365) to allow researchers to focus on the specific interlanguage feature(s) under scrutiny.

Furthermore, despite the fact that some of those responding critically to Firth and Wagner's (1997) views did not subscribe to the claim that SLA treats learners as deficient communicators, still others were ready to admit this, too. For instance, Poulisse (1997, 325) writes:

> [Firth and Wagner] begin by pointing out that this research [into Communicative Strategies in SLA] has been preoccupied with the foreign language learner's linguistic deficiencies and communicative problems. This is true, and there is a good reason for it. Linguistic deficiencies and communicative problems are relatively frequent in the speech of foreign language learners.

Kasper (1997, 310), too, admits that even though warnings have been sounded in SLA not to compare learners' "interlanguage" and native speakers' "correct" forms to each other (which is essentially the source of the deficit view), no one has paid much attention to these warnings (including Kasper herself, in her own words) (see Cook 2002, 8-9 for further defence of L2 speakers). The deficit paradigm in SLA is probably also due to the afore-mentioned fact that SLA takes the individual as its unit of analysis. As Brutt-Griffler (2002, ch. 7) writes, it is easy to accuse *individuals* of "errors" or defects where they deviate from the native speaker standard, while in the case of whole groups of people that would be politically out of line in modern linguistics (as in the case of, for example, AAVE or Indian English speakers). But perhaps the main source for the deficit paradigm, which is also important for our discussion, is the fact that learners are often compared to an idealized, "omniscient" native speaker (cf. e.g. Firth & Wagner 1997, 291) who speaks in normative standard language. If this is the taken-for-granted point of comparison for L2 speakers, and no attention is paid to how the "real" native speaker uses the language in real life situations it is easy to end up with ill-informed claims of L2 speakers "misusing" the language. This problem becomes particularly obvious in the volumes that list so-called common "learner errors" (cf. e.g. Turton and Heaton's *Longman Dictionary of Common Errors*, 1996) without actually having consulted any NS data for comparable features.

Finally, there is a long tradition in SLA to relate the "errors" that learners make to their first languages, in other words, errors are seen as "transfer" or "interference" from the learner's mother tongue. Although the original source for this model of explanation, Contrastive Analysis, fell out of fashion in SLA long ago (cf. Ellis & Barkhuizen 2005, 52), and although later studies in SLA have indeed shown that this explanation is far from being always valid, the tendency to refer to L1 interference as a kind of shortcut explanation has still lived on, especially in practical guidebooks for language teachers (cf. for example the volume *Learner English: A Teacher's Guide to Interference and Other Problems* edited by Swan and Smith 2001, where the title itself is rather revealing). This means that often the explanation for an error is sought in the speaker's mother tongue even when the exact same "error" seems to be common for learners from many typologically different first language backgrounds. This point is something that I will return to later.

But turning to the differences between learner language and English as a Lingua Franca research—how do the fields deviate from one another then? To answer this question, we can go back to Firth and Wagner's (1997) article. Many of the points they wanted to change in SLA are actually points that have been reconsidered in ELF and towards which ELF research has taken a different kind of approach compared to SLA (and very often that is in line with what Firth and Wagner suggested for SLA). First, ELF takes its interest expressly in how L2 English speakers *use* the language in their everyday and professional communication with—mainly—other L2 speakers, so the object of study is the observable "performance" of the speakers (in Chomskyan terms). Thus, ELF research does *not* seek to study, for example, how L2 speakers could "learn more" in order to become "more native-like" or how their knowledge of the L2 is stored in their language faculty and how to make it more similar to that of a native speaker. Secondly the focus of research is on a level above the individual, i.e. on larger groups of English L2 speakers and the way they interact and make use of their L2 resources in practice. To study this, ELF researchers aim to analyse naturally-occurring data instead of elicited samples so as to get to the actual, authentic language use.

Furthermore, native speaker speech is not a yardstick against which ELF speakers' speech is evaluated (as it is in SLA), but of course it provides a kind of baseline data for researchers to see what in ELF is different or, indeed, similar to NS speech (cf. Mauranen 2005, 275). I do not see a problem in using NS baseline data (as claimed by Firth and Wagner 1997, 292) as long as the purpose is non-evaluative. In other fields of linguistics, too, such as typology or variation and change, comparisons between varieties are made constantly without an intention of creating rank orders of languages or dialects. In L2 studies, comparable, naturally-occurring NS data can only help to get around the idealization of a native speaker as it gives us insights into how authentic native speech actually works.

It should be clear from the above that because ELF research is not interested in language acquisition as such, it also does not view its subjects as "learners" but L2 speakers or users. This is also justified by the contexts studied in ELF research: the speakers are not usually involved in an instructional setting and their primary goal is not to "learn more" English when they converse but to get whatever professional or personal business they have at hand done with their interlocutors. Thus, ELF conversations are approached in a similar fashion to any L1-L1 conversation in that ELF communication is seen as quite normal language use, and not as something exceptional deviating from a norm. Where L2 use is observed to deviate from L1 use, it is not automatically deemed defective or problematic, unless it causes problems in the communication at hand. This approach does away with the "deficit" paradigm of SLA and also resonates with Firth and Wagner's call for more participant-relevant analyses of L2 use. Moreover, because ELF speakers are not considered learners, they are not placed on an interlanguage continuum (cf. Jenkins 2006 for criticism on the interlanguage continuum) and are not viewed as striving for the NS goal in terms of their language use. Looking at L2 communication from the point of view of "normal" (however defined) communication, instead of the point of view of deviant linguistic activity, can actually make us see new things—or "old" things in new light, as I will try to demonstrate in the course of this article.

3. Spoken Language and Its Grammar

As pointed out above, one of the facts that has made L2 speakers' speech appear "deficient" or "wrong" is that their *spoken production* has often been compared with *standard language*—which is essentially based on written language norms. This is, of course, unfair in any linguistic sense, as written and spoken language operate on different premises and cannot be equated offhand. Thus such comparison needs to be taken under close scrutiny if we really want to give L2 users fair and full recognition as speakers.

As a matter of fact, it is not just SLA in linguistics that has long worked on an oversight of spoken language but, according to Linell (1982; 2005), the whole scientific study of language seems to be flawed with what he calls a "written language bias". This means that despite the fact that linguists agree that speech is the primary form of human language, both phylogenetically and ontogenetically, the main focus of linguistics has nevertheless rested on the study of the written mode, and this has led us to conceptualize *language* as a whole (including spoken language) in terms of the written mode. This is perhaps understandable in the light of tape recorders having become available for research purposes only in the 1950's—before that the only concrete evidence of language use for language researchers was embodied in written texts. But also the high recognition of written language *per se* has contributed to the fact that even the advent of recording devices does not seem to have remedied the situation entirely—the roots of linguistics lie too deep in the study of written language for fast reforms. Thus, although the study of spoken language really took off in the 1980's with various new research methods suited for this purpose (such as conversation analysis, discourse analysis and corpus-based analysis of transcribed speech), Linell (2005) can still find over a hundred points to demonstrate how the written language bias continues to affect the study and conceptualization of (spoken) language even today.

Since, according to Linell (2005, 14-15), foreign language teaching was one of the first domains that made extensive use of the written mode with large groups of people, it comes as no surprise that language pedagogy, too, should still suffer from this bias—as pointed out by McCarthy (1998, 18). In educational settings, most of the time the spoken input and the model for speech to be imitated by learners are based on written language grammar and vocabulary (McCarthy 1998, 15-20), and not on the way L1 speakers themselves use the language in *spoken* interaction. McCarthy (1998, 20) also regrets that despite the fact that we now know much more about how spoken language is really used—thanks to an increasing number of spoken corpora—there still seems to be a tendency in language pedagogy towards teaching what is *thought* to be proper language use instead of accepting descriptions of the spoken target language as it actually is between L1 speakers. In other words, L2 speakers' speech in classroom settings continues to be assessed against written (standard) language models. And this is particularly so with regard to grammatical constructions in speech.

Grammar seems to be particularly elusive in speech for us perhaps because, as Widdowson (2003, 39) puts it, we tend to "edit grammar out" when we listen to someone speak to catch the proposition of what was said. It follows from this "ignorance" that we *think* we employ the rules of written grammar even when we speak. Halliday's (1987, 57-58) recollection of his early experiences of recording and observing the properties of spoken language in the 1950's and 1960's illustrates this nicely: not only were the people he observed unconscious of the structures they had just used in their speech but also, when the structures were pointed out to them, they downright denied having used them in the first place and even claimed they could *never* say anything like that. Others, on the other hand, dismissed the structures as occasional slips. Yet, as Halliday remarks, many of these 'slips' occurred systematically in speech.

The moral of the story is, of course, that we cannot trust merely our intuition about grammar in speech but can become aware of its peculiarities only through careful study of real-life spoken data. However, it is, of course, unfortunate that even though we now have solid research findings on features in spoken grammar, it seems that it is particularly in grammatical structures where the difference between spoken and written language is the most difficult to accept. This explains why L2 speakers, too, are still penalized for constructions that could actually be just typical features of *spoken* grammar (cf. McCarthy 1998, 20). In pedagogy, these features continue to be treated as performance errors backed by the *belief* that L1 speakers would never use such constructions in their speech. So very often we are faced with a kind of double fallacy: L1 speakers are *thought* to speak in standard (written) language, and that is why L2 speakers should adhere to written grammar in their speech as well—as if their goal was to 'speak written language'.

But as, for example, Linell (2005, 14 and 26-27) reminds us, we cannot use written language as a proxy for spoken language because writing did not historically originate in attempting to record speech as it occurred but it had special functions of its own and consequently went through a number of adaptations for its own purposes. This same remark is also reflected in Miller and Weinert (1998, 23) who say that:

> The properties of spontaneous spoken language and the properties of formal written language both reflect the conditions under which they are produced. This does not mean that the properties of the former result from attempts to use the structures typical of the latter—attempts which fail because of the time constraints and the different tasks that claim attention in any face-to-face interaction. Rather, the structures of spontaneous spoken language have developed in such a way that they *can* be used in the circumstances in which conversation, for example, usually takes place. (emphasis in the original)

In other words, spoken language features are not "defects" caused by our inability to follow written norms in our speech but they emerge due to entirely different circumstances for use and thus follow their own norms. As so many researchers of spoken language have been saying all along: spoken language is not the corrupted version of written language—they both simply constitute modes of their own (see e.g. Mauranen 2006a).

For instance, Miller and Weinert (1998, 22) summarize some of the basic differences between spoken and written language as follows. Spontaneous spoken language is produced in real time with no opportunity for editing, while writing is usually produced with pauses for thinking and with much editing[1]. Spontaneous spoken language is also subject to the limitations of short-term memory: both speaker and hearer can hold only a limited number of items in their working memory at once. Speech is also typically produced face-to-face in a particular context, and it thus makes use of so-called paralinguistic features such as pitch, rhythm, and voice quality as well as gestures, facial expressions and body postures. According to Miller and Weinert (1998, 22-23) these characteristics naturally reflect in the linguistic properties of speech. For instance, information is carefully staged in speech meaning that only a small quantity of information is assigned to each phrase (cf. also Halliday 1987 who refers to this as 'low lexical density' pointing to a lower number of content words in a spoken phrase compared to a written phrase). Spoken language has also far less grammatical subordination and more co-ordination than writing, and the syntax of spoken language typically seems "fragmented" and "unintegrated" (from the written syntax perspective). Also, spoken language has grammatical constructions and patterns of its own that do not (typically) occur in writing, and vice versa. The writers find evidence for the last claim throughout their book in that similar kinds of features of spoken language occur in speech even *across* languages (English, French, Russian, and others).

The last claim about spoken language displaying grammatical constructions of its own is particularly important for us in the present discussion. In the following, I will look into some frequent grammatical features in ELF that are often deemed learner errors in English language teaching, but that might actually be just everyday features of *spoken* English grammar.

4. Verb-Syntactic Features in Spoken ELF

This section briefly presents three different non-standard verb-syntactic features in ELF and also takes a look at the same features in native-speaker data for comparative purposes. The reason for choosing to look into verb-syntactic features of all grammatical constructions lies in the fact that often verbs are considered to be the 'core' of an utterance (if the utterance has one in the first place), and thus important carriers of meaning and syntactic relations in an utterance. It is also interesting to note that especially in English, verb constructions are traditionally seen as providing some of the most "troublesome problems" for L2 speakers (cf. Leech 1987, 1). The selection of the three particular features in the present paper, on the other hand, is purely the result of their high frequency and recurrence in the ELF data studied. The findings presented below are still preliminary, however, as they come from a larger on-going research project which is sure to provide deeper insights into the features once finished.

4.1. The Data

The data for the present paper comes from the ELFA (*English as Lingua Franca in Academic Settings*) corpus, which is the first 1-million-word spoken corpus of academic ELF (see the corpus homepage at http://www.eng.helsinki.fi/elfa/elfacorpus.htm, and Mauranen 2003). The ELFA corpus comprises both monologic and dialogic speech events (e.g. lectures and seminar presentations as well as seminar discussions, PhD theses defence discussions, panel discussions etc.) conducted in English between—mainly—L2 speakers in four different universities in Finland. The academic domains covered in the corpus range from technology, natural sciences and medicine to humanities, behavioral sciences and social sciences. Also the range of speakers in ELFA is wide: the 650 speakers come from all over the world and represent 51 different first language backgrounds. (For more detailed descriptions of the corpus see Mauranen 2006b and Mauranen & Ranta 2008).

Academic settings are a particularly suitable domain for ELF research as English is the *de facto* lingua franca in the academia internationally, and many of the speakers use English regularly as their daily working language. In passing, the latter fact again renders the appellation 'learner' questionable, as some of the speakers have conducted their whole professional careers in English. It would, indeed, be patronizing to call such speakers 'learners' regardless how "near-native" they are. Another good reason for using academic speech for ELF studies is the fact that this domain is very demanding language-wise: the speakers have to be able to argue points, defend their views, elaborate their ideas etc.—and for ELF speakers, all this has to be accomplished in their second language with not much help from the physical context, as the topics discussed are often abstract. This puts pressure on language use particularly, and speakers who manage in these contexts can, for a good reason, be regarded as models for other ELF speakers as well.

For the purposes of the present study, a sub-corpus of ELFA of approximately 0.77 million words was compiled to ensure a maximally diverse representation of the speakers' first language backgrounds—and to further reduce the share of L1 Finnish speakers' production, which in the current database is approximately 16 %. In the following discussion, I will, nevertheless, refer to this sub-corpus as 'ELFA'. In addition to the ELF corpus, a comparable corpus from L1 native-speaker academic settings, MICASE (*The Michigan Corpus of Academic Spoken English*), was used as a reference corpus to explore similar constructions in NS speech (see http://lw.lsa.umich.edu/eli/micase/index.htm, and Simpson et al. 1999). MICASE comprises largely identical speech events to those in ELFA (lectures, seminars etc. from various academic disciplines) and stands at around 1.7 million words. Let us now turn to the features studied in these two corpora.

4.2. Hypothetical *if*-clauses

One of the recurrent non-standard grammatical features in the ELFA data is to be found in hypothetical *if*-clauses. *If*-clauses lay down a condition for a main clause, and the traditional, normative ELT paradigm distinguishes between three different kinds of *if*-clause+main clause – pairings, based on how "real" the condition is perceived to be. The paradigm is as follows:

- 1st conditional based on a "real" condition:
  constructed with *will* (in the main clause) +
  the present tense (in the *if*-clause), as in
  I will leave immediately if she comes.
- 2nd conditional based on an "unreal" condition:
  constructed with *would* + the past tense, as in
  I would leave immediately if she came.
- 3rd conditional also based on an "unreal" condition:
  constructed with *would have* + the past perfect, as in
  I would have left immediately if she had come.

The 2nd and 3rd conditionals represent hypothetical meaning with different degrees of hypotheticality (cf. Leech 1987, 116-118) and are the focus of our study here.

The non-standardness in ELF occurs in the hypothetical *if*-clauses as *would* and *would have* are used also in the *if*-clause instead of the normative past and past perfect tense respectively. Examples of such use from ELFA include:

(1) most people would choose video-on-demand over going to movie rental shop **if their price would be** the same
(2) but your requirement is stronger in the sense that **if you would implement** the fairness requirement in in some other way…
(3) i wanted to avoid this mine- if **if i would have just analysed** policies i there is this minefield of of party politics…
(4) because **if i would have left** in one month or something she wouldn't have fixed it

As hinted at earlier, this is one of the features that has often been considered "learner English", so not surprisingly the collection of learner

Englishes by Swan and Smith (2001) lists this feature as something causing problems for English L2 speakers from at least the following L1 backgrounds: Dutch, German, Italian, Portuguese, Greek, Russian, Polish, Turkish, Hindi, as well as Dravidian and West African languages. This non-standard use is also listed as an "error" in Turton and Heaton (1996, s.v. *would*). It is more interesting, however, that the cause for this "problem" in Swan and Smith (2001) is attributed to the respective L1s in almost all of the cases they mention (except for Hindi and Dravidian languages where this connection is not explicitly made). Sometimes the cause of the trouble is attributed to a lack of comparable construction in a learner's L1, sometimes to a different patterning of a similar construction—nevertheless, the outcome is always the same: use of *would* or *would have* in *if*-clauses. This certainly makes the reader doubt the validity of such an all-encompassing "L1-interference explanation". What is more, in the current ELFA data, this feature is attested in the use of speakers from 15 different L1 backgrounds, including Bulgarian, Czech, Dagbani, Danish, Dutch, Estonian, Finnish, German, Italian, Portuguese, Polish, Romanian, Russian, Somali and Swedish—which add a few more typologically very different languages to the ones in Swan and Smith. If the feature is so widely spread in L2 English, can it really be related to each and every speaker's mother tongue? What gives even more cause for concern about the validity of this explanation is Comrie's (1986) note on conditional constructions in the world's languages in general. He writes:

> Concerning time reference [...] backshifting of tense is found [...] crosslinguistically in conditionals with high hypotheticality; the commonest kinds of conditionals in actual use seem to be those of low hypotheticality with future time reference and those of high hypotheticality with past time reference. (Comrie 1986, 96)

Thus, globally speaking it seems that the patterning of hypothetical conditionals would be more or less the same as in English for many other languages in the world, which would mean that in global terms, English L2 speakers should not have particular problems with 'translating' this feature from their L1s into English. Consequently, one is tempted to look for reasons for such a feature in other sources than the speakers' respective mother tongues.

In fact, searching for *would/would have* in *if*-clauses in a native-speaker corpus, MICASE, reveals that the feature is present also in the speech of educated L1 speakers, as the following examples from MICASE manifest:

(5) if you do the reverse reacti- like **if you would add** something to that do you know what would happen?
(6) instead **if they would get** a profit, they'd make a lot more money
(7) we woulda been better off **if we would've done** this exercise, when you first got here
(8) do you think would've been more limited in their responses to non-native speakers **if they would've had** a spoken situation
(9) **if he wouldn't have burned** it it wouldn't- it would've been totally out of his character and wouldn't have represented, the first half of the novel at all.

Overall, the rate for using *would/would have* in hypothetical *if*-clauses for ELFA is 29 % and for MICASE only 2 %, but the difference is largely explained by the fact that in ELFA, *would* occurs much more frequently in 2nd conditional *if*-clauses (26 % of all 2nd conditionals) compared to MICASE, in which the percentage is 1.3 %. However, in the case of 3rd conditionals, the non-standard use becomes clearly more frequent in MICASE, too: ELFA speakers use *would have* in 3rd conditional *if*-clauses 75 % of the time, and MICASE speakers in 24 % of the instances. It is noteworthy that the figure for such a non-standard feature is close to 1/4 in the case of 3rd conditionals even for educated native-speakers. Miller and Weinert (1998, 84) have also found that the non-standard constructions (especially as regards 3rd conditionals) are becoming more frequent in native-speaker use, and have even found examples of such use in published L1 writing. Thus they declare unhesitatingly that: "[*Would/would have* in hypothetical *if*-clauses] are produced by educated speakers and are making their way into standard written English" (p. 84). And surely, by looking at the MICASE data, one could venture a hypothesis that if Miller and Weinert are right, the non-standard constructions might well be making their way into L1 English through the 3rd conditionals, where the non-standard use is already widely observable.

In addition to MICASE data, *A Handbook for Varieties of English* (edited by Kortmann & Schneider 2004) was consulted for the above constructions. The accounts of different spoken Inner and Outer circle varieties (as well as creoles) reveal that the same feature is also to be found to varying degrees at least in ten varieties of English world-wide ranging from South-eastern British English and Scottish English to AAVE, Newfoundland English, Fiji English, and beyond.

Thus, looking at the data above, it makes one rather uneasy to think that using *would* or *would have* in hypothetical *if*-clauses was a mere learner error. Quite the contrary, if this is something widely attested in different kinds of spoken Englishes all around the world, including educated native-speaker speech, could it be that we are dealing here with something else than "imperfect learning" or occasional "slips" in spoken interaction? Before answering this question, let us take a look at two more similar cases.

4.3. Existential *there is* + The Plural

Another non-standard verb-syntactic construction that L2 speakers are often penalized for has to do with subject-verb concord in the existential construction *there is* + *Noun*. According to normative grammar, the verb *be* should take the plural (*are/were/* etc.) if the noun following it is in the plural, as in:

There are some *people* outside waiting for you.

The "error" that L2 speakers are accused of here is, of course, that they "fail" to produce the plural form of the verb in above contexts and go on using the singular, be the following noun in singular or plural. Turton and Heaton (1996, s.v. *there*), among others, list this use as a "common learner error" in their dictionary.

Indeed, this feature is well manifested in the ELFA corpus. For the purposes of this paper, only 500 randomly sampled constructions in the present tense were retrieved from the data (both for *there is* and *there's*), yielding examples such as:

(10) [...] in honduras and in nicaragua but we have to see that **there is** er **some differences** between the countries
(11) democratic states should do this but er it it must be in a context where **there is multi-party er elections**
(12) the full sun production of coffee it's unshaded **there's no er shade trees** [...] in central america
(13) i've been looking for those projects in internet and i found few but they've been very small like **there's two computers** in one school and some NGOs supporting them

Also, looking at the L1 backgrounds of the speakers who used this construction in ELFA, we can see that the spectrum is wide. The relevant speakers' mother tongues include: Arabic, Bulgarian, Czech, Dutch, Finnish, French, German, Greek, Hindi, Italian, Kihaya, Lithuanian, Nepali, Portuguese, Romanian, Russian, Swahili, and Swedish. So again, one could assume that it is not the speakers' L1 that causes this feature in their speech.

Unlike in the case of hypothetical *if*-clauses, though, the use of the singular *be* with plural nouns in existential constructions is something that has drawn many researchers' attention even in native-speaker use. This non-standardness has been widely attested and discussed in many varieties of English (see e.g. Nevalainen 2009 and Tagliamonte 2009 for short reviews of the discussion), and it appears to be common also among the educated L1 speakers in the MICASE data. Again a random sample of 500 present tense existential constructions with *there is* or *there's* were retrieved. The results include, for instance:

(14) so um in the United States **there's a hundred to four hundred and fifty cases** of it.
(15) **there's example exams**, on the web or on the web page
(16) i just asked Julie cuz because i think **there is a lot of different issues** around **there's huge issues**
(17) well, **there's a lot of different levels** on which you can understand literature right?

However, there are again some statistical differences between the instances in ELFA and MICASE. First, *there is/there's* + the plural seems to be more common in the MICASE data (11 % of all possible combinations of the existential construction in the present tense in a random sample of 500 instances), whereas the ELFA speakers seem to be more norm-oriented in their use with only 5 % of the 500 randomly sampled occurrences showing this pattern. Secondly, the full construction *there is* (as opposed to the contracted *there's*) is used overall more in ELFA than in MICASE and in ELFA it also seems to take a plural noun more often (6.5 % of all the cases of *there is/there's* + plural) than the same construction in MICASE (where this sample yielded only one such instance, given in Example 16 above). Nevertheless, for both databases the overall tendency proved similar: it is the contracted construction (*there's*) that is followed by a plural noun more often than the non-contracted *there is*. The latter phenomenon has been found in other studies, too. For instance, Biber et al. (1999, 186) note that in their conversational data, plural nouns occur more frequently with the cliticized *there's* than the full construction *there is*. They suggest the reason for this is that the contracted *there's* has become a fixed expression, which does not distinguish between singularity or plurality anymore. Whatever the reason for this phenomenon might be, it is noteworthy that the L2 speakers in the ELFA data seem to show a similar linguistic behavior in their spoken grammar to that of native speakers in that *there's* 'attracts' the plural more often than *there is*.

Again, double-checking the reference materials (Kortmann & Schneider 2004) for this feature reveals that the pattern is, indeed, common in numerous spoken varieties of English all over the world, especially in the British Isles, North America, Australia, New Zealand and South Africa. So, in this light it needs to be asked whether it is reasonable and justified to claim that whenever L2 users employ the construction *there is/there's* + plural they are making a mistake, whereas L1 speakers of English uttering the same construction are only making use of the resources of the language. A third feature discussed next raises similar questions.

4.4. Embedded Inversions

The third feature looked into here concerns the so-called embedded inversions, by which I refer to indirect (i.e. embedded) questions with inverted word order. This feature thus relates more to the level of syntax and the position of the verb in it. Indirect questions can be divided into two categories: 'open-ended' *WH*-questions (see example (a) below), and *yes/no* -type of questions (as in example (b)). In both cases, however, the word order should, according to normative grammar, be uninverted (i.e. subject+predicate) as in the examples below:

(a) Do you understand **what he is saying**?
(b) I wonder **if they are coming**.

The "problem" for learners in such syntactic patterns is claimed to be that they invert the word order (i.e. predicate+subject) even in these embedded questions—although inversion should be restricted only to direct questions—producing utterances such as:

(a) Do you understand **what is he saying**?
(b) I wonder **are they coming**.

Turton and Heaton (1996) list this "common error" under several entries for question words (cf. s.v. *what*, s.v. *when*, s.v. *which*, and s.v. *why*) in their dictionary. Also the writers in Swan and Smith (2001) find word order in indirect questions problematic for learners at least from French, Italian, Spanish/Catalan, Portuguese, Polish, Farsi, Chinese and Korean L1 backgrounds as well as for L1 speakers of Dravidian and West African languages. Again, interference from the speakers' respective mother tongues is offered as an explanation for half of the cases (at least in the case of Portuguese, Polish, Farsi, Chinese and Korean), but for this feature also overgeneralization of the direct question word order is seen as a possible source of "error" (see e.g. Spanish, French). For Italian and Dravidian and West African languages no explicit source is suggested.

Yet again, exactly the same feature has drawn researchers' attention in many native-speaker vernacular varieties, too (see e.g. Filppula 1999, 167ff. and Filppula et al. 2008, 191ff.), and also according to Kortmann and Schneider (2004), embedded inversion is found to be frequent in 15 different vernacular varieties of English ranging from colloquial American English and Irish English to Indian and Singapore English to Australian and New Zealand English etc.

Retrieving this particular feature in corpus data is somewhat tricky, which is why the most often employed queries have utilized the matrix verbs preceding possible indirect questions. For the purposes of this paper, both ELFA and MICASE were searched for the matrix verbs *ask*, *wonder*, *see* and *understand* with the six most common question words (*what*, *when*, *where*, *who*, *why* and *how*) as context words, augmented by *if* and *whether*, and the three main auxiliaries (*be*, *do*, and *have*). Based on this sample, the overall rate for embedded inversions in ELFA was 19 % of all indirect questions, rendering examples such as:

(18) and i wonder **where does that concept** of mhm knowledge come from
(19) when you start to ask **how are they** bound together...
(20) we are correlating the signal with itself at different time (laps) to see **is it** correlated or **is it** uncorrelated
(21) if you know the code you may understand **what is it** about but...

In this sample, the feature manifests itself in the production of mother-tongue speakers of Bengali, Czech, Dangme, Danish, Dutch, Finnish, French, German, Hindi, Italian, Kikuyu, Polish, Portuguese, Romanian, Russian, Swahili, and Swedish.

For the MICASE data, the overall rate for embedded inversions was lower at 5 %, but the instances retrieved are very similar to those in ELFA, such as:

(22) now you might wonder **what is the purpose** of, cancer cells
(23) did you ask **is Shannon** done?
(24) they can do a lot of different tests they can look and see **how does that little rat** search for that platform
(25) because people really want to understand **why do we** get cycles

Also, when it comes to the matrix verbs, it seems on the basis of this sample that the extent to which each verb 'attracts' embedded inversion was similar (proportioned to the size of the two samples), so that *ask* attracted the most embedded inversion in both corpora, followed by *wonder*, *see* and *understand*. Further, considering the question words used in these queries, they, too, showed a similar pattern in each case: *what*, *why* and *where* being the most frequent question words 'causing' embedded inversion. In the case of auxiliaries (*be*, *do*, and *have*) versus *if* and *whether*, the difference in ratio between the corpora was very small: ELFA speakers formed *yes/no-* indirect questions with auxiliaries in 6.5 % of the relevant cases, whereas the percentage for MICASE speakers was 4.8 %.

So what we can conclude from here is that the patterns of use for embedded inversion appear to be very similar for both educated L1 and L2 speakers—it is only the slightly larger degree to which the feature can be found in L2 data that differentiates between the samples. All the same, the feature is there in (educated) native-speaker speech as well as in many other L1 vernacular varieties as discussed above. So is it an error? Probably not.

In the following discussion I will try to bring the pieces of evidence together and suggest a new way of looking at some of the features that have traditionally been put down to "imperfect learning" or characteristics of learner language in L2 use.

5. Discussion

By letting go of the restrictive learner/deficit paradigm—cast as the only possible mould for L2 speakers by SLA—and by setting L2 speech on a par with comparable L1 speech, we can actually gain fresh insights into spoken L2, as this paper has attempted to demonstrate. The fact that the three grammatical features discussed above are not only frequent in ELF data, but are also readily observable in (L1) spoken English varieties all around the world, including the speech of educated native speakers, forces us to reconsider the claims according to which these features are mere learner errors (caused by L1 interference). On the basis of the evidence above, it would seem, rather, that what we are facing here are structures typical of *spoken English grammar*. Why they are as they are is still something that cannot be answered directly within this study.

But as discussed above, spoken language functions on premises of its own and may also have structures of its own that have been 'smoothed out' of standard, written language. As spoken language has not been 'meddled with' as much as written language, it is also thought to reflect the 'natural' characteristics of each language better than the written mode. Consequently, researchers of English variation and change have begun to look into different spoken varieties of English in search for what have been termed 'vernacular universals' (Chambers 2004) or 'angloversals' (Mair 2003; see e.g. the studies in Filppula et al. 2009), i.e. features that appear to be similar in spoken Englishes around the world. The studies have not looked into L2 use, but based on the data above, one could hypothesize that also the structures discussed in this paper represent universal tendencies of spoken English rather than learner errors. (See Mauranen 2003, 515-516 for a discussion of different kinds of possible language universals in ELF.)

The features presented here must, of course, be studied further in more detail, but even at this preliminary stage they display surprisingly similar patterning to that in spoken NS data, as regards their syntactic characteristics. Similar tendencies appear in the proportions of use (e.g. non-standard *if*-clauses more frequent in 3rd conditionals than in 2nd, and *there's* attracting plural subjects more often than *there is*), and also in the syntactic environments where the features occur (e.g. embedded inversions most frequent after the matrix verb *ask* in an indirect question beginning with *what*). The main difference between the two databases in terms of the features retrieved lies in the overall frequency at which the structures are to be observed. But at the same time it is important to note that there is no straightforward connection between ELF and increased non-standardness. In the case of *there's/there is* + the plural it is the native speakers who display more non-standardness in their overall use of the feature. This could be yet another manifestation of the fact pointed out by Mauranen (2006a, 146) that—contrary to our common belief—in many corpus-based studies even L1 academic spoken language has been found to be *more* like spoken language in general than like academic written language. The evidence from this small-scale study also supports these findings as the same features are to be found both in academic and vernacular varieties of English.

On the other hand, two of the studied features did appear to have a stronger representation in the ELFA data than in MICASE, which could reflect the fact that ELF speakers may have even less 'obligation' to be norm-oriented and/or monitor their speech for standardness even in academic contexts than native speakers have. Thus, academic ELF speech might be even closer to everyday spoken English compared to academic L1 speech. Also the wider use of the progressive *–ing* forms, which I have discussed elsewhere (Ranta 2006) seems to support this, as it is a more frequent feature in ELF than in L1 data, but has been—as pointed out by Mair and Hundt (1995), and Smitterberg (2005)—on the increase even in native speaker varieties. Keeping in mind the influentiality of the academic speech genre and the fact that ELF speakers are in the majority of English speakers globally, one might even venture to hypothesize that we will see a further growth in the use of the features discussed here, as ELF speakers start leading the change in the language.

Hypotheses aside, the results of this study make it quite obvious that in many respects ELF speakers are just 'normal' speakers of the language (as opposed to deficient communicators postulated by SLA) when given a fair treatment in comparative analyses. This is not to suggest, though, that *all* features of ELF should represent universal characteristics of the language, but the present paper should make us aware of fact that not all features of L2 speech can be dismissed as 'deviation' caused by imperfect learning, either. Instead, we should take a closer look at the constructions to see which of them might be just features of spoken English grammar. The present study also makes void the often heard accusation from the critics of ELF that ELF is nothing but a chaotic bunch of idiolects grouped together. As we have seen, ELF speakers display strong similarities in their spoken grammar in many features, and also seem to reflect universal tendencies in the ways they make use of the resources of their second language. After all, what else could one expect from a 'universal' language?

Bibliography

Biber, D., S. Johansson, G. Leech, S. Conrad and E. Finegan, eds. 1999. *Longman Grammar of Spoken and Written English.* London: Longman.

Brutt-Griffler, J. 2002. *World English. A Study of Its Development.* Clevedon: Multilingual Matters.

Chambers, J. K. 2004. "Dynamic Typology and Vernacular Universals." In *Dialectology Meets Typology. Dialect Grammar from a Cross-Linguistic Perspective*, ed. B. Kortmann, 127-45. New York: Mouton de Gruyter.

Comrie, B. 1986. "Conditionals: A Typology." In *On Conditionals*, ed. E. C. Traugott, A. Ter Meulen, J. Snitzer Reilly & C. A. Ferguson, 77-99. Cambridge: Cambridge University Press.
Cook, V. 2002. "Background to the L2 User." In *Portraits of the L2 User*, ed. V. Cook, 1-31. Clevedon: Multilingual Matters.
Corder, S. P. 1967. "The Significance of Learners' Errors." *International Review of Applied Linguistics* 5 (4), 161-70.
ELFA corpus. http://www.eng.helsinki.fi/elfa/elfacorpus.htm (accessed May 30, 2009)
Ellis, R. and G. Barkhuizen 2005. *Analysing Learner Language*. Oxford: Oxford University Press.
Filppula, M. 1999. *The Grammar of Irish English. Language in Hibernian Style*. New York: Routledge.
Filppula, M., J. Klemola and H. Paulasto, eds. 2009. *Vernacular Universals and Language Contacts. Evidence from Varieties of English and Beyond*. New York: Routledge.
Filppula, M., J. Klemola and H. Paulasto 2008. *English and Celtic in Contact*. New York: Routledge.
Firth, A. and J. Wagner 1997. "On Discourse, Communication, and (Some) Fundamental Concepts in SLA Research." *Modern Language Journal* 81 (3), 285-300.
Gass, S. 1998. "Apples and Oranges: Or, Why Apples Are Not Oranges and Don't Need to Be. A Response to Firth and Wagner." *Modern Language Journal* 82 (1), 83-90.
Halliday, M. A. K. 1987. "Spoken and Written Modes of Meaning." In *Comprehending Oral and Written Language*, ed. R. Horowitz & S. J. Samuels, 55-82. London: Academic Press Inc.
Jenkins, J. 2006. "Points of View and Blind Spots: ELF and SLA." *International Journal of Applied Linguistics* 16 (2), 137-62.
Kasper, G. 1997. "'A' Stands for Acquisition: A Response to Firth and Wagner." *Modern Language Journal* 81 (3), 307-12.
Kortmann, B. and E. W. Schneider, eds. 2004. *A Handbook of Varieties of English*. Berlin: Mouton de Gruyter.
Leech, G. N. 1987. *Meaning and the English Verb*. 2nd ed. London: Longman.
Linell, P. 2005. *The Written Language Bias in Linguistics: Its Nature, Origins and Transformation*. London: Routledge.
—. 1982. *The Written Language Bias in Linguistics*. Linköping, Sweden: Department of Communication Studies, Linköping University.
Long, M. H. 1997. "Construct Validity in SLA Research: A Response to Firth and Wagner." *Modern Language Journal* 81 (3), 318-23.

Mair, C. 2003. "Kreolismen und verbales Identitätsmanagement im geschriebenen jamaikanischen Englisch." In *Zwischen Ausgrenzung und Hybridisierung*, ed. E. Vogel, A. Napp & W. Lutterer, 79-96. Würzburg: Ergon.

Mair, C. and M. Hundt 1995. "Why Is the Progressive Becoming More Frequent in English?" *Zeitschrift für Anglistik und Amerikanistik* 43 (2), 111-22.

Mauranen, A. 2006a. "Spoken Discourse, Academics and Global English: A Corpus Perspective." In *Spoken English, TESOL and Applied Linguistics*, ed. R. Hughes, 143-58. New York: Palgrave Macmillan.

—. 2006b. "A Rich Domain of ELF: The ELFA Corpus of Academic Discourse." *Nordic Journal of English Studies* 5 (2), 145-59.

—. 2005. "English as Lingua Franca: An Unknown Language?" In *Identity, Community, Discourse. English in Intercultural Settings*, ed. G. Cortese & A. Duszak, 269-93. Bern: Peter Lang.

—. 2003. "The Corpus of English as Lingua Franca in Academic Settings." *TESOL Quarterly* 37 (3), 513-27.

Mauranen, A. and E. Ranta 2008. "English as an Academic Lingua Franca—The ELFA Project." *Nordic Journal of English Studies* 7 (3), 199-202.

McCarthy, M. 1998. *Spoken Language and Applied Linguistics*. Cambridge: Cambridge University Press.

MICASE corpus. http://lw.lsa.umich.edu/eli/micase/index.htm (accessed May 30, 2009)

Miller, J. and R. Weinert 1998. *Spontaneous Spoken Language. Syntax and Discourse*. Oxford: Clarendon Press.

Nevalainen, T. 2009. "Number Agreement in Existential Constructions. A Sociolinguistic Study of Eighteen-Century English." In *Vernacular Universals and Language Contacts. Evidence from Varieties of English and Beyond*, ed. M. Filppula, J. Klemola & H. Paulasto, 80-102. London: Routledge.

Poulisse, N. 1997. "Some Words in Defense of the Psycholinguistic Approach: A Response to Firth and Wagner." *Modern Language Journal* 81 (3), 324-28.

Ranta, E. 2006. "The 'Attractive' Progressive—Why Use the *–ing* Form in English as a Lingua Franca?" *Nordic Journal of English Studies* 5 (2), 95-116.

Seidlhofer, B. 2004. "Research Perspectives on Teaching English as a Lingua Franca." *Annual Review of Applied Linguistics* 24, 209-39.

Selinker, L. 1972. "Interlanguage." *International Review of Applied Linguistics* 10 (3), 209-31.

Simpson, R. C., S. L. Briggs, J. Ovens and J. M. Swales 1999. *The Michigan Corpus of Academic Spoken English*. Ann Arbor: The Regents of the University of Michigan.

Smitterberg, E. 2005. *The Progressive in 19th-Century English. A Process of Integration*. Amsterdam: Rodopi.

Swan, M. and B. Smith, eds. 2001. *Learner English: A Teacher's Guide to Interference and Other Problems.* 2nd ed. Cambridge: Cambridge University Press.

Tagliamonte, S. A. 2009. "There *Was* Universals; Then There *Weren't*. A Comparative Sociolinguistic Perspective on 'Default Singulars'." In *Vernacular Universals and Language Contacts. Evidence from Varieties of English and Beyond*, ed. M. Filppula, J. Klemola & H. Paulasto, 102-29. London: Routledge.

Turton, J. and N. Heaton, eds. 1996. *Longman Dictionary of Common Errors*. London: Longman.

Widdowson, H. G. 2003. *Defining Issues in English Language Teaching*. Oxford: Oxford University Press

Notes

[1] See Halliday (1987, 70) for an illuminating example of what writing might look like if it included all the editing that was done to it during the writing process. It would turn out at least as "messy" as spoken language. The essential difference between writing and speech lies in the fact that a written text is a finished *product* whereas speech is an on-going *process*.

PRE-EMPTING PROBLEMS OF UNDERSTANDING IN ENGLISH AS A LINGUA FRANCA

JAGDISH KAUR

1. Introduction

The widespread use of English as a lingua franca (henceforth ELF) amongst its non-native speakers at the international level has become an everyday occurrence, a fact of life. In continental Europe, for instance, English today functions as "the *de facto* European *lingua franca*" (Jenkins 2003, 42). Similarly, McArthur asserts that "English is the lingua franca that Asians now share with one another and with the rest of the world" (2003, 22). The spread and use of English around the world, however, has resulted in the emergence of diverse varieties of English that display systematic variation in their use of the sounds, grammar and vocabulary of "standard" English. With so many different varieties of English in use, there is growing concern that these varieties may become mutually unintelligible, which may as a result impair international communications. Further, non-native participants in an international encounter are likely to display varying levels of competency in English, which can again impinge on the outcome of the encounter. There is also the issue of the ELF speaker's lingua-cultural background. It is often claimed that lack of shared knowledge and assumptions between ELF speakers of different linguistic and cultural backgrounds frequently lead to misunderstanding and communication difficulty as participants rely on the norms of their mother tongue and native culture to interpret meaning.

Regardless of the fact that communication in ELF may to some extent be disadvantaged, as a result of the aforementioned "problems", non-native speakers of English can and do manage to communicate quite successfully using ELF. Researchers working in the area of ELF, using naturally occurring data, are in fact making claims to dispute the popular belief that NNS interaction in English is rife with misunderstanding and non-understanding. House, for instance, talks about the "paucity of misunderstandings" (2002, 251) in ELF interaction and later says, "we found remarkably few misunderstandings … As opposed to the many misunderstandings I detected in my analyses of native-non-native talk" (House 2003, 567). Similarly, Meierkord, on the basis of her findings from ELF data, concludes that lingua franca communication in English is "a form of intercultural communication characterized by cooperation rather than misunderstanding" (2000, 11). Mauranen (2006), who also observes few instances of misunderstanding in her ELF data, suggests that this may be due in part to the participants' efforts in preventing such understanding problems from the outset. Such efforts, which she terms "proactive work", are said to be "a striking feature of this ELF interaction" (ibid., 135).

The interactional practices that participants utilize in order to pre-empt or avert problems of understanding contribute to the achievement of mutual understanding in ELF. It is therefore crucial that preventative procedures be examined in closer detail to obtain a more complete picture of how non-native speakers of English arrive at mutual understanding in this medium. The interactional procedures that have been identified for analysis in view of their salience in contexts where potential lack of understanding is clearly being addressed, as indicated by the participants' own orientations, are repetition and paraphrase. The paper will identify the interactional environments in which the aforementioned practices are used to pre-empt problematic understanding and shed light on how the practices are deployed in these environments. The Conversation Analysis (CA) methodology is employed to achieve these ends.

2. "Repair Strategies" in Conversation Analysis

Conversation Analysis, which advocates fine-grained examination of naturally occurring spoken discourse, regards practices such as repetition and paraphrase as repair strategies when they are used to address both real and potential problems of understanding in talk. Speech production difficulties, hearing problems and problems of understanding may trigger the initiation of repair by participants concerned with "trying to 'get things right'" (Sacks 1987, 66) in order that the talk is able to move forward. The notion of "repair", however, is, as Kurhila puts it, "widely defined" (2003, 43). It refrains from separating the functions that repair strategies perform in terms of whether they pre-empt problems of understanding or resolve them. The fact that "repair" refers to "practices for dealing with problems or troubles in speaking, hearing and understanding the talk in conversation" (Schegloff 2000, 207) presupposes that trouble has already occurred and the practices are therefore designed to resolve or remedy the problem. However, given Mauranen's observation that misunderstandings in her data are rare because ELF speakers employ such procedures to pre-empt problems of understanding, it becomes necessary to make a distinction between the use of these practices for preventative purposes as opposed to for remedial purposes. Participants who employ particular procedures to avert problems of understanding after all may be perceived as adopting a more proactive role in attempting to "anticipate and exclude misunderstanding thus securing understanding in advance" (Weigand 1999, 765). Do speakers of ELF take proactive measures to secure understanding in the light of the fact that English is not the native language of any of the participants concerned? The question can only be addressed if the notion of repair is seen to encompass both preventative and remedial strategies. The distinction, however, will have to take into account the local context in which the procedure is employed and the participants' own orientations and responses.

3. Methodology

The data comprises 15 hours of naturally occurring spoken interaction in English as a lingua franca. The participants are mainly postgraduate students pursuing an International Masters at an institute set up at a local university in Kuala Lumpur, Malaysia. The student community at this institute is said to be "truly international" (course prospectus, 2004-2005) in character and further, English is the established medium of instruction and communication for all concerned at the institute. For all the participants, English is a second or a foreign language. The students' English language proficiency appeared to range from intermediate to fairly advanced levels, although a couple of students displayed proficiency levels in English that tended towards the lower intermediate. The diversity of the participants' lingua-cultural backgrounds necessitated the use of a common language to facilitate communication among them and English was the preferred language.

22 participants recorded themselves as they conversed with each other about course-related matters or about more general or personal matters over a ten-week period. To ensure that the interactions recorded were naturally occurring, recordings were made without the presence of the researcher in the locations where the interaction would have taken place regardless of whether it was being recorded or not. With regard to data type, the range is wide and varied, from casual conversations to more task-based, goal-oriented discussions. The data can thus be said to reflect the varied kinds of talk that take place in this setting. What all the interactions have in common, however, is the fact that the participants concerned used

ELF to facilitate communication with fellow participants of different lingua-cultural backgrounds.

The recordings were transcribed using a slightly adapted version of the notation system developed by Gail Jefferson (see Appendix).

4. Analysis and Discussion

Instances of potential trouble in understanding were examined using CA procedures in order to describe and analyze how repetition and paraphrase were employed by the participants of the study to avert breakdown in understanding. The term "repetition" has been loosely defined by researchers such as Tannen (1987), Norrick (1987) and Johnstone et al. (1994) to include instances of paraphrase and reformulation of the prior utterance in addition to exact or identical repetition. However, given that "paraphrase is specifically an *alternative* to repetition (and to quotation) and involves very different uses for, and procedures of, constructing an utterance" (Schegloff 1996, 179), the practice of treating verbatim repeats and paraphrase as one and the same thing, or even as different forms along a continuum, needs to be treated with caution. The practice of paraphrasing, which constitutes operations that involve transformations in the syntactic structure and the lexical composition of a prior utterance, is after all qualitatively distinct from the mere re-saying of a prior utterance using substantially the same words. In ELF talk, this distinction is particularly important as it reflects on the non-native speaker's competence in using the different practices of talking strategically to address potential problems of understanding.

Following Schegloff (ibid.) then, the two practices are treated as different in this paper. The term "repetition" or "repeat" refers to the practice of re-saying some or all of the elements occurring earlier in an ongoing turn or in a preceding turn. The definition "allows for transformations geared to deixis, tense shift, speaker change etc., as well as change of prosody" but "excludes paraphrase and other substantial rewording of its target" (Schegloff 1997, 525). Further, the kinds of repetition that constitute the focus of the present paper are those that may be considered genuine or meaningful, namely, where the second occurrence of some earlier segment of talk can be seen to have a significant relation with the first occurrence.

Paraphrase, in turn, "entails displaying [this] given information in a new and different way, either by simplifying the form of the message or by expressing it in different words" (Neil 1996, 142). The extracts below illustrate how the participants of the study deploy the two practices to avert misunderstanding and non-understanding in specific interactional sites.

4.1. After Prolonged Silence

According to Sacks et al. "transitions (from one turn to a next) with no gap … are common" (1974, 708) because speakers seek the earliest possible start at a transition-relevance place as a means of securing the next turn. Thus, when the recipient refrains from taking up the next turn at a transition-relevance place, the speaker is likely to orient to this as suggesting a possible problem of hearing or understanding, particularly when the silence is prolonged and when some kind of response from the recipient may be considered appropriate. Although self-selection to speak at a transition-relevance place is optional, that the speaker chooses to recycle the segment of his or her talk preceding the extended silence before proceeding suggests that the repeat is designed to enhance the recipient's understanding in the face of possible difficulty in understanding. It is not the case here that a question is met with silence but rather that an expected response to a comment is not forthcoming. The next extract illustrates one such example:

Extract 1

D is telling M about a study that was conducted by a student of his.

01	D:		an:d the problem is one of er:: my students in Indonesia
02	M:		uhhuh
03	D:		they make a research about the effect of …(1.9) oh no no no
04			the::: relationship between: …(0.8) future performance
05	M:		uhhuh=
06	D:		=an:d CEO change
07	M:		uhhuh
08	D:		CEO change: an:d future performance
09	M:		°yes°=
10	D:		=okay …(1.3) the problem is …(0.9) the sample is only
11		→	seventeen: firms. …(1.2) seventeen firms
12	M:		seventeen firms=
13	D:		=huh and also: …(0.6) we divide between before an:d after
14			practice

The repetition that D produces in line 11 is very likely the result of his orientation to the preceding 1.2-second silence as a signal of a possible problem of hearing or understanding on M's part. The utterance in lines 10 and 11, which is syntactically complete and produced with terminal falling intonation, suggests that D has arrived at a possible completion point and is offering the turn to M. Having specified the problem that he alludes to in line 1, namely the small sample size, D very likely expects some reaction from M, or at the very least for her to produce a minimal response to signal receipt of the detail. While M has produced several minimal response tokens[1] at various points during D's extended turn, she fails to or refrains from doing so at this rather crucial point. Hence, when M fails to take up the turn, D repeats the critical detail to provide M with another opportunity to perceive this point. Further, it is likely that D is attuned to the possibility of mishearing occurring when numbers are verbally produced, e.g. "seventeen" versus "seventy". D, in fact, produces a sound stretch when pronouncing "seventeen" the first time around to possibly distinguish it from "seventy". The repeat results in M herself repeating this detail, in line 12, as a means of indicating receipt. This allows D to confirm the accuracy of her understanding, which he does in line 13, before proceeding with further talk. D's repetition, which provides redundant material, no doubt contributes to reinforcing M's understanding and succeeds in maintaining shared understanding.

In the next extract, the speaker's use of a comprehension check prior to paraphrasing a segment of his preceding talk, following a lengthy pause, provides strong evidence that the recipient's silence at the transition-relevance place is being oriented to as signaling a possible problem of understanding.

Extract 2

V is correcting K's misinterpretation of the topic of their presentation on "the global response of SMEs towards e-trade".

K: no I- I mean it's erm: …(3.4) this is to my understanding I
think that erm er: it-it's like erm: …(1.2) erm it's like erm why
SME in each regions need to go into e-trade I think this my
understanding of something like this.
V: no not- not need to go into e-trade. that's not what we're
considering. this global response has to:: …(0.7) has to deal
with …(0.7) either …(0.7) positive response or negative
response. now if we say this is why they have to go to e-trade
→ that means only positive …(2.7) do you understand me? this
→ global response we must think …(0.6) if it is positive …(0.6)
or negative in a particular country, we must state it and then …
(0.7) give the instances
K: °mm°

K's failure to say something at the transition-relevance place, in line 9, is clearly being oriented to as signaling a possible problem of understanding, as the comprehension check evidences. Given that V has just offered an interpretation of the topic that is different from the one provided by K, it is likely that he expects either an acknowledgement or a rejection at this point. The 2.7-second pause constitutes a rather lengthy waiting-out time during which the floor is clearly being made available for takeover by K. When K makes no move to take up the turn, V proceeds to check K's understanding of his preceding clarification. The paraphrase, following at the heels of the comprehension check, therefore seems specifically designed to enhance K's understanding and to possibly even secure it in the event that shared understanding has not yet been achieved.

In both the extracts above, the recipient was not selected to take up the next turn, as no question had been posed to him/her. For this reason, evidence of actual non-understanding is absent. The recipient's failure to self-select when given the opportunity to do so, however, seems to be interpreted as signaling a possible problem of understanding. The speaker's move to repeat or paraphrase a preceding segment of talk in this particular environment provides the support for this. The repeat in such instances provides redundant material while the paraphrase appears designed to amplify the meaning of the prior utterance and enhance the recipient's understanding of it. Thus, while there is no displayed evidence of non-understanding on the part of the recipient, both the repeat and the paraphrase nevertheless provide the recipient with another opportunity to make sense of prior talk and, in doing so, contribute towards maintaining shared understanding between the participants.

4.2. After Minimal Response

The participants of the study also frequently repeat or paraphrase a segment of the prior turn after it is receipted by a minimal response, particularly when the response token produced is muted, i.e. relatively softer in comparison to the surrounding talk. While response tokens such as "uhhuh", "mm", "yeah" and the like have frequently been treated as signaling understanding in the literature, Schegloff argues that these elements "at best *claim* attention and/or understanding, rather than *showing* it or *evidencing* it" (1982, 78).[2] Speakers who repeat or paraphrase themselves in this environment in fact appear to be orienting to the "equivocal" status of "uhhuh" as a display of understanding (ibid., 88). The next extract illustrates one example of repetition after a minimal response.

Extract 3

D is advising K to limit the time span of his study to ten years instead of thirty as originally intended by K.

K: and I think …(0.9) uhhuh I don't know how to do it maybe I
have to change the topic or: …(1.5) because it's hard to find
information …(0.6) related to …(0.6) education in nineteen:
seventy fi:ve …(1.7) (relations).
D: why not just your: focus at the: last ten: years
K: °uhhuh°
D: → the last ten years like er: from nineteen: ninety five to nine- to:
two thousand: …(0.6) five …(0.8) so you have to focus for:
ten years.
(2.0)
K: Doddy I have to really think.

D's suggestion in line 5 is receipted by a minimal response, in lowered volume, in the next turn. D, in turn, repeats the key point of his suggestion, i.e. "the last ten years" (line 7), before proceeding to elaborate on what he means. The elaboration is followed by a paraphrase of the original utterance in lines 8 and 9. The repeat, the elaboration and the paraphrase, following K's muted minimal response, collectively suggest that D is attempting to enhance K's understanding of his proposal. It is possible that D expects a response that "'does more' than receive the talk" (Wong 2000, 254) following his suggestion to reduce the time frame of the study. When such a response is not forthcoming, D employs repetition together with other understanding-enhancing procedures to facilitate K's understanding of his suggestion. Also, K's response, which is minimal in nature and stands alone (Wong 2000), in addition to being muted, may cause D to be a little unsure of the degree of understanding that has been achieved by K. While there is no displayed problem of understanding, D appears to be orienting to the possibility of the muted minimal response concealing a difficulty in understanding and thus attempts to forestall a problem from actually occurring.

The speaker's move to re-phrase a prior segment of talk, after the talk is receipted by a minimal response, provides further evidence that the speaker orients to such a response as failing to display unequivocally the recipient's understanding of the preceding talk.

Extract 4

M is telling S and K why she had to suspend her undergraduate studies.

01	M:	no in- in that company six years er first I join a: Korean
02		company it's ( )
03	S:	uhhuh
04	M:	elevator, escalator, TV:
05	K:	huh
06	M:	so they've got branch office in Burma
07	K:	°mm°=
08	M:	=so before I- I: get my degree I join because at that time you
09		know er eighty eight crisis in Burma
10	S:	°uhhuh°
11	M: →	er you know democra: democratic crisis in Burma sos ers
12		there's er university close about three years
13	K:	°huh°=
14	M:	=at that time I join: start working.

In lines 8 and 9, M explains that she had to interrupt her undergraduate studies to start work due to the "eighty eight crisis in Burma". Following a muted minimal response from S in the form of "uhhuh" (line 10), M clarifies the crisis being referred to by re-phrasing it in the form of "democratic crisis" (line 11). The paraphrase, coming at this point, suggests that M is cautious about accepting S's muted minimal response as a display of understanding. Since both S and K are Cambodian, it is likely that M is aware that the significance of the "eighty eight crisis", i.e. the year of the democratic uprising in Burma, may be lost on them. Thus, it appears that M is orienting to the assumed lack of shared knowledge between them, arising from their different national backgrounds, as a possible source of non-understanding. The use of the discourse marker "you know" prior to the first mention of this crisis (line 8) may reflect an attempt on M's part to check for shared knowledge (Schiffrin 1987)[3]. It is possible then that having made a move to do so, S's muted response fails to convince M that S understands the referent of the "eighty eight crisis". Her subsequent use of the discourse marker "you know" (line 11), prior to the paraphrase, suggests a further attempt to check for understanding before offering an alternative formulation of the potentially problematic item.

Since M is the narrator in the extract above, it is to be expected that S and K, the recipients, would assume a more passive role, confining themselves to the odd continuer to display "an understanding that an extended unit of talk is underway by another" (Schegloff 1982, 81). The minimal responses produced by both S and K are in fact of this nature.

M's paraphrase of a prior segment of talk in line 11, together with her use of the discourse marker "you know" preceding both the original formulation and the paraphrase, however, suggest that the minimal response in line 10 is being oriented to differently from the others. It is likely that the muted quality of S's response, in addition to M's own awareness of possible lack of shared knowledge between the recipients and herself, is the reason behind the move to paraphrase. By substituting "eighty eight" with the more transparent "democratic", M seeks to facilitate the recipients' understanding of her reason for suspending her undergraduate studies.

In the examples above, the speaker repeats or paraphrases a prior segment of talk when it is receipted by a minimal response. This happens when the speaker appears to expect some response other than a minimal one and when the minimal response is softer in comparison to the surrounding talk. Given their "shared incompetence" (Varonis & Gass 1985, 71) in the language, the participants seem to be somewhat cautious about accepting a minimal response as evidence of understanding. Wong suggests that a non-native interlocutor may use a minimal response token as "a face-saving acknowledgement token, displaying her or his orientation to the speaker's right to be heard but *not* necessarily to be understood" (2000, 263). In fact, the concept of "let-it-pass" that Firth (1996) raises may very well manifest itself through the recipient's use of such response tokens. Thus, Schegloff's (1982) observation that minimal responses are unreliable indicators of understanding in native speaker talk similarly applies to non-native speaker discourse. Although there is no overt display of non-understanding on the part of the recipient, a repeat or a paraphrase of prior talk provides the recipient with another opportunity to hear the prior turn to increase the chances of it being understood. In this way, problems of understanding are averted and shared understanding between speaker and recipient is maintained.

4.3. After Overlapped Talk

Both Neil (1996) and Gramkow Andersen (2001) have found ELF talk to constitute a highly collaborative style of discourse in which turn sharing[4] and cooperative overlaps contribute to the joint production of talk. Notwithstanding the above, overlap can, and does, create noise which may impair the recipient's hearing and understanding of the segment of talk produced in overlap. The participants of the study, who appear to be attuned to the potentially disruptive effect of overlap on the recipient's hearing and understanding, employ repetition and paraphrase in this environment to possibly avert a problem from occurring. That speakers tend to repeat themselves after simultaneous talk, has in fact been established by Schegloff (1987) who examined the phenomenon at turn beginnings in native speaker conversations. The practice, which is equally common in ELF talk, does not however appear to be confined to turn beginnings in this case. Given that simultaneous talk has been found to be common in ELF talk and not only confined to turn beginnings may therefore explain the high incidence of repetition after overlap in the data. Extract 5 below is a case in point:

Extract 5

M is telling S about the corrupt practices within the civil service in her country.

01	M:	yeah huhh.hhh so they: you know er their salary is not- not
02		more than fifteen US dollar per mo:nth but outside money is
03		about
04	S:	huhhuh [under the table
05	M: →	[eight hundred US dollar- eight hundred US dollar-
06		dollar: per month are for the lower=
07	S:	=°yeah°
08	M:	lower you know …(0.7) rank, for the higher rank they get a lot
09		of money.

In line 3, M, who uses the phrase "outside money" in place of "bribe", is about to tell S how much bribe a government officer receives when S chips in with an alternative term, i.e. "under the table". Neil terms this form of turn-sharing as "parenthetical elaboration" (1996, 117-119), whereby the recipient inserts an explanatory or qualifying remark within the speaker's turn as a means of actively engaging in the talk. S's contribution, however, overlaps with M's ongoing turn in which the amount of bribe received is indicated (line 4). M repeats the amount, i.e. eight hundred US dollar, before proceeding with the rest of her utterance. The fact that the repeat occurs where it does, namely immediately after the overlap, suggests that M is orienting to the overlap as having the potential to impair S's hearing and understanding of this piece of information. Hence, repetition is employed "as a way of repairing the possible impairment of a turn component by virtue of its having been in overlap" (Schegloff 1987, 76). The repeat, which provides S with another hearing of the detail, averts a problem of understanding that may have resulted from the noise created by the overlap.

The participants also sometimes paraphrase the segment of talk produced in overlap as an alternative to repetition. The next extract illustrates one such example:

Extract 6

A is asking D about his previous work experience.

01	A:		nineteen ninety eight, have you worked before in between? …
02			(0.7) [as a- [except the lecturer's job?
03	D:		[er: [no
04			yes no [no I'm jus::t]
05	A:		[so you carried on] teaching?
06		→	you were teaching?
07	D:		yes. …(0.7) [it's all] my: primary job.
08	A:		[okay]

In line 1, A enquires if D had worked elsewhere prior to assuming a teaching position at the university from which he had graduated. D's turn beginning (line 3), however, overlaps with A's move to add "optional post-completion elements" (Schegloff 1987, 73) after a 0.7-second pause. A's subsequent question (line 2), which is formulated to receive a confirming response, overlaps with D's response to the preceding question from line 1. Given that A has posed two consecutive questions, each making a different response relevant, D responds first in the affirmative and then again in the negative in line 4. D's attempt to elaborate on his response, however, overlaps with A's paraphrase (line 5) of the question from line 2. The overlap at this point creates more "noise" that could potentially impair D's hearing and understanding of A's enquiry in line 5. It is likely that A is in fact orienting to the effect that the overlapped talk might have on D's hearing and understanding of his enquiry when he produces a paraphrase of the question in line 6.

Like repetition, a paraphrase of the segment of talk produced in overlap is an effective means of providing the recipient with another opportunity to understand the segment in question, albeit worded differently. The question, however, arises as to why the speaker opts to paraphrase his question in line 6 rather than to repeat it. A candidate explanation for this may lie in the recipient's prior turn, which hints at possible trouble either in understanding the speaker or in producing a coherent answer. In line 3, D initiates his turn with a stretched hesitation marker. Further, in line 4, D's initial response in the affirmative is followed by a negative response token, which results in some degree of incoherence. Although this may be attributed to A's consecutive questions in the prior turn, it is possible that A orients to these features of D's talk as being indicative of a problem of understanding which a mere repeat of the original question may fail to address. Neil in fact suggests that "paraphrase is at times a more valuable strategic choice" in enhancing understanding (1996, 141). By substituting the phrasal verb "carried on" with "were", for instance, A makes his utterance in line 6 linguistically simpler and possibly more comprehensible for D.

Participants in talk do seem to orient to the fact that talk produced in overlap may not have been heard or understood completely by the recipient, as the immediate move to repeat or paraphrase the overlapped segment of talk suggests. Such a move generally reflects an attempt on the part of the speaker to pre-empt a problem of understanding rather than to resolve an actual problem as such. As Schegloff states, "simultaneous talk does not *necessarily* impair the hearing or understanding of any of its components" (1987, 75-76), rather it has the potential to do so. A repeat or a paraphrase of overlapped talk therefore serves to increase the comprehensibility of the segment in question and to enhance the recipient's understanding of it.

5. Conclusion

Instances of communication breakdown in the data are rare as the participants collaborate and engage in active negotiation, using procedures like repetition and paraphrase, to arrive at an adequate level of shared understanding that allows the talk to move forward. The participants' use of repetition and paraphrase after a muted minimal response or after overlapped talk, for instance, displays their perceptiveness to even the more subtle suggestions of trouble and their ability to draw upon the various interactional resources available to avert breakdown in intersubjectivity. While such practices to some extent disrupt the smooth flow of talk, it appears that what is of greater importance to the participants is the achievement of shared understanding.

Given the fact that most of the participants' utterances are marked by disfluencies and ungrammaticalities of one type or another throughout the data, the lack of communication breakdown is remarkable for it reflects on the participants' success in compensating their lack of linguistic competence in the language with increased use of interactional practices to bring about shared understanding. The participants' less-than-perfect grasp of the language therefore does not appear to detract from their ability to utilize the practices in question effectively. Although the participants' use of repetition or paraphrase frequently appears to be simply a matter of choice, there are many instances in the data where the participants make an informed decision to use a particular procedure. This decision may be influenced by the speaker's assessment of the source of the problem or by the local context, specifically the nature of the prior talk. The speaker, for instance, is likely to repeat a prior utterance when the potential problem is attributed to the recipient's difficulty in hearing rather than in understanding. Conversely, paraphrase is employed when the potential problem is perceived as being rooted in the recipient's difficulty in understanding, such as when the prior utterance appears vague or ambiguous with regard to the meaning it is intended to convey or when disfluency and ungrammaticality obscure the meaning of the utterance. The speaker thus seems attuned to the problematic nature of the prior turn and how this may potentially result in a problem in understanding. In such cases, the act of paraphrasing allows the speaker to address the inadequacies of the prior utterance so that meaning is clarified and understanding enhanced. That the prior utterance is problematic in the ways mentioned above is less apparent when repetition is employed to address a potential problem of understanding.

Regardless of their linguistic and cultural background, and their level of competency in English, all the participants employ repetition and paraphrase at some point or other as a means of pre-empting problems of understanding. It is likely that the participants' anticipation of difficulty in understanding, arising from the lingua franca context, gives rise to increased efforts at maintaining shared understanding. Mauranen (2006) suggests that ELF speakers make a concerted effort to avert misunderstanding and non-understanding possibly as a result of their own awareness of the heightened risk of communication breakdown arising from their lack of competence in the language. Neil affirms this when she says that, "in communication using a language which is the first language of neither participant, the need to collaborate in producing comprehensible meanings is heightened" (1996, 193). Mutual understanding in ELF is therefore not perceived as a given but rather something that has to be jointly worked at and monitored on a turn-by-turn basis. However, the fact that ELF is being used with success by its non-native speakers for a multiplicity of purposes, in myriad situations all over the world bears testimony to their ability and competence in making strategic use of various interactional practices to avert problems of understanding and, in doing so, to arrive at mutual understanding in ELF.

APPENDIX

The transcription notations used in this paper are as follows:

[	a left square bracket marks the onset of overlap
]	a right square bracket marks the end of overlapping talk; this feature, however, is only indicated when it can be accurately discerned
=	an equal sign marks latching
-	a hyphen marks a cut off
…(0.6)	a numeral placed within parentheses following three dots marks a pause of 0.6 seconds and above
:	a colon marks a stretched sound
?	a question mark marks rising intonation
.	a full stop marks falling intonation
,	a comma marks continuing intonation
.hhh	a series of 'h's preceded by a dot marks audible inhalation
hhh	a series of 'h's not preceded by a dot marks audible exhalation
°soft°	degree signs mark speech that is relatively softer than the surrounding talk
(see)	words within parentheses mark the transcriber's uncertainty of the actual words produced
( )	empty parentheses represent segments of talk that could not be transcribed

Bibliography

Firth, A. 1996. "The Discursive Accomplishment of Normality: On 'Lingua Franca' English and Conversation Analysis." *Journal of Pragmatics* 26 (2), 237-59.

Gramkow Andersen, K. 2001. *The Joint Production of Conversation.* Aalborg: Centre for Languages and Intercultural Studies, Aalborg University.

House, J. 2003. "English as a Lingua Franca: A Threat to Multilingualism." *Journal of Sociolinguistics* 7 (4), 556-78.

—. 2002. "Communicating in English as a Lingua Franca." In *EUROSLA Yearbook 2*, ed. S. Foster-Cohen, T, Ruthenberg & M.-L. Poschen, 243-61. Amsterdam: John Benjamins.

Jenkins, J. 2003. *World Englishes*. London: Routledge.

Johnstone, B. et al. 1994. "Repetition in Discourse: A Dialogue." In *Repetition in Discourse: Interdisciplinary Perspectives*, vol. 1, ed. B. Johnstone, 1-20. New Jersey: Ablex Publishing Corporation.

Kurhila, S. 2003. "Co-Constructing Understanding in Second Language Conversation." PhD diss., University of Helsinki.

Mauranen, A. 2006. "Signaling and Preventing Misunderstanding in English as Lingua Franca Communication." *International Journal of the Sociology of Language* 177, 123-50.

McArthur, T. 2003. "English as an Asian Language." *English Today* 19 (2), 19-22.

Meierkord, C. 2000. "Interpreting Successful Lingua Franca Interaction. An Analysis of Non-Native/Non-Native Small Talk Conversations in English." In *Conversation Analysis: New Developments*, ed. A. Fetzer & K. Pittner, Linguistik Online 5: 1/00 (Special Issue). http://linguistik-online.com (accessed October 21, 2004)

Neil, D. M. 1996. *Collaboration in Intercultural Discourse: Examples from a Multicultural Australian Workplace*. Frankfurt am Main: Peter Lang.

Norrick, N. R. 1987. "Functions of Repetition in Conversation." *Text* 7 (3), 245-64.

Sacks, H. 1987. "On the Preferences for Agreement and Contiguity in Sequences in Conversation." In *Talk and Social Organisation*, ed. G. Button & J. R. E. Lee, 54-69. Clevedon: Multilingual Matters.

Sacks, H., E. A. Schegloff and G. Jefferson 1974. "A Simplest Systematics for the Organization of Turn-Taking for Conversation." *Language* 50 (4), 696-735.

Schegloff, E. A. 2000. "When 'Others' Initiate Repair." *Applied Linguistics* 21 (2), 205-43.

—. 1997. "Practices and Actions: Boundary Cases of Other-Initiated Repair." *Discourse Processes* 23 (3), 499-545.

—. 1996. "Confirming Allusions: Toward an Empirical Account of Action." *American Journal of Sociology* 102 (1), 161-216.

—. 1987. "Recycled Turn Beginnings: A Precise Repair Mechanism in Conversation's Turn-Taking Organization." In *Talk and Social Organisation*, ed. G. Button & J. R. E. Lee, 70-100. Clevedon: Multilingual Matters.

—. 1982. "Discourse as an Interactional Achievement: Some Uses of 'uh huh' and Other Things That Come between Sentences." In *Analyzing Discourse: Text and Talk,* ed. D. Tannen, 71-93. Washington, DC: Georgetown University Press.

Schiffrin, D. 1987. *Discourse Markers*. Cambridge: Cambridge University Press.

Tannen, D. 1987. "Repetition in Conversation: Toward a Poetics of Talk." *Language* 63 (3), 574-605.

Varonis, E. A. and S. Gass 1985. "Non-Native/Non-Native Conversations: A Model for Negotiation of Meaning." *Applied Linguistics* 6 (1), 71-90.

Weigand, E. 1999. "Misunderstanding: The Standard Case." *Journal of Pragmatics* 31 (6), 763-85.

Wong, J. 2000. "Delayed Next Turn Repair Initiation in Native/Non-Native Speaker English Conversation." *Applied Linguistics* 21 (1), 244-67.

Notes

[1] M's minimal response tokens appear to function as "continuers" (Schegloff 1982) in this context. In essence, they reflect the recipient's understanding that a multi-unit turn is in progress and that the recipient has no intention of taking up a fuller turn.

[2] Schegloff's (1982) observations, which are based on native speaker conversations in English, appear equally relevant to ELF talk.

[3] Schriffin's work on discourse markers is based on native speaker conversations in English. However, her findings on the use of the discourse marker "you know" seem applicable and relevant in this context.

[4] The concept of "turn-sharing" that Neil proposes regards interjections from the recipient as "prompts or cues which facilitate the development of the narrative" (1996, 121) rather than as interruption or attempts to take over an ongoing turn.

PART II:

CONTEXTS OF USE: ELF IN DIFFERENT COMMUNITIES

ENGLISH AS A LINGUA FRANCA IN MULTINATIONAL CORPORATIONS—EXPLORING BUSINESS COMMUNITIES OF PRACTICE

SUSANNE EHRENREICH

1. Introduction

Doing research on English as a lingua franca (ELF) means doing research in a vibrant and fast-paced field. This also means we can no longer start our papers and presentations by lamenting the lack of data-driven studies, and how this lack of empirical work needs to be redressed. Since 2005, a relatively large number of such studies has been published, investigating various aspects of "what ELF users actually do when they communicate with each other" (Seidlhofer & Jenkins 2003, 139). We are therefore now in a much better position to compare recent findings, approaches, methodologies and theoretical frameworks. Yet, with ELF being a field of research still in its infancy, many open issues on several levels remain. Of these the following four issues in particular are taken up in my study on English as a business lingua franca in German multinational corporations (MNCs).

First, on the level of research methodology, Barbara Seidlhofer and her team have pointed out the need for "clearly situated qualitative studies with a strong ethnographic element" (Seidlhofer et al. 2006, 21). I will demonstrate later how a truly emic perspective, i.e. a perspective from the participants' point of view, can in fact only be gained by a close collaboration with the research participants. Second, with regard to language attitudes towards ELF the main focus has been on the professional fields of applied linguistics and ELT, providing us with revealing insights into the rather guarded, or even sceptical feelings towards ELF held by linguists and teachers. These are important findings, however, the language attitudes characteristic of other professions and domains should not be neglected. With ELF being part and parcel of a whole range of "influential frameworks" (House 1999), often involving high status and elite users, there is, consequently, a need to include not only other domains, but also a "studying up" approach (Nader 1988) in ELF research activities. This, although gaining access to the field in domains such as international business can pose an enormous challenge (Yunick Van Horn 2006). In a similar vein, with many ELF studies building on samples in which female research participants are in the majority, I believe we need to make a gender-critical effort of a new kind so as not to practically exclude men and their voices from our research. Finally, on the theoretical level, it has been suggested that ELF users can usefully be conceptualized by applying the notion of "community of practice" (Wenger 1998, cf. also House 2003, Jenkins 2007, Poncini 2007 and Seidlhofer 2007). While this is a helpful starting point, detailed and empirically grounded explorations of the analytical value of this concept are still scarce (Poncini 2007, Schaller-Schwaner 2005).

This last point will be taken up and considered in some detail in this paper, which is structured into two main parts. The first part addresses the question of how ELF speakers can usefully be conceptualized. It will be shown how the sometimes puzzling differences in attitudes towards ELF as articulated by different groups of speakers of English can, in a first step, be illuminated by drawing on the sociological concept of "subjective relevances". Identifying the role linguistic issues play in an individual's "relevance system" proves to be a valuable explanatory starting point, allowing us to differentiate between language-focussed speakers of English and content-focussed speakers of English (as a lingua franca). Building on this, the concept of "community of practice", which has already been successfully employed in sociolinguistic research, will be discussed in terms of its potential relevance to ELF research. In the latter part preliminary findings of my research project, in which I investigate ELF and how it is used by a group of business executives in a German multinational corporation, will be presented, applying the community of practice approach. I conclude this paper by bringing together again the language- and content-focussed perspectives on English.

2. Conceptualizing ELF Speakers: Subjective Relevances and Communities of Practice

The necessary conceptual distinction between different types of Englishes, e.g. English as a native language (ENL) and English as a lingua franca (ELF), has been convincingly argued for (Seidlhofer 2001; 2004). Large corpora of ELF have been compiled (e.g. ELFA / English as a Lingua Franca in Academic Settings, and VOICE / Vienna-Oxford International

Corpus of English) and corpus-based linguistic descriptions of ELF are currently under way. In light of the fact that the majority of ELF research hitherto has been small-scale work, and not, in the technical sense of the word, corpus-based, these are extraordinary achievements. Ideally, however, research of this kind should be complemented by approaches which go beyond the corpus, 're-embodying' as it were ELF data again by taking a closer look at the people producing these data, thus exploring in detail who uses the language, how, why and in which contexts, as well as developing adequate theoretical frameworks which help us to conceptualize ELF speakers.

2.1. A Sociological Perspective: Relevance Systems

One of the most fundamental and far-reaching distinctions which needs to be built into an empirically grounded conceptualization of ELF speakers, the distinction between language-focussed speakers and content-focussed speakers, can be illustrated quite nicely with the origins of my research project. Why did I, an applied linguist and teacher educator, develop an interest in English as it is used and perceived in the world of international commerce? The reason for this lies in my observation of what seemed to me strikingly different attitudes towards English (as a lingua franca) among students or teachers of English and people working in international business. On the one hand, I had noticed in a previous research project on study abroad and teacher education (Ehrenreich 2006; 2008) that despite the fact that my research participants (students and teachers of English) had had substantial and first-hand experience in ELF interactions with their international friends, they nevertheless saw ELF communication as something hugely flawed and remained ardent supporters of ENL. On the other hand, listening to stories told by friends and family members working in different business sectors about the role and effects of English as an international language, I was surprised by the relaxed pragmatism they seemed to have developed when it came to dealing with the linguistic challenges in their jobs.

How could this remarkable discrepancy in attitudes towards English as an international language be explained best? Drawing on the sociological concept of "subjective relevances" (Hitzler & Eberle 2004, 70) as used in phenomenological life-world analysis, and the way in which these relevances shape the perceptions and "shared meaning schemata" (*Deutungsschemata*) of members of different "small social life-worlds" (Luckmann 1970) provides us with a first theoretical underpinning for the observed differences in language attitudes. Among the professional groups of linguists and language teachers, linguistic issues take centre stage in their particular relevance systems, which are intersubjectively shared and obligatory for successful participations (Hitzler & Eberle 2004, 70). For non-linguists, e.g. for people working in the domain of international business, different kinds of knowledge are relevant. Quite clearly, for business professionals business matters most, with language skills only being assigned a subordinate function. Thus, a sociologically based conceptual distinction is possible between language-focussed speakers of English and content-focussed speakers of English. How the different relevance systems translate into distinct ways of dealing with, as well as interacting in and identifying with English as a lingua franca will be shown later using examples taken from my study on ELF in German multinational companies.

2.2. A Sociolinguistic Perspective: Communities of Practice

We have seen that, as a variable, a speaker's sociological background, in this case his or her professional background, may influence to a considerable degree the way ELF is perceived. Similarly, a speaker's professional background may influence his or her personal target model. Finding themselves in ELF situations some speakers still strive for an ENL approximation, as has been shown to be the case with the majority of non-native speaker teachers and linguists. This could be different for speakers with a non-linguistic background, who may happily identify with being an ELF speaker. So far, however, we still know relatively little about these issues because ELF research has only begun to address the question of how ELF functions in its social contexts of use (e.g. Mauranen 2005).

Let us take a quick look back to gauge the extent to which ELF research has so far embraced a sociolinguistic perspective in terms of taking account of the specific relationship between the social backgrounds of individuals or groups of ELF speakers and their specific language use/s. Quite clearly, while data collection in simulated situations may have been a legitimate approach in the very early phases of ELF-oriented research, the sociolinguistic insights which can be obtained using such contrived data are rather limited. One of the problems concerning those early studies which were actually based on real ELF data is the fact that, at times, the findings of these studies have been over-generalized beyond their original sociolinguistic and pragmatic contexts, thus generating some myth-like assumptions about the use of ELF and its speakers (cf. Cogo & Dewey 2006).

Recently the attitudes and identities of one specific group of English (as a lingua franca) speakers, namely non-native speaker English teachers, have been studied empirically based on concepts and methodologies from sociolinguistics and social psychology (Jenkins 2007). However, to what extent and in which pedagogical and non-pedagogical contexts English teachers do in fact qualify as ELF speakers, may need further investigation. Similarly, and drawing on the above mentioned conceptual distinction between language-focussed and content-focussed speakers, it remains to be seen how far findings pertaining to ELT professionals can be extended to other social or professional groups.

On the conceptual level, there is general agreement that established notions and frameworks may no longer be able to capture the new (socio-) linguistic realities of ELF communication adequately (Seidlhofer 2007, 310). One such example is the sociolinguistic notion of speech community with its characteristic features of stability and relative homogeneity. House (2003), for example, has suggested that instead of basing ELF research on the concept of speech community the concept of "community of practice" (Wenger 1998) should be considered as a possible theoretical alternative. Originally the concept of "community of practice" (CofP) was developed by Wenger and his colleagues (Lave & Wenger 1991, Wenger 1998) as an integral part of a social theory of learning, and it has been introduced to sociolinguistics and language and gender research in particular by Eckert and McConnell-Ginet (1992, 464), who define it as follows:

> A community of practice is an aggregate of people who come together around mutual engagement in an endeavour. Ways of doing things, ways of talking, beliefs, values, power relations—in short, practices—emerge in the course of this mutual endeavor. As a social construct, a community of practice is different from the traditional community, primarily because it is defined simultaneously by its membership and by the practice in which that membership engages.

The concept has been used in a number of recent ELF-related publications to refer to different types of ELF-speaking groups. However, the process of exploring in detail the relevance of the concept for ELF research and its specific analytical value has only just begun. For example, one of the issues that requires careful consideration is the scope of the concept, which according to Wenger is a "midlevel category" (1998, 124). Thus the "CofP domain is rather smaller than that usually circumscribed by the term 'speech community'" (Meyerhoff 2002, 526). This suggests that the concept cannot usefully be applied to ELF speakers in general, but rather unfolds its analytical potential when applied to particular CofPs in which ELF is used for communication.

In the ELF literature we find some instructive pointers which help to build useful links to the three dimensions of a CofP (characterized in detail below), which comprise "mutual engagement", a "joint enterprise" and a "shared repertoire". House (2003, 561) talks about English (as a lingua franca) being used for "various 'pockets of expertise'", Mauranen and Metsä-Ketelä (2006, 2) about ELF being used by a "plethora of in-groups and special domains" and, finally, Seidlhofer (2007, 314) about global communities whose "'dislocated' interactions [are] driven by *needs* and *wants* in specific domains of use" (my italics). Seidlhofer mentions as examples academic research communities, economic communities, chatrooms and gamers in cyberspace. Essentially, ELF research adopting a sociolinguistic perspective is interested in the social meaning ELF and other languages have taken on in individual CofPs. Its aim is to explore contextual conditions of use as well as to identify processes of socialization and learning which shape the members' emerging sociolinguistic competence, i.e. their knowledge about what constitutes "appropriate" English within their community.

2.3. Defining Communities of Practice

In the following, I will outline the three criteria which define a social group as a "community of practice" (Wenger 1998, 72-85) using examples from my research in a German multinational company—referred to as TechComp in this paper—in order to illustrate their explanatory potential. The reader is invited to keep the above mentioned or other candidates for CofPs in mind and decide for themselves whether or not these can in fact be usefully described in terms of an ELF-speaking CofP.

The first criterion is "*mutual engagement*", which means that the members need to get together, interacting with each other and thus building relationships. The group of business executives I studied can be characterised by simultaneous memberships in several CofPs which have evolved in response to respective enterprise- or project-related needs. These CofPs typically comprise an international mix of divisional heads, project managers, and engineers from within TechComp, but also from companies representing their customers or suppliers. The members of each CofP regularly interact with each other face-to-face in various types of settings (in their offices, in corridors, during meetings, over lunch or dinner) or via different channels of telecommunication (phone, email, internet). As a consequence, diverse and complex interpersonal relationships develop, in which collegiality and competition are played out in various and highly dynamic ways. Probably a feature of today's global business, the individual CofPs I observed in TechComp are in a state of constant flux with new people joining and others leaving a community. Therefore a manager, apart from simultaneously taking on different functional roles in different CofPs, may also find himself in the role of a fairly neophyte member in one community as well as, at the same time, in the role of an experienced member in another CofP.

The second criterion involves a "*joint enterprise*", which is some kind of goal or purpose which is defined explicitly or implicitly and shaped by the participants creating among them "relations of mutual accountability". These include, for example, a shared perspective on "what matters, and what does not" (Wenger 1998, 81). Meyerhoff (2002, 528) points out that a community's enterprise should be "reasonably specific and not very general or abstract". Therefore,

> [s]ociolinguists who wish to use the notion of CofP in their analyses have to exercise caution and ensure that as researchers they are not attempting to constitute 'CofPs' for which a shared enterprise is explanatorily vacant. (Meyerhoff 2002, 528)

The overall goal of business CofPs, such as the ones to which TechComp business executives belong, is of course the corporate objective of profit-making. This translates into the members' individual contributions towards this goal, such as negotiating and securing national and international contracts as well as monitoring the process of delivering high quality products according to a specified time frame. Exactly how to accomplish these goals is a matter of negotiation among the members of the CofPs, through which they define "what matters" as well as what is "appropriate" in which context. Being able to observe TechComp managers at work has taught me a lot about particular "relevance systems" and context-specific or task-specific interpretations of "appropriateness". I therefore subscribe fully to what Wenger, after a period of participant observation in an insurance company, says:

> Their pragmatic resourcefulness sometimes surprised me in my newcomer's eagerness to be thorough, but I had to admit that the job could not reasonably get done without it. (Wenger 1998, 80)

In TechComp, "the job" involves dealing and coping with technical, financial, legal, intercultural, communicative and many more challenges, and newcomers are socialized into shared practices by learning from more experienced members.

The third criterial characteristic of a CofP concerns the production of a "*shared repertoire*", linguistic, symbolic, or material etc., over time, as a resource for the negotiation of meaning within the community. The linguistic aspects of this shared repertoire, its components and its formation are, of course, what is of particular interest to ELF research:

> It is not necessary that a repertoire be completely locally produced. In fact, the bulk of the repertoire of most communities of practice is imported, adopted, and adapted for their own purpose—if only the language(s) they speak. (Wenger 1998, 126)

The shared repertoire as it is used by the TechComp managers includes German, English and many more languages, as well as documents such as drawings, charts, power point presentations or websites, models of different parts of their products, and, on a more abstract level, certain "ways of doing things" (Wenger 1998, 83). Appropriateness in the sense of "does it serve the purpose it is intended for?" is the guiding principle which has shaped this repertoire. Shortcuts to communication and jokes reflect the CofP's history of mutual engagement. The amount of innovative and 'unorthodox' language use illustrates the processual character of the repertoire and how its elements can continually be "re-utilized to new effects" (Wenger 1998, 83).

In addition to these three abstract criteria, Wenger provides as a supplementary heuristic tool a list of features which help to decide whether a community of practice has formed and whether or not it is therefore justified to view a social group as a CofP or, rather, as a much broader configuration (cf. Wenger 1998, 127):

1) sustained mutual relationships—harmonious or conflictual
2) shared ways of engaging in doing things together
3) the rapid flow of information and propagation of innovation
4) absence of introductory preambles, as if conversations and interactions were merely the continuation of an ongoing process
5) very quick setup of a problem to be discussed
6) substantial overlap in participants' descriptions of who belongs
7) knowing what others know, what they can do, and how they can contribute to an enterprise
8) mutually defining identities
9) the ability to assess the appropriateness of actions and products
10) specific tools, representations, and other artifacts
11) local lore, shared stories, inside jokes, knowing laughter

12) jargon and shortcuts to communication as well as the ease of producing new ones
13) certain styles recognized as displaying membership
14) a shared discourse reflecting a certain perspective on the world. (Wenger 1998, 125-6)

Again, it may be helpful to try and answer on the basis of this list the question "Has a community of practice formed?" for groups as diverse as, for example, a cohort of ERASMUS students in Trieste, a research network of international scientists, a New Zealand government policy unit (Holmes & Meyerhoff 1999), claims processors in an insurance company (Wenger 1998), wine producers, vineyard owners and journalists during a winery visit in Italy (Poncini 2007), or multilingual academics at a Swiss university (Schaller-Schwaner 2005).

2.4. Some Implications

Based on this brief characterisation of the concept of CofP I would like to discuss some implications for ELF research. First and as already mentioned above, "using / speaking ELF" in itself is not only too abstract to represent a meaningful and therefore explanatorily productive "joint enterprise", but is also too broad in scope. Applying the concept to ELF speakers in general would therefore be stretching the idea as Wenger points out with respect to the "English-speaking world" or "a language" (Wenger 1998, 122/127). In the same way, a profession, e.g. ELT professionals or linguists, do not constitute one unified CofP, but should rather be conceptualized as "*constellations* of interconnected practices" (Wenger 1998, 127).

Second, with the CofP being considerably smaller in scope than, for example, the notion of speech community, there is a clear need to distinguish between *different* ELF-using CofPs, in which, consequently, linguistic issues may play fundamentally different roles. Also, how individual CofPs communally assess "appropriateness" with respect to their language-related practices may vary significantly (cf. Mauranen 2005, 291).

As a third point I would like to point out that the centrality of the dimension of a "jointly negotiated enterprise", in conjunction with the requirement of continuous "mutual engagement", makes it evident that for one-off constellations or ad hoc groupings of ELF speakers, the CofP approach is probably not applicable. For these groups, alternative conceptual frameworks may have to be developed.

Fourth, examining in detail the role language, or English in particular, plays in a CofP, the concept can help us explain the markedly different attitudes towards ELF and processes of linguistic change between different CofPs. In probably all CofPs within linguistics and the ELT profession "English" constitutes the very core of the communities' "joint enterprises". Quite understandably, changes affecting this core have the potential of exerting a troubling impact on the members' constructions of professional identity. Therefore, taking into account the nature of the communities' joint enterprises provides us with a plausible explanation for the widely observable attitudes of reservation and scepticism towards ELF among linguists and ELT professionals (Jenkins 2007, Seidlhofer 2007). In other CofPs or "*constellations* of practices" English does not form a part of the joint enterprises, but is used as one resource together with other resources in their "shared repertoires". For these communities linguistic variation and change have far less existential repercussions.

Also, choosing a CofP approach has methodological implications in that it requires an ethnographic multi-method research design going beyond an exclusive focus on speech data and including interview and observational data. The reservations Meyerhoff has expressed with respect to the use of archival material in language and gender research equally apply to corpus-based research in general:

> It remains to be seen whether the CofP contributes much insight into the interaction of social and linguistic processes when researchers are restricted to using archival materials. (Meyerhoff 2002, 542)

Finally, the 'beauty' of the concept CofP lies in the fact that it is an integral part of a social theory of learning which criticizes traditional models of learning where learners are abstracted from their normal interactional contexts. Instead, it defines learning as a fundamentally social process through which we "learn to perform appropriately in a CofP as befits our membership status" (Holmes & Meyerhoff 1999, 174). As a welcome consequence, this approach makes obsolete the controversial questions whether or not or to what extent ELF speakers are (still) learners of English. Researchers are invited to rethink their own notions of 'learner' and ask novice as well as expert members of different ELF-speaking CofPs what it is they have to learn about languages, and English in particular, in order to become fully functional members in their respective CofPs.

I hope I have been able to show that the concept of CofP promises to be a useful framework for a contextualized exploration of the many ways in which ELF is used in different ELF-speaking communities and the social meanings associated with it. However, in order to be able to gauge the true potential of the concept and its actual contribution to ELF research and theory building, we still need to fill 'the empirical gap'. In the following section one such empirical analysis of an ELF community will be presented.

3. ELF in a German MNC—Preliminary Findings

The two main research questions I seek to answer in my study are concerned with ELF discourses and contexts as well as the professional-linguistic identities of ELF users in multinational corporations:

1) Discourses and contexts: When, where and how is English used in German multinational corporations? What are the salient features of ELF communication in business contexts? What are the principles governing ELF communication? How do ELF users define successful ELF communication?
2) Professional-linguistic identities of ELF users: What are the users' attitudes towards English as an international business lingua franca? How do they perceive and manage intercultural issues arising in their daily business interactions?

The two companies in which I carried out my research are both global players in their fields, one a supplier for train systems with an international workforce of 12,000 employees at 60 locations in 25 countries, the other a major car manufacturer with an international workforce of 350,000. Although in my study I mainly concentrate on the first company, TechComp, data collection in a second corporation was deemed important for general comparative purposes. Access to these two companies was possible through two personal contacts. With respect to data collection I adopted an ethnographic, multi-method approach in order to capture the multidimensional realities of my research topic as comprehensively as possible. And although I had been aware of Wenger's concept of "communities of practice" and its potential analytical value for my study from the beginning in 2005, the design of data collection procedures was not shaped by any specific theoretical framework, but was guided by general principles of qualitative research (Flick et al. 2004). My data consists of:

1) 28 in-depth interviews (60-120 mins),
2) (mostly non-participant) observation of various types of meetings, phone conferences and dinners (16 events),
3) shadowing of two managers for a whole working day,

4) 9 recordings of phone calls, phone conferences and meetings (totalling 300 mins).

All in all, more than thirty days were spent on site at the two companies. Needless to say that arranging and conducting interviews with and observation of members of a business elite of this kind poses very specific challenges to the linguist researcher (see e.g. Welch et al. 2002 and Lueders 2004). Among my interviewees and observees in TechComp were board members, CEOs, high level executives and project managers as well as engineers and a few assistants. The majority of my interview partners were German, the nationalities of the observees included Italians, French, British, American, Chinese and Spanish. However, at events such as the international executive meeting, held annually at the headquarters in Germany, more than 20 nationalities were gathered together. The fact that women play a very marginal role in my study is a correct reflection of TechComp's and its customers' (upper) managements.

In the following I will describe a number of salient features of the ELF communicative practices that have been established among the managers in TechComp (and beyond) applying, as far as this is possible, conceptual elements of the CofP framework. As this is still work in progress, I would like to add the caveat that a final and comprehensive interpretation of my findings can only be offered once all my data has been fully analyzed.

3.1. Efficiency and Appropriateness

At TechComp the use of English in international business is a huge issue. At the same time, it is an issue about which a human resources officer told me this: "We don't have the time to think about it" (cf. Kleinberger Günther 2003, 91). This statement is clearly indicative of the fact that one of the results of this community's ongoing process of negotiating their joint enterprise is the shared perspective that linguistic issues 'do not matter' (Wenger 1998, 81), or at least, do not matter enough to be given special prominence. Interestingly though, my interviews seem to have been a welcome opportunity for my interview partners to do exactly this: taking some time out and, prompted by my questions, reflecting on and articulating, often for the very first time (cf. Wenger 1998, 81), how they actually use English and other languages in their daily business and how they feel about the necessity to get their work done in and via English.

Overall—and not surprisingly—in the business domain, efficiency is the key criterion governing communication (cf. Seidlhofer 2001, 141; Kleinberger Günther 2003, 92), a criterion which is played out on several levels and in numerous ways. Similar to how the community negotiates "what matters and what does not", the participants have developed a shared perspective on what they judge as appropriate or not (Wenger 1998, 81/125; cf. Seidlhofer 2007, 315). Becoming an expert member of an ELF-speaking business CofP is therefore very much about acquiring this new, enterprise-related as well as efficiency-governed notion of appropriateness concerning the use of English, no matter how far removed this may be from previous (e.g. educational) experiences, and acting competently according to it.

3.2. Englishes and Other Languages

Linguistic plurality is one of the most salient features of the managers' shared repertoire in TechComp. According to the interviewees' personal estimates, 70 per cent of the communication conducted in English is communication among non-native speakers. What is therefore required of them is a well-developed competence in (World) English*es*, as highly complex interactions have to be managed with speakers of English as a second or foreign language of varying linguistic proficiencies as well as with native speakers of English from almost all 'Inner Circle' countries (cf. Kachru 1982/1992). A concrete example based on my one-day shadowing of one of the managers illustrates this quite nicely. His daily discourse activities show a geographic structure. Early in the morning, phone calls have to be made with China, where he has to deal with Chinese English of varying proficiency levels. During the day German face-to-face exchanges alternate with spoken or written interactions with European suppliers or customers in English or in other languages. Later in the day, phone calls are made to the United States or Canada, this time involving various regional varieties of English as a native language. ELF contexts are thus, by nature as it were, multilingual situations with languages other than English being used for various functional purposes (cf. Cogo, this volume; Klimpfinger, this volume). Also, I noticed that often several communicative tasks are carried out simultaneously. A manager might be talking to someone on the phone while checking his emails, or listening to a presentation at a meeting while working on his laptop. In the process several languages may be involved at the same time. In a similar vein, if in an international meeting held in English a quick exchange of information among compatriots is necessary, this is often done in their own language, simply because this *is* more efficient.

3.3. 'Linguistic Respect'

For a CofP "accountability to their enterprise includes … being responsible to others by not making their lives more difficult" (Wenger 1998, 81). For this reason, 'linguistic respect' is another principle governing international business communication (and one often in conflict with the principle of efficiency). In TechComp, there is almost unanimous tacit agreement that as soon as a non-German-speaking person is present, the language mode is switched to English. Most of the time this is unproblematic, particularly among representatives of top management, who are generally expert communicators, irrespective of their English skills in traditional terms. Occasionally, however, this is a problem and may sometimes result in near-absurd situations. One example in this context was a discussion in which fifteen German engineers representing supplier and customer—most of them with a very poor command of English as well as poor communicative and strategic skills, for that matter—had to negotiate technical details in English, which was a struggle that lasted more than two hours, just because two Americans and one Chinese were present, albeit in receptive roles only. Unlike what has been reported to be occasionally the case in Finnish and Dutch business contexts (cf. Louhiala-Salminen 2002, 218/234), at TechComp headquarters in Germany, English is practically never used within Germans-only groups. As soon as everybody involved realizes that there is no need to speak English, they will switch back to German.

3.4. Endonormativity

For me, the linguist observer, the self-confident and efficient (as in 'appropriate-to-their-enterprise') use of ELF by members of this business community initially came as a surprise. Later on, I will illustrate with the help of a text sample just how efficiently ELF is employed for the communication of enterprise-related content topics. At TechComp ELF in its spoken and in most of its written forms (e.g. emails, memos, slides etc., excluding some official documents as well as contracts) is used virtually endonormatively. With regard to speaking, planning how one is going to say something so as not to 'make mistakes' is only possible to a very limited extent anyway. The only other option of making sure not to violate exonormative standards is to remain silent, an option which some neophyte members occasionally resort to, but soon learn to give up because such behaviour is just not "appropriate". As far as most written texts are concerned, again there is generally neither time nor even a perceived need for planning, drafting, or a revision of texts. Slightly more time is devoted to the linguistic quality of what are considered "important" texts, such as emails or letters to the customer. However, exonormative tools such as dictionaries are rarely used even for these purposes. If a manager is not sure and wants to have an "important" email or letter checked, the resource that is employed is a (German) colleague or his (German) assistant, whose English is considered "good" or "better than mine".

In the same way, testing an applicant's proficiency in English is done by asking him or her a few questions in English during the job interview, which is in most cases conducted by a group of Germans. An "appropriate" procedure indeed, because who else would be able to judge the "appropriateness" of the applicant's English more competently than the members of the relevant CofP?

There are many more ways in which the managers I observed act as creative change agents of the English language. Coining and establishing new words and phrases, ad hoc meaning-making as well as culturally enriching the language by spontaneous translations of mother-tongue metaphors and idiomatic expressions are only some additional examples of their "pragmatic resourcefulness" (Wenger 1998, 80), which reflects their essentially pragmatic attitude towards language innovation and variation (cf. Meyerhoff 2002, 538).

3.5. Attitudes and Intelligibility

Besides this generally self-confident and largely endonormative stance towards ELF, the whole gamut of emotional reactions towards English as the business lingua franca can be found. On the one hand, we find bitter frustration over unintelligible Chinese English or impatience because it takes a German colleague forever to explain something in English. On the other hand, we find an overall appreciation of one's international workplace environment as well as, on a concrete level, fun and laughter (Wenger 1998, 125) in meetings and over dinner as a clear sign of the fact that "'feeling good'" in ELF (cf. Jenkins 2007, 122) is possible. At least in this non-linguistically focussed community.

When asked which English they understand best, many of the German managers said, not surprisingly, German English was the easiest to understand, closely followed by American English. Serious intelligibility problems occur in interactions with Indians. In general, Indian English seems to be a linguistic mystery to everybody involved. Yet, another candidate for 'difficult English' is British English. Comments such as the following were frequently made: "Too sophisticated, you never really know what they are getting at." However, these are relatively abstract and (over-)generalized statements reflecting the members' initial reactions to different varieties of English. The idea that intelligibility is, in fact, a highly dynamic and subjective concept becomes apparent in the interviewees' narratives about their "history of mutual engagement" (Wenger 1998, 83). The longer they have been working with an international partner whose variety of English may indeed have been almost unintelligible to them in the beginning the easier mutual understanding gets.

3.6. Cultural Hybridity

Refreshing insights can also be gained in terms of the language-and-culture link. In ELF the norms or rules for international interaction are not pre-established, but have to be co-constructed by those involved. At TechComp I observed managers of diverse international backgrounds interacting and doing business successfully in English, expressing their individual 'web of cultures', their national, regional or business cultures as well as the cultures of their specific positions, functions and areas of expertise, face-to-face in personal encounters or via the phone or in emails in what they call a linguistic "tool", the lingua franca. Forms of address, for example, (titles, surnames, first names etc.) are used according to their own socio-cultural norms even in English interactions or according to what has been negotiated as appropriate in specific constellations. On the receptive level, the way one is addressed by international colleagues is generally handled with great tolerance. Most interview partners actually prefer such a multicultural mix of social deixis to a homogenized approach, which might be imposed on them in the name of a 'corporate culture'. They prefer this authentic mess of the local cultures involved. Also, as one manager put it, why should Germans give up their German approach in international interactions, after all, some of their business partners chose to do business with them because they value German 'virtues' such as efficiency, reliability and directness. Therefore, the fact that the use of ELF in this community does not defer to ENL cultural norms, by no means transforms these exchanges into culture-neutral or culture-free interactions.

3.7. Illustrating the Shared Repertoire—An Example

The following telephone conversation between a German project manager and a Chinese sales manager illustrates the communicative challenges which have to be mastered in international business communication and are, in this case, mastered with remarkable ease. The reader is reminded of the fact that his or her experience of reading this transcript (transcribed according to the VOICE transcription conventions 2.1) is far removed from the actual situation in which the two participants find themselves, having to process and respond immediately to their interlocutor's spoken utterances. I would like to point out that for Western listeners (for example at conferences when the recording of this telephone call is presented to the audience) the Chinese manager's English, which is spoken very fast and is 'heavily accented', seems to be particularly difficult or even impossible to understand. It is therefore the audio-file rather than its transcript which serves as evidence for the two managers' shared repertoire and their membership in the same CofP.

In this sample we can again identify efficiency as the key principle governing business communication. The Chinese interlocutor is boarding a train, i.e. he is on the move. Even so, less than two minutes are long enough for the two to tackle some issues concerning their joint enterprise. As this is a routine situation in this community, several of the typical features of a CofP are exemplified even in this very brief exchange. What follows after a less than rudimentary "introductory preamble" (turns 2-5) is a "very quick setup of [the] problem to be discussed" (Wenger 1998, 125). In the course of the exchange "knowing what others know" facilitates several "shortcuts to communication" (Wenger 1998, 125). These features account for the fact that for outsiders, i.e. non-members of this community, it is almost impossible to make sense of this conversation, even though it is of a fairly general nature and includes virtually no technical jargon. For the two interlocutors, however, mutual understanding is possible on account of their shared repertoire resulting from a long-standing working relationship.

The following transcript reproduces the entire telephone conversation, which takes just over one and a half minutes. It is a company-internal call, in which the German project manager (S1) seeks to receive a brief update on a joint project before S2, the Chinese sales manager, goes on holiday for a few days.

{S1 dials, phone rings (5)}
(1) S1: <L1de> ach </L1de> {S1 hangs up, dials again, phone rings (42)}
(2) S2: hello?
(3) S1: hello [S2] it's [S1] (.) hi (1)
(4) S2: hi <pvc> [S1] </pvc>
(5) S1: how are you? is it <1> possible </1>

(6) S2: <1> i am </1> in [placech1] station and er i will start my <clears throat> my leave (.) yeah?
(7) S1: okay. well then i just picked you how many minutes do you still have?
(8) S2: er (.) and i will stay in [placech1] i will stay with my family until next tuesday and er next tuesday i will go to [placech2] and wednesday i will stay in office=
(9) S1: =okay
(10) S2: and <un> xx </un> and after eleven thirty and i will leave
(11) S1: okay (.) okay then it then j- only just two very f:ast questions (.) erm (.) the one have you received any further information of venezuela [product1]? (.) er sorry erm: <smacks lips> erm sudan (.) sudan <2> project </2>
(12) S2: <2> sudan </2> yes (.) yes actually and this morning i got some information. and er the car builder contact me actually i contacted them first (.) and then car builder told me and er they just er finished a visit to venezuela= {both know that they are talking about the sudan project!}
(13) S1: =yeah
(14) S2: a:nd er (.) er (.) er: (.){chinese voices in background} they will they will come to <un> xx </un> <fast> sorry i'm just er because i'm just er i'm just gonna try to go on board the <3> er <3/>
(15) S1: <3> ok-</3>
(16) S2: the coa- the <4> train </4>
(17) S1: <4> okay </4>
(18) S2: anyway and this time (.) and this they affirmed that (.) that er: december a- and they er probably work out the order i mean the contract will be effective </fast>
(19) S1: okay (.) <5> so </5>
(20) S2: <5> <un> x </un> </5>
(21) S1: then maybe afterwards we can proceed?
(22) S2: yeah and after i am on the train <pvc> chair </pvc> i will call you later again=
(23) S1: =okay. okay thank <6> you then </6>
(24) S2: <6> <soft> <un> xx </un> <soft> </6>
(25) S1: yeah=
(26) S2: =bye bye
(27) S1: bye bye [end 0: 02:19]

Their "history of mutual engagement" within the same CofP enables them to skilfully exploit the second characteristic of a shared repertoire, its inherent "ambiguity", which is played out in this conversation on several linguistic levels (phonology, grammar, semantics, discourse), but is obviously not a source of obstacles for the two participants (Wenger 1998, 83-4). Consequently, the degree of (non-)conformity with Standard English is clearly not a central issue here, the factors which define the nature and functionality of this kind of successful ELF interaction have to be located elsewhere:

> The real problem of communication [...] then is to situate ambiguity in the context of a history of mutual engagement that is rich enough to yield an opportunity for negotiation. (Wenger 1998, 84)

With respect to earlier ELF research it should be noted that what happens in turns 11-12 could easily be identified by the linguist analyst as an exemplification of what has been called the "let-it-pass"-principle (Firth 1996; cf. Cogo & Dewey 2006, 66) and has frequently been interpreted as some kind of consensus-oriented avoidance behaviour. Such a perspective, however, does not capture what is going on here. Getting the names of the two projects mixed up and not putting them right may create confusion on the part of an outsider trying to make sense of this transcript. For the two managers, however, this mix-up did not even represent an actual ambiguity let alone deserve time to be addressed, as the German manager told me afterwards, confirming yet again what Wenger says about a CofP's repertoire:

> Indeed, mismatched interpretations and misunderstandings need to be addressed and resolved directly only when they interfere with mutual engagement. (Wenger 1998, 84)

Finally, one of the most intriguing observations and one which has major implications for the way we approach ELF data was the following comment by a key informant. I replayed several times a passage of a telephone conversation between him and a Chinese colleague, which I just could not decipher. After listening intently he said: "I can tell you what he [i.e. his Chinese colleague] is talking about, what he wants from me, but I can't tell you the single words he uses to articulate this." My point is that while bottom-up approaches such as, for example, Jenkins' research on the Lingua Franca Core (Jenkins 2000) are important, this comment indicates a clear need to include holistic top-down approaches (cf. Nelson 2008) into ELF research as well. For these, evidently, a close collaboration with the research participants is required.

3.8. Implications for Future ELF Research and Theory Development

As has been shown, some of my findings support, others throw new light on what has been said earlier about ELF uses as well as ELF users and their attitudes. This concerns, for example, issues such as the de facto endonormative and relatively self-confident use of ELF, which may prove to be a characteristic feature of non-language focussed ELF-speaking groups such as business CofPs (Charles 2007, see also Mauranen 2005). A clear conceptual distinction between different ELF-speaking communities therefore seems helpful in explaining diverging ways of dealing with ELF. Consider, for example, the following statement by Seidlhofer concerning the possible recognition of new conceptual frameworks in English studies. Having discussed the shortcomings of traditional concepts such as 'speech community' and 'variety' for an adequate interpretation of ELF communication she goes on to explore as possible alternatives 'community of practice' and 'register', anticipating the following:

> While this [the conceptual reframing] may seem difficult at present, my prediction is that in ten or twenty years these new concepts will be taken for granted and *people will wonder what the fuss was all about.* (Seidlhofer 2007, 310, my italics).

In English studies (including applied linguistics and ELT), the recognition of ELF and a concomitant conceptual reframing may indeed still take some time. However, based on the findings of my study of international business CofPs, I could safely transform Seidlhofer's prediction into a statement describing, in empirical terms, the present state of affairs as well as the prevalent attitudes: What *is* all this fuss about?

What follows are, very briefly, some of my suggestions for future ELF research and theorizing, addressing issues of adequate conceptualizations, research methodologies as well as the nature and make-up of data used in ELF research.

On the basis of my study, an optimistic conceptualization of ELF speakers as 'highly proficient' turns out to be a somewhat unjustified idealization. Indeed sometimes, the speakers who participate in ELF events are 'highly' non-proficient speakers of English or, more generally, insecure communicators, causing more or less visible communicative problems of various kinds. This is a fact which should not be glossed over too quickly, but which needs careful consideration in empirical as well as in theoretical terms. With respect to research methodologies, the study presented in this paper has, hopefully, helped to illustrate the considerable potential of ethnographic approaches to studying ELF-speaking communities. More such ethnographic studies and micro-analyses of ELF-speaking business communities and other CofPs are needed to capture in context-sensitive detail the linguistic behaviour and social characteristics of these communities. Finally, although what constitutes 'representative' ELF data is still very much an open question, some recommendations concerning the kind of data used in ELF research can nevertheless be made. First and foremost, as simulations are not able to reproduce the complex realities of ELF use, only naturally occurring discourse recorded in authentic settings (as documented, for example, in the two ELF corpora ELFA and VOICE) should be used as databases. Also, care has to be taken to incorporate and devote sufficient attention to competitive talk (which may, however, be difficult for the researcher to get access to) as not all of ELF is informal and consensual. With regard to genres such as presentations in business meetings, for example, a similar case can be made of monologic speech, which is an important feature of real-life ELF talk in some CofPs and should therefore be represented in ELF data (cf. the lecture mode in ELFA). While there is good reason, in general, to keep the proportion of ENL and ESL speaker data fairly low in ELF corpora and other ELF data bases, these speakers and the roles they play in what may be predominantly ELF settings nevertheless remain important issues to research. Therefore, the fact that these speakers are, at least in some contexts, a regular part of communicative events, means that such data should not be excluded altogether, but should be included as representative of the respective ELF-speaking contexts.

4. Conclusion

By applying the "community of practice" framework of Wenger's social theory of learning, the managers I studied can usefully be conceptualized as *life-long learners*, moving in and out of different ELF-speaking CofPs as well as adapting to and actively shaping their communities' socially shared repertoires. This process of being socialized into international business CofPs involves leaving behind traditional notions of appropriateness as experienced in ELT classrooms during secondary and tertiary education and adjusting their use of English to what is required and therefore 'appropriate' in these professional communities. My interviews provide ample and highly informative evidence of how challenging the task of acquiring this new sociolinguistic competence in business ELF has been for most of them.

A relevant point to note in this context, Business English trainers generally do not have a history of socialization into business CofPs, where "appropriateness" is defined according to business goals and is not part of the members' joint enterprise (but is 'relegated' to being one of many components of a shared repertoire). This partly accounts for the often observed mismatch between supply and demand with respect to language training. Another challenge for trainers lies in the fact that what is "appropriate" with regard to the use of English in one business CofP may be different in another:

> The extent to which practices at one workplace differ from those at another has implications for people who join these workplaces, and also *for outsiders who want to interact with those members effectively.* (Holmes & Meyerhoff 1999, 177, my italics)

In other words, for Business English trainers to be able to deliver effective and truly customized training, they first need to 'learn from their learners' as it were, familiarizing themselves with the highly contextualized communicative practices of the respective workplace CofPs.

The majority of managers I observed have successfully developed into skilful and self-confident users of English as a business lingua franca, for whom (in most cases) *what* they say in ELF is by far more relevant than *how* they say something (cf. Jenkins 2007, 73). Even so, memories of past memberships still exist. In fact, most managers are well aware of the fact that their (linguistic) practices "may be contentious and externally problematized" (Meyerhoff 2002, 540), especially by language professionals. This explains why first encounters with me, 'the linguist', regularly triggered comments such as "So you have come here to study our business pidgin" and why I was often asked why their "bad English" was something that I was interested in. Similarly, seeing me taking field notes during meetings sometimes evoked questions such as "Ah, are you writing down the mistakes we make?" By the same token, when asked in my interviews where they thought they might need additional language training, their answers (grammar, vocabulary) may have to be treated as a reflection of previous educational memberships rather than as an accurate needs analysis.

Judging from their feedback during and after the interviews, I think I have been able to convey to the interviewees what I also intended to communicate in this paper: Being able to do research in this multinational corporation has taught me a lot about the skilful and creative ways in which the managers utilize ELF as part of their communicative repertoires in order to get their work done efficiently.

As pointed out above, further exploration of ELF-speaking CofPs through ethnographic studies like the one presented in this paper is clearly needed. Only then will we be able to make valid generalisations about ELF speakers and their uses of ELF which transcend individual CofPs. We may then want to move our analyses to a higher-level category examining, for example, Wenger's concept of "*constellations* of interconnected practices" (Wenger 1998, 126-31) and the ways in which typical features of and perspectives on the use of ELF can be described as being characteristic of a whole company, organization, sector or even domain.

Bibliography

Charles, M. 2007. "Language Matters in Global Communication: Article Based on ORA Lecture, October 2006." *Journal of Business Communication* 44 (3), 260-82.

Cogo, A. this volume. "Accommodating Difference in ELF Conversations: A Study of Pragmatic Strategies."

Cogo, A. and M. Dewey 2006. "Efficiency in ELF Communication: From Pragmatic Motives to Lexico-Grammatical Innovation." *Nordic Journal of English Studies* 5 (2), 59-93.

Eckert, P. and S. McConnell-Ginet 1992. "Think Practically and Look Locally: Language and Gender as Community-Based Practice." *Annual Review of Anthropology* 21, 461-90.

Ehrenreich, S. 2008. "Sprachlernsituation Ausland—Sprachbad-Mythen und Lingua-Franca-Realitäten." [Language Learning in a Study Abroad Context. Linguistic Immersion Myths vs Lingua Franca Realities.] In *Auslandsaufenthalte in Schule und Studium—Bestandsaufnahmen aus Forschung und Praxis*, ed. S. Ehrenreich, G. Woodman & M. Perrefort, 105-21. Münster: Waxmann.

—. 2006. "The Assistant Experience in Retrospect—An Interview Study Examining Its Educational and Professional Impact in Teachers' Biographies." In *Living and Studying Abroad*, ed. M. Byram & A. Feng, 186-209. Clevedon: Multilingual Matters.

ELFA corpus. English as a Lingua Franca in Academic Settings. http://www.eng.helsinki.fi/elfa/elfacorpus.htm (accessed April 24, 2009)

Firth, A. 1996. "The Discursive Accomplishment of Normality: On 'Lingua Franca' English and Conversation Analysis." *Journal of Pragmatics* 26 (2), 237-59.

Flick, U., E. von Kardorff and I. Steinke, eds. 2004. *A Companion to Qualitative Research*, translated by B. Jenner. London: Sage.

Hitzler, R. and Th. S. Eberle 2004. "Phenomenological Life-World Analysis." In *A Companion to Qualitative Research*, ed. U. Flick, E. von Kardorff & I. Steinke, translated by B. Jenner, 66-71. London: Sage.

Holmes, J. and M. Meyerhoff 1999. "The Community of Practice: Theories and Methodologies in Language and Gender Research." *Language in Society* 28 (2), 173-83.

House, J. 2003. "English as a Lingua Franca: A Threat to Multilingualism?" *Journal of Sociolinguistics* 7 (4), 556-78.

—. 1999. "Misunderstanding in Intercultural Communication. Interactions in English-as-lingua-franca and the Myth of Mutual Intelligibility." In *Teaching and Learning English as a Global Language*, ed. C. Gnutzmann, 73-93. Tübingen: Stauffenburg.

Jenkins, J. 2007. *English as a Lingua Franca. Attitude and Identity*. Oxford: Oxford University Press.

—. 2000. *The Phonology of English as an International Language*. Oxford: Oxford University Press.

Kachru, B. B. 1982/1992. "Models for Non-Native Englishes." In *The Other Tongue. English Across Cultures*. 2nd ed., ed. B. B. Kachru, 48-74. Urbana, IL: University of Illinois Press.

Kleinberger Günther, U. 2003. *Kommunikation in Betrieben*. [Communication in Companies]. Frankfurt: Lang.

Klimpfinger, T. this volume. "'She's mixing the two languages together'—Forms and Functions of Code-Switching in English as a Lingua Franca."

Lave, J. and E. Wenger 1991. *Situated Learning. Legitimate Peripheral Participation*. Cambridge: Cambridge University Press.

Louhiala-Salminen, L. 2002. "The Fly's Perspective: Discourse in the Daily Routine of a Business Manager." *English for Specific Purposes* 21 (3), 211-31.

Luckmann, B. 1970. "The Small Life-Worlds of Modern Man." *Social Research* 4, 580-96.

Lueders, C. 2004. "Field Observation and Ethnography." In *A Companion to Qualitative Research*, ed. U. Flick, E. von Kardorff & I. Steinke, translated by B. Jenner, 222-30. London: Sage.

Mauranen, A. 2005. "English as Lingua Franca: An Unknown Language?" In *Identity, Community, Discourse*, ed. G. Cortese & A. Duszak, 269-93. Frankfurt: Peter Lang.

Mauranen, A. and M. Metsä-Ketelä 2006. "Introduction." *Nordic Journal of English Studies* 5 (2), 1-8.

Meyerhoff, M. 2002. "Communities of Practice." In *Handbook of Language Variation and Change,* ed. J. K. Chambers, N. Schilling-Estes & P. Trudgill, 526-48, Oxford: Basil Blackwell.

Nader, L. 1988. "Up the Anthropologist—Perspectives Gained from Studying up." In *Anthropology for the Nineties*, ed. J. B. Cole, 470-84. New York: The Free Press.

Nelson, C. L. 2008. "Intelligibility since 1969." *World Englishes* 27 (3/4), 297-308.

Poncini, G. 2007. "Communicating within and across Professional Worlds in an Intercultural Setting." In *The Use of English in Institutional and Business Settings. An Intercultural Perspective*, ed. G. Garzone & C. Ilie, 283-312. Frankfurt: Lang.

Schaller-Schwaner, I. 2005. "Ecological Niches, Emergent Genres and Emergent Communities of Practice? English as an Academic Lingua Franca at the French-German Bilingual University of Fribourg-Freiburg." Paper presented at *Bi- and multilingual universities—Challenges and Future Prospects conference*, University of Helsinki, September 1-3, 2005. Available at http://www.palmenia.helsinki.fi/congress/bilingual2005/presentations/SchallerSchwaner.ppt. (accessed November 3, 2008)

Seidlhofer, B. 2007. "English as a Lingua Franca and Communities of Practice." In *Anglistentag 2006 Halle Proceedings*, ed. S. Volk-Birke & J. Lippert, 307-18. Trier: Wissenschaftlicher Verlag Trier.

—. 2004. "Research Perspectives on Teaching English as a Lingua Franca." *Annual Review of Applied Linguistics* 24, 209-39.

—. 2001. "Closing a Conceptual Gap: The Case for a Description of English as a Lingua Franca." *International Journal of Applied Linguistics* 11 (2), 133-58.

Seidlhofer, B. and J. Jenkins 2003. "English as a Lingua Franca and the Politics of Property." In *The Politics of English as a World Language*, ed. C. Mair, 139-54. Amsterdam: Rodopi.

Seidlhofer, B., A. Breiteneder and M.-L. Pitzl 2006. "English as a Lingua Franca in Europe." *Annual Review of Applied Linguistics* 26, 1-34.

VOICE corpus. Vienna-Oxford International Corpus of English. http://www.univie.ac.at/voice/. (accessed April 24, 2009)

VOICE Transcription Conventions [2.1]. http://www.univie.ac.at/voice/voice.php?page=transcription_general_information. (accessed November 3, 2008)

Welch, C., R. Marschan-Piekkari, H. Penttinen and M. Tahvanainen 2002. "Corporate Elites as Informants in Qualitative International Business Research." *International Business Review* 11 (5), 611-28.

Wenger, E. 1998. *Communities of Practice. Learning, Meaning, and Identity*. Cambridge: Cambridge University Press.
Yunick Van Horn, S. 2006. "World Englishes and Global Commerce." In *The Handbook of World Englishes*, ed. B. B. Kachru, Y. Kachru & C. L. Nelson, 620-42. Oxford: Blackwells.

No Joke—This is Serious! Power, Solidarity and Humour in Business English as a Lingua Franca (BELF)

Patricia Pullin Stark

1. Introduction

Research into English as a lingua franca (ELF) is a relatively new field and the concept of ELF itself is still in a formative stage. Nevertheless, there is now an increasing body of research on ELF in a range of contexts, drawing on both discourse analysis and corpus linguistics. These include: Cogo & Dewey 2006, Firth 2008, House 1999 and 2002, Jenkins 2000 and 2007, Mauranen & Metsä-Ketelä 2006, Meirkord 2002, Seidlhofer 2002 and 2004. Further studies, notably: Bargiela-Chiappini & Harris 1997, Firth 1995, 1996 and 2008, Louhiala-Salminen 2002, Louhiala-Salminen et al. 2005, Nickerson 2005, Poncini 2001, 2002 and 2003, Rogerson-Revell 2007 and 2008 have focused on the use of ELF for business. The term Business English as a lingua franca (BELF) was coined by Louhiala-Salminen (2002).

In this paper, I will consider humour as an aspect of relational work amongst speakers of Business English as a lingua franca (BELF) in a series of meetings recorded in Switzerland. Particular focus will be on the Chair's strategic use of humour to manage the group and achieve his goals, balancing the inherent power of his role with the need for solidarity with his staff. Solidarity amongst group members will also be considered.

A number of management researchers have underlined the importance of relationships in the workplace in terms of promoting harmony and consequent productivity (Fletcher 1999, Holden 2002, Wong 2005), although they point out that relationships are often undervalued. The ways relationships are built and maintained, both within and outside the workplace, have also been studied by linguists, using a range of terms to describe the phenomenon. Holmes and Marra (2004, 377) refer to "relational practice" as supportive and collaborative talk that nurtures solidarity and improves productivity in the workplace. They identify two basic functions that underlie the realisation of relational practice (ibid. 2004, 381). Firstly, relational practice functions in constructing and nurturing good workplace relationships, in establishing and maintaining solidarity between team members and in creating new relationships. Secondly, relational practice helps to construct and maintain workers' "dignity", saving face and reducing the likelihood of offence, mitigating potentially threatening behavior, minimising conflict and negotiating consensus. Similarly, Spencer-Oatey (2000, 2002, 2005) uses the term "rapport" in relation to the "relative harmony and smoothness of relations between people" and Locher (2004, 322) refers to "relational work" as "the process of shaping relationships in interaction by taking face into consideration".

Humour, which is discussed in further detail below, has been identified as a powerful and flexible tool in managing relations in the workplace (Attardo 1994, Holmes & Marra 2002, Holmes & Stubbe 2003).

2. Data and Methodology

The data analysed in this paper are drawn from three meetings, recorded in part of a larger study in an international import/export company based in Switzerland. The transcription conventions are given in Appendix A and details regarding participants and the meetings are set out in Appendix B. The five participants are of particular interest for ELF research as they each have a different mother tongue and speak at least two other languages in addition to their mother tongue. Further, not all of them work together regularly. One of the women, Marie, is on a short visit from the Middle East and another participant, Rui, only works with the others on an occasional basis.

Business meetings were chosen for analysis as bounded speech events, allowing fine-grained analysis of goal-related interaction over a series of turns, which is clearly important in analysing the building, maintenance and repair of relationships. The study is data-driven with the main analytical tool being discourse analysis. It draws on politeness theory (Brown & Levinson 1987) in terms of the strategic use of language and face. In addition, the heuristic model of Small Cultures (Holliday 1999) is used as it fits well with the notion of ELF in allowing the exploration of emergent behaviour in groups, as opposed to beginning with pre-determined categories such as "native speakers" and "non-native speakers" or nationalities. The focus of this study is thus on the speakers' use of English as a lingua franca "in its own right" (Jenkins 2007, xii), and the nature and effectiveness of their communication in context. The aim is thus to avoid comparison with native-speaker models, which may highlight "defective" usage (Seidlhofer 2004) instead of exploring speakers' interactional "achievement" (Firth 2008).

The study also involved an ethnographic strand, which allowed triangulation of the data through semi-structured interviews with the Chair and time spent with the group outside the meetings.

3. Humour

For the purpose of this study, I have drawn on Holmes' (2000, 163) in defining humour as "utterances [...] identified by the analyst, on the basis of paralinguistic, prosodic and discoursal cues, as intended by the speaker(s) to be amusing by at least some participants". It is also important to consider laughter, which is relevant for the analyst in identifying uptake of humour (Jefferson et al. 1987), although laughter may not always signal amusement. It can, for example, be a sign of embarrassment or surprise. In addition, differentiation between "conversational humour", as analysed in this paper, and scripted or "canned" jokes (Norrick 2003), i.e. as included in books of jokes, is a key factor in analysing humour in context. Whereas the former is context dependent, interactive and jointly achieved, and therefore of considerable relevance to relational work, the latter tend to be monologic and do not depend on the context.

Humour appears to play a key role in constructing and nurturing relationships in the workplace, in addition to mediating power and solidarity. Holmes and Stubbe (2003, 117) argue that:

> humour is used to construct and preserve good workplace relations, to indicate positive intent and concern for the feelings of addressees and to mitigate overt realisations of power—in other words to express politeness.

Humour tends to be viewed as a positive social device used to amuse and create rapport. It can, of course, be used repressively by those in power, to enforce their authority and even demean those under them, whilst maintaining a veneer of collegiality (Hay 2000, Holmes 2006). Whilst such "negative" instances of humour are not apparent in the data analysed here, not all of the instances reflect pure amusement. However, each instance of humour analysed below is seen to contribute to the building, nurturing or repair of workplace relations.

4. Power, Solidarity and Face

Power is intrinsic to the workplace (Holmes & Stubbe 2003). Those in power have certain rights and obligations (Boden 1994, Thomas 1995) in ensuring work is done and goals achieved. However, they also need their staffs' collaboration, which implies showing respect and nurturing solidarity. Locher (2004, 2) underlines the relational nature of power and notes the importance of face in relational work. She states that:

> The exercise of power is assumed to occur in and around relationships, negotiating symmetrical and asymmetrical relations between interactants. This means that power also reflects the degree of solidarity between interactants. One may, for example, exercise power merely to prove that one is in a more powerful position, thus emphasising difference. Or one may show restraint in the way power is exercised, taking the addressee's face needs into consideration and thus indicating some degree of solidarity as well.

Humour can be helpful in managing power relations in the workplace, in mitigating power and thus increasing solidarity, for example in softening face-threatening acts such as directives or criticism (Holmes & Stubbe 2003). Diamond (1996, 12) points to the dynamic nature of power:

> power is not merely a quality which is assigned or earned; it is also an interactional *skill* and *process*. (original emphasis).

The Chair of the meetings analysed in this study was a mature and experienced manager. He used humour not only in mitigating his power and hence nurturing solidarity, but also in wielding it in maintaining control over the group as its leader. The success of his use of humour reflects not only social competence, but also management skill.

A further factor in relational work, which relates specifically to power and solidarity, is face. The notion of face is difficult to pin down. However, a straightforward definition of face and facework, which is relevant to this study, is provided by Tracy (1990, 210):

> Whereas face references the socially situated identities people claim or attribute to others, facework references the communicative strategies that are the enactment, support, or challenge of those situated identities.

Tracy (1990) argues that whilst face is probably a universal phenomenon, its enactment is highly dependent on situation, culture and individual differences. She notes that in certain situations, particular facets of face will be more salient. For example, in the workplace people are more likely to value being seen positively for their professional competence. Indeed, Holmes and Marra (2004) emphasise that in the workplace relational practice is often directed at workers' need for recognition of their expertise or skills and their value as team members. Such orientation to face can be equated with Brown and Levinson's (1987) notion of positive face. Similarly, Harris (2003, 33) refers to negative face strategies which "serve institutional as well as interpersonal goals in helping to avoid confrontation and possible breakdown in communication". Attention to face in the workplace thus reflects the "simultaneous yet conflicting interactive goals" in the "need for connection" alongside the "need not to be excessively impinged on by others" (Tannen 2005, 202).

5. Humour in Context

5.1. The Multiple Functions of Humour

In this section, the two excerpts analysed illustrate the way humour can serve a number of functions simultaneously and hence its power as a management tool. Here humour is used to mitigate power and create or nurture solidarity in the first instance and to protect face and create a pleasant atmosphere conducive to good working relations in the second.

5.1.1. Excerpt 1: Joe 'Croaker'

Humour often occurs at transitional phases in meetings (Holmes & Stubbe 2003) such as the beginning or end, or it fills in gaps, for example when work is temporarily suspended. This is the case in Excerpts 1 and 2 (see Appendix A for transcription conventions).

Excerpt 1

Context: Four participants waiting for a late arrival before beginning a meeting.

Joanne	1	this this weekend have you seen Joe Cocker
Researcher	2	no I didn't I would have liked to go
Joanne	3	oh wonderful really wonderful ((coughing))
Herbert (Chair)	4	Cocker croaker () he's not called croaker () ((laughter))
	5	he's standing up there croaking all the time
		((humorous banter continues for 5 minutes on the topic of music until the awaited participant arrives))
Herbert	6	okay Alex is just coming um do you mind if we start

When one of the participants was late for the start of this meeting, the Chair and the other two participants indulged in humour embedded in small talk, whilst waiting for his arrival. Such uses of humour not only avoid awkward silences, but also serve to mitigate power and nurture solidarity. One of the participants had been to a Joe Cocker concert and asked if I had attended it. This led to a lively exchange on rock music. Herbert, the Chair, made various humorous remarks, for example playing on words (line 4) by referring to the singer as "Croaker". This humorous banter continued for five minutes covering sub-themes ranging from heavy metal to The Spice Girls, who Herbert said had "voices flat like cardboard". The talk resulted in much laughter and a relaxed atmosphere. In joining in this talk, and initiating much of the humour, the Chair is participating as an equal, drawing on common ground in a non-work-related topic, and thus mitigating his power, whilst building solidarity with the group. Holmes and Stubbe (2003, 80) note that:

> Humour typically constructs participants as equals, emphasising what they have in common and playing down power differences.

The choice of topic is also of relevance to (B)ELF in that music tends to transcend national borders and is an uncontroversial subject to discuss.

However, once the awaited participant arrived, Herbert cut short this talk quite abruptly, although politely (line 6), to begin the meeting. This reflects his right as Chair to control the extent of such talk and his obligation to "get the job done" (Thomas 1995). In general conversation, such abrupt shifts would usually be inappropriate. However, swift transitions from "play" to work seem to be common in workplace communication, in contrast to informal conversation, where humorous talk can become an extended focus of interaction *per se*.

Finally, the meeting was fairly stressful, with considerable resistance from the floor to changes the Chair wished to institute. At the end of the meeting, Herbert alluded to Cocker again, saying he would sing a Cocker song, if I would turn the recorder off. This resulted in laughter and release of tension. Holmes and Stubbe (2003) have noted the power of humour to release tension at the end of a stressful meeting and help participants to return to normal collegial relations. This short excerpt shows the multi-functional and flexible use of humour, indicating its power as a tool in managing relations in the workplace.

5.1.2. Excerpt 2: Not Portuguese

In this excerpt, humour is used to overcome potential tension and also to protect face. At this stage, one meeting had just finished and some members of the first group left, whilst Rui joined the group for another meeting. Herbert welcomed him and then asked if I would like to stay on to record the second meeting. Of course, he had to gain Rui's agreement, which could have been face threatening to someone who did not operate in English regularly. This led to the first instance of humour.

Excerpt 2

Context: Three participants—beginning of meeting on IT problems in Middle East office.

Herbert (Chair)	we will not talk Portuguese as I normally do with
	you ((laughter)) I will talk French () we go in English ()
Rui	((much rustling of paper)) () speak English yes (..)
	it's recorded?
Herbert	only if you agree (..) if not=
Rui	=I can agree now it's () ((laughter)) okay
Herbert	no it's okay you know it's recorded to work how we do
	it

Herbert firstly jokes about not speaking Portuguese, as usual, although he doesn't speak Portuguese, and their normal lingua franca is French; this invokes laughter from all present. The ironic humour and general laughter help to diffuse any tension that might have been caused for Rui by my presence, the use of the recorder, and the potential face threat relating to the unexpected request to speak English. Rui agrees to speak English, but notices the recorder and seems to hesitate. Herbert then offers him the option of agreeing to the arrangement or not. In terms of Brown and Levinson's (1987) framework, this is a case of negative politeness where the speaker offers the hearer an option in not assuming his willingness to speak English or coercing him to do so. The humour used here also serves to start the meeting on a pleasant note, which is clearly important for harmonious and effective working relations.

5.2. The "Achievement" of Collaborative Humour

The next excerpt involves an example of "jointly constructed", "conjoint" (Holmes 2006), or "collaborative humour" (Coates 2007). Both Holmes (2006) and Coates (2007), in analysing instances of such humour in native speaker discourse, have noted its highly co-ordinated nature that appears almost to have the qualities of music in its synchronisation and the way it reflects the "in-tuneness" of the participants. Holmes (2006, 37) notes the "level of skill involved in such collaborative floor work". What is of interest here is the "extraordinary accomplishment" (Firth 2008, 6) of these speakers of BELF, meriting analysis *per se*, leaving behind notions of "standards" promoted in language classrooms (Firth 2008, Mauranen & Metsä-Ketelä 2006, Seidlhofer 2004). The language used here is not standard, but it is effective on a number of levels, as the analysis shows.

5.2.1. Excerpt 3: "Them" and "Us"

The use of humour in sharing problems, notably in mild criticism of absent others, can be a means reinforcing solidarity by differentiating between "insiders" and "outsiders" (Boxer & Cortés-Conde 1997, Holmes 2000). Here, the participants are discussing problems with clients in the Middle East and develop a "them" and "us" dichotomy in the discourse. The humour here is at the expense of the client or clients and results in extended banter and much joint laughter, which appeared to have functioned in releasing tension over what was quite a serious and long-standing problem.

Excerpt 3

Context: Four participants discussing problems with difficult clients in the Middle East who hassle them to process orders quickly.

Herbert	1	{yeah} they push you know {()} they send you today the
	2	order and tomorrow you get the first phone call
Marie	3	yeah for example you know Mr A. well
Herbert	4	yeah {yeah} he's but okay uh yes I know I mean they are
	5	they screw pressure on our {I know} and you know they talk not
	6	very nicely because this is a woman
		((mimicking an angry voice))
	7	() I sent (), and you told me you will, no okay ()
Marie	8	okay no problem ()=
Herbert	9	you have to be tough with them
Joanne	10	tell them to call me ((laughter))
Herbert	11	I wouldn't mind I wouldn't mind eh
Marie	12	((loudly—joking tone)) they are very very interested to talk
	13	with you
		((some overlap and lack of clarity))
Joanne	14	since I had () before you know X when they are calling
		((X = name of country))
	15	() ((further imitation of an angry voice))
	16	Mr General Manager, Mr General Manager
	17	() not satisfied= ((much laughter))
Herbert	18	((imitating an angry voice)) what are you thinking
	19	((laughter)) you don't respect us
	20	okay, okay so, information flow eh in the end what I tell you
	21	we have to come to a system where you do NOT need to
	22	follow up orders

Holmes (2006, 33) notes that in such jointly constructed humour sequences:

> [p]eople extend and build on one another's humorous comments [...] the process is generative or circular, since this kind of humor constructs and contributes to the solidarity of a group.

The joint construction of humour is a considerable linguistic and social achievement and the non-standard usage here does not detract from its effectiveness. One turn flows into the next, as in line 3, where Marie offers an example of the type of client Herbert has just referred to, indicating that they are "on the same wavelength". There are also several minimal responses in the initial lines. Coates (1997) points out that minimal responses such as "yeah" and "I know" occur more frequently in collaborative floors than when one speaker holds the floor. She argues that these responses signal the listeners' presence and involvement. The frequent simultaneous laughter in this excerpt functions in a similar way. It also reflects the "playful" nature of the talk and signals rapport.

The collaborative floor and notion of a "play frame" (Bateson 1972, Coates 2007, Davies 2003) are further exemplified in the way both Herbert and Joanne mimic the client in lines 7, 16-17 and 18-19. There is evidence of a patterned "performance" here, which some researchers have compared to jazz, with speakers' voices interweaving as they improvise on a theme (Coates 2007). Production is shared between the three speakers, showing their shared knowledge and viewpoints. Indeed, Davies (2003, 1368) argues that:

> A play frame can only be sustained if all conversational participants collaborate in sustaining it. This inevitably makes such talk solidary, since co-participants collaborate not only in sustaining a particular topic but also in sustaining a particular way of talking. Successful collaboration arises from shared understandings and shared perspectives, and is a strong demonstration of in-tune-ness.

Further, Tannen (1989, 110) remarks that material represented as dialogue is often constructed rather than real. She argues that:

> casting ideas as dialogue rather than statements is a discourse strategy for framing information in a way that communicates effectively and creates involvement […] it is not reported speech but constructed dialogue.

There also appear to be several levels of humorous meaning operating within this excerpt. Herbert has made the point, in lines 5 and 6, that the clients in question tend to lack respect towards women, "they talk not very nicely because this is a woman", and in line 9, Herbert says "you have to be tough with them". Joanne responds in the following line suggesting he tell them to call her. This implies that *she* is tough and will not be pushed around. Given that she has shown considerable resistance to some of the changes Herbert wishes to institute, this is quite ironic and represents a joke within a joke.

Similarly, Marie joins in with swift repartee in lines 12 and 13 saying "they are very very interested to talk with you". Her tone implies that more is meant than is directly stated and she seems to imply irony in that these men, who lack respect for women (which Herbert evokes explicitly in line 19) also find them difficult to resist. Drawing on Gumperz (1982) and Chafe (1982), Tannen (1989, 23) notes that a sense of rapport can arise in conversation when speakers are understood without having expressed their meaning explicitly. Tannen (1989, 23) argues that "requiring the listener or reader to fill in unstated meaning […] contributes to a sense of involvement through mutual participation in sensemaking." Finally, after much joint laughter, Herbert redirects the group back to the business in hand.

Boxer and Cortés-Conde (1997, 283) argue insightfully that joking at the expense of absent others allows speakers to affirm and reaffirm relationships, and yet remain vague about the specific nature of these relationships. They maintain that:

> Bonding against others perceived as different allows us to become a unit without having to define what we are for each other. What makes us part of an 'in-group' is having in common an 'out-group'. […] there is identity display through reducing the 'others' to some laughable characterization that makes them different from us.

This is particularly important in a group such as this, comprising very different others with major social, cultural and generational differences, and in particular where one member is physically present only on rare occasions. Bonding in this way reinforces group cohesion, rather than allowing differences to divide group members.

This instance of humour enacted by speakers of BELF is thus not just an example of linguistic accomplishment, but also of social bonding and the effective use of humour in relational work. It is interesting to note how successful the participants are as speakers of English as a lingua franca in using humour strategically and collaboratively. This would seem to imply that the effective use of humour may be just as, if not more, reliant on social and interpersonal skills as on linguistic competence.

5.3. Dealing with Problems—Humour and Boundaries

A number of studies on ELF and BELF, involving participants from a wide range of backgrounds, have shown that, whilst there will always be tensions and communication problems in any group, on the whole, ELF/BELF communication is effective, and notably characterised by an orientation towards solidarity and consensus (Firth 1996, House 2002, Meierkord 2002, Poncini 2001, Seidlhofer & Jenkins 2003). Some studies of BELF have found links between different communication styles, for example involving more or less "small talk", and communication problems (Louhiala-Salminen et al. 2005). However, these problems did not lead to conflict or breakdown in communication.

However, House (2002) argued that superficial consensus may hide communication problems at a deeper level and Seidlhofer (2004, 219) notes that "findings available to date result from research on a fairly limited database". One problem in collecting data is that researchers are unlikely to gain access to settings where there is overt conflict. Nevertheless, as speakers of (B)ELF are human beings and not necessarily given to continual co-operation, it is likely that disputes also arise amongst them.

In the data I collected in this study, there was one instance of extended disagreement. This is not analysed here, but an example of humour that followed the incident, relating to the delineation of boundaries with respect to appropriate behaviour (Hay 2000), is discussed below. Again, this illustrates not only the power of humour in relational work, but also the skill and resourcefulness of speakers of BELF in using humour to both "do" and "contest" power (Holmes & Marra 2002, Holmes & Stubbe 2003). "Doing" and "contesting" power refers here to the exercise of power by those in authority and subordinates' direct or indirect resistance to this.

5.3.1. Excerpt 4: Sarcasm and Power

In this case, it is important to understand the preceding incidents. A problem had been identified with one of the orders and Joanne decided to telephone the office in Germany during the meeting to clarify some details. The conversation became heated, with Joanne shouting at her interlocutor in High German. Meanwhile, Alex, whose German was very basic, tried to intervene with suggestions for action. Joanne then abruptly interrupted the telephone call, laying the receiver on the desk, and told Alex in an angry tone that she would pass the call to him in his office. Alex did not budge and they subsequently entered into a 'slanging match', carried out in French. Finally, Herbert came into the office and, after saying "ciao" to the person waiting on the telephone in Germany and putting the phone down, tried to calm the situation. He was initially greeted by a tirade from Joanne in Swiss German about Alex's meddling, which clearly represented a face threat to her in terms of negative face in impinging on her 'territory' and positive face in indirectly questioning her ability to make the right decision. Herbert defused the situation by saying firmly but calmly (in English) that they would deal with the matter the following week. He then asked for the file on the issue (line 1) and deftly used humour to conclude the exchange.

Excerpt 4

Context: Three participants (no chair) joined at this stage by Herbert, discussing problem orders.

Herbert	1	can I have this dossier and I can look at it
Joanne	2	you can yes look [at it]
Herbert	3	[don't worry] keep going handling your problems
Joanne	4	I do ((laughs))
Marie	5	[what does it said]
Herbert	6	[drink a glass of water] I'll put in each 20 grams of rum ((Herbert leaves the room with Alex and the file to go to Herbert's office))

Hay (2000, 720) notes that humour can be used to delineate boundaries if a member of a group has "overstepped the boundaries of acceptability", as in the confrontation preceding this excerpt. Humour also functions here as a form of "damage control" (Holmes & Marra 2004, 377). Herbert remarks in a sarcastic tone (line 4): "don't worry keep going handling your problems". Despite the sarcasm, the humour serves to defuse the situation and Joanne disarmingly says "I do" and laughs. Her response may also imply that whatever the problems, she intends to deal with them herself and will not tolerate interference from Alex. As such, her use of humour is "contestive" (Holmes & Marra 2002), and shows that she may also be testing the boundaries of power, implicitly re-asserting her own power, even if only by implying that she will live to fight another battle on her terms. Before leaving, Herbert also says (line 6) "drink a glass of water I'll put in each 20 grams of rum". This may reflect his military background, as he was previously a professional army officer, and be an allusion to the serving of rum to soldiers before going into battle; if so, it would be particularly ironic given the preceding 'battle' and Joanne's slightly subversive response to his reprimand. Thus unraveled, even a short instance of humour can be seen to contain several 'layers' of meaning that reflect the participants' dynamic relationships, and their mediation through the skillful use of power and humour. Once again, this also demonstrates the accomplishment of BELF in context.

The use of sarcasm is also of interest. Sarcasm tends to be associated with negative instances of humour such as put downs. However, this is not the case here. Kotthoff (2003, 1393) cites Schütte (1991), who studied the language of musicians in a professional orchestra. She found that sarcastic remarks were exclusively made by the conductor, i.e. the person with the highest status. Schütte (ibid.) thus linked sarcastic or ironic humour with status and viewed irony in a professional context as a social procedure for avoiding conflict and securing co-operation. In this instance, such well placed humour, even if it involves sarcasm, conveys a clear message concerning the inappropriacy of the previous exchange, but also respects Joanne's positive face. Respect is essential from a boss to maintain social cohesion within a group.

Holmes and Stubbe (2003, 114-115) argue that humour can serve the strategic function of "disarming criticism" in relation to positive face threats and add that: "Without humour [...] public reprimands would be harsh indeed". Direct criticism of Joanne on the way she had handled the problem would probably have resulted in offence and may have set the dispute off again. Holmes and Stubbe (2003, 116) also point out that:

> The requirements of institutional roles at work often make face-threatening acts unavoidable; in such contexts, humour provides an acceptable attenuation strategy. It is coopted as a strategy for mediating between competing discourses—those of politeness and power.

Finally, individual style is also apparent here. Tannen (1984, 132) claims that: "One of the most distinctive aspects of any person's style is the use of humor." Individuals are likely to use humour in different ways and to a greater or lesser extent, depending, for example, on how well they know each other and, in the case of the workplace, roles and hierarchical differences. In this group, Herbert most frequently initiated instances of humour, using different forms of humour effectively as a management tool. On the one hand, such uses of humour probably reflect his lengthy experience and skill in a senior management role. On the other hand, they may also be an indication of a "competence". Attardo (1994, 1) notes that humour is: "a competence [...] something that speakers know how to do, without knowing how and what they do". Joanne also showed quick wit and was able to use humour in subtly contesting power and defending her position.

5.3.2. Excerpt 5: Returning to Normality

Excerpt 5 follows directly from the previous excerpt. The two men leave the room and Joanne and Marie are then alone together (apart from my presence).

Excerpt 5

Context: as for Excerpt 4—Marie and Joanne now alone.

Marie	1	what did he ((Marie spills her tea)) oh sorry I'm so sorry
Joanne	2	don't don't worry
Marie	3	I'm so so sorry whoop
Joanne	4	don't worry don't worry
Marie	5	I'm so sorry
Joanne	6	((humorous tone)) no not on the documents but{()} come
Marie	7	°do you have a tissue°
Joanne	8	°I have a little one°
		((Joanne tells Marie what was said and then turns to me))
Joanne	9	muss nicht Fernseh ga gell ((to me)) ((laughs)) hhh
		((you don't need to watch telly, eh))

Marie does not understand French or German and was clearly quite upset by the outburst. As soon as the others have left, she begins to query Joanne on the conversation, but then spills her tea. She apologises repeatedly and it is interesting to see in line 6 how Joanne jokes about the need to avoid the liquid going on the documents and offers Marie a "little" tissue (line 8). She seems to have overcome her anger and is now more concerned about Marie, whom she can see is upset. Her humour probably helps Marie to relax. In lines 10-21, Joanne then explains the problem, as she sees it. Marie, who speaks with the voice of experience, comments "yeah I again there is a complaint", showing empathy towards Joanne. At this point, they raise their glasses and say "cherrio/cheery" and laugh together. This appears to provide closure before they move on to another subject, and is typical of the transitional function of humour.

However, Joanne also turned to me, whom she seemed to have forgotten, despite the room being very small and my sitting almost directly opposite her, and said in Swiss German "muss nicht Fernseh ga gell", which roughly translated meant that one does not need to watch the television, implying reality shows as a source of amusement. This comment, with its self-mocking humour, would seem to reflect protection of the speaker's positive face, in coping with embarrassment (Hay 2000).

Nevertheless, despite considerable tension, Joanne was able to use humour to "come down to earth", and it certainly seemed to help in returning to normality. Joanne and Alex spoke to me about the incident later and were clearly rather embarrassed. The group were functioning perfectly normally in the next meeting I taped that week, indicating a sufficient degree of solidarity to overcome such a robust clash.

Finally, the constant switching of languages in this episode may reflect the fact that with emotions running high, the issues had become personal and were no longer purely task focussed. The speakers seemed no longer to be aware of which language they were speaking, as Joanne's addressing me in Swiss German could not have a rational foundation, given that she did not know me well and it was unlikely that I would understand Swiss German. In addition, whilst it might have appeared rude to leave Marie out, by not speaking English, Alex and Joanne seemed to forget her presence, as they did the person on the telephone. Finally, the presence of other languages reflects one of the realities of ELF, which is inherently embedded in the context of at least one other language and whose speakers are often multilingual (Poncini 2001, 2002, 2003; Pölzl & Seidlhofer 2006).

5.4. From Language Problems to Language Play

The final two instances of humour analysed here relate to language. In Excerpt 6 an example of misunderstanding, apparently due to a lack of language knowledge, is analysed, showing how speakers deal with failed uses of humour. Excerpt 7, on the other hand, is an example of a playful use of humour, based on the use of language itself, and reflects the speakers' multilingualism.

5.4.1. Excerpt 6: Failed Humour

In this excerpt, the group are discussing the problem of overcoming hierarchical resistance to extending the use of the intranet to lower levels of staff in the Middle East office.

Excerpt 6

Context: Three participants—beginning of meeting on IT problems in Middle East office. As for Excerpt 2.

Rui	1	they (the Middle East office) know [who is]
Herbert	2	[the right contact]
Rui	3	they have defined that's the rule of Z the rules in Z for the
	4	countries, that's why for me when you come to me and you say
	5	okay what can we do for connecting them to [Z?]
Herbert	6	() we take them over, we change them into a Z office then
	7	you take them over.
Rui	8	you cannot change=
Herbert	9	=no we take them over, we buy them {ah} ((look of recognition from Rui and smiles))
	10	we put them onto our empire
Rui	11	Yeah: of course

The solution to the problem is apparently going to be difficult to find and Herbert jokingly suggests that the Swiss branch "take over" the office in the Middle East (line 6). Initially, Rui seems to ignore this comment, focussing on the word "change", but Herbert repeats the phrase several times in a lively, joking tone. However, Herbert, possibly sensing a linguistic problem, rephrases his point, using the term "buy" (line 9). At this point, Rui seems to understand the joke. The group did not dwell on the point, possibly as it had been rather belaboured and also perhaps as further expansion on a gap in a participant's linguistic knowledge could be face-threatening.

It has been noted that misunderstandings are not frequent in non-native speaker interaction (Seidlhofer 2004, 218), but when they do occur, they tend to be resolved either by topic change or accommodation (Cogo & Dewey 2006) through communication strategies such as rephrasing or repetition, as in this case. Firth (1996) has also referred to the "let it pass principle" in relation to ambiguity, where non-native speakers accept a certain amount of ambiguity in lingua franca communication and are not worried about occasional incomprehension. Interestingly, Seidlhofer (2002), in noting inevitable communication problems due to lack of lexis, draws attention to misunderstanding resulting from idiomatic speech used by one speaker that another may not know. She refers to this as "unilateral idiomaticity" (Seidlhofer 2002, 220). This seems to have been the cause of misunderstanding in the above excerpt. The fact that the attempt at humour was not totally successful, did not seem to affect the atmosphere in the meeting or group cohesion and is an example of the "robust" nature of (B)ELF (Firth 1996). As Seidlhofer (2004, 222) notes:

> Another important insight from the study of intercultural ELF interactions is that proficiency in the language code only accounts for part of the success or failure of communication; at least as important is a more general communicative capability, such as sensitivity to the limits of shared systemic and schematic knowledge, as well as accommodation skills.

Nevertheless, referring to communication in academic settings, Mauranen (2006, 148) notes that:

> A distinct orientation toward content allows minor imperfections to pass, but only as long as they do not hamper intelligibility; maintaining a sufficient level of intelligibility is constantly monitored in cooperative interaction.

The same point would also seem to be relevant with regard to ELF in business settings, where misunderstandings can result in loss of time and money. Indeed, Pitzl (2005) demonstrates the way miscommunication is signalled and resolved through negotiation in business communication, whilst maintaining a co-operative stance. In the instance above, the apparent lack of lexis as the root of the problem was not dwelt on, but the meaning was clarified, even though it was "only a joke".

5.4.2. Excerpt 7: A Linguistics Class

The final excerpt deals with humour as a form of language play.

Excerpt 7

Context: As for Excerpt 5. The two women are alone, the men having left earlier, and are nearing the end of the meeting.

Joanne	1	Khrazem?
Marie	2	rr razem ((pronounces the word correctly))
Joanne	3	Rrahzem
Marie	4	rrahZEM not ze
Joanne	5	ZEM khraZEM khraZEM
Marie	6	not kr rh ((laughter))
Joanne	7	kraZEM
Marie	8	yeah good ((laughter)) hu a linguistics class () okay

Coates (2007, 46) points out that "playful talk is fun", it makes people feel good and nurtures solidarity. The focus of humour here is the language itself. The excerpt illustrates the protean and spontaneous nature of humour, which are key aspects of its attraction.

Excerpt 7 hinges on foreign language pronunciation and reflects the multilingual speakers' natural interest in language. Rogerson-Revell (2008) has noted that speakers of BELF tend to avoid correcting other speakers' language and it is noteworthy that Marie does not correct Joanne's pronunciation until Joanne questions it herself with rising intonation, in line 4, and a questioning look. The ensuing "linguistics class" (line 13) entails intense repetition and correction and elicits mutual laughter. Such "correction" would probably be face threatening to a monolingual speaker, even if invited, as it could be demoralising. Joanne, however, speaks several languages and clearly enjoys the challenge. Humour here provides a break in a gruelling meeting at the end of a long day, and also helps to reduce tension and lighten the atmosphere. As Boxer and Cortés-Conde (1997, 293) remark: "we all enjoy a good laugh".

Further, such an exchange would not be possible without a certain degree of solidarity and it also serves to reinforce this existing solidarity.

6. Conclusions

In this paper, I have explored uses of humour in workplace meetings between speakers of English as a lingua franca. The focus has been on humour in relation to power and solidarity in relational work. Whilst the study is small in scale, the data are rich and show that BELF speakers use humour as a powerful, multifunctional device in managing relations in the workplace and hence promoting the effectiveness of their collaboration. Humour, however, requires subtle and quick reactions and it is in analysing instances of humour in BELF that the resourcefulness and sheer achievement of lingua franca usage is apparent.

Analysis of the data in this study has shown that humour is a particularly powerful management tool for bosses and serves a number of functions. Humour can be used to mitigate power and thus nurture solidarity; its use reduces hierarchical distance in the workplace, for example in instances of collaborative humour or humour deriving from small talk. Such humour tends to be based on common ground, which is particularly important for speakers of English as a lingua franca, as it can help to foster a feeling of belonging or bonding amongst people whose identities reflect more differences than areas of similarity.

A range of different types of humour was used in the meetings, from witty quips and word play to sarcasm. The instances of humour analysed were shown to be context based and not dependent on cultural knowledge. This reflects the tendency indicated in earlier research on ELF towards group alignment in relation to culture, based on common ground and identity, in this case that of business, rather than national origins (Meierkord 2002). One unsuccessful instance of humour also illustrated the flexible and non-critical nature of BELF and the linguistic awareness of multilinguals, which may contribute to effective relational management in BELF.

The paper has also shown ways in which humour can be used to mitigate face threats, both to self and others. Power can be actively wielded through the use of humour, notably in delivering criticism, whilst still respecting face. However, uses of humour were also present in the data where participants contested power and subtly asserted their independence. The quick wit and subtle irony that occurred in the meetings appeared to be based as much on social skills as on language. Nevertheless, the enactment of collaborative humour reflected considerable linguistic achievement with language used in an almost virtuoso manner, as participants built on each others' contributions, evoking both explicit and implicit meanings.

Given the important role humour has been shown to play in lingua franca discourse, further research could explore how far speakers of ELF enact humour through the transfer of social skills used in their mother tongue and in what ways they may adapt such uses of humour when in ELF contexts.

Another area that would seem to be of interest for future research is with regard to the use of humour between native and non-native speakers. There is some evidence to suggest that whereas ELF speakers manage very well amongst themselves, despite linguistic limitations, contact with native speakers can prove problematic (Rogerson-Revell 2007), perhaps because humour becomes more culturally-based and its interpretation is dependent on "insider" knowledge.

In conclusion, the subtle and complex uses of humour analysed in this study provide examples of interactive "achievement" in BELF, illustrating its "robust" nature (Firth 1996) and thus supporting earlier findings on ELF. The speakers in this study manage to deal effectively with the conflicting interactional goals of power and solidarity, whilst paying attention to face and relational issues and achieving their goals. This communicative effectiveness, which is not reliant on standard language usage, also underlines the need to avoid systematic reference to native-speaker models as points of comparison or teaching models (Firth 2008, Mauranen 2006, Seidlhofer 2004).

APPENDIX A

Transcription conventions

?	Rising intonation (final sentence)
.	Falling intonation (sentence-final)
/ \	Rising and falling intonational contours
,	Continuing intonation (final clause, 'more to come', lists)
TEXT	Stress (syllable or word) or longer utterances spoken loudly
(0.6)	Pause (tenths of a second)
(..)	Pauses of one-half second or less
<text>	Spoken slowly
>text<	Spoken rapidly
:	Lengthened syllable (ha:rd)
-	Word cutoff (abrupt self-termination, because speaker stops speaking or another interrupts)
=	Latched talk (lack of temporal gap between two speakers—typically used at end of 1st speaker's line and at beginning of next speaker's utterance)
{ }	Backchannel {S:OK}
[ ]	Overlapping speech
°text°	Text spoken softly
H	Clearly audible breathing (general breath sounds)
.h .hhh	In-breath (.h = inhalation / .hhh = longer inhalation)
h hhh	Out-breath (as above)
((behavior))	Transcriber's comments (e.g. whispers, coughing, laughter)
( )	Unclear or intelligible speech (unclear/questionable words appear within the parentheses)

Source:

Dressler, R. A. and R. J. Kreuz 2000. "Transcribing Oral Discourse: A Survey and a Model System." *Discourse Processes* 29 (1), 25-36.

APPENDIX B

Overview of data

NB. All names have been changed for confidentiality.

Mtg code	Subject	Length of mtg (mins)	Name	Sex	Age	Position & Role	Mother tongue
CH2	Order forms and procedures	60	Joanne	F	41-50	Logistics Assistant	French
			Marie	F	31-40	Middle Management	Armenian
			Alex (no Chair)	M	21-30	Herbert's Assistant	Rumanian
CH3	Review of meetings on orders	62	Herbert (Chair)	M	60+	Senior Manager Meeting Chair	Swiss-German
			Joanne Marie Alex				
CH4	Intranet connections in Middle East offices	22	Rui	M	21-30	Middle Management IT Specialist	Portuguese
			Herbert (Chair) Alex				

Bibliography

Attardo, S. 1994. *Linguistic Theories of Humor.* Berlin: Mouton de Gruyter

Bargiela-Chiappini, F. and S. Harris 1997. *Managing Language: The Discourse of Corporate Meetings*. Amsterdam: John Benjamins.

Bateson, G. 1972. *Steps to an Ecology of the Mind.* San Francisco: Chandler Publishing Company.

Boden, D. 1994. "Agendas and Arrangements: Everyday Negotiations in Meetings." In *The Discourse of Negotiations: Studies of Language in the Workplace*, ed. A. Firth, 83-99. Oxford: Pergamon.

Boxer, D. and F. Cortés-Conde 1997. "From Bonding to Biting: Conversational Joking and Identity Display." *Journal of Pragmatics* 27 (3), 275-94.

Brown, P. and S. Levinson 1987. *Politeness: Some Universals in Language Usage*. Cambridge: Cambridge University Press.

Chafe, W. 1982. "Integration and Involvement in Speaking, Writing, and Oral Literature." In *Spoken and Written Language*, ed. D. Tannen, 35-53. New Jersey: ABLEX Publishing Corporation.

Coates, J. 2007. "Talk in a Play Frame: More on Laughter and Intimacy." *Journal of Pragmatics* 39 (1), 29-49.

—. 1997. "The Construction of a Collaborative Floor in Women's Friendly Talk." In *Conversation: Cognitive, Communicative and Social Perspectives*, ed. T. Givon, 55-89. Amsterdam: John Benjamins.

Cogo, A. and M. Dewey 2006. "Efficiency in ELF Communication: From Pragmatic Motives to Lexico-Grammatical Innovation." *Nordic Journal of English Studies* 5 (2), 59-94.

Davies, C. 2003. "How English-Learners Joke with Native Speakers: An Interactional Sociolinguistic Perspective on Humor as Collaborative Discourse across Cultures." *Journal of Pragmatics* 35 (9), 1361-85.

Diamond, J. 1996. *Status and Power in Verbal Interaction. A Study of Discourse in a Close-Knit Social Network.* Amsterdam: John Benjamins.

Dressler, R. A. and R. J. Kreuz 2000. "Transcribing Oral Discourse. A Survey and a Model System." *Discourse Processes* 29 (1), 25-36

Firth, A. 2008. "The Lingua Franca Factor." Paper presented at the *1st International Conference on English as a Lingua Franca*, University of Helsinki, March 6-8, 2008.

—. 1996. "The Discursive Accomplishment of Normality: On 'Lingua Franca' English and Conversation Analysis." *Journal of Pragmatics* 26 (2), 237-59.

—. 1995. *The Discourse of Negotiation: Studies of Language in the Workplace*. Oxford: Pergamon.
Fletcher, J. 1999. *Disappearing Acts. Gender, Power, and Relational Practice at Work*. Cambridge: MIT.
Gumperz, J. 1982. *Discourse Strategies*. Cambridge: Cambridge University Press.
Harris, S. 2003. "Politeness and Power: Making and Responding to 'Requests' in Institutional Settings." *Text* 23 (1), 27-52.
Hay, J. 2000. "Functions of Humor in the Conversations of Men and Women." *Journal of Pragmatics* 32 (6), 709-42.
Holden, N. 2002. *Cross-Cultural Management: A Knowledge Management Perspective*. Harlow: Pearson Education Limited.
Holliday, A. 1999. "Small Cultures." *Applied Linguistics* 20 (2), 237-64.
Holmes, J. 2006. "Sharing a Laugh: Pragmatic Aspects of Humor and Gender in the Workplace." *Journal of Pragmatics* 38 (1), 26-50.
—. 2000. "Politeness, Power and Provocation: How Humour Functions in the Workplace." *Discourse Studies* 2 (2), 159-85.
Holmes, J. and M. Marra 2004. "Relational Practice in the Workplace: Women's Talk or Gendered Discourse?" *Language in Society* 33 (3), 377-98.
Holmes, J. and M. Marra 2002. "Having a Laugh at Work: How Humour Contributes to Workplace Culture." *Journal of Pragmatics* 34 (12), 1683-710.
Holmes, J. and M. Stubbe 2003. *Power and Politeness in the Workplace*. Edinburgh: Pearson Education Limited.
House J. 2002. "Communicating in English as a Lingua Franca." In *EUROSLA Yearbook 2*, 243-61. Amsterdam: John Benjamins.
—. 1999. "Misunderstanding in Intercultural Communication: Interactions in English as a Lingua Franca and the Myth of Mutual Intelligibility." In *Teaching and Learning English as a Global Language*, ed. C. Gnutzmann, 73-89. Tübingen: Stauffenburg.
Jefferson, G., H. Sacks and E. Schegloff 1987. "Notes on Laughter in the Pursuit of Intimacy." In *Talk and Social Organisation*, ed. G. Button & J. Lee, 152-205. Clevedon, Philadelphia: Multilingual Matters Ltd.
Jenkins, J. 2007. *English as a Lingua Franca: Attitude and Identity*. Oxford: Oxford University Press.
—. 2000. *The Phonology of English as an International Language*. Oxford: Oxford University Press.
Kotthoff, H. 2003. "Responding to Irony in Different Contexts: On Cognition in Conversation." *Journal of Pragmatics* 35 (9), 1387-1411.

Locher, M. 2004. *Power and Politeness in Action: Disagreements in Oral Communication.* Berlin: Mouton de Gruyter.

Louhiala-Salminen, L. 2002. "The Fly's Perspective: Discourse in the Daily Routine of a Business Manager." *English for Specific Purposes* 21 (3), 211-31.

Louhiala-Salminen, L., M. Charles and A. Kankaanranta 2005. "English as a Lingua Franca in Nordic Corporate Mergers: Two Case Companies." *English for Specific Purposes* 24 (4), 401-21. Special issue on English as a lingua franca in international business contexts, ed. C. Nickerson.

Mauranen, A. 2006. "Signaling and Preventing Misunderstanding in English as Lingua Franca Communication." *International Journal of Sociology of Language* 177, 123-50. Special issue, ed. C. Meierkord.

Mauranen, A. and M. Metsä-Ketelä 2006. "Introduction." *Nordic Journal of English Studies* 5 (2), 1-8. Special issue on English as a Lingua Franca, ed. A. Mauranen & M. Metsä-Ketelä.

Meierkord, C. 2002. "'Language Stripped Bare' or 'Linguistic Masala'? Culture in Lingua Franca Conversation." In *Lingua Franca Communication*, ed. K. Knapp & C. Meierkord, 109-33. Frankfurt am Main: Peter Lang:.

Nickerson, C. 2005. "English as a Lingua Franca in International Business Contexts." *English for Specific Purposes* 24 (4), 367-80. Special issue on English as a lingua franca in international business contexts, ed. C. Nickerson.

Norrick, N. 2003. "Issues in Conversational Joking." *Journal of Pragmatics* 35 (9), 1333-59.

Pitzl, M.-L. 2005. "Non-Understanding in English as a Lingua Franca: Examples from a Business Context." *VIenna English Working PaperS* 14 (2), 50-71. http://www.univie.ac.at/Anglistik/Views0502mlp.pdf. (accessed 22 October 2008)

Pölzl, U. and B. Seidlhofer 2006. "In and on Their Own Terms: The "Habitat Factor" in English as a Lingua Franca Interactions." *International Journal of the Sociology of Language* 177, 151-76.

Poncini, G. 2003. "Multicultural Business Meetings and the Role of Languages Other than English." *Journal of Intercultural Studies* 24 (1), 17-32.

—. 2002. "Investigating Discourse at Business Meetings with Multicultural Participation." *International Review of Applied Linguistics* 40 (4), 345-73.

—. 2001. "Business Relationships and Roles in a Multicultural Group: An Investigation of Discourse at an Italian Company's Meetings of Its International Distributors." PhD diss., University of Birmingham.

Rogerson-Revell, P. 2008. "Participation and Performance in International Business Meetings." *English for Specific Purposes* 27 (3), 338-60.
—. 2007. "Humour in Business: A Double-Edged Sword: A study of Humour and Style Shifting in Intercultural Business Meetings." *Journal of Pragmatics* 39 (1), 4-27.
Schütte, W. 1991. *Scherzkommunikation unter Orchestermusikern*. Tübingen: Narr.
Seidlhofer, B. 2004. "Research Perspectives on Teaching English as a Lingua Franca." *Annual Review of Applied Linguistics* 24, 209-39.
—. 2002. "The Shape of Things to Come? Some Basic Questions about English as a Lingua Franca." In *Lingua Franca Communication*, ed. K. Knapp & C. Meierkord, 269-302. Frankfurt am Main: Peter Lang.
Seidlhofer, B. and J. Jenkins 2003. "English as a Lingua Franca and the Politics of Property." In *The Politics of English as a World Language*, ed. C. Mair, 139-54. ASNEL Papers 7, Amsterdam—New York.
Spencer-Oatey, H. 2005. "(Im)politeness, Face and Perceptions of Rapport: Unpacking Their Bases and Interrelationships." *Journal of Politeness Research* 1 (1), 95-119.
—. 2002. "Managing Rapport in Talk: Using Rapport Sensitive Incidents to Explore the Motivational Concerns Underlying the Management of Relations." *Journal of Pragmatics* 34 (5), 529-45.
—. 2000. "Rapport Management: A Framework for Analysis." In *Culturally Speaking*, ed. H. Spencer-Oatey, 11-46. London: Continuum.
Tannen, D. 2005. *Conversational Style: Analyzing Talk among Friends.* 2nd ed. Oxford: Oxford University Press.
—. 1989. *Talking Voices: Repetition, Dialogue, and Imagery in Conversational Discourse*. Cambridge: Cambridge University Press.
—. 1984. *Conversational Style: Analyzing Talk among Friends.* Norwood, NJ: Ablex.
Thomas, J. 1995. *Meaning in Interaction*. Harlow: Longman Group Limited.
Tracy, K. 1990. "The Many Faces of Facework." In *Handbook of Language and Social Psychology*, ed. G. Howard & P. Robinson, 209-26 Chichester: John Wiley & Sons Ltd.
Wong, P. 2005. "Lessons from the Enron Debacle: Corporate Culture Matters." In *Organizational Culture: An Introduction*, ed. N. Taher, 180-92. Hyderabad, India: ICFAI University Press.

Students on Exchange in Scandinavia: Motivation, Interaction, ELF Development

Philip Shaw, Tim Caudery and Margrethe Petersen

1. Introduction

An English as a lingua franca (ELF) situation is defined by extra-linguistic criteria—it is one in which a group is communicating in English but this is not the native language of any of the speakers (Mauranen 2005, Jenkins 2000 and 2006ab, Seidlhofer 2001). Studies of lingua franca situations may focus descriptively on their linguistic (phonological, syntactic, lexical-semantic, or pragmatic) features. At the same time they often examine sociolinguistic parameters such as norms and attitudes or their implications for language teaching.

The ELF situations reported in the literature vary quite widely in terms of their communicative demands but there are similarities as well as differences in the patterns of pragmatic behaviour these give rise to. For example, Firth's (1996) classic study of lingua-franca English telephone interaction examined situations with high stakes but a relatively narrow range of topics and functions. Both partners knew they were talking about buying and selling dairy products, both knew that they needed to do business, and neither could use any channel other than auditory, since they were telephoning. These features led to a pragmatic pattern of persistence, tolerance, and successful inferencing about the other's intentions. Björkman (this volume), House (2002) and Meierkord (1998; 2004) find similar efficiency and adaptability in their studies.

A number of studies seem also to have found a degree of uniformity on the lexico-grammatical level. Björkman (this volume), Mauranen (2005), and for example Seidlhofer (2004; 2006) list similar sets of features, although the details vary across lists and further research may be tending to suggest more differentiation.

Meierkord (2004) implies that pronunciation in ELF situations is that of the speaker's home variety, but the discussion of this issue has been influenced by Jenkins' (2000) lingua-franca core for pronunciation, which would suggest that some pronunciation features would be rapidly adapted so that lingua-franca communication in English could be efficient.

One might therefore expect the language used in lingua-franca situations to have certain pragmatic, lexico-grammatical, and even pronunciation features in common. If there is not one single lingua-franca variety of English, then there is probably at least a class of lingua-franca varieties with shared features.

2. Background

2.1. Exchange Students as an ELF Community

ELF situations are easily recognizable and quite frequent. By contrast, the notion of ELF community seems more elusive. Some writers (such as Jenkins 2006b, 45) speak of ELF users as members of a community, but it would seem more realistic to think of those involved in ELF situations as members of a variety of more-or-less tightly-knit communities or networks. Educationists meeting for a discussion a few times a year (Penz 2008) do not seem to belong to the same community or the same sort of community as dairy-industry negotiators discussing a particular problem on the phone (Firth 1996), or engineering students trying to solve a set problem (Björkman, this volume). In fact, House (2002, 244) says that "lingua franca speakers must always work out anew a joint linguistic, intercultural and behavioural basis for their communication."

One might, however, hypothesise that something like a lingua-franca English community would arise where speakers of different languages live in fairly tightly-knit groups over an extended period of time. Members of such groups would not need to work out norms anew with every interaction, but would learn reusable local norms. One good place to look for such communities would be international organizations (Kirkpatrick 2007 reports on ASEAN as such a community). Another would be the groups of exchange students or other "international" students now found at universities all over Europe. The increasing trend for these groups to be taught in English even in non-English-speaking countries (Coleman 2006) and the increasing trend for all their members to have English as their best second language suggest that in many countries these students are likely to use English rather than the language of the host country as their medium. It is also a common experience throughout the world that it is difficult for international students to make friends with local students so that it would be no surprise if they socialized mainly with members of their own speech community or with other international students in English throughout their stay abroad.

2.2. Accommodation

Where people with different varieties of the same language meet and form a new community, various linguistic processes happen. Over two or three generations a new variety emerges of the type called koiné (Kerswill 2002)—usually a generalized and simplified version of the varieties, influenced most by the ones most frequent in the community. New Zealand English is a variety of this kind, as documented by Trudgill (2004), who could actually show that the English of the first New-Zealand-born generation was still unfocussed, while their children spoke a relatively uniform and recognizably New Zealand variety. A somewhat similar pattern, involving more phonological change and simplification, has been recorded for Modern Hebrew, a language all of whose early speakers were non-natives (Siegel 1997). This process of variety formation is obviously irrelevant to ELF, which is not acquired naturalistically by children and whose "communities" are temporary.

A process that is much more likely to be at work in ELF interaction is accommodation. Jenkins (2006a) refers, for example, to the importance of accommodation skills for ELF interaction. Speakers who feel solidarity with one another adjust their language patterns in actual interaction to match those of their interlocutors. That is, they use the parts of their linguistic repertoire that match those of the group that they happen to be in just at that moment, if they feel solidarity with that group. The features adopted are those that are frequent in the partner's speech (the "behavioural-frequency model", Kerswill 2002). Jenkins seems to envisage the adoption of features chosen to facilitate communication, which we could call a communicative model of accommodation. Kerswill (2002, 690) cites Auer (1998) arguing that "accommodation may not be in response to a particular interlocutor, but to images, or stereotypes, of the group the interlocutor belongs to, or of a socially attractive group not actually represented in the immediate context". This is the "identity projection model" of accommodation. The first stage of koinéization is hypothesized to be "long-term accommodation", in which repeated adjustments of the same kind become habitual in the speech of adults interacting with interlocutors with different varieties. "Long-term accommodation" states Kerswill (2002, 689) "results from the cumulative effect of countless acts of short-term accommodation in particular conversational interactions."

Where lingua-franca users are in contact with one another for a reasonable length of time and feel solidarity with one another, one might hypothesize that they would accommodate and start to use shared features. Of course we can observe accommodation on the micro-level, agreeing on appropriate lexical items, for example, in individual conversations. But this type of accommodation might be expected to cover more, not only the morphosyntactic features that are fairly well documented as appearing in lingua-franca discourse, but also accent features, since it is these that are most prominent in discussions of accommodation phenomena.

It is difficult to see what suggestions that ELF is some kind of variety based in some kind of community could refer to other than the results of a process in which adults who habitually engage in interaction with other L2 users show long-term accommodation to the features of their joint speech. Clearly this could be behavioural-frequency accommodation to what they actually hear, communicative accommodation to the most efficient forms, or identity-projection accommodation to their conception of the speech of "a socially attractive group not actually represented in the immediate context". The positive evaluation of the dynamism of US English among young people world-wide (Söderlund & Modiano 2002, Mobärg 1998, Kim 2007) might suggest that Americans are a candidate for such a "socially attractive" group, though the issue is unclear (Garrett et al. 2005, Ladegaard 1998).

This leads us to the issue we intend to investigate. Do exchange students form a closely-knit group who identify themselves as users of L2 English (Erling & Bartlett 2006) and feel solidarity for one another? If so, do they use English much in lingua-franca situations and with speakers of many different varieties (or, for example, mainly with L2 speakers whose L1 is the host country language)? If they appear to be in the type of situation where one would expect interaction patterns to lead to long-term accommodation and so to development towards a more uniform pattern of usage, is there evidence of such a development? If so, is this pattern "ELF" (behavioural-frequency or communicative accommodation or conceivably ELF identity-projection accommodation with a non-native norm not represented in the "community") or "native-like" (exonormative identity-projection accommodation)?

If, contrary to expectation, we did not find much ELF interaction then we would have to rethink our preconceptions of the role of English among international youth groups, or of the social patterns of exchange students.

If we, on the other hand, find an intense ELF "community" and accommodation to norms which are similar to characteristics suggested for ELF, we have shown that solidarity and identification have indeed led to something like an incipient variety, even though we are dealing with adults over a fairly short period, and we can probably remove the scare quotes from *community*.

If we find an intense ELF "community" and accommodation to native (say US) norms, then we have to suspect that identification and solidarity in this group are essentially with US popular culture as a world norm, as suggested by Engle and Engle (2004), who refer to "the increasing prevalence of English as a nearly universal lingua franca, the daily reality of instant electronic communication, and the near omnipresence of certain realities and symbols of American pop culture" (p. 221).

And finally, if we find an intense ELF "community" but do not find (much) accommodation then we have shown that more than six months or a year of interaction is necessary to produce long-term accommodation, and therefore that not many speakers will have a chance to adopt ELF norms from one another. Such ELF norms as exist are likely to be due to shared simplification of what one might call "native-speaker nonsense", that is, bits of morphosyntax which do not affect meaning and are difficult to learn (compare Klein & Perdue 1997) rather than to community construction of new conventions. We note that Meierkord's study (2004) of interactions in international student group in the L1 English environment of London University found little evidence of any of the focussing characteristics of new-variety formation (cf. Trudgill 2004).

3. Subjects and Methods

Our study is of approximately 240 exchange students at four institutions in Stockholm, Sweden and Aarhus, Denmark — two traditional universities (University of Aarhus (AU) and Stockholm University (SU)) and two specialised ones (Royal Institute of Technology, Stockholm (KTH) and Aarhus School of Business[1] (ASB)). The students in the study were exchange students whose first languages were one of the following: German, Dutch, French, Spanish, Italian, Polish, Czech. None of them was a specialist language student. They were planning to stay at the host institutions for a period of one or two semesters. They were interviewed around the start of the teaching semester, half-way through the semester and at the end of the semester; in the case of those students who stayed a year, they were interviewed once more just before they left. In addition to being questioned about their language experiences while in the host country (who they interacted with; which languages they used, and with whom; what difficulties if any they experienced with communication in different languages) and such matters as their motivation for coming on exchange, they were also given brief language tests in English and Danish/Swedish at each interview, in the form of a picture description and Scandinavian-language vocabulary test. Data collection, which took place over a three-year period, is complete, but analysis of the data will take a considerable time, and in this paper we present some results that cover only sub-groups of the students and sections of the data. The trends identified must therefore be regarded as provisional.

4. Results

In what follows, we report on three aspects of the study: the students' motivation for going on exchange to Scandinavia (see also Caudery et al. 2008), in particular their tendency to view themselves as users (rather than learners) of L2 English; their patterns of interaction while on exchange, in particular their use of English in lingua-franca situations with speakers of many different varieties; and their language development during the study abroad period, in particular any development towards a more uniform pattern of usage, whether "ELF" (behavioural-frequency or communicative accommodation) or "native-like" (identity-projection accommodation).

4.1. Motivation

One factor which might affect the formation of an "ELF community" among exchange students abroad and the students of the host university is the motivation that the exchange students have for going on exchange, particularly with regard to language learning. One might feel that students going to a country where they already speak the local language as an L2 could reasonably be assumed to have as a goal some sort of development of their skills in that language—in their ability to use it fluently and confidently, if not in terms of expanding their knowledge of grammar, vocabulary, etc. Maiworm (2001) showed that this was indeed the case in his survey of more "traditional" Erasmus students going to study abroad through the medium of the language of the host country: improving language skills was one of the major motivations for going on exchange. In the case of students coming to Scandinavia, however, relatively few exchange students speak the local language before they arrive in the host country, and they are, in general, expecting to use English as a working language for study, not the local language. Are they motivated, then, to expand their knowledge of English in the same way as traditional exchange students wish to expand their knowledge of the host country language? Are they motivated to attempt to learn the local language? Or are other motivations paramount? If there are strong language learning motivations, this could affect conscious decisions made about language use—whether to avoid speaking L1, whether to seek out opportunities for practising the language of the host country, or whether to make determined efforts to practise and learn English rather than using it purely as a tool to facilitate the academic and life-experience aspects of the exchange visit.

There was no particular reason to expect our subjects to form a homogenous group with respect to perceived motivation for coming on exchange, in terms of language learning ambitions or anything else; they had certain basic factors in common (the fact that they were students, for example), but there were also many differences, for example in terms of their pre-exchange level of proficiency in English, their interest in languages generally, the amount of choice they had in where they came on exchange, and so on. This means that while there were certain frequently occurring motivations for coming on exchange at all, and for choosing to come to Sweden or Denmark, there were also considerable differences between individuals.

Students were asked open-ended questions with respect to their motivation, and the answers were then grouped into categories. Students could name as many motivations as they wished. Improving English skills figured prominently in the motivations for coming on exchange. Table 1 shows percentages from a total of 194 students coming from all four institutions who mentioned a particular type of motivation.[2]

The three most frequently mentioned motivation categories were improving English skills, personal development and a new life experience, and encountering a new culture. Motivations in these three categories were spontaneously mentioned by 42, 44 and 47% of students respectively. If students did not spontaneously mention improving their English skills, then they were specifically asked whether this was one of their goals; 60% of students agreed that they wanted to improve their English, which also means that 40% of students actually denied that improving their English was among their goals. Those who agreed after prompting that improving English skills was a goal may have simply forgotten to mention this at first, but in many cases they seemed to regard it as more of a secondary goal.

Table 1. Exchange students' reasons for deciding to study abroad, academic year 2005-2006, N=194

Reasons for Studying Abroad	**% of subjects mentioning**				
	AU	**SU**	**KTH**	**ASB**	**Total**
Improving English language proficiency (spontaneous mention)	42	38	41	50	42
Total mentioning English, including after prompt	62	54	59	68	60
Experience, travel, fun	52	42	36	41	44
Encounter a new culture (and language)	44	54	46	47	47
Experience a new study environment	27	16	13	9	18
Meeting new people	23	4	18	12	15
Exchange mandatory/recommended by university	4	8	5	21	8
Own/friends' experience	8	2	5	6	6
Career benefit	6	16	8	44	15

We thus see a division among the students. There were those for whom improving English skills was a strong motivation for coming on exchange to a country where English would be used as a lingua franca, showing that ELF can replace the local language in being viewed as providing an opportunity to improve proficiency. There were also those who felt that their English could be improved and did not regard it as impossible or unlikely that their stay in Denmark or Sweden would contribute to this. And finally, there were a substantial minority who apparently saw themselves much more as ELF users rather than English learners; their English knowledge was already sufficient to make the exchange possible, and they did not envisage further improvement to their language skills as a result of using their English.

These three sample responses to the question "Why did you decide to study abroad?" give an indication of the way students expressed their motivations:

(a) A student who gave a high priority to learning English:
Oh. Why? Mmm— just to improve my English, definitely. To meet some people, mmm, I don't know, get to know another country, such things.

(b) A student who had to be prompted to acknowledge English learning as a goal:
I would like to see how it is in different countries and meet many people and learn about the culture and see how they behave how it look like in their countries and gaining friends and I think that is some kind of adventure it's something that will never happen to me again.
(What about improving your English?)
Yes, mm-hmm, I would like to improve my English, mm-hmm.

(c) A student who denied that English learning figured among his motivations for exchange:
Actually just for the experience and because it's so easy doing an exchange programme. I wanted to take part in an exchange programme before I finished my studies. It's not so much that I need to do the credit points here because I'm almost finished my studies in Germany. I wanted to stay for a longer time in Scandinavia. Just live here. Because I've spent a lot of summer holidays in Finland, Sweden, Norway and Denmark but that was like only three weeks in August or July but I was interested in living, really living in Scandinavia. I've always liked it and I was interested in the culture and I hope that I will get to know a lot of Danes here.
(Did you have any motives such as learning more language?)
Yes, I hope when I leave I will be able to do some talking in Danish.
(And did you think about improving your English here?)
No, definitely not, no.

There were small differences in the division of motivations among students at different institutions, as Table 1 indicates. These differences suggest that students coming to the two specialised universities (KTH and ASB) might have had slightly stronger instrumental motivations than those at the two traditional universities (consider the percentages mentioning career benefits of the exchange, for example), but students at the two specialised institutions had the lowest and the highest levels of interest in improving English language skills (perhaps reflecting the degree of importance that communication skills in English were seen as having for their careers).

While some of the students who were interested in learning Danish or Swedish might have included mention of this under the category "encountering a new culture", a question on the specific reasons for choosing Denmark or Sweden as the country for exchange was more likely to prompt mention of an interest in learning Danish or Swedish. Once again, there were differences between institutions (see Table 2), but relatively few people mentioned an interest in learning the local language; and among those that did express such an interest, it was often a question of learning *any* new language rather than a specific desire to learn this *particular* language that contributed to the reasons for choosing to come to Scandinavia.

Table 2. Exchange students' reasons for studying at a particular institution/in a particular city or country, academic year 2005-2006, N=194

Reasons for choosing country/institution	**% of subjects mentioning**				
	AU	**SU**	**KTH**	**ASB**	**Total**
Interest in country/ city	41	52	36	41	43
Limited choice/ Exchange agreement with university	45	20	26	71	39
Study environment/ quality	30	24	31	29	28
Interest in Scandinavia/ somewhere exotic	25	20	18	41	25
Learn Danish/Swedish or "a new language"	23	22	36	3	22
English medium	24	24	28	35	27
Personal recommendations/know people in this city/ institution/country	18	12	21	21	18

All in all, the majority of students had some language learning motivation connected with their exchange visit, though a substantial minority stated no interest whatsoever in language improvement (see Table 3). Of those that had a motivation for language learning, the main motivation was for learning English; some students were *also* interested in learning the local language, while a small number were *only* interested in learning the local language.

Table 3. Summary of language motivation, academic year 2005-2006, N=194

Language motivation expressed	% of subjects mentioning				
	AU	SU	KTH	ASB	Total
No language motivation	32	20	23	9	23
Motivation for English only	46	34	33	88	48
Motivation for Danish/Swedish only	4	18	18	0	10
Motivation for both/other languages	18	28	26	3	20

The differences between institutions are not easy to explain. It would appear that there is a country effect; of students going to Sweden (SU and KTH), almost half expressed an interest in learning Swedish, either as the only language that interested them or in addition to English. Only 22% of students at the University of Aarhus indicated that a wish to learn Danish was among their reasons for coming on exchange to Denmark, while at Aarhus School of Business virtually no students expressed an interest in learning Danish. The last effect may be due to the fact that the exchange students enrolled at ASB were, with a few rare exceptions, not allowed to join courses run in Danish. As for the country difference, it may indeed be the case that students opting to go further north are more specifically interested in the Swedish culture than those venturing no further than Denmark. Exchange students in Sweden seem to get more opportunities to take some of their courses in Swedish, too, a situation which might well encourage those with an interest in language learning to opt to study there. Taking courses conducted in Swedish might also prompt students to "remember" a motivation for learning Swedish, even if this was not in fact a particularly strong motivation at the time they chose their exchange destination. The reverse effect might be apparent in Denmark, where their academic studies are almost exclusively in English (though there is the option of taking Danish language classes). It is also possible that part of the difference can be accounted for by experimental effects of some kind, such as the more or less rigorous exclusion from the study in the different countries of people with a prior knowledge of the local language.

If students' motivations for coming on exchange and for choosing a particular country were then to lead to a decision on their part to try to pattern their interactions with other people in such a way as to best enhance the opportunities to practice the languages desired, then we would expect those students who were motivated to improve their language skills to avoid interacting with their compatriots, or at least only to do so in the company of third parties who did not speak their common language. A number of people could be expected to attempt to create opportunities for interacting in the local language; often this would have to be outside the academic classroom, since students' academic studies were in many cases exclusively conducted in English. Up to 60% of the students would wish to get practice in English, and thus would have a motivation for becoming part of an ELF community, with membership consisting of other exchange students, local students, and perhaps other people.

However, students' interactions are not governed purely by motivation. Clearly other factors are relevant—for example, their communicative needs in their studies and everyday lives, the opportunities presented for interaction by the way their lives were organised in the exchange situation, and the desire to speak their own language at times. Of particular importance in relation to practising the local language may be the fact that, as our language tests suggest, many students never reach a "threshold level" at which meaningful interaction becomes practicable, and thus they may abandon any attempt to use the local language. Even those students who feel that they can make an attempt to interact in the local language may find that their native interlocutors lose patience and prefer to switch to English, their common language. Quite apart from the effects of students' motivation, then, it is to be expected that events will tend to create situations in which exchange students work in English, except when interacting in groups of speakers of their own language.

4.2. Patterns of Interaction

As mentioned above, a study of exchange students who are not language students is particularly interesting for a discussion of the existence of ELF communities. Such students live in the host environment over an extended period of time and are, therefore, not unlikely to provide good candidates for lingua franca communities. Furthermore, a study of this kind may reveal (a) whether the students form closely knit groups; (b) if so, whether the groups consist of speakers of a variety of languages; and (c), crucially, whether a similar variety of languages or, alternatively, English is the preferred medium of communication within such groups. In what follows, we consider these three issues.

As regards closely knit groups, one sufficient characteristic of such a group would presumably be its lack of communication with outsiders. For the purpose of determining whether this characteristic applied to the subjects in the study, we asked them about the extent to which their communication with others was with students. The replies offered varied from a total of 30-100% (in first interviews) to a total of 50-99% (in third interviews). On average, however, around 85-90% of the subjects' interaction was with other students and, conversely, 10-15% with other groups, which included academic staff, university library staff, shop assistants, bus drivers, employers, etc.

As regards the second issue, i.e. who the subjects communicated with, three categories of student communication partners were considered: (a) native speakers of the subject's first language (below, we refer to this category as a "same-language" one); (b) other international students; and (c) native speakers of the official language of the host country, i.e. Danish or Swedish (we refer to this category as a "local" one). While perceptions of the extent of communication with same-language students varied somewhat among institutions in that, on average, subjects at the two traditional universities reported around 30-32% of their communication to be with this group, and subjects at ASB and KTH gave figures corresponding to 37-40% and 35-42%, respectively, communication with other international students averaged around 45-50%[3] of total communication with students at all four institutions. By contrast, communication with local students totalled approximately 18-20% at ASB and SU; 21-25% at AU; and 9-17% at KTH.

The third issue of interest, i.e. the language(s) of communication used by the subjects in interaction with other students, was also addressed in the interviews. The same three categories of student communication partners were considered with the subjects providing estimates of the extent to which their communication with each category was in their own native language, the local language, English, or some fourth language. As regards communication with same-language students, this was to a considerable extent, but by no means exclusively, in the subjects' native languages. This reflects tendency to switch to English when speakers of other languages are present but not active participants. At AU and SU, this applied to approximately 61-67% and 60-64%, respectively, of such communication, while the corresponding figures were around 76-79% for ASB subjects and 65-73% for KTH subjects. Although by the time of the third interview subjects at KTH, in particular, did report some limited use (less than 5%) of Swedish and other languages with communication partners in this category, the remainder of the subjects' interaction in same-language groups was almost exclusively in English. The reason typically given for using English with same-language partners was a wish not to exclude any speakers of other languages who might be present during such interaction.

Regarding communication with other international students, subjects at all four institutions reported this to be overwhelmingly in English: at AU, the figures totalled around 94-96% on average; at SU, 90-94%; at ASB, 91-93%; and, at KTH, 84-90%. It follows that, at AU, other languages were barely used for communication with these students. At the other three institutions, however, subjects did—admittedly to a rather limited extent—communicate in their own language, a fourth language, or even the local language.

Finally, language use with local students was also reported to be largely in English, although at three of the institutions there was some development away from English over the semester. This was least pronounced at AU, where an average of approximately 91% of communication with these students was in English but, by the time of the third interview, the figure had dropped to 89% with a corresponding increase in the use of Danish. Similarly, SU subjects reported a development from 84% to 77% on average with the remainder largely being covered by Swedish, which went from 5% at the time of the first interview to 17% by the end of the teaching semester. The pattern was not entirely dissimilar at KTH, although the use of English with Swedish students was estimated to average around 75% at the time of the first interview, 80% at the second and, again, 75% at the third. While mirroring the converse pattern in the use of the subjects' own language, the development also reflected a steady increase in the use of Swedish from 8% to 22% on average. The only institution at which subjects reported a different pattern was ASB: communication in English amounted to around 94% on average at the time of both first and third interviews with a slight drop to 92% at second interviews. This corresponded to a temporary increase in the use of the subjects' own language and of Danish, in particular.

In sum, the average subject communicated extensively with other students and very little with "outsiders". Approximately half of the student communication in which s/he engaged was with other international students while almost one third—or, if the subject was from one of the two specialised universities, up to 40-42%—was with speakers of the subject's own language. By implication, the remainder of his/her communication was with local students. Turning to the medium of communication, we found that, although interaction with same-language students was mostly in the subject's own language, a surprisingly large proportion, varying from approximately 20% to 40%, was actually in English. Less surprising perhaps were the findings that the average subject's communication with other international students was almost exclusively in English and that, at the Danish institutions in particular and to a slightly lesser extent at the Swedish institutions, a not entirely dissimilar situation was true of his/her communication with local students: such interaction was overwhelmingly in English.

4.3. Language Development

It appears so far that many of our subjects were in a group in which a great deal of English was spoken and with which they felt a good deal of solidarity. As individuals are members of the group for six months or a year, some degree of long-term accommodation is possible. We can judge language development, and thus the degree and form of accommodation, from reported perceptions and from language samples in the form of the picture descriptions mentioned above.

The subjects' perceptions give a great deal of credence to the view that they belong to a lingua-franca English community. Subjects with relatively low proficiency on arrival report improvement, and those with very high proficiency report 'degradation' of their English, which can usually be interpreted as accommodation to the lingua franca environment. A Mauritian with French as mother-tongue but near-native in English reported after a year that her English had got worse, and explained that speaking English to non-natives meant that she habitually avoided expressions which she had observed to cause difficulties. A French student who had previously spent six months on exchange in Britain judged that he had continued to become more fluent in English, but that his vocabulary and pronunciation had not developed in the same way. Similar indications that the international student community becomes accustomed to a somewhat stable lingua franca which differs in some respects from native norms come from less proficient students who answer the question "Now at the end of your stay are there any groups you have trouble communicating with" by saying "Yes, Americans...and also Australians. They are very friendly but I can't understand them" or "I can understand the English and the South Africans, but the Americans, they don't pronounce all the sounds." Perhaps the most revealing quotation, though, is from a Spanish student who answered this question in the first interview by saying "In my corridor there are some French students and I'm afraid to speak it [English] because their English is different from my English" and in her third "There are people who I don't feel comfortable to speak with…now it's not a problem of the country they are coming from, now it's more a problem of personality."

Transcription and inspection of a selection of individuals (n=20, 9 L1 speakers of French, 8 of Spanish and 3 of German, 12 women, 8 men) of the picture-description tests from the first and last interviews suggests that there is accommodation to discourse norms of some kind. As Figure 1 shows, one striking development was in discourse markers: a reduction of the number of instances of *I think* and *maybe*, which corresponded to an increase in *well* and *like,* suggesting a collective move towards a wider and more balanced range of discourse management devices. The change in *I think* was spread across all users, showing co-evolution of the register even among speakers with different initial levels of proficiency. It is significant that this appears to be co-evolution, rather than frequency-based establishment. That is to say, although most subjects seemed to use *I think* a great deal at the beginning, high frequency did not lead to mutual accommodation and establishment as lingua-franca usage (which would have been behavioural-frequency adaptation). Rather the development was towards a new norm, presumably because the more fluent members of the community modelled other devices (identity-projection accommodation).

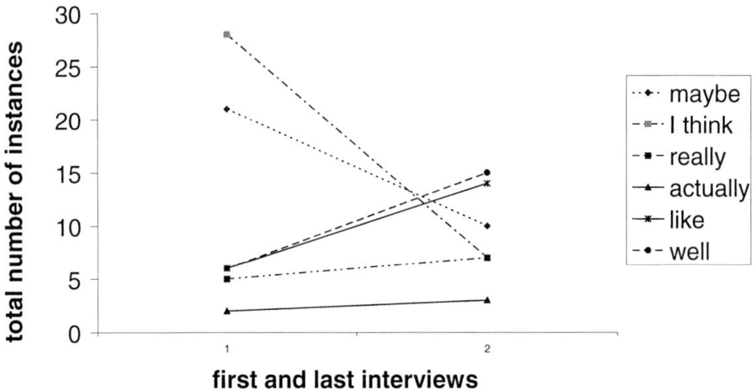

Figure 1. Development in discourse markers (N=20)

As regards accent, it may change in two ways. Pronunciation of individual phonemes or intonation contours might develop towards some norm, and choice of phonemes in individual lexical items or syllable positions might change.

Most subjects pronounced the individual lexical item *clothes* in non-native ways (/klo(u)θɪz/, /klo(u)ð/, /klo(u)zɪz/ and nearly all pronounced the word in the same way in both interviews. In this respect the majority seemed to have adapted neither to each other nor to a native norm. This is an illustration of the very general stability of most individuals' phonological representations.

On the level of development of individual phonemes, Table 4 shows change in the picture-description recordings in terms of two parameters, chosen because they are easy to identify and potentially contrasted in terms of their significance. The first is rhoticity. Pronunciation of non-prevocalic <r> in words like *party* or *farm* is indexical of a US rather than a British model, but also a potential lingua-franca feature because it increases the transparency of phoneme-letter relations. It might also be a feature of some less proficient learner usage pronunciation based on spelling. The procedure adopted was to identify instances of non-prevocalic <r> in the transcripts and then listen to the recording, marking each instance as 0 (non-rhotic), 1 (rhotic) or 0.5 (uncertain). The transcripts were then assessed as 0 (wholly non-rhotic), 0.5 (predominantly non-rhotic), 1.0 (with equal proportions of both types of realization), 1.5 (predominantly rhotic) and 2 (wholly rhotic). The assessments for the first and second interviews were then compared to obtain a judgement of the direction of change, if any. Table 4 shows that there was no particular pattern of change, with similar figures for increase and decrease. Stability could mean staying fully rhotic, staying fully non-rhotic, or staying mixed. On the surface there was no adaptation to a shared norm. It is, however, significant that the decreases in rhoticity were mostly among the least proficient speakers and the increases among the more proficient ones. A possible interpretation is that the decreasers were mainly moving from a spelling-based pronunciation to one more like the majority (which, on the evidence of this sample, was definitely non-rhotic), while the increasers were adopting a more US-style pronunciation. The last hypothesis is supported by the recordings in which one (highly proficient) L1 German speaker became more rhotic, as this was accompanied by other US features.

Table 4. Selected phonological development, N=20

Development of rhoticity and flapping	**Rhoticity**			**Flapping**		
	stable	**increasing**	**decreasing**	**stable**	**increasing**	**decreasing**
French L1 (9)	4	2	3	9		
Spanish L1 (8)	2	3	3	4	1	3
German L1 (3)	2	1		2	1	

The other feature examined in detail was flapping of alveolar stops in words like *eating*, *sitting* and *party*, and their elision in *twenty*, etc. Most subjects neither flapped nor elided and there were a good number of both proficient and less proficient rhotic speakers who did not flap. The German speaker mentioned and one Spanish speaker went from non-flapping to predominantly flapping, thus reducing transparency but approaching high-status usage (identity-projection adaptation). But there was also at least one proficient rhotic speaker who abandoned flapping either because he was accommodating to the usage around him (behavioural-frequency accommodation) or because this increased comprehensibility (communicative adaptation).

More impressionistically it may be said that realizations of *th-* as [sz] tended to decline sharply, while realizations as stops were fairly stable. Our impression is that the group stigmatized sibilant realizations but accepted stops.

To sum up, in discourse markers this study showed some signs of mutual accommodation on a set of discourse markers, including the characteristic ‘youth’ marker *like.* On the other hand, the study showed little tendency to focus on shared norms for pronunciation, whether lingua-franca or US, and in fact little change overall. Within this general stability there seemed to be more change towards rhoticity, which would imply accommodation both to US norms and to clarity, than towards flapping, which would imply preference for US norms at the expense of clarity.

5. Discussion

As the results above show, the majority of our subjects' motivation suggested that they saw English as the natural vehicle for international or intercultural experience, but a large minority held to a more traditional view of language learning as a part of such experience. Once in Scandinavia, most of our subjects (including many who had initially been motivated to improve both languages) found themselves in an ELF bubble where contact with Danes/Swedes was more a matter of the locals entering the international community rather than vice versa. A telling example here is a German student who said that his motivation for coming abroad was having been part of the exchange student community at his home university, noticing how much his English improved as a result of just that, and wanting more of this experience. His motive was explicitly integration into the international student group. The group is cohesive, and efficient lingua-franca communication develops so that subjects no longer have difficulty with other non-native accents and can even find native speech more difficult than non-native, as one would expect from the literature on ELF interaction.

Our first two research questions can thus be answered by saying that a proportion of the subjects do have a lingua-franca attitude to the language they use (they are users not learners, or at least more users than learners), and a large proportion find themselves in a fairly dense network of interactions in English with other non-natives, which they experience as fairly efficient.

Our third question was whether this is reflected in any long-term accommodation in their language use. Here we would need to distinguish between majority usage and norms. Majority usage would simply be the usage of a numerically predominant proportion of the exchange students who are interacting with one another. Norms would be the usage of groups or individuals regarded as speaking in a desirable way. Examination of a sample suggested quite substantial accommodation on the discourse level. This was not simply accommodation to majority usage, but rather the majority accommodated to a particular usage, possibly one associated with American youth. It does however suggest shared values in the "community" since all involved moved in the same direction. For pronunciation, there was less unambiguous evidence of adaptation and in fact, within the small sample, there was evidence of several different kinds of change: some accommodation to US norms even when they are not efficient for lingua-franca communication (flapping), but also some shift away from US towards majority usage (the majority does not flap) or communicative efficiency; rather more accommodation to US norms where they coincide with efficiency (rhoticity) but also some accommodation to majority usage (non-rhoticity) among less proficient speakers.

The mixture of communicative accommodation with behavioural-frequency and identity-projection accommodation might reflect the status of the group as cohesive but partly exonormative, basing itself partly on its own international-ELF values and partly on US youth culture.

Bibliography

Auer, P. 1998. "Structural Convergence and Interpersonal Accommodation in a Theory of Language Change." Plenary paper presented at the *European Science Foundation Network* on *The Convergence and Divergence of Dialects in a Changing Europe*. University of Reading, September 17-19, 1998.

Björkman, B. this volume. "From Code to Discourse in Spoken ELF."

Caudery, T., M. Petersen and P. Shaw 2008. "The Motivations of Exchange Students at Scandinavian Universities." In *Students, Staff and Academic Mobility in Higher Education*, ed. M. Byram & F. Dervin, 114-30. Newcastle-upon-Tyne: Cambridge Scholars Publishing.

Coleman, J. 2006. "English-Medium Teaching in European Higher Education." *Language Teaching* 39 (1), 1-14.

Engle, L. and J. Engle 2004. "Assessing Language Acquisition and Intercultural Sensitivity Development in Relation to Study Abroad Program Design." *Frontiers: The Interdisciplinary Journal of Study Abroad* 10, 219-36.

Erling, E. J. and T. Bartlett 2006. "Making English Their Own: The Use of ELF among Students of English at the FUB." *Nordic Journal of English Studies* 5 (2), 9-40.

Firth, A. 1996. "The Discursive Accomplishment of Normality: On 'Lingua Franca' English and Conversation Analysis." *Journal of Pragmatics* 26 (2), 237-59.

Garrett, P., A. Williams and B. Evans 2005 "Attitudinal Data from New Zealand, Australia, the USA and UK about Each Other's Englishes: Recent Changes or Consequences of Methodologies?" *Multilingua* 24 (3), 211-35.

House, J. 2002. "Communicating in English as a Lingua Franca." In *EUROSLA Yearbook 2*, ed. S. Foster-Cohen, 242-61. Amsterdam: John Benjamins.

Jenkins, J. 2006a. "Current Perspectives on Teaching World Englishes and English as a Lingua Franca." *TESOL Quarterly* 40 (1), 157-81.

—. 2006b. "Global Intelligibility and Local Diversity: Possibility or Paradox?" In *English in the World: Global Rules, Global Roles*, ed. R. Rubdy & M. Saraceni, 32-9. London: Continuum.

—. 2000. *The Phonology of English as an International Language*. Oxford: Oxford University Press.

Kerswill, P. 2002. "Koineization and Accommodation." In *The Handbook of Language Variation and Change*, ed. J. K. Chambers, P. Trudgill & N. Schilling-Estes, 669-702. Oxford: Blackwell.

Kim, Y. S. 2007. "Korean Adults' Attitudes towards Varieties of English." MSc diss., The University of Edinburgh. http://hdl.handle.net/1842/1903.

Kirkpatrick, A. 2007. *World Englishes: Implications for International Communication and English Language Teaching*. Cambridge: Cambridge University Press.

Klein, W. and C. Perdue 1997. "The Basic Variety (Or: Couldn't Natural Languages Be Much Simpler?)." *Second Language Research* 13 (4), 301-47.

Ladegaard, H. J. 1998. "National Stereotypes and Language Attitudes: The Perception of British, American and Australian Language and Culture in Denmark." *Language and Communication* 18 (4), 251-74.

Maiworm, F. 2001. "Erasmus: Continuity and Change in the 1990s." *European Journal of Education* 36 (4), 459-72.

Mauranen, A. 2005. "English as Lingua Franca: An Unknown Language?" In *Identity, Community, Discourse: English in Intercultural Settings*, ed. G. Cortese & A. Duszak, 269-93. Bern: Peter Lang.

Meierkord, C. 2004. "Syntactic Variation in Interactions across International Englishes." *English World-Wide* 25 (1), 109-32.

—. 1998. "Lingua Franca English: Characteristics of Successful Non-Native-/Non-Native-Speaker Discourse." *Erfurt Electronic Studies in English* (EESE) 1998. http://webdoc.sub.gwdg.de/edoc/ia/eese/artic98/meierk/7_98.html/ (accessed May 25, 2009)

Mobärg, M. 1998. "Media Exposure vs. Educational Prescription: The Case of British and American English in Sweden." In *The Major Varieties of English: Papers from MAVEN 97*, ed. H. Lindquist, S. Klintborg, M. Levin & M. Estling, 249-62. Växjö: Acta Wexionensia.

Penz, H. 2008. "What do we mean by that?—ELF in Intercultural Project Work." Paper presented at *The Ninth International Conference of the*

European Society for the Study of English. University of Aarhus, August 22-26, 2008.

Seidlhofer, B. 2006. "English as a Lingua Franca in the Expanding Circle: What It Isn't." In *English in the World: Global Rules, Global Roles*, ed. R. Rubdy & M. Sarceni, 40-50. London: Continuum.

—. 2004. "Research Perspectives on Teaching English as a Lingua Franca." *Annual Review of Applied Linguistics* 24, 209-39.

—. 2001. "Closing a Conceptual Gap: The Case for a Description of English as a Lingua Franca." *International Journal of Applied Linguistics* 11 (2), 133-58.

Siegel, J. 1997. "Mixing, Levelling, and Pidgin/Creole Development." In *The Structure and Status of Pidgins and Creoles*, ed. A. K. Spears & D. Winford, 111-49. Amsterdam: John Benjamins.

Söderlund, M. and M. Modiano 2002. "Swedish Upper Secondary School Students and their Attitudes Towards AmE, BrE and Mid-Atlantic English." In *Studies in Mid-Atlantic English*, ed. M. Modiano, 147-71. Gävle: Högskolan i Gävle.

Trudgill, P. 2004. *New-Dialect Formation: The Inevitability of Colonial English*. Edinburgh: Edinburgh University Press

Notes

[1] The Aarhus School of Business is now a fairly autonomous unit with the University of Aarhus, but it was completely independent of the University at the time the data for this study was collected.

[2] The results in tables 1, 2 and 3 were first published in Caudery et al. 2008.

[3] Percentage ranges indicate variation in results from the first, second, and third rounds of interviews.

EMIC EVALUATIONS AND INTERACTIVE PROCESSES IN A CLASSROOM COMMUNITY OF PRACTICE

UTE SMIT

1. Introduction

With globalisation and internationalisation in full swing, it practically amounts to a commonplace to comment on the globalised role of English in an ever growing range of domains. As the most prominent language of international business, media, politics and academia (e.g. Crystal 2003), English has certainly attracted substantial interest and attention, also in terms of academic discussions and explorations (Graddol 2006). Although delayed by a few years, sociolinguistic interest in English as a lingua franca (ELF) has also been burgeoning lately (e.g. Gnutzmann & Intemann 2005; Jenkins 2006; *Nordic Journal of English Studies* 5 (2), 2006; *International Journal of the Sociology of Language* 177/2006; Seidlhofer, Breiteneder & Pitzl 2006), paying tribute to the immense impact that the (post-)modern role of English as only shared medium of communication amongst multilinguals might have on using the language itself (e.g. Jenkins 2000, Mauranen 2006, Seidlhofer 2001).

Of the numerous domains of interest, higher education is arguably a central one, with various supporting factors coming together: English as leading academic language (Ammon & McConnell 2002), students as a relatively mobile group (Smith 2004), universities attracting international students for reasons of increased reputation and, more mundanely, increased finances (Wilkinson 2004). In view of the centrality of internationalisation in higher education, it is surprising to find this domain rather underrepresented as a focus of interest in the ELF literature. After a decade of no relevant studies, the first to be announced were those based on the ELFA corpus (Mauranen 2003) and the present one (Smit 2003). In the meanwhile, a few more have followed (e.g. Björkman 2008; this volume). ELF in educational settings is thus moving into the investigative limelight. At the same time, it is interesting to note that these investigations are based on the presently accepted methodology of ELF research and provide cross-sectional snapshots of language use in the classroom and/or other academic settings, therefore sidelining a crucial feature of any kind of education—its longitudinality. Not only is the time factor central to teaching and learning in general (e.g. Marton & Tsui 2004), but it is also integral to the interactional processes that develop within the specific group of learners and teachers; the more so in view of the conception of ELF users as (emerging) communities of practice (House 2003).

In an attempt to address this issue and, at the same time, heed Seidlhofer, Breiteneder and Pitzl's (2006, 21) advice for future ELF researchers "to proceed by way of clearly situated qualitative studies with a strong ethnographic element", the study reported on in this contribution approaches ELF as classroom language, i.e. "the language of all main classroom talk" (Smit 2008a, 73), from a longitudinal perspective by focussing on one specific tertiary educational programme that is undertaken in ELF (Smit 2003; 2008a).[1] This paper will describe the emic evaluations of learners and teachers on using ELF as classroom language as well as two classroom interactional patterns of dealing with instances of unintelligibility and control acts. As the respective thematic and discourse-pragmatic analyses could draw on two longitudinal corpora of interviews and classroom interaction, the insights gained reflect centrally time-dependent developments and changes.

Before these findings can be discussed (Section 4) and interpreted (Section 5), Section 2 offers a brief sketch of the rather limited literature on English as a lingua franca in tertiary education, arguing for a highly situated and dynamic conceptualisation of ELF as classroom language. The corresponding research methodology is introduced in Section 3, together with the study site of the discourse-pragmatic ethnography reported on in this paper.

2. ELF in Tertiary Classrooms—Basic Considerations

While ELF research has so far mainly focussed on domains other than education, the recent developments in mainland European tertiary education towards considerably more English-medium educational programmes has not gone unnoticed in applied linguistic circles. On the contrary, recent conferences and ensuing publications on 'integrating content and language' in higher education (Fortanet-Gómez & Räisänen 2008, Wilkinson 2004, Wilkinson & Zegers 2007), vouchsafe for an impressive diversity of concerns pursued. Reflecting the complexity of applied linguistic considerations integral to educating professionals in and through an additional language, the research undertakings range from the macro-level of policy decisions and their implementation, via the meso-level of curricular developments and course adaptations to the micro-level of language use and learning. More precisely, micro-level analyses have thrown light on questions such as students' and teachers' levels of language proficiency considered appropriate for the respective educational programme, language support for students and teachers, or the relationship between educational success and learning in a second language. In other words, research along such lines reveals the implicit conceptualisation of the medium of instruction as the participants' second language which is in need of improvement. While this might very well be an important issue in many settings, by framing participants as primarily lacking certain linguistic skills, analyses of their discourse are predisposed to highlight deviances from what is assumed to be L1 discourses. By implication, they run the danger of sidelining typical and/or constitutive discursive features or patterns that would allow a careful description of what characterises the respective classroom discourse. And it is exactly this latter point that, I wish to argue, calls for integrating the ELF paradigm into analysing international higher educational discourse.

As explicated in more detail elsewhere (e.g. Introduction to this volume, Gnutzmann & Intemann 2005, Seidlhofer 2001), 'English as a lingua franca' gives centre stage to the increasingly relevant communicative function of English outside English-speaking countries as the only common language of multilingual interlocutors in pursuing their communicative aims (cf. Smit 2005, 67). As argued in detail in Smit (2008a, chs. 1-2), this definition gains in conceptual strength when combining it with Hall's (1993) model of the 'oral practice', Wenger's (1998) model of the 'community of practice' and James's (2005; 2006) trichotomous approach to 'social language'.

As a constructivist reinterpretation of Hymes's (1972) speech event, oral practices refer to "face-to-face interaction[s] by which members create, maintain and/or modify their collective history" (Hall 1993, 146), thus stressing the two-layered relevance of verbal engagements for situated meaning-making as well as group formation processes. This two-layeredness is particularly relevant for educational processes, which are by definition both moment-specific as well as long-term. Furthermore, the *mutual engagement* in momentary and long-term discourse combines well with the *joint* educational *enterprise* of students and teachers constructing knowledge by drawing on ELF as developing *shared repertoire*. As the three processes rendered in italics indicate, such educational practices take place in 'communities of practice' (cf. Corder & Meyerhoff 2007), a central practice of which is co-constructing their educational discourse (cf. also House 2003).

This dynamic practice draws on three resources (for more details cf. Smit 2008a, 54-63), viz. the community members' *individual repertoires*, *established practices* of varyingly relevant educational and professional cultures, but most centrally, on the process of *communicating* in the here and now of the respective classroom. The first resource relates to the individuals' diverse backgrounds as regards lingua-cultures represented in a certain community of practice, but also as regards English learning and using backgrounds; the second pays tribute to the diversity of professional and educational language practices drawn upon. Both resources are seen as dynamic and varying in their influence on the ongoing classroom discourse. On the other hand, the third resource, *communicating*, is always of central relevance as it pertains to the central aim of using a lingua franca, i.e. constructing classroom talk.

While the resulting conceptualisation of ELF as classroom language thus recognises the relevance of educational oral practices and their established and well documented discourse structures and patterns (e.g. Cazden 2001, Christie 2002, Drew & Heritage 1992, Edwards & Westgate 1994, van Lier 1988, Walsh 2006), it lays special emphasis on the high degree of contextualisation and local dynamics that need to be given centre-stage, also when undertaking research. In contrast to the widespread practice of describing educational discourse as social practice, but analysing it cross-sectionally (e.g. Kasper 2001, Markee 2000), I support other educational ethnographers (e.g. Lazarton 1995, Watson-Gegeo 1997) in their call for research methodologies that take the qualitative and longitudinal theoretical assumptions on board. In this light, the study introduced in the next section analyses the ELF classroom practices of one tertiary educational programme in their full contextualisation and dynamic developments.

3. The Study

The tertiary setting in question is a two-year international hotel management programme set at a hospitality educational centre in Vienna, Austria. The programme leads to a diploma in hotel management focussing explicitly on introducing newcomers to the field and providing them with the knowledge and some initial experience relevant for securing career-oriented positions in hospitality businesses. While its main thrust is thus job-oriented rather than academic, the diploma is accepted as first part of respective BBA programmes at other hospitality educational institutions.

Reflecting its practical nature, the programme offers a broad introduction to the various areas of expertise central to the hospitality industry, such as hotel management, accounting, marketing or public relations, as well as typical hospitality skills, such as serving, cooking or front office computer programmes. This has resulted in a dense study programme of on average 34 contact lessons per week. Additionally, students are required to do a three-month internship in a hospitality business of their choice between the first and second year of studies, thus gaining what is the first practical experience for most of them.

In accordance with the research methodology argued for above, I accompanied one group and their teachers (henceforth HMP, short for 'Hotel Management Programme') for the whole duration of their studies, starting on their very first day and acting as non-participant observer throughout the four semesters until their graduation, all of which took place in the first decade of the 21st century (cf. Smit 2008a for the detailed study report).[2] The student group was truly international as the following brief description underlines: the 28 students had 14 different nationalities, reported to use 14 different home languages and eight further languages of communication, and had previously stayed in all continents apart from Australia. The ten teachers involved in the study, on the other hand, reflected the local setting more clearly: apart from a native Brit, they were Austrians with extensive international work experience. Heterogeneity amongst them becomes apparent when turning to their professional backgrounds: apart from their different areas of expertise, the lecturers came with diverse backgrounds in teacher education and teaching experience, ranging from full studies and/or many years of teaching to none at all. As regards English, a similar range of background and experience could be observed among both students and teachers. While some had used English extensively in education before, others had studied the language as a subject only and/or used it for professional or private reasons. The group can thus be described as heterogeneous in terms of lingua-cultures, educational and professional backgrounds as well as English language proficiency levels.

In line with the theoretical and methodological considerations sketched in Section 2, the study reported on here is a 'discourse-pragmatic ethnography' of the HMP, i.e.

> a qualitative applied linguistic investigation that combines discourse analytical and pragmatic approaches with (educational) ethnography and aims at a principled analysis and informed interpretation of the HMP classroom interaction. (Smit 2008a, 80)

Put briefly, it follows educational ethnographic research (Davis 1995, Lazarton 1995) in that it aims to "understand the social organization and culturally-based perspectives and interpretations of specific interactions" (Watson-Gegeo 1997, 136). In the present case this resulted in an extensive pilot phase of more than one year, which not only introduced me to the research setting, but also to how the participants viewed their educational and interactional dynamics, thus laying the foundations for the two-year study of the HMP.

In view of my research interest on classroom interaction, qualitative applied linguistics and its focus on researching language use suggested itself, integrating discourse analytical and pragmatic methods and categories (Blum-Kulka 1997, Nikula 2002). By doing so, the centrally insider or emic research perspective of ethnography was complemented by the interactional data as main source of analysis and interpretation regarding the interlocutors' language use. In other words, the emic perspective was enriched by the analyst's etic research perspective and the detailed interactional analyses that both—emic and etic—perspectives support and allow. The resulting triangulation in research methodology not only leads to the 'thick' description relevant to ethnographic studies in general, but also adds to the carefully developed and argued "grounded theory [... that] potentially allows for transfer to a wide range of [...] social situations" (Davis 1995, 441). In other words, it is the methodological triangulation that adds to the trustworthiness of the analysis (Bloome et al. 2005, 433) and the transferability of findings (Lazarton 1995, 461).

Table 1. The data collected in the HMP

Data	Semester 1	Semester 2	Semester 3	Semester 4
Emic	qu* 1; 28 int* with students		4 group int.*; qu* 2	
		15 int.* with teachers		
	informal talks			
Interactional	observations and recordings of 126 lessons (33 transcribed)			

* 'qu'= questionnaire, filled in by all students;
'int' = interviews (where not specified further: one-on-one)

Table 1 illustrates the types of data collected as well as their temporal overlap. The emic data were collected from day one of the programme until its very end and contain two open-ended questionnaires filled out by the 28 students and 49 transcribed semi-guided interviews with all students and teachers. Additionally, I engaged in informal talks with the social actors at all times during the HMP. The interactional database consists of 126 observed and mainly audio-recorded lessons, 33 of which were chosen for detailed transcription in preparation for discourse-pragmatic analyses according to the three parameters time, subject and teacher. While the latter two refer to a fair representation of the subjects and teachers involved, the former takes into consideration the longitudinal character of the study. Based on the emic insights gained during the pilot phase, three moments in time were singled out as especially relevant to the developing community:

T1 (the introductory two weeks): the short phase during which the students and teachers got to know each other, starting to develop their community of practice;

T2 (the second half of semester 1): the phase during which the students started to be introduced to the varied subject matters of the programme;

T3 (semester 3): the first half of the second year of studies and the time after all students had gathered some hotel-related experience during their internships in hospitality businesses.

As can be gleaned from the overview of the interactional data in Table 2, approximately 10 lessons were chosen for each moment in time. Overall, ten teachers and eleven subjects were involved, with the corpus amounting to 24.5 hours of classroom talk and almost 228,000 words.

Table 2. Interactional data

Subject	Lecturer	T1	T2	T3	Sum
Financial Management	TON	2	2	2	6
Hotel Operations	OUL	2	-	-	2
Front Office / F&B Management	AKL	2	-	2	4
Hotel Management	LER	2	1	2	5
Marketing	NER	2	-	2	4
Austrian Law	XEN	2	2	-	4
Cooking	RER	-	2	-	2
Service	FER	-	1	1	2
Human Resources	OPP	-	2	-	2
Public Relations	MER	-	-	2	2
Totals, lessons		*12*	*10*	*11*	*33*
time (mins)		554	436	469	1459
words		80,303	68,140	79,222	227,665

In combining both sets of data, the analysis of classroom talk in ELF gains in detail and depth, as the following section will illustrate.

4. Findings

While this study has led to a broad variety of insights and a resulting grounded theory of ELF as classroom language in the HMP (Smit 2008a), I will discuss three central findings here by way of illustrative examples in the form of interview 'quotes' and classroom talk 'extracts', and, where applicable, supportive quantifications underlining frequencies and longitudinal developments. To begin with (see 4.1), the voices of the participating students, teachers and administrators are heard as regards their views on the HMP and English as classroom language. This strongly emic approach is then complemented by interactional analyses (see 4.2) as regards reaching intelligibility (Smith & Nelson 1985) as well as formulating speech functions (in)directly (Meierkord 1996, Nikula 2002, Trosborg 1994). Due to the longitudinal nature of the study, the emic and interactional analyses go beyond discussions of momentary instances by embedding them in detailed analyses of perceptions and discursive processes over time.

4.1. Insiders' Views on the HMP

Given that more than 40 social actors can be expected to have diverse ideas and opinions, it is noteworthy that the HMP teachers and students voiced remarkably similar views on the main orientation of the HMP and on the functions English played in their community. As regards the former, the headmaster described the original motivation for the English-medium international hotel management programme as responding to 'the demand from non-German speaking countries for Austrian tourism education' (Quote 1); a call which was reflected not only in the composition of the student group, but also in their motivation to join (Quote 2) as well as the teachers' interest in teaching there (Quote 3). The generally positive evaluation of the international character of the HMP was also explicitly linked to the thoroughly international character of the hospitality industry and the need for all future hotel managers to function in an international work environment (Quote 4).

Quote 1. Head-master (2nd sem, 1st mth):[3]

<on starting the programme> dass man für die Nachfrage aus dem Ausland und zwar dem nicht deutschsprachigen Ausland die nach österreichischer Tourismusausbildungsstandard […] befriedigen soll.
so that we answer to the demand from non-German speaking countries for Austrian standards in tourism education

Quote 2. Kama (2nd sem, 1st mth):

a lot of international students and I really enjoy that.

Quote 3. RER (2nd sem, 2nd mth):

ich unterricht eigentlich recht gern in englischer Sprache weil ma des […] so ein bisschen internationalen […] Flair […] gibt.
I like teaching in English because it adds some international flair

Quote 4. Cana (2nd sem, 1st mth):

er it's interesting. I think it makes erm things much easier later on. […] ja I think it's more difficult for them [=students doing same programme in German] afterwards to to work in a hotel and to use English than it's going to be for us, because they have to they know everything in German and they have to translate it first in their heads like, they are not used to we hear the same expressions the whole day. So we know the expression by heart. […] I don't think I would choose to study medicine in English or something. But […] but hotel management I would.

Concerning English as their classroom language, all teachers and students agreed on it being an additional language to all. Therefore, they saw themselves as 'sitting in the same boat' as the Public Relations teacher put it so succinctly (Quote 5). Furthermore, language proficiency was not evaluated in absolute terms, but in relative ones, regarding what was considered necessary for the communicative tasks to be met (Quote 6). This clear focus on community-internal needs and requirements also came to the fore in the members describing their interactions and how successful they seemed to the group. Right from the start of the HMP, the students were clearly aware of the lingua-culturally based differences amongst them and willing to invest the time and effort necessary to make communication work (Quote 7). While this readiness did not change with time, community members reported on decreasing communicational difficulties in interviews after the third month. Obviously, the increase in familiarity amongst themselves and with the programme had smoothed communicational processes (Quote 8).

Quote 5. MER (3rd sem, 3rd mth):

also ich denk immer wir sitzen alle im selben Boot ich sag ihnen in der ersten Stunde mein Englisch ist auch nicht perfekt, ich hab's nicht als Muttersprache ah wenn irgendwas unklar ist sollen's bitte schreien wenn ich ein Wort nicht weiß wer ich selber sagen bitte wie heißt das ah und so geht's sicher vielen anderen auch deren Muttersprache nicht Englisch ist.

I always think we are in the same boat, I tell them in the first class that my own English isn't perfect either, it's not my mother tongue. if something's unclear they need to make themselves heard. When I don't know a word myself, I'll say myself excuse me, what is it called? (.) And this is most likely what many others feel like whose mother tongue isn't English.

Quote 6. Alac (2nd sem, 1st mth):

ja I mean they know basic they know good Austrian English that's about what I would say [...] some teachers have better vocabularies than others I guess, [... but] you don't really need a high level of English cause that's not really the point I think. I mean as long as they get it across what they want to- what is important for this subject, if they don't have a fluent perfect English doesn't make a difference

Quote 7. Anns (1st sem, 4th mth):

they do get on in class, but yes there are differences, some people are it is hard for them to understand because the way they have learnt English, is different. I mean even if you take the (Koreans) they have an accent. [...] when they speak sometimes yes the others don't understand. but we yes we try to communicate with each other without fight and stuff so we understand each other well. because they sometimes that what I speak maybe she doesn't understand or another person then I explain them.

Quote 8. Kail (2nd sem, 3rd mth):

uhm language wise it is fine I guess, we (2) it's no problem and generally especially now after a year I think everyone has integrated with the environment here I feel like it's a good group

In sum, the students and teachers unanimously described the HMP as truly international in orientation and in character. Correspondingly, they identified English as everybody's additional language and communicational success as central and worth working for jointly, irrespective of the obvious diversity in language proficiency levels. In view of the definitions given above, this means that they saw English as their lingua franca. Additionally, their emic perspectives revealed that they experienced their shared repertoire as developing group-internally by mutually engaging in their joint teaching and learning enterprise. In other words, they evaluated their social activities as structuring a developing classroom community of practice with one central practice being their community-specific communication in English as a lingua franca (cf. House 2003).

4.2. Classroom Discourse Patterns

This section turns to the interactional patterns that the discourse-pragmatic analysis of the HMP classroom talk has brought to light. More precisely, I will illustrate two such patterns with special focus on their longitudinal developments. The first picks up on the generally established consideration that encounters between multilingual English speakers of varied lingua-cultural backgrounds can be characterised by frequent instances of unintelligibility (e.g. Jenkins 2000, Wagner & Firth 1997). The second pattern focuses on control acts as a typical speech function of classroom talk (e.g. Iedema 1996, Kasper 2001, Lemke 1990) and discusses the preference for directness with which these acts are verbalised.

4.2.1. Unintelligibility in ELF as a Temporary Phenomenon

The question of (un)intelligibility, i.e. of (not) recognising words or phrases (Jenkins 2000, 78), is central to talk in general because it amounts to the first step in reaching understanding or "finding a situated meaning and appropriate response" (Linell 1995, 184). At any moment in ongoing discourse, interactants need to make, and find, the previous words or utterances, as Smith and Nelson (1985) put it, firstly intelligible (recognisable) before they can be comprehensible (recognising their meaning) and interpretable (recognising the speaker's intention). These three subprocesses require a great deal of communicative competence and shared sociocultural background. By definition this is, however, not an integral feature of an ELF setting, in which "speakers 'have little in common' apart from their [... varying proficiencies in the] L2 and the mutual desire to achieve a particular goal" (Jenkins 2000, 73-74). This means that the interactants need to bridge their divergent backgrounds and proficiency levels with regard to all three levels of understanding, first and foremost as regards intelligibility.

Communicative trouble in this regard was also identified as such by the students and teachers of the HMP, many of whom mentioned the hard times they experienced in trying to understand each other (Quote 9). Interestingly, these problems were reported on as alleviating during the first semester. After the first three months, understanding each other was evaluated as having become easier (Quotes 9 and 10).

Quote 9. Jenz (2nd sem, 2nd mth):

> <as regards understand teachers> oh ja ja that was hard. that was hard. because you have to figures out all the different character personality the way they talk, it was very hard, for first semester for first three months it was hard.

Quote 10. Elig (1st sem, 4th mth):

> I think we all got used to each other. doesn't mean we're speaking English better, but we speak in a way that we definitely understand each other I guess

In view of the discrepancies between self-reported and actual linguistic behaviour, these emic perspectives need to be complemented by an interactional analysis of actual problems of intelligibility. In this context, the investigation of repair work suggests itself as it offers a broad and well established theoretical and methodological frame of analysis (e.g. Markee 2000; McHoul 1990; Schegloff, Jefferson & Sacks 1977; van Lier 1988). Put briefly, interactants identify instances of lacking understanding as 'repairables', which they submit to 'repair' so as to reach the degree of shared understanding regarded as sufficient at the moment of interaction. While a detailed discussion would extend the present needs (but cf. Dalton-Puffer 2007, ch. 8; Smit 2008a, ch. 5), problems of intelligibility can be analysed as triggering repair on 'mishearings', i.e. problems in identifying words and utterances spoken (Linell 1995, 188). As illustrated in Extract 1, the repair exchange starts with the repairable 1 (turn 2) being identified in hindsight through a repair initiation (turn 3), which leads to a repair response (turn 4). Alternatively, the repair can be undertaken in one turn, as regards repairable 2 in Extract 1 (turns 4 and 5).

Extract 1. Front Office Management (T1)

1 AKL	well it's belongs to holiday inn=		
2 Kosk	**=sheraton**	*repairable 1*	
3 AKL	sorry?	*initiation 1*	
4 Kosk	**sheraton**	*response 1*	*repairable 2*
5 AKL	sheraton is a separate chain again		*repair 2*

While the actual repair exchanges and how students and teachers handled them in the HMP are worth dealing with in themselves (cf. Smit 2007), the focus here is on the longitudinal development that repair on mishearing underwent during the HMP. As a basis of such a description, repair on mishearing will be compared with repair on other repairable categories, such as factual information issues (see repairable 2 in Extract 1). For that purpose the repair exchanges were analysed in detail in a sub-corpus of the interactional data consisting of 9 lessons, i.e. 3 per time phase (cf. Smit 2008a, ch. 5). As discernable from Table 3, four main repair categories could be identified: factual information on instructional and classroom regulative issues, lexical items and mishearing.[4]

Table 3. Main repair categories, per moment in time

Repairable categories	**Sum N**	**T1 N**	**T1 %**	**T2 N**	**T2 %**	**T3 N**	**T3 %**
facts (instructional)	125	41	*32,8*	50	*40,0*	34	*27,2*
facts (regulative)	32	11	*34,4*	12	*37,5*	9	*28,1*
lexical items	70	25	*35,7*	21	*30,0*	24	*34,3*
mishearing	**66**	**36**	***54,5***	**21**	***31,8***	**9**	***13,6***
Total	293	113	*38,6*	104	*35,5*	76	*25,9*

chi-square=13.21, df=6, p=0.0398

The absolute frequencies in Table 3 show that mishearings account for about a fifth of all repair exchanges, approximating the number of instances of unknown lexical items. As regards temporal developments between the three moments in time, however, repair exchanges on mishearing display a unique pattern in that there is a statistically significant decrease in frequency, with more than half of all instances having taken place in the introductory phase (T1) and a further third during T2. A year later, only a handful of instances of mishearing could be identified. In other words, intelligibility problems clearly decrease with time and the corresponding increase in familiarity between the interactants. This long-term development within the HMP classroom talk is revealing in that the preponderance of problems of intelligibility identified as typical of ELF communication finds support, but is specified further in that the developments away from repairing mishearings to co-constructing (views on) topics suggests that problems of intelligibility characterise ELF talk only at an initial stage. Once an ELF community of practice has established itself, difficulties of intelligibility become less relevant in their discourse.

4.2.2. Directness as Increasingly Preferred Strategy in Control Acts

As one of the main speech functions in general, control acts, such as "open the window" or "pass the salt", have been analysed widely and in diverse domains, such as home, work or formal education (for an overview cf. Smit 2008a, 208-213; Vine 2004, 16-19). While individual studies tend to deliver situation-specific results on how social actors demand goods and services (Halliday 2004, 107), recent investigations agree that the relevant factor for the type of control act carried out is 'power', especially when considered in a complex way as product and as process (e.g. Holmes & Stubbe 2003, Vine 2004). In brief, power as product becomes apparent in the relative institutional status of the interactants and the type of control act carried out by the speaker. Power as process, on the other hand, becomes apparent in the speaker's formulation and the hearer's handling of the control act (Vine 2004, 30-31). As the present study is concerned with discourse in a tertiary classroom, it is important to keep in mind the generally asymmetrical power relations between teacher and (adult) students. Especially in traditional classrooms (Cazden 2001) like the HMP, the teacher generally acts as main provider of subject-relevant information as well as leading organiser of classroom talk and activity (e.g. Widdowson 1990, 181-191).

Concerning control acts, the teacher's institutional status—and thus power as product—is reflected in their leading role in constructing control acts. This is also confirmed in the HMP control acts (see Table 4 below), practically all of which were uttered by teachers. Power as process, on the other hand, rather comes to the fore in how control acts are formulated and taken up by those addressed. Here, relevant studies have pointed out the degree of (in)directness and kinds of modifications with which control acts are formulated (e.g. Blum-Kulka, House & Kasper 1989). While, again, results tend to be contingent on specific settings and generalisations thus difficult and potentially misleading, the only study into ELF control acts, undertaken for casual conversation (Meierkord 1996), has so far identified rather direct formulations with little modification as preferred option. Regarding educational settings, studies undertaken at various educational levels have shown that direct formulations seem to be more likely with younger learners (Iedema 1996) and a feature of increased familiarity between teachers and learners (Kasper 2001). Studies focussing on second language learners have identified further influencing factors, such as language proficiency levels, lingua-cultural patterns or individual communicative styles (Dalton-Puffer 2005, House & Kasper 1987, Nikula 2002).

Against this brief sketch of the relevant literature, let us now turn to the degree of (in)directness with which control acts were uttered in the HMP. Based on a sub-set of the interactional corpus,[5] I could identify 139 control acts, all of which were uttered by teachers, thus underlining their special institutional status and interactional role. As discernable from Table 4, the instances represent the six strategies originally established by Blum-Kulka, House and Kasper (1989) and frequently employed in diverse studies (e.g. Dalton-Puffer 2007, ch 7; Trosborg 1994), but do so in highly diverse frequencies. More than half of all control acts fit to strategy VI with less than 10 percent being elliptical phrases. This means that about half of all control acts reveal a clearly direct, imperative form. While this preponderance could be expected at primary level (Holmes 1983, 96), it is rather unusual at upper-secondary (e.g. Lemke 1990, 63) and, by extension, tertiary levels. Conventionally indirect formulations aiming at ability and willingness (strategy II) are, on the other hand, considerably less frequent and appear in less than 20 percent of all instances. Additionally, more than 60% of them come from T1, thus pointing at a sudden decrease in rather indirect strategies with the HMP progressing, favouring more direct ones such as strategies IV and VI after the introductory phase.

Table 4. Strategies of control acts

(In)directness		Strategy	T1	T2	T3	Total	Total (%)
indirect	I	hint	6	3	5	14	*10*
conventionally indirect	II	ability/willingness	**14**	1	7	**22**	*16*
	III	wants/needs	4	2	4	10	*7*
	IV	obligation	4	2	8	14	*10*
direct	V	performative	0	2	1	3	*2*
	VI	imperative (+ elliptical phrases)	29	20	27	**76**	*55*
		Total	*57*	*30*	*52*	*139*	*100*

In other words, the HMP control acts present an unusual preference for direct rather than conventionally indirect strategies. This could be interpreted as an indication that the HMP teachers were not particularly polite; or that they displayed rather idiosyncratic speech styles. But as none of the students made any comments in this regard in the many interviews and informal conversations conducted with them, this seems a highly improbable possibility. Rather, the complete lack of awareness amongst the students of this verbal practice shared by all teachers seems to indicate that directly formulated teacher control acts were jointly established as fulfilling their discursive function and as appropriate in the HMP community of practice.

More substantiation for this interpretation can be gained from a discussion of four extracts, which display typical as well as atypical examples in order to sketch the breadth of control acts as well as the longitudinal development towards directness as preferred strategy. To begin with, Extract 2 represents a conventionally indirect control act (strategy II), which is modified by the politeness marker *please*. What is interesting is that this relatively indirect speech act was produced at the very beginning of the HMP. In TON's lessons at T2 and T3 his control acts tended to be imperatives with occasional lexical or external modifiers (cf. Extract 3).

Extract 2. Financial Management (T1)

1	TON	could you, **could somebody please arrange** then to give this back .

Extract 3. Financial Management (T2)

1	TON	**read the question** there . what are they asking you to do ?

Extract 4. Human Resources (T2)

1	OPP	**close the window** .

More generally, control acts at T2 and T3 were seldom modified (see Extract 4), which seems to hint at a possible communicational need. Too much modification could end up to be experienced as counterproductive to the main aim of teacher-whole class interaction, namely to make the intention of control act transparent to all involved. Extract 5 is a case in point.

Extract 5. Public Relations (T3)

1	MER	you missed one quiz.
2	Elig	when was this ?
3	MER	four weeks ago.
4	Elig	oh really ?
5	MER	**would you be prepared to** repeat what we discussed last week ? (.) so you make up for the quiz that you missed ?
6	Elig	ua:: ?

7	MER	**could you give us** an overview about the media landscape ? (.) the topic we discussed last week , which media exist and ?
8	Elig	oh yes .

MER, the Public Relations teacher, for whom this is the first semester of teaching this group, wants to ask Elig, an Austrian student, to review the preceding lesson. The teacher's first control act in turn 5 is syntactically and lexically modified in a highly atypical way. The modal verb *will* is generally barely used for control acts, as is the phrase *be prepared to*. In addition, the teacher chooses the past tense. The student's reaction in turn 6—an unspecified sound in interrogative intonation—shows that she cannot interpret the teacher's intention. It could, of course, be argued that Elig has a semantic problem, but this is not very likely as she was a very experienced and proficient user of English. So, instead of a lexical gap, it is more likely that the student has encountered a pragmatic one insofar as, after more than a year of HMP interaction, she does not associate such a formulation with teacher control acts. The teacher's paraphrase in turn 7 includes the relevant 'trigger word' *can* in combination with the past tense, which, as Elig's reaction in turn 8 shows, leads to the desired interpretation.

In sum, this analysis has confirmed the expected, namely that control acts in the HMP reflect the formal educational setting and the special social role fulfilled by the teachers as classroom organisers and managers. More interestingly, however, the analysis has brought to light a preference for (almost) direct strategies of formulating control acts; a preference that can be described as growing with time, but also as shared by teachers and students. The former increasingly employed unmodified imperative constructions and the latter arguably accepted them as default strategy, with less direct formulations potentially leading to non-understanding (see Extract 5). While individual examples cannot be taken as hard and fast proof, they indicate that after the introductory phase members of the HMP community of practice increasingly considered directly verbalised control acts (see Extracts 3 and 4) as meeting the community-internal 'norm' in numeric but also pragmatic terms.

5. Conclusions

This contribution focuses on tertiary education as one domain that has so far attracted ELF research interests only in the Finnish ELFA project (e.g. Mauranen 2003), although internationalisation and concurrently the use of English is rapidly spreading at tertiary institutions all over mainland Europe. As, furthermore, the presently wide-spread constructivist understanding of education arguably requires qualitative and longitudinal applied linguistic research, the study reported on here has investigated one specific tertiary educational programme within an ethnographic framework and analysed classroom discourse from a combination of emic, etic and interactional points of view (Smit 2008a). The educational programme in question was a two-year hotel management programme designed for and attended by a truly international student group and taught by mainly local, i.e. Austrian, teachers with international work experience in their respective areas of expertise.

The detailed and in-depth discourse pragmatic ethnography of one year group (referred to as HMP) has allowed a multi-layered description of ELF as classroom language. There is firstly the researcher's etic evaluation of English as "the language of all main classroom talk" (Smit 2008a, 73), i.e. as the HMP's classroom language, and, at the same time, as the only language shared by all HMP members, i.e. as their lingua franca. Such outsider descriptions gain in depth when complemented by insider or emic views. Here, teacher and student opinions put into relief the preconditions of and developments while 'doing education' in a lingua franca. The analysis has shown that such an educational undertaking presupposes that the participants welcome the socio-cultural diversities as an asset and as fitting to their professionalization. They furthermore need to (learn to) recognise the use of a lingua franca as a resource to the developing community of practice which requires some investment of time and effort in developing their shared repertoire to make ELF classroom talk work out. When considered successful, participants develop a relativistic understanding of necessary levels of language proficiency by identifying them in relation to what the ongoing classroom discourse requires. This 'good enough' evaluation is not only considered relative to the discourse aims and topics, but also to the interactants, as all must take an active role in co-constructing successful talk (Quote 11).

Quote 11, Anns (4th sem, 1st mth):

> <on other students having improved their English> yeah, [...] I mean, [...] cause when she <Anle> talks to me I understand everything and yeah sometimes when she's not able to say a word, then I complete it, it doesn't matter.

These dynamic insider views on ELF as classroom language stand in a complementary and mutually enriching relationship to the long-term interactional data. The former identify critical phases in classroom discourse, which in turn open up a rich source of information and insights on ELF interactional dynamics complementing the respective emic assessments.

The two discourse patterns chosen for discussion in this paper illustrate the complex relationship between insider evaluation and actual discursive behaviour. The first discussion on instances of (un)intelligibility, which were numerous and central during the introductory phase of the HMP only, decreasing rapidly thereafter, finds a corresponding reflection in the emic evaluations. The second interactional issue discussed, however, arguably took place below the level of conscious awareness as it was not mentioned in the emic data at all. The point at stake here is the degree of directness with which teachers formulated control acts. As the analysis has shown, directly phrased commands were not only the increasingly preferred option, but also the one considered appropriate by the community members, in that they not only went by unnoticed; the rare indirectly formulated control acts were also considered difficult to interpret. While this result is interesting in itself, it gains in relevance as it exemplifies a strong and growing discursive preference for directness and explicitness established in further analyses of other discourse functions, such as questions or explanations (Smit 2008b). In other words, direct control acts illustrate that the HMP classroom talk reveals a generally strong preference for realising speech functions in illocutionarily explicit ways, thus displaying an interactional 'principle of explicitness'.

In addition to the new insights into ELF as classroom language brought to light here, the study of the HMP and its innovative research methodology can, I wish to suggest, be beneficial to further research undertakings. As the brief discussion has intended to show, the fully contextualised and longitudinal discourse-pragmatic and ethnographic approach allows for a multi-layered, step-by-step and in-depth description of oral practices, combining momentary meaning-making processes with community-building (verbal) activities over time as well as insider perspectives. In other words, this methodology offers an investigative framework to observe such developments 'live' with the aim to provide evidence of the dynamic nature claimed likewise for education and English used as a lingua franca.

APPENDIX

Transcription conventions

3-letter pseudonyms (in capitals)	refer to teachers
4-letter pseudonyms	refer to students
(.)	pause shorter than a second
(2)	pauses, timed in seconds
exte:nsion	noticeable extension of a syllable or sound
cut off wo-	cut off word or truncated speech
text= =text	latching utterances
.	falling intonation
?	rising intonation
,	level intonation
[...]	deletion of text
<text>	added explanations
text	translation from the original German
text (in Excerpts)	material which is currently under discussion

Bibliography

Ammon, U. and G. McConnell 2002. *English as an Academic Language in Europe. A Survey of its Use in Teaching*. Frankfurt: Lang.

Björkman, B. this volume. "From Code to Discourse in Spoken ELF."

—. 2008. "'So where we are?' Spoken Lingua Franca English at a Technical University in Sweden." *English Today* 24 (2), 35-41.

Bloome, D., S. P. Carter, B. M. Christian, S. Otto and N. Shuart-Faris 2005. *Discourse Analysis and the Study of Classroom Language and Literacy Events—A Microethnographic Perspective*. Mahwah, New Jersey: Erlbaum.

Blum-Kulka, S. 1997. "Discourse Pragmatics." In *Discourse as Social Interaction. Discourse Studies: A Multidisciplinary Introduction*, ed. T. A. van Dijk, 38-63. London: Sage.

Blum-Kulka, S., J. House and G. Kasper, eds. 1989. *Cross-Cultural Pragmatics: Requests and Apologies*. Norwood, New Jersey: Ablex.

Cazden, C. 2001. *Classroom Discourse: The Language of Teaching and Learning*, 2nd ed. Portsmouth, NH: Heinemann.

Christie, F. 2002. *Classroom Discourse Analysis*. London: Continuum.

Corder, S. and M. Meyerhoff 2007. "Communities of Practice in the Analysis of Intercultural Communication." In *Handbook of Intercultural Communication, HAL* 7, ed. H. Kothoff & H. Spencer-Oatey, 441-61. Berlin: Mouton.

Crystal, D. 2003. *English as a Global Language*, 2nd ed. Cambridge: Cambridge University Press.

Dalton-Puffer, C. 2007. *Discourse in Content and Language Integrated Learning (CLIL) Classrooms*. Amsterdam: John Benjamins.

—. 2005. "Negotiating Interpersonal Meanings in Naturalistic Classroom Discourse: Directives in Content and Language Integrated Classrooms." *Journal of Pragmatics* 37 (8), 1275-93.

Davis, K. A. 1995. "Qualitative Theory and Methods in Applied Linguistics Research." *TESOL Quarterly* 29 (3), 427-53.

Drew, P. and J. Heritage 1992. "Analyzing Talk at Work: An Introduction." In *Talk at Work: Interaction in Institutional Settings*, ed. P. Drew & J. Heritage, 3-65. Cambridge: Cambridge University Press.

Edwards, A. P. and D. P. G. Westgate 1994. *Investigating Classroom Talk*, 2nd ed. London and Washington D.C.: Palmer Press.

Fortanet-Gómez, I. and C. A. Räisänen, eds. 2008. *ESP in European Higher Education. Integrating Language and Content*. Amsterdam: John Benjamins.

Gnutzmann, C. and F. Intemann, eds. 2005. *Globalisation of English and the English Language Classroom*. Tübingen: Narr.

Graddol, D. 2006. *English Next. Why Global English Might Mean the End of 'English as a Foreign Language'*. British Council.

Hall, J. K. 1993. "The Role of Oral Practices in the Accomplishment of Our Everyday Lives: The Sociocultural Dimension of Interaction with Implications for the Learning of Another Language." *Applied Linguistics* 14 (3), 145-66.

Halliday, M. A. K. 2004. *An Introduction to Functional Grammar*, 3rd ed. London: Arnold.

Holmes, J. 1983. "The Structure of Teachers' Directives." In *Language and Communication*, ed. J. C. Richards & R. W. Schmidt, 89-115. London: Longman.

Holmes, J. and M. Stubbe 2003. *Power and Politeness in the Workplace. A Sociolinguistic Analysis of Talk at Work*. London: Longman.

House, J. 2003. "English as a Lingua Franca: A Threat to Multilingualism?" *Journal of Sociolinguistics* 7 (4), 556-78.

House, J. and G. Kasper 1987. "Interlanguage Pragmatics: Requesting in a Foreign Language." In *Perspectives on Language in Performance. Studies in Linguistics, Literary Criticism and Language Teaching and*

Learning. To Honour Werner Hüllen on the Occasion of his Sixtieth Birthday, ed. W. Lörscher & R. Schulze, 1250-88. Tübingen: Narr.
Hymes. D. 1972. "Models of the Interaction of Language and Social Life." In *Directions in Sociolinguistics: The Ethnography of Communication*, ed. J. Gumperz & D. Hymes, 35-71. New York: Holt, Rinehart and Winston.
Iedema. R. 1996. "'Save the talk for after the listening': The Realisation of Regulative Discourse in Teacher Talk." *Language and Education* 10 (2-3), 82-102.
International Journal of the Sociology of Language 177, 2006. (Special issue on lingua franca language use).
James, A. 2006. "Lingua Franca English as Chimera: Sociocultural and Sociolinguistic Perspectives." In *Cultural Studies in the ELF Classroom*, ed. W. Delanoy & L. Volkmann, 221-32. Heidelberg: Universitätsverlag Winter.
—. 2005. "The Challenges of the Lingua Franca: English in the World and Types of Variety." In *The Globalisation of Englsh and the English Language Classroom*, ed. K. Gnutzmann & F. Intemann, 133-44. Tübingen: Narr.
Jenkins, J. 2006. *English as a Lingua Franca: Attitudes and Identity*. Oxford: Oxford University Press.
—. 2000. *The Phonology of English as an International Language: New Models, New Norms, New Goals*. Oxford: Oxford University Press.
Kasper, G. 2001. "Classroom Research on Interlanguage Pragmatics." In *Pragmatics in Language Teaching,* ed. K. R. Rose & G. Kasper, 33-60. Cambridge: Cambridge University Press.
Lazarton, A. 1995. "Qualitative Research in Applied Linguistics: A Progress Report." *TESOL Quarterly* 29 (3), 455-72.
Lemke, J. L. 1990. *Talking Science. Language, Learning and Values*. Norwood, N.J.: Ablex Publ.
Linell, P. 1995. "Troubles with Mutualities: Towards a Dialogical Theory of Misunderstanding and Miscommunication." In *Mutualities in Dialogue*, ed. I. Markova, C. Graumann & K. Foppe, 176-213. Cambridge: Cambridge University Press.
Markee, N. 2000. *Conversation Analysis.* Mahwah, New Jersey: Erlbaum.
Marton, F. and A. B. M. Tsui 2004. *Classroom Discourse and the Space of Learning*. Mahwah, New Jersey: Erlbaum.
Mauranen, A. 2006. "Signaling and Preventing Misunderstanding in English as Lingua Franca Communication." *International Journal of the Sociology of Language* 177, 123-50.

—. 2003. "The Corpus of English as Lingua Franca in Academic Settings." *TESOL Quarterly* 37 (2), 513-27.
McHoul, A. W. 1990. "The Organization of Repair in Classroom Talk." *Language in Society* 19, 349-77.
Meierkord, C. 1996. *Englisch als Medium der interkulturellen Kommunikation. Untersuchungen zum non-native- / non-native-speaker Diskurs*. Frankfurt: Lang.
Nikula, T. 2002. "Teacher Talk Reflecting Pragmatic Awareness: A Look at EFL and Content-Based Classrooms." *Pragmatics* 12 (4), 447-68.
Nordic Journal of English Studies 5 (2), 2006. (Special issue on English as a lingua franca).
Schegloff, E. A., G. Jefferson and H. Sacks 1977. "The Preference for Self-Correction in the Organization of Repair in Conversation." *Language* 53 (2), 361-82.
Seidlhofer, B. 2001. "Closing a Conceptual Gap: The Case for a Description of English as a Lingua Franca." *International Journal of Applied Linguistics* 11 (2), 133-58.
Seidlhofer, B., A. Breiteneder and M.-L. Pitzl 2006. "English as a Lingua Franca in Europe: Challenges for Applied Linguistics." *Annual Review of Applied Linguistics* 26, 3-34.
Smit, U. 2008a. *Classroom Interaction in English as a Lingua Franca. A Discourse Pragmatic Ethnography in International Tertiary Education*. Unpublished 'Habilitationsschrift', University of Vienna.
—. 2008b. "What I think is important [is] to know how to explain it." Explaining Lexical Items in English as a Lingua Franca in International Higher Education." In *Sprachen lernen—Menschen bilden. Dokumentation zum 22. Kongress für Fremdsprachendidaktik der Deutschen Gesellschaft für Fremdsprachenforschung (DGFF) Gießen, Oktober 2007*, ed. E. Burwitz-Melzer, W. Hallet, M. K. Legutke, F.-J. Meißner & J. Mukherjee, 279-88. BFF—Beiträge zur Fremdsprachenforschung, Band 10. Hohengehren: Schneider Verlag.
—. 2007. "ELF (English as a Lingua Franca) as Medium of Instruction—Interactional Repair in International Hotel Management Education." In *Empirical Perspectives on CLIL Classroom Discourse*, ed. C. Dalton-Puffer & U. Smit, 227-52. Frankfurt am Main: Lang.
—. 2005. "Multilingualism and English. The Lingua Franca Concept in Language Description and Language Learning Pedagogy." In *Mehrsprachigkeit und Kommunikation in der Diplomatie. Favorita Papers 4*, ed. R. Faistauer, C. Cali, I. Cullin & K. Chester, 66-76. Vienna: Diplomatic Academy.

—. 2003. "English as a Lingua Franca (ELF) as Medium of Learning in a Hotel Management Educational Program: An Applied Linguistic Approach." *VIEWS (Vienna English Working Papers)* 12 (2), 40-75. http://www.univie.ac.at/Anglistik/views.htm (accessed May 3, 2008).

Smith, K. 2004. "Studying in an Additional Language: What is Gained, What is Lost, What is Assessed." In *Integrating Content and Language. Meeting the Challenge of a Multilingual Higher Education*, ed. R. Wilkinson, 78-93. Maastricht: Universitaire Pers

Smith, L. E. and C. Nelson 1985. "International Intelligibility of English: Directions and Resources." *World Englishes* 4 (3), 333-42.

Trosborg, A. 1994. *Interlanguage Pragmatics. Requests, Complaints and Apologies*. Berlin: Mouton de Gruyter.

Van Lier, L. 1988. *The Classroom and the Language Learner*. London: Longman.

Vine, B. 2004. *Getting Things Done at Work*. Amsterdam: John Benjamins.

Wagner, J. and A. Firth. 1997. "Communication Strategies at Work." In *Communication Strategies. Psycholinguistic and Sociolinguistic Perspectives*, ed. G. Kasper & E. Kellerman, 323-44. London: Longman.

Walsh, S. 2006. *Investigating Classroom Discourse*. London: Routledge.

Watson-Gegeo, K. A. 1997. "Classroom Ethnography." In *Encyclopaedia of Language and Education. Vol. 8: Research Methods in Language and Education*, ed. N. H. Hornberger & D. Corson, 135-44. Dordrecht, The Netherlands: Kluwer Academic Publishers.

Wenger, E. 1998. *Communities of Practice. Learning, Meaning, and Identity*. Cambridge: Cambridge University Press.

Widdowson, H. 1990. *Aspects of Language Teaching*. Oxford: Oxford University Press.

Wilkinson, R., ed. 2004. *Integrating Content and Language. Meeting the Challenges of a Multilingual Higher Education.* Maastricht: Universitaire Pers.

Wilkinson, R. and V. Zegers, eds. 2007. *Researching Content and Language Integration in Higher Education.* Maastricht: Universitaire Pers

Notes

[1] This study has been made possible by a research grant of the Austrian Science Fund; the transcriptions have in part been financed by a grant of the 'Wiener Hochschuljubiläumsstiftung'.
[2] As there are very few such hospitality educational centres in Vienna, I wish to respect the participants' anonymity by, firstly, not revealing any exact dates and, secondly, referring to the participants by arbitrarily chosen pseudonyms, with four-letter combinations referring to students and upper-case three-letter ones to teachers.
[3] For the transcription conventions see the Appendix.
[4] The other categories of repairables, such as pronunciation or grammar, have turned out as numerically minor, with less than 15 instances overall and between 2 and 6 instances per time phase.
[5] The sub-corpus consists of 9 lessons, 3 each for T1, T2 and T3 and is thus similar in size and weighting as the one used for the repair analysis, but contains different lessons.

FROM CODE TO DISCOURSE IN SPOKEN ELF

BEYZA BJÖRKMAN

1. Introduction

For an applied linguist, any ELF setting with its intrinsic multilingual nature is a very exciting research environment. Such settings are diverse by nature: each speaker has preconceptions and beliefs s/he carries into the setting. Users' language skills show tremendous variation. Such contexts are known to include numerous linguistic forms that clearly diverge from standard prescriptive forms.

Of all possible ELF contexts, academia is among the most interesting ones. As anglification of universities throughout the world surges onward, an increasing number of higher education institutions are adopting English as the medium of instruction for parts of their education. Most universities in continental Europe have become ELF settings where English is spoken by a wide spectrum of first-language users for various purposes, be it for academic activity or social interaction. We are slowly beginning to understand the implications of functioning in a foreign language which is no one's native language in a university classroom.

This study investigates the usage of English of teachers and students in a setting such as the one described above. The aim is to look at the morphosyntactic non-standardness in their speech, and to investigate how they adopt and adapt the language to get the job done, to find out whether any type of non-standardness causes communication breakdown and/or irritation, which can adversely affect communication. This paper attempts to take the progress from consideration of code to consideration of discourse and presents a selection of the results of the present study.

2. Background

Although ELF is still a relatively new field of research, the proliferation of investigations that are being carried out on different aspects of it is dramatic. Research so far has already had an impact on the growth of the field and its future developments. Space here does not allow an extensive coverage of all the valuable work carried out so far, but some of the contributions dealing with ELF will be referred to with respect to form and communicativeness.

Among the wide variety of valuable studies, some have dealt with phonology (Jenkins 2000), pragmatics (Firth 1996; Firth & Wagner 1997; Meierkord 1996, 1998, 2000; House 2002; Lesznyák 2004; Mauranen 2006a) and morphosyntax (Seidlhofer 2004; Breiteneder 2005; Ranta 2006).When it comes to pragmatics, a study that later became a seminal work for ELF research investigates business telephone conversations and points to the effectiveness of the speakers' conversations where interactional work is done despite potential problems (Firth 1996). Problem-solving mechanisms deployed by speakers in ELF situations ease communication and help achieve effectiveness (Firth & Wagner 1997). In line with these results are findings reported in another study that has analyzed the discourse features of students' small-talk conversations in a student hall in the UK. The results show that ELF communication includes shorter turns and more pauses compared to native-speaker communication, but it is also characterized by cooperation (Meierkord 1998). European students' topic management has been analyzed in another study, and the results indicate that they efficiently make decisions in simulated meetings (Lesznyák 2004). With their dynamic topic management, the students find a common ground and achieve communication. Similar results have been reported in studies that have investigated misunderstandings. Despite the diverse nature of ELF settings, not so many cases of misunderstandings occur in ELF speech. Mutual cooperativeness to prevent misunderstandings and the presence of signaling of comprehension is an apparent characteristic of ELF interaction (Mauranen 2006a, 146).

The work on pragmatics was followed by studies concerning morphosyntax. Some studies have reported on the instability and lack of systematicity of syntactic features of informal ELF conversations (Meierkord 2004, 117). Other work has focused on commonalities of ELF communication, perhaps the best known one being the documentation of the most common features of ELF usage by Seidlhofer (2004). A number of smaller-scale studies that investigate these reported features in detail followed this work, preceding the launch of the VOICE corpus (VOICE). Some of the most popular areas of research have been high-frequency items e.g. the third person *–s*. An investigation reporting on the variations of this construction from group discussions among EU officials actually reports that 80% of all the instances in the ELF speech investigated conformed to standard forms (Breiteneder 2005). It is suggested that a mix of linguistic and extra-linguistic environments could lead to divergent forms of the third person *–s*. Another structure that occurs frequently in ELF discourse is the widespread use of the progressive form. It has been argued that ELF speakers use the progressive form for prominence and salience. In fact, highlighting the verb in such a manner could be contributing to success in ELF communication (Ranta 2006, 112-113).

It has been suggested that there is an inherent link between lexicogrammar and pragmatics and that users' lexicogrammatical choices are determined by pragmatic motives (Cogo & Dewey 2006). The variation in lexicogrammar caused by pragmatic needs and the interrelationship between the two are significant elements in understanding the dynamics of ELF interaction. It seems like it is the area between lexicogrammatical variation and communicative effectiveness that calls for further investigation.

3. Data

The present study focuses primarily on form but also on communicativeness of ELF and investigates non-standardness in spoken ELF as the academic language at a Swedish university. It is important for teaching purposes (Jenkins 2000) to find out what specific types of non-standardness occur in ELF settings and whether they do interfere with communication.

With 123 reported English-taught programs in 2007 (Wächter & Maiworm 2008, 24), Sweden was number four on the list of the leading countries as providers of English-medium tuition in continental Europe (Wächter & Maiworm 2008, 29). The present investigation was carried out at a leading technical university which produces about one third of the country's engineers. It is also a significant provider of the country's technical research. Engineering is the subject area in which English-taught programs are most-frequently found across Europe, with 27 % of all (Wächter & Maiworm 2008, 12). This trend can be observed in the present engineering setting, where English is used extensively to allow for academic mobility of students and scholars and to prepare students for the global job market among other reasons. Such practices have resulted in a large number of incoming exchange students and foreign scholars who communicate with each other through English. English is the language of instruction in the more advanced stages of many programs, and international Master's programs and higher levels have been fully anglified. Doctoral theses are almost exclusively written in English.

The data used for the present paper are made up of student group-work discussions and lectures from twelve different departments[1], totaling to 70 hours of recordings (28 hours of classroom group-work, 42 hours of lectures, captures an estimate of 502 000 words). There are a total of twenty different first language backgrounds, namely Arabic, Catalan, Chinese, English, Finnish, French, German, Greek, Icelandic, Italian, Persian/Farsi, Polish, Punjabi, Russian, Serbian, Somali, Spanish, Swedish, Turkish and Uzbek, in alphabetical order. 50% of the students were exchange students from different countries, 25% were ethnically Swedish and another 25% were ethnically non-Swedish, i.e. residents in Sweden who have another home language than Swedish. When it comes to lecturers, 54% were Swedish and 46%, speakers of other languages. None of the foreign languages in the material dominated over another one. A total of 63 speakers were recorded for the investigation. The recorded speech events have been divided up into two categories as 'monologic' and 'dialogic', thereby taking interactivity into consideration as in the ELFA corpus (English as a Lingua Franca in Academic Settings, cf. Mauranen 2003). The present paper refers to the lectures as 'monologic' speech events and student group-work as 'dialogic'.

The lectures[2] and student group-work sessions were digitally recorded and all analyzed for the present project. The recording stage was accompanied by observation with a protocol, which will be discussed later on in the paper.

Compared to working with a corpus that is already available for utilization, compiling what Swales calls a "specialized micro corpus" (2002), is often a time-consuming and complex endeavor. However, for a task of this kind, it was necessary to have a specialized corpus rather than a broader corpus. Since variability is a characteristic of ELF situations, it is important to have a subset of users and look at their usage closely. This created some challenges; it was not possible or feasible to transcribe all the recordings within the scope of this investigation in an individual research project of this scale. This work investigated a large corpus extensively, but analyzed a subset of it intensively. The combination of extensive and intensive analyses allowed the study both to outline general practices in morphosyntactic usage by the subjects and to give more detailed information, using the subset of the large material to achieve the latter.

Only data from authentic high-stakes technical speech have been used in the present investigation. All the recordings were obtained from content courses. A small comparative corpus from language courses at the same university (within the same study but not included in this paper) has indicated that, quite naturally, students have a completely different focus in language courses and their production is highly dependent on this focus with the extra attention they pay to linguistic forms. Another important issue, and quite possibly another strength of the present investigation, is the inclusion of two different genres. Group-work has been included in the investigation. Recording group-work sessions is much more complex than monologic speech events in general, and requires a great deal of coordination. They are worth the effort however; such highly interactive speech events are immensely rich in terms of examples of usage, reveal considerable data that are not necessarily observable in other speech events, and therefore, useful discoveries are likely to be made through investigation of such authentic speech. Apart from the ELFA corpus, authentic group-work as a genre has been almost ignored in the research into spoken university registers (cf. Biber et al. 2002, 9).

4. Methods and Results

In this section, the methods and the results of both dimensions of the present study will be presented.

4.1. Dimension 1: Form

The present corpus resembles the ELFA corpus in several ways (see Mauranen 2006b; Mauranen & Ranta 2008). The first resemblance has to do with the authentic data as discussed in the previous section. It deals with different genres and has a large number of first language backgrounds. There are naturally differences as well since ELFA is a macro corpus and the present corpus a specialized micro corpus. ELFA is a large-scale project, being a product of a team of scholars. Unlike ELFA, the present corpus is not accessible by other parties since the subjects were assured of this during the compilation stage.

In order to describe morphosyntactic usage in this lingua franca setting and examine the commonalities, the material was checked for non-standard and non-prescriptive features. The recording stage was accompanied by observation with a protocol. During the listening stage, timed notes were made, so the features of interest were retrieved with ease. The exact points were opened in separate Audacity windows for further investigation if necessary. All the occurrences of morphosyntactic non-standard usage from the group-work sessions and lectures were identified, noted down and transcribed.

To ensure the accuracy of this procedure, there were a minimum of three full listenings of each recording to make sure all the potential non-standard features present were included in the investigation. Quite naturally, there were ambiguous cases. There are differences of what is standard and therefore acceptable even within varieties of native

Englishes. In such doubtful cases, the feature was not included as a case of non-standard usage. An example of such a case is 'travels slower', i.e. using 'slower' instead of the standard adverb form 'more slowly'. 'Travels slower' occurs in standard usage and native speaker discourse although the prescriptive form is 'travels more slowly', where an adverb is used to describe how the action is performed.

In the next stage, the following criteria were applied: a feature had to be used by different speakers of different first language backgrounds, in different types of speech events and for a minimum of ten times in order to be regarded as a commonality in the material. The ones that matched the criteria were subsequently grouped as 'Morphological' or 'Syntactic' features. The findings in the syntactic category were then divided into phrase and clause levels, (PL) and (CL), and the phrase level was further divided into 'Noun phrase' (NP) and 'Verb phrase' (VP). This was done to avoid an accumulation of incidental findings since investigating corpora can result in incidentalism (Swales 2002).

It is obvious that a single researcher cannot categorize all forms as non-standard or standard in an intersubjectively valid way. To overcome this problem and check for outright error and oversight, four lectures and four student group-work sessions, each around 45 minutes, were fully transcribed. These texts had already been surveyed by the researcher and the results established. A second linguist then applied the same criteria without reference to the results already established, and resurveyed the material. The two judges together had standardization meetings. The aim of the meetings was to estimate the rate of error in the analyses as a whole. Three lecture and group-work sessions were fully transcribed, analyzed and discussed, false negative and positives were determined, and out of all the cases of non-standard usage, the error rate was calculated as approximately 12%. So what have been included as data in the present investigation have been cases that clearly diverged from prescriptive L1 forms.

The non-standardness was categorized into syntactic deviation and morphology. Syntactic non-standardness was further classified according to level, into those which formed deviant phrases and those in which deviation was only apparent at the clause level. In the following, the findings on both morphological and syntactic features are presented.

4.1.1. Morphology

In the morphological part, the commonalities are 'Non-standard word formations', 'Analytic comparative' and 'Non-standard plural forms/Countability'. The speakers produce non-standard forms in word formation as in (1) and (2):

(1) There is **discriminization** against women engineers in our society (PLEL-21-2)[3]
(2) Today I am going to try to **levelize** the knowledge here (FARE-RENEW-21-1)

the analytic comparative as in (3) and (4):

(3) It's **more easy** to find a matrix B which creates the recommendations... (BODA-120207-4)
(4) It's **more cheap** to build hydropower station. (SATH-RENEW-18-3)

and non-standard plural forms/countability as in (5) and (6):

(5) **how many hydrogen** you have around these carbons. (FARE-21-1)
(6) One unit has **very much disadvantages**. (BAAN-RENEW-25-1)

4.1.2. Syntax

Phrase level: Noun phrase

At the phrase level, starting with the noun phrase (NP), the features found comprise 'Not marking the plural on the noun', 'Non-standard usage of articles', and 'Double comparatives/superlatives'.

Not marking the plural on the noun

'Not marking the plural on the noun' is a significant type of non-standard usage especially in the present domain since expressing quantity and using quantity bundles (Biber 2006, 170-171) and units are frequent features of engineering discourse. The speakers in this investigation seem to indicate the plural meaning merely by numerals, adverbs or determiners before the noun but leave the noun itself without a declension. Some examples of this are given below (7)-(11):

(7) Above **500 meter** you have to consider Pelton turbines. (BA-RW-2)
(8) Typically you want to have **5 kilogram** oxygen. (KA-RW-13-2)
(9) ...**two different reactor**: reactor X and reactor Y. (VP-190407)
(10) He said you can reduce from **8000 hour** per year to **6000 hour** per year. (VP-200407-2)
(11) In the literature you can find the **two definition** for the word 'coal'.

(FR-RW-22-3)

and (12)-(13):

(12) because we would need **all the detail** from the new equipments… (VP-200407-2)
(13) You can actually compare **several process** and improve the use of the utilization and make it more… (SM-RW-11-1)

It is possible that some of the –s's were omitted to avoid difficult consonant clusters. For example, Chinese speakers often have problems with the plural ending *–s*, e.g. in *parts*.

Article usage

Also, non-standard usage of articles is common, as exemplified in (14)-(17):

(14) This is a typical comparison between **a** old runner and a new runner. (BA-RW-25-2)
(15) **The** Einstein… (KA-RW-16-1)
(16) Pure hydrogen comes from **the** natural gas. (PM-RW-23-1)
(17) So question, what is renewables? Anybody can define **the** renewability? (FR-RW-21-1)

Zero article is another common non-standardness as exemplified in (18)-(20):

(18) From those figures, you can have **Ø** idea what reasonable speed runner size… (BA-RW-25-2)
(19) Who has paid for the infrastructure? That's always **Ø** interesting question. (PL-111006-3)
(20) L2 is **Ø** liquid. (OJ-080207-3)

Double comparatives and superlatives

There are also examples of 'double comparatives/superlatives' in the material such as:

(21) I would say this one here is much **more safer** and much **more wider**. (HEHE-RENEW-10-2)
(22) The generator gets **more and more bigger**. (ACTH-RENEW-18-1)
(23) …the **most cheapest** available biowaste… (ACTH-RENEW-4-1)

Phrase level: Verb phrase

The main cases of non-standard usage in the verb phrase (VP) are 'Lack of Subject-verb agreement', 'Tense and aspect issues' and 'Non-standard usage of passive voice'.

Lack of subject-verb agreement

To start with, there are many cases of lack of subject-verb agreement in the material, a feature often found in L2 speech. The material in the present study has examples of this (24)-(28):

(24) **People gets** mad because they want water there. (KA-RW-13-1)
(25) That's what essentially the **electrons does**. (KA-RW-16-1)
(26) So you end up with **a nice mechanism which do not** really contain the surface (PL-021006-2)
(27) I call this A, which is a function of past history, what **a catalyst have seen** in its life. (PL-111006-3)
(28) One of the drawbacks is the amount of fluid **this require**. (SM-RW-11-2)

Tense and aspect issues

The overuse of the progressive in ELF settings has been reported on before as a common feature of non-standardness in ELF (Ranta 2006). However, this is not a feature unique to ELF settings. It is also observed in interlanguage and has been on the increase in general for several hundred years (Smitterberg 2005). The speakers in the present context often produce utterances referring to scientific or technical phenomena that are always true or valid, and despite this, they use the progressive instead of the simple form, as in (29)-(33):

(29) And this **is showing** a Kaplan turbine. (BA-RW-25-2)
(30) In water turbines the water **is flowing** along buckets before it leaves the runner. (BA-RW-25-2)
(31) But **is that increase reflecting** that we are dealing with a limited resource? (HH-RW-10-1).
(32) Do you understand **how this is working** not what it is but how it is working? (WJ-140906-2)
(33) According to United Nations majority of the world's population **is living** in large city areas. (PL-RW-8-1)

Passive voice

Although used frequently in engineering discourse, passive voice is rare in spoken university registers (Biber 2006, 65). Correspondingly, there are few occurrences of deviant passive voice in the present material but enough to be included in the study. See the examples below (34)-(37):

(34) I think it's a rather huge **project that built** underground. (PE-120207-1)
(35) Certain steels **are not corrode** very quickly in alcohol environment. (PM-RW-23-1)
(36) **Are we asking** in the computer lab to to find the minimum mass. (BODA-050207)
(37) **What does it mean by** molar fraction vapor (OJ080207-2)

Clause level

The second main section in the syntactic analysis is the investigation of the clause level. At this level, there are three interesting cases of non-standard usage, namely 'Non-standard question formulation', 'Word Order' and 'Negation'.

Non-standard question formulation

To start with, there are numerous cases of non-standard question formulation in the corpus as shown in (38)-(45), observed both in Wh- and Yes/No questions:

(38) Why is such a difference in the diagram here between the blue and the red then? (HH-RW-10-1)
(39) How many pages we have now? (PE-120207-1)
(40) What means two pages? (EC-090307-2)
(41) Which kind of the vortex we should have? (AP-190407-1)
(42) Why has ASTRA 18 hours? (AP-200407-2)
(43) So from which point you started? (EC-090307-1)
(44) So anybody can read the first sentence? (FR-RW-22-1)
(45) Where is written or you know why does the question come up? (BODA-050207)

So speakers in ELF contexts sometimes seem to disregard question word order and ask questions mainly by using interrogative pronouns e.g. what, why in Wh- questions and follow the affirmative sentence word order in Yes/No questions. This type of usage is found mainly in the dialogic material in the present study as in group-work, speakers often raise questions to complete the task whereas in lectures, it is not so often that the lecturer directs questions to the floor. This type of deviance differs from all others discussed here since it is the only one that sometimes disturbs communication and leads to repetition and rephrasing in some cases.

Word order issues

The next point deals with word order issues. Although some of the instances here seem to deal with reported questions, they were categorized in this way since they were in declarative constructions. The material has examples of non-standard word order, most of which have to do with indirectness and speech subordination such as in (46)-(51):

(46) The system shows what kind of a system **are you going** to be using. (KA-RW-13-1)
(47) Salinity can affect what kind of material **can you use** and what type of X **can you use**. (SM-RW-11-1)
(48) So that's more or less what **was it**. (SM-RW-19-1)
(49) You are welcome to see how **does it work**. (FR-RW-21-2)
(50) You get a feeling of **how is the cost developing** for wind power. (AT-RW-4-1)
(51) We can't judge how solid **is the ground**. (ST-RW-17-2)

Negation

Another quite interesting area is the relatively high frequency of unraised negation. Not raising negation from the subordinate clause to the main clause and not incorporating it in the verb phrase seem to be common especially in the dialogic material (52)-(55) with some examples also in the monologic material, (56)-(57):

(52) This point is supposed to **not** move. (BD-050207-3)
(53) It looks **not** good. (PE-120207-1)
(54) But that caught fire **not** because of the hydrogen. (HH-RW-10-1)
(55) Do you have any nons that lead **not** to zero here? (EC-090307-3)
(56) It has **not** always a low complexity. (HH-RW-10-1)
(57) It is a **not** very good generator. (ST-RW-17-1)

4.1.3. Dimension 1: Summary of Results

It cannot be argued that the features reported here are necessarily unique to a lingua franca context. A corpus of native speech would probably turn up some of these features as well. The number of occurrences for each feature exemplified above is shown in Table 1.

Table 1. The number of occurrences of the non-standard morphosyntactic features found both in the dialogic and monologic corpus.

			Features	**Dialogic**	**Monologic**	**Σ**
MORPHOLOGY			NonS word forms	10	6	16
			NonS analytic comparative	16	18	34
			NonS Plural forms	22	33	55
SYNTAX	**PL**	**NP**				
			Not marking the plural on the noun	39	156	195
			NonS article usage	37	178	215
			Double comparative/ superlatives	16	8	24
		VP				
			Subject-verb disagreement	57	135	192
			NonS tense and aspect	34	135	169
			NonS passive voice	11	14	25
	CL					
			NonS question formulation	59	20	79
			NonS word order	23	32	55
			NonS negation	17	13	30

4.2. Dimension 2: Communicativeness

At this stage, communicativeness was investigated through examining overt disturbance, clarification of discourse and irritation by listeners.

4.2.1. Overt Disturbance

In this part of the study, communication breakdowns were investigated. Whether a feature is 'disturbing' or 'non-disturbing', indicating respectively 'causing overt comprehension problems' or 'causing no comprehension problems' was looked into.

The sound files were carefully examined through listening. The surrounding discourse and the questions raised were paid attention to since they are important indicators of disturbance in communication. Overt comprehension problems are relatively easy to spot in student group-work. Problems in communication generally result in questions raised by the students working together on a given task. Even if they choose not to reveal problems in comprehension, miscommunication or lack of comprehension becomes apparent at a later stage of the group-work since, in such an event, they fail to get to the intended outcome, e.g. solving the problem assigned to them. Lectures are, however, much harder, if not impossible, to analyze when it comes to comprehension. The present study relies on the questions raised during lectures by the students, which are infrequent.

As briefly touched upon in the methods section, in spite of the divergence from standard forms, very few cases of overt disturbance were found in the investigation. More significantly, among all the forms analyzed closely, only non-standard formulation of questions resulted in communication breakdown. Also, this could only be detected in the dialogic material (See Björkman 2008 for a discussion of the results regarding the dialogic material exclusively). In some cases, such constructions were followed by questions, leading to the repetition of the same form or a form that slightly differs from the first uttered form, paraphrasing of the question or self-correction as in (58), (59), (60) and (61) respectively:

(58)
<S1> in the outlet , what we have in the outlet </S1>
<S2> mhm , huh </S2>
<S1> in the outlet what we have </S1>
<S2> (xx) </S2> (OJ-080207-1)

(59)
<S1> why it is black </S1>
<S2> huh </S2>
<S1> why it is black </S1> (OJ-080207- 4)

(60)
<S1> how is the length of this <P:03> i mean how many pages you will work on this , i mean if you count for how much part in your work </S1>
<S2> ahh , just two or three pages i think </S2> (PLEL1060207-1)

(61)
<S1> it is given </S1>
<S2> huh </S2>
<S1> is it given </S1>
<S2> yes </S2> (OJ-080207-3)

4.2.2. Analysis at the Discourse Level

After the investigation of non-standard morphosyntactic forms, the emphasis was put on the discourse level for further examination. This part of the investigation was designed subsequent to the completion of the first stage, which revealed very few cases of communication breakdown caused by divergence from standard morphosyntactic forms.

Because communication seemed to take place virtually without much breakdown despite frequent and considerable divergence from standard forms, it was quite likely that there were discourse strategies where meaning was negotiated or clarified among the speakers. To reach a better understanding of the material at hand, four lectures and four group-work sessions (each 45-50 minutes long) were analyzed in depth to look into the number of occurrences of clarification strategies used by the speakers.

The investigation of discourse level revealed some examples of number and types of clarification. Penz's study (2008) on multicultural, English-medium seminars at the European Center for modern languages has been followed as a model here because her data shows parallelisms with the data and methods in the present project: the multicultural nature of the setting, using a micro and specialized corpus, the incorporation of group-work discussions, and the data collection methods (participant observation and recording). Clarification of terms and concepts, details, comment on intent, clarification of/metadiscursive comment on discourse structure, discourse context and common ground have been looked into along with backchanneling and repetition (cf. Cogo and Dewey 2006) and point abandonment. The results are shown in Table 2:

Table 2. Types of clarification in sample lectures (L) and group-work sessions (G).

DISCOURSE FEATURES	L1	L2	L3	L4	G1	G2	G3	G4	Σ
Clarification of terms and concepts	3	1	3	1	-	4	-	-	12
Clarification of details and content of task	-	26	9	16	6	5	15	33	110
Metadiscursive comment on discourse structure	1	9	4	5	13	3	3	-	38
Metadiscursive comment on discourse context	9	10	12	11	12	35	8	-	97
Metadiscursive comment on intent	3	8	1	1	11	4	4	-	32
Metadiscursive comment on common ground	60	64	17	-	26	68	76	63	374
Backchannelling					57	177	174	88	496
Repetition (other)					11	19	7	8	45
Point abandonment	-	-	-	-	-	-	-	-	-

All the strategies mentioned above were more frequent in group-work than in lectures, the most frequent being clarification of common ground, content, task or topic. The following are some examples (62)-(69):

Clarification of terms and concepts

(62) what is steam reforming , this is as i already mentioned a very very commercial way to produce hydrogen (PEMI-RENEW-23)

Clarification of details and content of task

(63) i don't know if we're supposed to know the code during the lab i think we're just supposed to know it so we can model it later (BODA-00407)

Metadiscursive comment on intent

(64) yeah i just wanted him to repeat that (PEAV-200407)

Metadiscursive comment on discourse structure / labeling speech acts

(65) first we went through the time frame (PEAV-200407)

Metadiscursive comment on discourse content

(66) yeah that's my question (BODA-050207)

Metadiscursive comment on common ground

(67) we have to check the distillation process (PEAV-200407)

Backchanneling

(68)
<S2> it means we can only have flutter results with computers </S2>
<S3> yeah </S3> (BODA-050207)

Repetition

(69)
<S1> so you just put a mass without any stiffness </S1>
<S2> without any stiffness </S2> (BODA-050207)

4.2.3. Irritation Study

This part of the study is different from the other parts with regard to data collection. The data came from a lab situation and not an authentic communication setting. However, it was important to get data on irritation since constant irritation can adversely affect communication. It was suggested as early as in the 1980s that comprehensibility and irritation are "intricately linked" (Ludwig 1982).

When investigating attitudes and irritation in general, the problem the researcher faces is that the object is not overtly observable. This requires a subjective data collection method, namely surveys and questionnaires where the subject himself/herself expresses an opinion on the point of investigation. In this study, whether a feature is 'irritating' or 'non-irritating' was investigated to examine attitudes and listener-friendliness using the data that were obtained through a survey, which is in a way a 'tolerance test'.

The survey was designed subsequent to the investigation of the non-standard morphosyntactic structures that were discovered in the first stage of the investigation. Two to three examples of each structure, a total of 34 utterances, were recorded into Audacity by different speakers[4]. Because most authentic utterances included more than one non-standard example of morphosyntactic usage, some non-standardness was removed in some of the re-recorded utterances. Only one non-standard example of usage per utterance was left in order to direct the respondents to a certain structure.

Two non-native speakers of English with moderate non-native accents were chosen to read the sentences into Audacity for recording. One of the speakers was a native speaker of Swedish with a slight Swedish accent, and the other, a native speaker of German with a slight German accent. These two speakers were chosen to be representative of the type of English that is most frequently heard in the setting. In order to avoid getting responses on accents instead of the inquired morphosyntax, some groups listened to Speaker A and some, Speaker B, who read the same sentences from the material. The number of groups listening to each speaker was kept equal.

In the administering stage, content courses with English as the language of instruction were selected. The classes were given brief information about the present research project, and they all agreed to spend some of the classroom time on this survey (convenience sampling). The respondents, a total of 100, were all volunteers; they simply listened to the sentences and ticked the corresponding answer on the questionnaire sheet under perceived communicativeness and irritation. Extra space was provided for those who wanted to write down additional comments (see Appendix). Table 3 below shows each feature and one hundred respondents' answers.

The columns 'Perfectly OK' and 'Comprehensible but wrong' have been merged in the 'Communicativeness' results. Similarly, the columns 'Not irritating' and 'Somewhat irritating' have been merged under 'Irritation'. This was done in case the respondents had been steered towards irritation in the experiment for legibility.

Table 3. Results of the irritation survey in percentages.

Feature	**Communicativeness**		**Irritation**	
	Comprehensible (either 'Perfectly OK' or 'Comprehensible but wrong')	Incomprehensible	No irritation (either 'Not irritating at all' or 'Somewhat irritating')	Very irritating
Word order	71	29	72	28
Question formulation	83	17	77	23
Countability/Plural forms	80	20	80	20
Passive voice	80	20	81	19
Negation	89	11	81	18
Subject-verb agreement	73	27	85	15
Analytic comparative	80	20	86	14
Articles	76	24	87	13
NonS word formulation	85	15	88	12
Tense usage	81	19	90	10
Double comparatives/ superlatives	97	3	91	9
Not marking the plural	88	12	91	9

The category 'very irritating' is not a frequent answer. However, it seems to indicate a general pattern of irritation, which can be observed in the table above. The table has been sorted according to what the respondents thought were very irritating, from the highest to the lowest figure. It is interesting that non-standard question formulation, which is the only feature that seems to disturb communication, is also high up on the irritation scale. The only feature that is more irritating than non-standard question formulation is word order. Both these categories are actually concerned with the order of constituents.

Respondents who expressed their irritation towards the divergent forms reported here wrote comments like the ones below on the questionnaire sheet, in the space provided for comments:

> I feel my comprehension of all these incorrect sentences is problem-free, but it is quite annoying with such basic grammar mistakes and I hope I won't have lecturers with this poor English grammar.

> The teachers' English isn't that good, leading to difficulties listening to what they're saying.
>
> I wish those giving lectures in English would go through some sort of training before taking on something like this.
>
> Understanding bad English is challenging.

The ones who did not find morphosyntactic non-standardness irritating wrote comments like the following two:

> For me the language is not an issue. I only care about the subject itself.
>
> I don't understand what this is about. This sounds like any professor talking that is deep in thought. So as long as you understand it is OK.

It must be mentioned, that in a lab situation, there is certainly more focus on form than there would be in a real-life situation. Nonetheless, it is noticeable that there is some irritation towards non-standard forms.

5. Discussion

The fairly detailed illustration of examples from the materials report from a Swedish ELF setting. This is the first study that looks into an ELF setting in Sweden. There are several insights about spoken ELF discourse in the present study, about the quality and the quantity of non-standard forms, about the discourse structure of sample speech events and speaker reactions towards non-standardness. These results add to the mounting body of evidence which exists today on ELF from different settings.

The results, first of all, indicate that communication takes place without much disturbance in lingua franca settings. The twelve different types of morphosyntactic non-standard usage at word, phrase and clause levels do not impede communication with the exception of non-standard question formation in this engineering setting. This is in line with earlier findings in ELF research from other settings. It is significant that most of the ELF features reported earlier on (e.g. Seidlhofer 2004) are present in this corpus. This seems to indicate that, although ELF is not a variety and ELF speakers have highly diverse backgrounds, code features seem to be similar across different settings. This means that the code features found in highly specialized high-stake environments are the same sort of features found in other LF environments. So there is considerable evidence to suggest that the code features are not affected by the setting and by how high or low the stakes are. There is naturally the proficiency issue. Speaker proficiency affects both the quality and quantity of code features, in that less proficient speakers will have more non-standardness and more types of non-standardness.

What seem to be affected by the situation are pragmatic features. The small-scale investigation of pragmatic features in the present study reveals a considerable number of clarification techniques in the dialogic part of the material. It is possible that, due to the very high stakes, the speakers want to make sure that they understand each other and carry out the task by following the instructions. Differences may be expected in other settings where the stakes are not equally high. The topic avoidance in Meierkord's (1996) study does not seem to be present in this study, which is likely to be due to the very high-stakes nature of the present data. In a task where there is a problem to be solved and a solution to be presented in the form of a presentation or report, topic avoidance is unlikely to take place. Thus the results here show a certain resemblance to Penz's results (2008), which are also based on high-stakes group-work discussions. The only noticeable difference between Penz's results and the results in the present paper seems to be the absence of the clarification of terms in the present study, which can perhaps be explained by the familiarity of the speakers with the field and the task. Since the students here take the same course, receive the same instructions for the task and refer to the same reference materials to carry out the task, they are familiar with the terminology required for the task. With all these, it could be argued that pragmatic features are affected by the nature of lingua franca setting unlike the code features that are not.

The other significant finding is the level of irritation in relation to non-standardness regardless of comprehensibility. The respondents who report irritation are greatly outnumbered by those who do not, and 'very irritating' is not a common answer altogether. However, a remarkably high percentage (See Table 3) of the respondents say that they find certain non-standardness incomprehensible. Among these features is the lack of subject-verb agreement, which is a redundant feature of English and therefore not necessarily critical for actual comprehension. Since redundant features do not generally cause communication breakdown, it is suggested here that such responses are emotive and were caused by the listeners' irritation. This kind of investigation cannot distinguish between responses based on emotion or actual comprehension.

On the basis of these preliminary results, it appears that some respondents do react to these minor and redundant features. There seems to be supportive evidence for this. A study on CLIL (Content and

Language Integrated Learning) that investigated teachers' attitudes towards language inaccuracies found out that content teachers who had no EFL qualifications were irritated by low-level mistakes of redundant features e.g. 3rd person *–s* and said they would correct their students (Dalton-Puffer, forthcoming). On the other hand, teachers with EFL training who teach a second language through the medium of English said they regarded language issues secondary and that they would be more tolerant towards inaccuracies in a content course. Dalton-Puffer's study did not look at students' attitudes but one of the teacher respondents mentioned in an interview that her students are actually more concerned about linguistic correctness than they are given credit for.

The results in the present study indicate that whether students' irritation might interfere with lecturing in ELF more than any actual failure to understand is worth further consideration (see e.g. Suviniitty 2008). Constant irritation might take resources away which would otherwise be given to comprehension processing. Anything we are conscious of can slow down processing and create competition, which in turn will affect the capacity of attentional resources and allocation of attention (Robinson 2003, 633).

6. Conclusion

The present investigation and the compilation of the present corpus was motivated by the pedagogic needs of teachers and students in the present setting who have found themselves in the endeavor of operating in a foreign language. English-medium instruction is on the increase in continental Europe, so the number of lecturers and students in similar settings are finding themselves in very similar circumstances. To be able to understand the demands of such an environment, more work within applied linguistics must be carried out, which in turn will contribute to the common understanding of today's international academia. It is those who need to operate in ELF settings that research should prioritize. Authentic data from real-life contexts that result in research-based theory have potential and actual relevance for daily practice.

It is hoped that the illustration from this engineering setting will be a valuable contribution to the existing knowledge we have regarding ELF usage.

Acknowledgements

I wish to thank my supervisor professor Philip Shaw for the guidance and feedback he provided me with on this paper. I am also grateful to Anna Mauranen and Elina Ranta for their meticulous revision of this paper. Any remaining errors are my own. Special thanks go to the Unit for Language and Communication at the Royal Institute of Technology (Stockholm), especially Margaretha Andolf, for providing financial support for this work.

APPENDIX

QUESTIONNAIRE ON ENGLISH AS A LINGUA FRANCA
Please tick all the appropriate boxes after you have listened to each sentence. You must tick at least one box from each column.

Ex/ Sentence X It is much more clearer than you think.

COMMUNICATIVENESS	ATTITUDES
Sentence X □ Perfectly OK ☑ Comprehensible but wrong □ Incomprehensible	□ Not irritating at all ☑ A bit irritating □ Very irritating

COMMUNICATIVENESS	ATTITUDES
Sentence 1 □ Perfectly OK □ Comprehensible but wrong □ Incomprehensible	□ Not irritating at all □ A bit irritating □ Very irritating
Sentence 2 □ Perfectly OK □ Comprehensible but wrong □ Incomprehensible	□ Not irritating at all □ A bit irritating □ Very irritating
Sentence 3 □ Perfectly OK □ Comprehensible but wrong □ Incomprehensible	□ Not irritating at all □ A bit irritating □ Very irritating
Sentence 4 □ Perfectly OK □ Comprehensible but wrong □ Incomprehensible	□ Not irritating at all □ A bit irritating □ Very irritating
. . [Rows omitted here for brevity] .	

Sentence 32 □ Perfectly OK □ Comprehensible but wrong □ Incomprehensible	□ Not irritating at all □ A bit irritating □ Very irritating
Sentence 33 □ Perfectly OK □ Comprehensible but wrong □ Incomprehensible	□ Not irritating at all □ A bit irritating □ Very irritating
Sentence 34 □ Perfectly OK □ Comprehensible but wrong □ Incomprehensible	□ Not irritating at all □ A bit irritating □ Very irritating

What is/are your native language/s?

____

Any other comments:

____

Thank you very much for your cooperation.

Bibliography

Biber, D. 2006. *University Language: A Corpus-Based Study of Spoken and Written Registers*. Amsterdam: John Benjamins.

Biber, D., S. Conrad, R. Reppen, P. Byrd and M. Helt 2002. "Speaking and Writing in the University: A Multidimensional Comparison." *TESOL Quarterly* 36 (1), 9-48.

Björkman, B. 2008. "'So where we are': Spoken Lingua Franca English at a Swedish Technical University." *English Today* 24 (2), 11-17.

Breiteneder, A. 2005. "The Naturalness of English as a European Lingua Franca: The Case of the 'Third Person –s'." *VIenna English Working PaperS* 14 (2), 3-26.

Cogo, A. and M. Dewey 2006. "Efficiency in ELF Communication: From Pragmatic Motives to Lexico-Grammatical Innovation." *Nordic Journal of English Studies* 5 (2), 59-93.

Dalton-Puffer, C. (forthc.) "Outcomes and Processes in Content and Language Integrated Learning (CLIL): Current Research in Europe." In *Future Perspectives for English Language Teaching*, ed. W. Delanoy & L. Volkmann. Heidelberg: Carl Winter.

ELFA corpus. English as a lingua France in Academic Settings. http://www.eng.helsinki.fi/elfa/elfacorpus.htm (accessed May 26, 2009)

Firth, A. 1996. "The Discursive Accomplishment of Normality: On 'Lingua Franca' English and Conversation Analysis." *Journal of Pragmatics* 26 (2), 237-59.

Firth, A. and J. Wagner 1997. "On Discourse, Communication, and (Some) Fundamental Concepts in SLA Research." *Modern Language Journal* 81 (3), 285-300.

House, J. 2002. "Developing Pragmatic Competence in English as a Lingua Franca." In *Lingua Franca Communication*, ed. K. Knapp and C. Meierkord, 245-69. Frankfurt: Peter Lang.

Jenkins, J. 2000. *The Phonology of English as an International Language*. Oxford: Oxford University Press.

Lesznyák, Á. 2004. *Communication in English as an International Lingua Franca. An Exploratory Case Study*. Norderstedt: Books on Demand GmbH.

Ludwig, J. 1982. "Native-Speaker Judgments of Second-Language Learners' Efforts at Communication: A Review." *Modern Language Journal* 66 (3), 274-83.

Mauranen, A. 2006a. "Signaling and Preventing Misunderstanding in English as Lingua Franca Communication." *International Journal of the Sociology of Language* 177, 123-50.
—. 2006b. "A Rich Domain of ELF: The ELFA Corpus of Academic Discourse." *Nordic Journal of English Studies* 5 (2), 145-59.
—. 2003. "The Corpus of English as Lingua Franca in Academic Settings." *TESOL Quarterly* 37 (3), 513-27.
Mauranen, A. and E. Ranta 2008. "English as an Academic Lingua Franca—The ELFA Project." *Nordic Journal of English Studies* 7 (3), 199-202.
Meierkord, C. 2004. "Syntactic Variation in Interactions Across International Englishes." *English World-Wide* 25 (1), 109-32.
—. 2000. "Interpreting Successful Lingua Franca Interaction: An Analysis of Non-Native/Non-Native Small Talk Conversations in English." *Linguistik Online 5*. http://www.linguistikonline.com/1_00/ index.htm. (accessed June 5, 2005)
—. 1998. "Lingua Franca English: Characteristics of Successful Non-Native–Non-Native Speaker Discourse." *Erfurt Electronic Studies in English 1998*. http://webdoc.sub.gwdg.de/edoc/ia/eese/eese.html. (accessed June 5, 2005)
—. 1996. *Englisch als Medium der interkulturellen Kommunikation. Untersuchungen zum non-native-/non-native speaker—Diskurs*. Frankfurt am Main: Lang.
Penz, H. 2008. "'What do we mean by that?'—ELF in Intercultural Project Work." Paper presented at the *ESSE conference*, University of Aarhus, August 22-26, 2008.
Ranta, E. 2006. "The 'Attractive' Progressive—Why Use the *–ing* Form in English as a Lingua Franca?" *Nordic Journal of English Studies* 5 (2), 95-116.
Robinson, P. 2003. "Attention and Memory during SLA." In *The Handbook of Second Language Acquisition*, ed. C. H. Doughty & M. H. Long, 631-79. Oxford: Blackwell Publishing.
Seidlhofer, B. 2004. "Research Perspectives on Teaching English as a Lingua Franca." *Annual Review of Applied Linguistics* 24, 209-39.
Smitterberg, E. 2005. *The Progressive in 19th-Century English. A Process of Integration*. Amsterdam: Rodopi.
Suviniitty, J. 2008. "Good, Poor, or Excellent—Students' Perception of Lecturers' English and Comprehension of Lectures." In *The 2nd International Multi-Conference on Society, Cybernetics and Informatics: Proceedings Volume IV*, ed. F. Welsch, F. Malpica, A. Tremante, J. Vicente Carrasquero & A. Oropeza, 187-90. Winter

Garden, Florida: International Institute of Informatics and Systematics (IIIS).

Swales, J. 2002. "Integrated and Fragmented Worlds: EAP Materials and Corpus Linguistics." In *Academic Discourse*, ed. J. Flowerdew, 150-164. Harlow, UK: Longman.

VOICE corpus. The Vienna-Oxford International Corpus of English (version 1.0 online). http://voice.univie.ac.at (accessed May 26, 2009).

Wächter, B. and F. Maiworm 2008. English Taught Programmes in European Higher Education. Bonn: Lemmens.

Notes

[1] Sustainable Energy Engineering; Sustainable Technology; Energy Technology; Machine Design; Communication Systems; Computer and Systems Science; Electronic, Computer and Software Systems; Chemical Engineering and Technology; Chemical Reaction Engineering; Transport Phenomena; Energy Processes; Aeronautical and Vehicle Engineering.

[2] Ten of the lecture recordings come from already recorded lectures from one of the departments.

[3] The corpus uses special codes for each speaker and recording, all based on pseudonyms that cannot be tracked down to the speakers' identities.

[4] These speakers were not among the subjects but were academics working at the same university.

PART III:

FEATURES OF ELF IN INTERACTIVE DISCOURSE

ACCOMMODATING DIFFERENCE IN ELF CONVERSATIONS: A STUDY OF PRAGMATIC STRATEGIES

ALESSIA COGO

1. Introduction

It is now commonly known that in today's global world and globalised societies people often use English with other bilinguals in lingua franca communication. English as a Lingua Franca (ELF) speakers conduct various communicative tasks, from business meetings, academic presentations, service transactions to casual chat and small talk, in a language that is neither their L1 nor the L1 of most of their interlocutors. These speakers, who come from different linguistic and cultural backgrounds, have to operate efficiently in diverse and fluid situations, where the common ground cannot be presumed and diversity needs to be negotiated locally. Their challenge is managing difference in communication and finding out how speakers negotiate differences in conversation. One way speakers can do this is to change their speech patterns to resemble those of their interlocutors, e.g. through other-repetition or code-switching.

Adapting one's speech or altering it for certain communicative purposes concerns the phenomenon of accommodation, i.e. the process by which speakers adjust their communicative behaviour to that of their interlocutors in order to facilitate communication. This paper discusses the accommodation strategies that speakers employ in order to adapt to the communicative situation they find themselves in, that is, to accommodate to their interlocutors, for communicative efficiency and cooperation. Such purposes may not be the only ones, though. In the conclusion to this paper I suggest that ELF speakers may strategically use repetition and code-switching in terms of signalling affiliation to their community, and these may be two of the possible accommodation strategies that identify them as members of one of the multilingual ELF communities.

In this paper, I provide a brief overview of accommodation research in ELF pragmatics, concentrating on the studies that have looked at cooperative, convergent strategies. Then I analyse some examples of naturally occurring communication in an ELF community and focus on accommodation strategies, such as other-repetition and code-switching.

2. The Focus: Accommodation Strategies in ELF Pragmatics

Research on ELF pragmatics has spawned quite a good number of studies which have dealt with a wide range of issues in various settings. From academic and business communication to small talk, ELF pragmatic research has covered the negotiation of non-understanding, the use of interactional features, discourse markers and code-switching (for an overview see Seidlhofer, Breiteneder & Pitzl 2006).

That all speakers need to cooperate to make communication work goes without saying, and the interest here lies in finding out what strategies they use to suit different communicative conditions. Basically, accommodation is concerned with the different ways of adjusting speech to facilitate communication. Research in social psychology (Giles & Coupland 1991, Giles et al. 1987) has looked into how this is done, especially the tendency to change one's speech to make it more intelligible or sometimes converge one's spoken habits to resemble those of one's interlocutors.

Jenkins (2000) has investigated ELF phonology and, when proposing the Lingua Franca Core, she has underlined how this would help to preserve phonological intelligibility, but, by itself, would not be enough. Jenkins argues that "speakers need to develop the ability to adjust their pronunciation according to the communicative situation in which they find themselves" (2000, 166) and she points out how using certain phonological features depends crucially on who is talking with whom, and not on the imitation of native speakers' pronunciation. She also goes on to highlight how accommodation is key for successful ELF pronunciation. Accommodating to certain shared variants in the local context, rather than conforming to some ideal notion of correctness, may not only ensure intelligibility between interlocutors, but also signal solidarity between them.

Accommodation also figures as a way of overcoming possible difficulties in naturally occurring conversations and the area of problematic talk has provided interesting results for ELF communication. Though supposedly predisposed to misunderstandings because of the variety of lingua-cultures involved, ELF communication displays surprisingly few problematic moments, and the participants show skilful use of various strategies to prevent non-understanding and ensure the smooth running of talk (Cogo 2007; Cogo & Dewey 2006; Kaur, this volume). Research has also shown how ELF speakers deal with non-understanding appropriately in a range of situations: business meetings (Pitzl 2005), academic exchanges (Mauranen 2006a) and casual conversations (Meierkord 2000). Initial findings have demonstrated how adapting to the interlocutor's linguistic and cultural expectations can be used to pre-empt a possible cause of misunderstanding.

Mauranen (2007), for instance, has investigated ELF speech in academic communities in Europe and has highlighted how speakers "engage in a variety of adaptive strategies, among which cooperation and explicitness hold an important place." (Mauranen 2007, 257). Three main strategies emerge from Mauranen's ELFA corpus: self-rephrasing, negotiating topic and discourse reflexivity. Self-rephrasing, as a change of the original utterance by the same speaker, has been found to be used more often as an adjustment of form, rather than a change of meaning. These adjustments then, by following immediately the original phrasing, are aimed at improving clarity and increasing explicitness. For example,

> the poor nutrition level this poor diet
> (Mauranen 2007, 251)

is a straightforward reformulation of the original utterance ("the poor nutrition level") by the same speaker, which retains the meaning while changing the form.

Negotiating topic is also used as a way of making discourse explicit and clearer to the interlocutor. In this strategy, the speaker would introduce a new topic or referent by using a noun phrase and a coreferential subject pronoun. For instance:

> Estonia and Latvia **they** have this problem with Russian minority (ibid., 253).

Here the explicitness is created by a feature of spoken grammar that is particularly frequent in the ELFA corpus (Mauranen 2006b). Similarly, explicitness and clarity can be favoured by using discourse reflexivity, as in:

> I would like to ask about what do you mean about (ibid., 256),

where the use of "ask" makes explicit that a question is following, and helps in organising the ongoing exchange.

Like Jenkins's participants in the ELF phonology research, Mauranen's speakers adapt their speech to the communicative situation, rather than moulding it to resemble the native speaker ideal. As Mauranen points out, ELF speakers make use of these strategies as "a way of overcoming linguistic and cultural barriers in the situation" (2007, 257) and they promote "communicative clarity by making utterances more explicit" (ibid., 258). All these examples of explicitness, clarification and pre-empting strategies are ways in which speakers change their linguistic and cultural patterns to make communication as intelligible as possible to their interlocutors. This way, ELF speakers are sensitive to linguistic and cultural differences that might create misunderstanding, and therefore are prone to taking certain steps in order to avoid possible misunderstanding at the onset. In other words, not only have ELF speakers been found to deal with potentially problematic situations carefully and appropriately, but they also use pragmatic strategies to enhance their communication.

In addition, Mauranen's study concentrates on self-repetition, instead of other-repetition, where the participants change their own speech completely or partially as a way of anticipating moments of non-understanding in communication, or as a way of making explicit and framing what they are going to say to avoid potential non-understanding. Similarly to Mauranen's research, where speakers accommodate to their interlocutors in pre-empting moves, my research deals with other-repetition as an accommodation strategy together with code-switching, as two of the more commonly found pragmatic strategies within my transcribed data.

In the remainder of this paper, I will explore how ELF speakers skilfully make appropriate and extensive use of accommodation strategies for cooperation and engagement, but also to enhance efficiency of communication, i.e. to allow their exchanges to be more intelligible than if they had referred to "standard native-speakers' norms".

Before I move on to the analysis of some examples of naturally occurring ELF conversations, I will briefly describe the corpus and the participants involved.

3. The Data and Participants

This research constitutes a case study of an ELF community of practice (Wenger 1998, Seidlhofer 2007) whose members are teachers of modern foreign languages, coming from various cultural backgrounds and working together in an institution of higher education. The community members regularly collaborate, negotiate, and create a common identity as they interact. As groups of people sharing common interests and coming together for certain periods of time to engage in particular activities, communities of practice is a notion describing collectivity which seeks to avoid essentialisations. In this research, the concept of "community of practice" helps to frame the discourse activities and conventions of this group, which may not be intelligible or acceptable within the dominant ideology of that institution, and at the same time offers the opportunity to observe and understand precisely those discourse activities in context.

The exchanges collected are mainly casual conversations, the kind of small talk that has no immediate work-related purpose (Eggins & Slade 1997), and, though the participants are colleagues and see each other more frequently in their work-environment, the interactions that constitute the data are recorded during social events or breaks from work.

In terms of methodology, the conversations were transcribed using conversation analytic tools complemented by an ethnographic perspective (Gumperz 1999). The conversation analytic approach was deemed as the most appropriate to analyse data constituted exclusively by naturally occurring conversations, as its focus on the turn-by-turn description of the conversation "machinery" allows for a more emic perspective (Seedhouse 2004), with the focus on the participants' co-construction of meaning in interaction. However, because of the closeness of the researcher to the community and access to its participants, a "pure" conversion analytic approach did not seem appropriate, and an ethnographic perspective was also adopted. The researcher was at times a participant and at other times an observer. This provided important access to the communicative practices of the community as well as the individual spoken practices of each participant. First-hand experience of the community, the individual spoken practices and the styles of its members allowed, on the one hand, the analyst to handle data with more sensitivity and, on the other, the participants to give feedback to the researcher in the form of comments and retrospective interviews.

The data consist of more than 40 hours of digitally recorded conversations, collected through ethnographic participant and non-participant observations. So far 82 speech events have been transcribed for a total of around 10 hours. The recorded conversations arose naturally among the participants during periods of relaxation, and took place in non-instructional (i.e. non-classroom) settings, such as the staff room, the cafeteria or the house of one of the participants. In total, there were numerous members in the community, but 14 participants, between the ages of 32 and 55, were involved in the recorded conversations. They are of both sexes, speak seven different mother tongues and can all be considered fluent or expert users of ELF. Out of the 14 participants, 4 constituted the main speakers in the recorded events, as they shared a working space and therefore appeared more frequently in the conversations. These main participants were also the ones who provided retrospective comments on the recordings and were interviewed by the researcher.

4. Examples of Accommodation Strategies: Repetition and Code-Switching

In this section I show how repetition and code-switching are used as accommodation strategies in order to achieve efficiency and, at the same time, to show cooperation among speakers. In this function as accommodation strategies, they signal agreement, listenership and engagement in conversation.

I have three main points to make about these strategies. First, while traditional views of repetition and code-switching in the learning or communication strategies literature see these as compensatory actions taken by learners in a problematic exchange or helping strategies to make up for non-understanding, in the ELF conversations analysed they appear as accommodating strategies, whereby speakers adapt to the speech of their interlocutors in the conversation, i.e. strategies they use to sound similar to the interlocutors or to align to their strategic use. Secondly, their functions in ELF are multiple and overlapping. They are used in order to acknowledge understanding, ensure the smooth development of the conversation, the synchrony of its delivery, and alignment. Thirdly, in this last function of alignment, accommodation strategies such as repetition and code-switching suggest affiliation and membership in the same community of multilingual ELF speakers.

Finally, to underpin these three points, I suggest that, in the cases below, questions of social identity are at issue. When speakers switch between languages in the course of a single interaction, language diversity does not necessarily serve as a social indicator, but it constitutes a resource that can be drawn upon by the speakers to represent aspects of their identity or membership in their community.

I will start by introducing the first accommodation strategy—repetition—and, in order to do this, I will present some of the concepts concerning repetition that are relevant to my analysis of the data which follows.

4.1.Repetition in ELF Discourse

Johnstone (1994) has pointed out that "we find repetition in everything" (p. 15) and that repetitions are part of our daily communicative practices. Bearing in mind that repetitions are omnipresent, it is important to set some criteria in order to recognise them in discourse. First of all, repetition is used here to refer to instances of "other-repetition", i.e. the repetition performed by *another* speaker, as opposed to "self-repetition", i.e. the repetition performed by the *same* speaker of the original utterance. Secondly, repetition is also used in this paper when the interlocutor replicates *part of or all* the utterance produced by a previous speaker within the *same conversation*. In this sense, the two criteria for recognising repetitions are i) that an original utterance, or a prior text, must be identified, and ii) that this is found within the same conversation as the repeated text. Though it is important to recognise that repetitions can be performed on speech pronounced outside the conversation, since this study is an investigation of ELF talk in interaction, only repetitions occurring in the same speech event as the original utterance will be considered.

As to the formal aspects, repetitions are a multifaceted phenomenon and can appear in various forms: they can occur as a whole, i.e. word-by-word, or as partial. A third type of repetition is the paraphrase, where only the original concept is repeated (as in the examples by Mauranen 2007 above). In terms of functions, repetitions are a powerful and versatile tool that can provide a linguistic resource for facilitating rhythm and group synchrony, providing time to catch up on the missed discourse (e.g. when attention has lapsed for a moment), or buying time to think of what to say next (Merritt 1994). Repetition is also seen as a strategic resource that can be used quickly and clearly to show alignment with the speaker of the original utterance (Kangasharju 2002, Lichtkoppler 2007). It is precisely in all these functions that the ELF speakers in this paper strategically use repetition in their discourse. While at times one function may be prevalent over the others, on most occasions speakers display numerous and overlapping motivations for their strategic use of repetition.

But this is not all. Three more points need to be made about repetition used as an accommodation strategy as a whole. The accommodation repetition does not appear in a problematic exchange as a face saving or helping strategy to make up for non-understanding, but as a cooperative strategy meant to show alignment and solidarity, as well as affiliation with the previous turn. Its rationale is threefold. It is used to acknowledge understanding and confirm the original turn. This way it is consequently also used to ensure the smooth development of the conversation and the synchrony of its delivery. This is in contrast to what would happen if speakers altered their original utterance, thus slowing down the exchange and causing asynchrony in tempo, as well as creating friction between the participants. Finally, repetition is used to show alignment and solidarity with the interlocutor, to invoke their approval and possibly to suggest affiliation and membership into the same community of multilingual speakers. All three points are going to be explored in more detail below.

In the following examples from my ELF corpus the repetition is often produced latching to the previous original utterance, which helps to keep the same rhythmic delivery of the speech while at the same time performing other possible functions. For instance, Extract 1 shows clearly how repetition is used to quickly signal alignment as well as maintaining rhythmic synchrony. This extract is a conversation about summer holidays, where Karen tells Daniela that she went to Salzburg, but she did not like it. (See Appendix for transcription conventions.)

Extract 1

(Karen: L1 German; Daniela: L1 Italian)

1	KAREN:	actually … I didn't like Salzburg a lot … I think	
2		it's very … very traditional	
3	DANIELA:	*(laughing)*	
4	KAREN:	it was nice to be there …	[two days
5	DANIELA:		[one day
6	KAREN:	yeah=	
7	DANIELA:	=**it's small**=	
8	KAREN: →	=yeah **it's small** and … people are very unfriendly there	

Karen tells Daniela that she did not like Salzburg because it is a traditional town, and Daniela starts engaging with Karen, providing her own feedback on Salzburg. First, Daniela performs a completion overlap (line 5) where she, ironically, suggests that "one day" in Salzburg is enough, and Karen accepts this comment by saying "yeah", while she has said before (line 4) that she spent "two days" there, not one. Karen is being factual in her providing the exact time she spent in Salzburg, while Daniela is being ironic in saying that one day in this town is sufficient. Karen's agreement in line 6 is therefore a signal of accommodating to Daniela's ironic tone. Secondly, Daniela again provides her opinion on Salzburg by saying that it "is small", and Karen agrees by performing a repetition (line 8) and then expanding on it by talking about Salzburg inhabitants.

This repetition in line 8 is particularly interesting because it seems to be performed not only to converge to the interlocutor's irony, but also to support it further with a stronger evaluation of the place. The irony, which was initiated by Daniela in line 5, is continued in line 7, where "it's small" offers a justification for staying only "one day" in the town. Karen's repetition in line 8 then shows agreement but also serves as a way of introduction to the rest of the utterance, where Karen provides further support to Daniela's opinion by saying that "people are very unfriendly there". Here Karen quickly latches to Daniela's speech and then provides another reason for disliking Salzburg. The repetition is therefore used as a strategic device, a timely alignment to the interlocutor's speech and a further support of the interlocutor's position.

Alignment and support also come through the repetition in Extract 2, but in this conversation the strategy is even more powerful as Sila is accommodating to a "non-standard" utterance provided by Chako in a previous turn. Chako and Sila are talking about the Mandarin language, and Chako is enquiring about language variation in Mandarin.

Extract 2

(Chako: L1 Japanese; Sila: L1 Mandarin)

1	CHAKO:	my [specific interest in point
2	SILA:	[yeah
3	CHAKO:	when did language I mean ... **because [of revolution,**
4	SILA:	[mhm mhm
5	CHAKO:	did language change?
6	SILA:	yeah [it's it changed
7	CHAKO:	[specifically intentionally
8	SILA: →	**because of revolution** ↓ but it also changed from the
9		beginning of the twentieth ce [ntury
10	CHAKO:	[yeah

Chako is interested in finding out when Mandarin started to change (lines 1-3), so she explicitly asks whether Mandarin changed because of the revolution (lines 3-5) and she uses the utterance "because of revolution" without definite article "the". In line 8 Sila is repeating Chako's utterance and accommodating from a grammatical point of view, for she repeats the zero article that Chako uses in the previous turn. That, with the repetition of zero article, Sila is actually converging to Chako's talk and not simply omitting a grammatical item is evidenced in the remainder of the conversation. From line 8 onwards, Sila uses definite articles where she could have used a zero article instead (for instance in the expression "from *the* beginning of *the* twentieth century"). From other transcriptions it is possible to confirm that the general tendency is for Sila to use the definite articles, which corroborates the evidence that line 8 is an instance of accommodation, i.e. Sila changed her speech style to resemble that of Chako.

Nonetheless, that is not the only reason for accommodating to Chako. Sila's accommodation has two different purposes: efficiency and alignment. In the first sense, Sila is repeating exactly the original utterance to ensure that the synchronic delivery of her speech keeps up with the rhythm of the encounter. In the second, she is displaying attentiveness to Chako's earlier contribution, as well as confirming it and aligning with it and with the interlocutor's knowledge. If, on the contrary, Sila had repeated the utterance introducing the article she would have done a repetition with variation. This change would have probably meant that Sila wanted to perform a repair and thus show non-alignment with Chako. The fact that Sila did not make any change to the original utterance is meaningful in the sense that it proves the intention to align towards Chako.

4.2. Code-Switching in ELF Discourse

In the previous section I considered repetition as an accommodation strategy in ELF discourse and commented on its functions. In this part I will consider another strategy which is used to accommodate diversity, i.e. code-switching. In contrast to the SLA approach which sees code-switching as a learner strategy that lower proficiency learners may adopt to compensate for their linguistic deficiency, the approach taken in this paper is a sociolinguistic one. From a sociolinguistic perspective, code-switching is an expression of the bilingual or multilingual competence of the participants (and not of their deficiency) being able to draw on their multifaceted linguistic repertoire (Gross 2000, Myers-Scotton 2000).

The sociolinguistic approach aims to investigate the reasons why speakers switch languages and the sociolinguistic parameters that surround language alternation. Research has focused either on the macro level, that is language choice at the community level, or on the micro level, where code-switching is analysed in discourse, in terms of the functions it serves as talk in interaction and how social meaning is created by the code-switching participants. In respect of the latter, Gumperz (1982) employs the term *conversational* code-switching and observes that bilinguals constantly make choices about the code to be used during interactions, and suggests that code-switching has important discourse functions for them. Bilingual and multilingual speakers jointly construct social meaning in interactions, assigning different functions to different codes. These functions range from conveying referential meaning to signaling the social identities of the speakers involved. In this sense, language carries significant symbolic meaning, values and identities and the switch from one language to another would index certain views, values and identities. For instance, according to House (2003), ELF could be seen as a neutral instrument for international communication, while other local languages could be used to index culture and identity. Blommaert (2003), on the other hand, points out that the binary distinction between language for communication and language for identification "is considerably more complex" (p. 620). In the same way, as shown below, the participants' use of languages other than English is so intrinsic to ELF as to be seen as a constituted and constitutive part of it.

Following from this, another way of researching code-switching sociolinguistically views language alternation itself as more important than the symbolic meanings that a language is associated with. That way, the speakers' switch from X to Y or Y to X is more meaningful than the sociolinguistic categories associated with X or Y (Auer 1998, Gafaranga 2007, Li 1998). Li (1998) clearly distinguishes the two approaches by referring to the "brought-along meaning", i.e. the macro approach where the symbolic references associated with different codes are brought along into the conversation to index the participants' individual associations and values, and the "brought-about meaning", which refers to the meaning, views and values negotiated through code-switching in conversation, with new meaning created as a result of the negotiation itself. In other words, while recognising the importance of the social values, power and ethnic relations associated with certain codes to make sense of societal code-switching, there is no simple one way link between languages and social values and functions. In the same way, one cannot assume that ELF conversations serve a transactional, business-like function or that speakers' L1 talk has an identificatory value, especially when, as in ELF talk, code-switching becomes part of ELF interaction, as shown below. In the ELF context below, the meanings and motivations of code-switching are brought about and negotiated by the speakers in interaction.

Things get even more muddled when considering the linguistic repertoire of the participants involved in ELF talk, particularly in this study. ELF speakers in general are at least bilinguals, in the sense that they have more than one variety / language / code in their repertoire, and the participants in this study have most often more than two at their disposal. This makes things more difficult as switching within ELF conversation may happen not only from English to their L1/s or vice versa, but also from English to any Ln (variety / language / code). It is therefore impossible to identify a clear symbolic association between each variety in their repertoire and certain social values. Each participant may have different preferences, perspectives and expectations associated with their linguistic repertoire. In this sense, Li warns researchers against "bringing along" their assumptions concerning the social values and functions in the interpretation of code-switching.

A further complication concerns the participants' linguistic repertoire and their competence in their Ln. As mentioned before, the ELF speakers in this community have a pool of linguistic resources to draw upon in their ELF conversations, but they do not all have the same competence in those resources and, more importantly, they may not have full competence in any. Apart from their different linguistic repertoires, as well as their competence in their L1 and Ln, Jenkins (2006) points out that the proficiency levels of ELF users is diverse and it would include speakers that are still learners, speakers that stopped learning at some point short of expert level and competent ELF users. Despite different proficiencies in their linguistic repertoire and their different sociocultural backgrounds, participants in this study are found to use code-switching successfully and in various conversational functions.

In the following, I use three examples of code-switching to illustrate the functions it covers in ELF discourse. The first, Extract 3 below, concerns the end of a dyadic conversation. Closings of conversations can be potentially problematic moments for the speakers, because they might risk ending the exchange abruptly or not sensitively enough for the interlocutor. That is why, as Schegloff and Sacks (1973) explain, participants engage in sometimes quite long closing sequences and initiate them with pre-closing signals, such as repetitions, "we-el!, "ok", "so-oo" and others. Repetitions are evidently used as pre-closings in the following terminal exchange, but, instead of stopping the conversation after them, the participants take greater care in crafting the closing section by engaging in code-switching and elaborating on their multilingual repertoire.

Daniela and Karen have met to discuss some work practice that they have been involved in. The discussion has been friendly and relaxed and they are about to reach the end of their meeting.

Extract 3
(Daniela: L1 Italian; Karen: L1 German)

1	DANIELA:	*(low)* yeah
2	KAREN:	yeah
3	DANIELA:	ok

4	KAREN:	e:h ok
5	DANIELA:	grazie
6	KAREN: →	yeah ok … **grazie e:h danke: thank you for you** eh
7		how do you say thank you eh **danke an dich**
8	DANIELA:	**grazie a te**
9	KAREN:	*(laughing)* yeah

The repetitions of the pre-closings "yeah" (lines 1 and 2) and "ok" (lines 3 and 4) signal the first part of the closing section. In line 5 Daniela codeswitches to Italian to say "thank you" ("grazie") and in line 6 Karen starts an elaboration on the thanking theme: first, she repeats the Italian version, then translates it into German ("danke:") and then re-translates it into English ("thank you for you"). The last part of the English translation ("for you") is then followed by a hesitation ("eh") and a word search ("how do you say thank you"). Here, it is obvious that Karen knows how to say "thank you" but is actually looking for the expression 'danke an dich' (line 7) in Italian, and the "for you" in line 6 corresponds to "an dich" in German. Daniela finally translates into Italian, "grazie a te" (line 8), and, with the laughing and "yeah", the conversation is eventually ended.

The use of "for you", "an dich", "a te" illustrates not only the level of cooperation and engagement in this final part of the conversation, but also the willingness of the participants to put extra care in the shaping of final thank-yous. In line 6, Karen initiates an expansion of the closing sequence by converging to Daniela in her switch to Italian, and then asking her how to translate the expression "thank you for you" or "danke an dich". This kind of negotiation of final thanking turns and display of multilingual repertoire is frequently used in the ELF corpus analysed. The interesting observation is that their code-switching is performed with expertise, a certain nonchalance and playfulness typical of speakers who habitually accept and make use of this strategy in their conversations.

A certain feeling of membership to a "different" community of speakers, a multilingual community, is also transported in the following extract. Here the same participants are talking on the subject of Karen's bag.

Extract 4

(Anna: L1 Italian; Karen: L1 German; Daniela: L1 Italian)

1	ANNA:	you've got a very nice bag
2	KAREN:	bought in China … maybe fifty p
3	ANNA:	really? … gosh it's really nice
4	DANIELA: →	=**bella**=

5 ANNA: =nice=
6 KAREN: =I don't know how long it takes until it's … broken …
7 but I still

In line 2 Karen specifies that the bag was bought in China and that it was very cheap, only "fifty p". Anna is surprised and self-repeats when she says it is a "nice" bag. In line 4 Daniela takes the turn and uses the word "bella" to describe the bag, and then Anna self-repeats again with "nice". The interesting point in this extract is Daniela's use of "bella". Her code-switching does not seem to be justified by any functional reasons: firstly, it does not fill in a word search moment, since Anna has already used the word "nice" two times. Secondly, it would not even be a choice justified by efficiency, in the sense that Daniela's processing time might have been even faster (though the whole conversation is already in fast tempo, signalled by the latchings) if she had just repeated Anna's word "nice". Instead, her language alternation may signal her "Italianness", while at the same time getting the other speakers' approval by using an expression that is known by them and generally widespread in the multilingual world of the participants.

While in the previous conversation the language that Daniela codeswitches to (i.e. Italian) is her mother tongue, in the following extract the speakers codeswitch to a third language which is the first language of none. In the "Galletas" conversation Chako (Japanese) is offering some biscuits to Anna (Italian). Chako uses the Spanish "galletas" to refer to the biscuits.

Extract 5

(Chako: L1 Japanese; Anna: L1 Italian)

1 CHAKO: → Anna … **galletas**
2 ANNA: mhm (0.5) nice
3 CHAKO: take two
4 ANNA: no one is en-
5 *(Chako signals with hand to take two and Anna*
6 *takes two)*
7 ANNA: thank you *(Chako goes back to her desk)*
8 (0.5)
9 ANNA: ah:: with nuts=
10 CHAKO: =nuts and chocolate
11 ANNA: mhm … ni::ce=
12 CHAKO: → =**te gusta?**=
13 ANNA: =**mucho**

In this extract there are two instances of code-switching (in line 1 and in lines 12-13). The first occurs in line 1 where Chako offers Anna some home-made biscuits using the Spanish word "galletas". Chako insists on Anna taking two (lines 3-6) not just one (line 4). Anna accepts and comments on what ingredients the biscuits contain, i.e. nuts and chocolate. Chako resumes the code-switching when asking Anna if she likes the biscuits ("te gusta" in line 12) and Anna replies in Spanish saying "a lot" ("mucho" in line 13).

The interesting point about this extract is that both participants codeswitch not to their L1s (Japanese or Italian) but to a third language, i.e. Spanish. Both participants are fluent speakers of Spanish, but Chako's motivation for initiating the codeswitch to Spanish is double. Firstly, the nearest language to Italian that Chako speaks is Spanish, therefore she uses Spanish knowingly because of its similarity with Anna's L1. In the retrospective interview, Chako explained that she codeswitched to Spanish because of the contextual elements: in the conversation she is offering biscuits, which she made at home, and feels this is a homely situation. The language she would use at home in the same situation is Spanish (apart from Japanese, Chako speaks Spanish at home, because this is her husband's L1), and here it is also the language spoken by both participants in a friendly and relaxed moment.

One final point to make is that, as with the previous extracts, Chako and Anna are code-switching without flagging it. There is no signal of surprise, uneasiness or language negotiation in the conversation, although neither participant is Spanish. They easily choose and accept speaking in a third language, and do not show hesitation or any other elements of flagging. Thus code-switching even in a third language is considered "normal", the unmarked choice for this multilingual and multicultural community of ELF speakers.

In conclusion, contrary to the assumption that code-switching is evidence of linguistic deficiency in bilingual or multilingual speakers, the data analysis suggests that code-switching is used as an additional resource to achieve particular conversational goals in interactions with other intercultural speakers. The first function of code-switching consists in offering an extra tool in communication that is at the disposal of multilinguals and allows for meaning making and greater nuances of expression (Extract 4). The second function is that code-switching is used in intercultural communication to ensure understanding beyond cultural differences and the efficient delivery of talk. In this function it is sometimes used to make up for temporary lapses or word-search moments, and it constitutes an extra strategy that ELF speakers employ to ease potentially risky moments of talk, such as closings (Extract 3).

The third code-switching function draws on issues of cultural and social identity. Participants codeswitch not to compensate for some linguistic deficiency but as a strategy for signalling solidarity and membership into the same community, i.e. the community of multilingual speakers who can codeswitch into a third language which is none of the speakers' mother tongues (Extract 5). If we accept that social identities are made visible through talk (Auer 1998, Sebba & Wootton 1998), it is important to emphasise that in this ELF community participants' affiliations, values and identities do not rest with one precise code or language in their repertoire, but they are brought about and negotiated in ELF interaction. There is no evidence showing that when participants use their L1s they express their identity, whereas when they use ELF they are talking with some sort of transactional purposes. As seen from the data, ELF speakers make creative use of their multilingual repertoire, while maintaining social relations and showing membership in a certain group.

Certain communities, as the one described in this paper, may use code-switching as their default practice for conversation even when speakers are not completely fluent in all the codes involved. Even more significantly, from the speakers' perspectives the codes used in the code-switching may not be clearly indexing any social or functional purpose. In these communities, code-switching is part and parcel of the communities' communicative activities, as their normal everyday practice.

5. Conclusion

The focus of this paper has been on the accommodation strategies that ELF speakers use to facilitate communication and deal with diversity. Despite that diversity, ELF communication is far more effective and less problematic than one might assume (cf. Mauranen 2006a and Pitzl 2005): non-understandings are fairly uncommon and generally avoided by pre-empting strategies (Kaur, this volume). ELF speakers seem to be able to negotiate meaning, accept a plurality of cultural and linguistic backgrounds and accommodate it in their conversations.

I have argued that in ELF pragmatics accommodation is key to the successful accomplishment of ELF communication and it is realized through a number of convergence strategies. ELF speakers in the community analysed in this paper use repetition and code-switching as two important strategies in various functions. The flexible use of multilingual resources and recycling of speakers' utterances through repetition also resonate with other current research findings in ELF communication (Hülmbauer, this volume; Klimpfinger 2007; Metsä-Ketelä 2006) and supports the view that successful ELF communication relies on crucial adaptive accommodation skills along with appreciation and acceptance of diversity.

The selection of data examined here has focused on small talk events taking place among language teachers in a higher education institution. It may be argued that the skilful use of such strategies as repetition and code-switching may be due to the speakers being language professionals and therefore expert communicators, capable of employing different strategies for various purposes, but that other "non-linguist" participants may behave differently. The most empirical way of dealing with this assumption is to indeed compare the results with similar research conducted in other communities. Recent developments in this sense have shown that in different contexts these practices are widely used (cf. Klimpfinger 2007, Lichtkoppler 2007), and more research in this direction is undoubtedly needed.

I began by pointing out the need for more research concerning accommodation in ELF discourse and I would like to close by emphasising how repetition and code-switching are two vital and creative strategies of ELF talk which contribute to accommodate linguistic and cultural differences to make communication successful. The ELF communication explored in this paper is also, as Jenkins (2009) puts it, evidence of "the fact that a language does not have to be a mother tongue in order to be capable of expressing aspects of a speaker's social identity" (p. 165). In the same way, the accommodation strategies explored are testimony to the creativity of ELF speakers, who use language skilfully, drawing on their multilingual and multicultural repertoire, not only to make ELF communication successful, but to enrich it with their own flavour, to make it their own.

APPENDIX

Transcription Conventions

=	latching
…	short pause (unmeasured)
(0.5)	measured pause
[ ]	overlapping speech
?	rising intonation
↓	falling intonation
underlining	used to highlight parts of the transcript discussed in the text

Bibliography

Auer, P. 1998. "Introduction: Bilingual Conversation Revisited." In *Code-Switching in Conversation. Language, Interaction and Identity*, ed. P. Auer, 1-24. London: Routledge.

Blommaert, J. 2003. "Commentary: A Sociolinguistics of Globalization." *Journal of Sociolinguistics* 7 (4), 607-23.

Cogo, A. 2007. "Intercultural Communication in English as a Lingua Franca: A Case Study." PhD diss., King's College London.

Cogo, A. and M. Dewey 2006. "Efficiency in ELF Communication: From Pragmatic Motives to Lexico-Grammatical Innovation." *Nordic Journal of English Studies* 5 (2), 59-93. https://guoa.ub.gu.se/dspace/bitstream/2077/3148/1/5-2-Cogo-Dewey.pdf (accessed April 19, 2009)

Eggins, S. and D. Slade 1997. *Analysing Casual Conversation*. London: Cassell.

Gafaranga, J. 2007. *Talk in Two Languages*. Basingstoke: Palgrave Macmillan.

Giles, H. and N. Coupland 1991. *Language: Contexts and Consequences*. Milton Keynes, UK: Open University Press.

Giles, H., A. Mulac, J. Bradac and P. Johnson 1987. "Speech Accommodation Theory: The Last Decade and Beyond." In *Communication Yearbook 10*, ed. M. McLaughlin, 13-48. Beverly Hills, CA: Sage.

Gross, S. 2000. "Intentionality and the Markedness Model in Literary Code-Switching." *Journal of Pragmatics* 32 (9), 1283-303.

Gumperz, J. 1999. "On Interactional Sociolinguistic Method." In *Talk, Work and Institutional Order*, ed. S. Sarangi & C. Roberts, 453-71. Berlin: Mouton de Gruyter.
—. 1982. *Discourse Strategies*. Cambridge: Cambridge University Press.
House, J. 2003. "English as a Lingua Franca: A Threat to Multilingualism?" *Journal of Sociolinguistics* 7 (4), 556-78.
Hülmbauer, C. this volume. "'We don't take the right way. We just take the way that we think you will understand'—The Shifting Relationship between Correctness and Effectiveness in ELF."
Jenkins, J. 2009. *World Englishes*. 2nd ed. Oxon: Routledge.
—. 2006. "Points of View and Blind Spots: ELF and SLA." *International Journal of Applied Linguistics* 16 (2), 137-62.
—. 2000. *The Phonology of English as an International Language*. Oxford: Oxford University Press.
Johnstone, B. 1994. "Repetition in Discourse: A Dialogue." In *Repetition in Discourse: Interdisciplinary Perspectives*, vol. 1, ed. B. Jonhstone, 1-20. Norwood, NJ: Ablex.
Kangasharju, H. 2002. "Alignment in Disagreement: Forming Oppositional Alliances in Committee Meetings." *Journal of Pragmatics* 34 (10), 1447-71.
Kaur, J. this volume. "Pre-Empting Problems of Understanding in English as a Lingua Franca."
Klimpfinger, T. 2007. "'Mind you, sometimes you have to mix'—The Role of Code-Switching in English as a Lingua Franca." *VIenna English Working PaperS* 16 (2), 36-61. http://www.univie.ac.at/Anglistik/Views_0702.pdf (accessed April 20, 2009)
Li, W. 1998. "The 'Why' and 'How' Questions in the Analysis of Conversational Code-Switching." In *Code-Switching in Conversation. Language, Interaction and Identity*, ed. P. Auer, 156-79. London: Routledge.
Lichtkoppler, J. 2007. "'Male. Male.'—'Male?'—'The sex is male.'—The Role of Repetition in English as a Lingua Franca Conversations." *VIenna English Working PaperS* 16 (1), 39-65 http://www.univie.ac.at/Anglistik/views_0701_pdf. (accessed April 20, 2009)
Mauranen, A. 2007. "Hybrid Voices: English as the Lingua Franca of Academics." In *Language and Discipline Perspectives on Academic Discourse*, ed. Kjersti Fløttum, 243-59. Newcastle, UK: Cambridge Scholars Publishing.
—. 2006a. "Signaling and Preventing Misunderstanding in English as a Lingua Franca Communication." *International Journal of the Sociology of Language* 177, 123-50.

—. 2006b. "A Rich Domain of ELF—The ELFA Corpus of Academic Discourse." *Nordic Journal of English Studies* 5 (2), 145-59.

Meierkord, C. 2000. "Interpreting Successful Lingua Franca Interaction: An Analysis of Non-Native/Non-Native Small Talk Conversations in English." www.linguistik-online.de/1_00/MEIERKOR.HTM (accessed April 20, 2009)

Merritt, M. 1994. "Repetition in Situated Discourse—Exploring Its Forms and Functions." In *Repetition in Discourse: Interdisciplinary Perspectives*, vol. 1, ed. B. Jonhstone, 23-36. Norwood, NJ: Ablex.

Metsä-Ketelä, M. 2006. "'Words are more or less superfluous': The Case of *more or less* in Academic Lingua Franca English." *Nordic Journal of English Studies* 5 (2), 117-43. http://gupea.ub.gu.se/dspace/handle/2077/3151 (accessed April 20, 2009)

Myers-Scotton, C. 2000. "Explaining the Role of Norms and Rationality in Code-Switching." *Journal of Pragmatics* 32 (9), 1259-71.

Pitzl, M.-L. 2005. "Non-Understanding in English as a Lingua Franca: Examples from a Business Context." *VIenna English Working PaperS* 14 (2), 50-71. http://www.univie.ac.at/Anglistik/Views0502mlp.pdf. (accessed April 20, 2009)

Schegloff, E. A. and H. Sacks 1973. "Opening Up Closings." *Semiotica* VIII (4), 289-327.

Sebba, M. and T. Wootton 1998. "We, They and Identity. Sequential Versus Identity-Related Explanation in Code-Switching." In *Code-Switching in Conversation. Language, Interaction and Identity*, ed. P. Auer, 262-86. London: Routledge.

Seedhouse, P. 2004. "Conversation Analysis Methodology." *Language Learning* 54 (1), 1-54.

Seidlhofer, B. 2007. "English as a Lingua Franca and Communities of Practice." In *Proceedings of Anglistentag 2006 Hall*, ed. S. Volk-Birke & J. Lippert, 307-18. Trier: Wissenschaftlicher Verlag.

Seidlhofer, B., A. Breiteneder and M.-L. Pitzl 2006. "English as a Lingua Franca in Europe." *Annual Review of Applied Linguistics* 26, 1-34.

Wenger, E. 1998. *Communities of Practice. Learning, Meaning and Identity*. Cambridge: Cambridge University Press.

FLUENT SPEAKERS—FLUENT INTERACTIONS: ON THE CREATION OF (CO)-FLUENCY IN ENGLISH AS A LINGUA FRANCA

JULIA HÜTTNER

1. Introduction

The label fluency is used pervasively and with deceptive ease to describe the language proficiency of speakers (cf. e.g. Chambers 1997, Guillot 1999 for overviews), and most language users share some ideas of what is meant when referring to somebody as a fluent speaker of a particular language. Intuitively, fluency seems to capture different aspects of language proficiency than other labels, such as 'proficient' or 'near-native' would, which might also be the reason why the label fluency has been used to describe English as a lingua franca (ELF) speakers, for instance in definitions such as "fairly fluent speakers from a wide range of first language backgrounds" (Seidlhofer 2004, 219) or as "highly competent and fluent users of ELF" (Seidlhofer et al. 2006, 14). Thus, there is something about fluency that lay people, teachers and researchers can relate to and which makes it an attractive starting point in trying to introduce ways of distinguishing between diverse ELF speakers or, as I shall argue below, between diverse ELF interactions.

Despite this apparent accessibility, the label fluency is not unproblematic, especially when applied to an ELF context. One of the main problems is that it is usually used in educational or psycholinguistically experimental situations to refer to individual non-native speakers, who are being compared, implicitly or explicitly, to native speakers of the target language. Apart from the fact that such a conceptualization does not allow for non-native fluency as distinct from native fluency, a number of further problems surround such a use of the label fluency. Notably, these problems relate to the mismatch between a comparatively narrow view of fluency, relating it mostly to speed of language production, and a broad, more encompassing view of fluency, relating to general aspects of oral language proficiency or some level of perceived 'smoothness', which seems to be evoked in many lay perceptions (cf. Lennon 1990 for the distinction between broad and narrow fluency). The difficulties surrounding a clear-cut definition of fluency that takes into account actual language performances serve as a starting point for questioning whether such a speaker-oriented use of the label fluency is indeed the only appropriate one, and for re-visiting previous research on fluency. Importantly, the relevance of using the concept fluency is brought to the test by relating it to ELF language use, which seems characterized by perceptions of varying degrees of smoothness. As I shall discuss, such fluency in ELF cannot, however, be compared usefully to native-speaker language use or be measured using only the parameters of psycholinguistic studies.

This contribution proposes a new conceptualization of fluency, which moves from viewing fluency as a descriptor of individual speakers to one of individual interactions. The focus of this paper is thus to propose a dialogic conceptualization of fluency, focusing on interactivity as a crucial characteristic of it, and fluency as an enactment of a speaker's language competence adjustable to contextual conditions.[1] In order to frame this argument, this paper will present an outline of previous research into fluency, which uses native speaker norms as the only applicable yardstick as it has mostly taken place in paradigms that view non-native speakers as language learners only. Studies from a psycholinguistic background and those conducted in a more pragmatic-oriented framework will be presented and then linked to previous related research into ELF. An analysis of two extracts will support the possibility of applying fluency also in an ELF context and highlight some features that might contribute to the perception of dialogic fluency.

2. Investigations of Fluency

2.1. Psycholinguistics

Within linguistics, fluency has had a rather chequered history as an object of inquiry, and a careful re-analysis of previous work seems timely before an attempt can be made of turning fluency into a helpful and systematic descriptor of ELF language use. After Fillmore's influential (1979) paper, descriptions and investigations of fluency have diverged in a number of directions. Considering first psycholinguistics as arguably the most prolific area of fluency investigation, the so-called 'narrow' definition of fluency, focusing on the automatization of language encoding processes, was proposed by Lennon (1990) and views it as the perception on the part of the listener that the "psycholinguistic processes of speech planning and speech production are functioning easily and efficiently".[2] A similar definition, focusing on the speaker, is found in Rehbein (1987a, 104) who views fluency as indicating that "the activities of planning and uttering can be executed nearly simultaneously by the speaker of the language". Underlying this view of fluency is the notion that a higher speech rate with fewer discontinuities is indicative of a higher degree of automaticity in the translation of thought into language and studies have attempted to establish which factors are most prominent in the evaluation of speakers as fluent. Findings are not unambiguous, but suggest that rate of speech (usually measured in syllables per minute), pace (i.e. number of stressed words per minute), mean length of runs, and with some caution, number of disfluencies and pauses (including filled and unfilled pauses; use of lexical fillers) are the most relevant factors. Additionally, the overall amount of speech, phonological features (e.g. intonation contours) and the use of formulaic language have been used as measures of fluency. (Findings are summarised here from studies by Ejzenberg 2000, Freed 1995 and 2000, Kormos & Denes 2004, Kormos 2006, Lennon 1990 and 2000, Prodromou 2008, Riggenbach 1991, Towell et al. 1996, Wennerstrom 2000, and Wray 2002).

Formulaic language is one feature often considered evidence of a higher degree of automatic language processing and thus also as linked to the creation of fluency. Such a focus assumes that the use of formulaic sequences, which are learnt and used as holistic units, enables speakers (and listeners) to free vital processing time and so tackle the limitations posed by the constraints of human working memory capacities (cf. Hüttner 2007, 67ff. for a discussion). Evidence in support of the role of formulaic language for the creation of fluency is found in Ellis (2001; 2003), Nattinger and DeCarrico (1992), Pawley and Syder (1983), and Wray (2002). In the framework of ELF, Prodromou (2008) has linked fluency to the use of formulaic language, as will be discussed in greater detail in section 3. All these investigations support the notion that through conventionalised use of formulaic language users and learners (both L1 and L2) are better equipped to function linguistically. Thus, by tacit agreement on particular collocations or sequences, expectations of both speakers and listeners are fulfilled, attention guided to particular parts in the texts, and language-processing resources made available. Several researchers, e.g. Bolander (1989), Hüttner (2007), Linnakylä (1980), Myles et al. (1999), Rehbein (1987b), Schmidt (1983), Wong Fillmore (1979) and Yorio (1989), have shown how non-native speakers of a language use formulaic sequences, both for pragmatic reasons, such as being able to enter into children's games, to function at school, to indicate the presence of genre moves in writing, and as a step in their language learning (usually unconsciously), by first acquiring a set of formulaic sequences unanalysed (e.g. *I don't know*) which are at a later stage analysed with regard to their syntactic patterns.

The ability to use a stock of formulaic sequences arguably supports both the production and the perception of fluent speech by firstly, freeing language processing resources for the production of the non-prefabricated parts of the utterance and secondly, by guiding the listeners' attention through the use of recurring phrases, often in expected situations or positions in the discourse (cf. Wray 2002, 97). This can be considered support for the notion of dialogic fluency in that the benefits for listeners of the use of formulaic sequences indicate a certain degree of interactivity in the creation of fluency. However, the relationship between the amount of formulaic language used and the perception of fluency appears to be non-linear in that there is a 'right level of formulaic language use'. While an under-use of formulaic language might make a speaker sound stilted or slightly odd, an over-use might make a speaker appear clichéd and can well be inappropriate in specific situations. Additionally, what remains problematic in viewing fluency as largely equal to using formulaic sequences is the existence of "false fluency" (cf. Lennon 2000) or even pathological 'superfluency'.[3] Both of these concepts refer to speakers producing long stretches of discourse without noticeable pauses or disfluencies by relying mainly or solely on formulaic sequences. However, "false fluency" is thus because the speech so produced is "conceptually, communicatively, formally and functionally impoverished" (Lennon 2000, 28), even though "time is filled with talk" (Fillmore 1979). "Superfluency" relates to the pathological, extreme form, where patients speak fluently, and often rapidly, but their speech is meaningless to listeners. In sum, then, while there are reasons to assume that the process of idiomaticity, i.e. the ability to use chunks of language rather than assembling every stretch of language piece by piece, furthers productive fluency, the actual forms or frequency of formulaic sequences are harder to link to perceptions of fluency.

Even though psycholinguistic studies have so far been the most prolific area in fluency studies, there are some limitations that appear to be recurring in much of the research conducted in this framework, and these limitations make it difficult to apply the underlying concept of fluency of these studies to an ELF context. Firstly, while there are numerous studies of automaticity—and in that sense also fluency—related to L1 use, as soon as L2 speakers are the focus of investigation, their patterns of behaviour are judged according to L1 types of behaviour. Thus, rate of speech and pauses are compared to typical or expected L1 patterns (even if this typicality is generally not established empirically). This is problematic on several counts; firstly, there are slow and fast speakers in any language, who are not necessarily perceived as more fluent if fast and less fluent if slow. Thus, there is a considerable speaker-inherent factor that ought to be taken into account systematically, ideally by obtaining L1 data of the speakers involved and by using L1 speakers rather than target language speakers (also) as raters of fluency levels. This reliance on L1 patterns as norms might additionally affect the evaluation of pauses, especially in connection with turn-taking patterns. In these instances, pausing can have different meanings in different lingua-cultures, so that answering a question by latching on or with overlap might be expected in some lingua-cultures, e.g. Italian and partly US-American, but it might be an indication of hierarchies not being observed or of not taking the question seriously in others, e.g. Japanese (cf. Bowe & Martin 2007, 65-66). Thus, the pragmatically correct use of pauses in some lingua-cultures might well not correspond to the expected L1 pattern of, say, English. Another factor to be considered is the potential of an 'ideal speed' at which to talk, dependent on the characteristics of the other interlocutors (for example, whether they are adults or children; L1 or L2 speakers; and if L2 speakers, their levels of proficiency) and on the situation (casual conversations vs. educational discourse or formal interviews).

As has been criticised by Kormos and Denes (2004, 146), research into fluency within this psycholinguistic framework has also suffered from methodological shortcomings. These include a paucity of longitudinal research to address the development of fluency (*pace* Towell et al. 1996), and the use of very few subjects (e.g. Ejzenberg 2000, Freed 1995, Lennon 1990, Riggenbach 1991), as well as usually excluding non-temporal variables that might contribute to the perception of fluency, such as linguistic ones (e.g. lexical range, grammatical accuracy) or interactional ones.

Finally, taking only the language behaviour of one speaker, usually the non-native one, into account ignores the attested influence of the interlocutor, often the native-speaker, on the perceived level of fluency (cf. Brown 2005, Lorenzo-Dus & Meara 2005). In normal language use one might, however, argue that all speakers involved in an interaction contribute to its fluency by gauging their own speech patterns to the expectations and abilities of their interlocutors. In this sense, all parties involved in an interaction need to 'do their conversational work-load' in order to achieve fluency. This is seen as prime support in considering fluency itself a dialogic phenomenon and an indication that there are contextual conditions encouraging a speaker to access his or her language resources in such a way to increase the perceived level of fluency.

2.2. Studies of Fluency outside Psycholinguistics

Investigations into fluency that assume an equation of fluency with automaticity of language planning and processing have not, despite being prolific, been the only focus of studies of fluency. Fillmore (1979), for instance, in his early treatment of the topic views fluency as a rather general feature of language competence, and indeed focuses on L1 language competence. Fillmore includes among the parameters of fluency speed and continuity or "the ability to fill time with talk" (1979 [2000], 51), which is taken on most prominently in psycholinguistic studies that use measures of rate of speech and number of pauses as operationalised criteria. Further criteria proposed by Fillmore include coherence or "the ability to talk in coherent, reasoned and 'semantically dense' sentences". The third dimension of fluency proposed is context-sensitivity or "the ability to have appropriate things to say in a wide range of contexts". Clearly, this sense of fluency relates mostly to socio-pragmatic abilities, and as Fillmore points out, might be diverse for the same speaker in different situations; again, this might be considered support for a re-conceptualisation of fluency as a descriptor of interactions rather than of speakers. After all, if a speaker can be diversely fluent in different settings, fluency is hard to conceptualise as a speaker-inherent trait. The fourth type of fluency according to Fillmore is creativity, as evidenced in the ability "to express ideas in novel ways, to pun, to make up jokes [...] to vary styles, to create and build on metaphors". One of the aspects most noticeable in Fillmore's dimensions or types of fluency is that arguably only the first one of these, "the ability to fill time with talk", has become part of more generally used linguistic definitions of fluency; the others, especially context-sensitivity and creativity, have been treated as separate types of language ability. While one might reasonably find that Fillmore's definition of fluency encompasses *too* wide a range of abilities and might prove virtually impossible to operationalise, it is a worthwhile counterpoint to more narrow definitions of fluency and challenges the implicit assumption underlying many investigations of L2 fluency that *all* (and possibly only?) L1 speakers are to be regarded as fluent speakers of their language. If we question such a link with L1 speakers and fluency, the need to clearly define fluency also for L2 speakers, becomes even more apparent.

As regards the focus on 'monologic' fluency, Riggenbach's (1991) study marks an important point in fluency research by introducing interactional features as measures of L2 fluency. She proposes "conversational fluency", considered as "the ability to appropriately claim or surrender turns, pause or overlap, or to provide other evidence of alignment with the interlocutor (e.g. collaborative completion)". Some caveats apply relating to the lack of discussion of what exactly is "appropriate" and how to differentiate fluency from general conversation management abilities in these contexts. Apart from various turn change types, Riggenbach lists further interactive phenomena, namely backchannelling behaviour, echoing, questions, repair initiations and laughter particles. Interestingly, the frequency of self-repairs was not found to be indicative of being perceived as in the high or low levels of L2 fluency, but rather diverse patterns of self-repair were observed at diverse proficiency levels. Laughter was not found to contribute to perceptions of either higher or lower levels of fluency. Riggenbach (1991, 439) lists the following as emerging fluency-related phenomena:

1. demonstrated ability to initiate topic changes (e.g. using questions, initiating repair when necessary)
2. demonstrated ability to "carry weight" in a conversation as manifested in the show of comprehension—not only through backchannels but also through substantive comments and responses
3. ability to show anticipation of end-of-turns as evident by appropriate latching and overlapping
4. [...] the amount of speech produced relative to the other interlocutor

While Riggenbach's is quite clearly a study that moves the discussion of fluency forward in acknowledging a greater range of factors, she herself acknowledges the difficulties of analysing many of these factors. Additionally, with a database of only six subjects, any findings must be viewed as highly tentative. In her later work, Riggenbach (1998) points out that many of these more interactional aspects of fluency are inhibited in the setting of a formal language proficiency interview with the inherent asymmetry of the interlocutors. Her suggestion of using an interlocutor familiar to the test-taker and conduct a conversation in a private setting, however, seems to venture into the other extreme and to underestimate the importance of the interlocutor, who—if highly adept and collaborative—might take on a major share of the conversational workload.

Within an approach to fluency that focuses on the more pragmatic aspect of this ability, Sajavaara's (1987) notion of fluency is highly relevant as it relates it to "the communicative acceptability of the speech act, or 'communicative fit'". This idea is developed in House (1996, 228) into pragmatic fluency, defined as "a dialogic phenomenon that combines both pragmatic appropriateness of utterances and smooth continuity in ongoing talk". House (1996, 229) classifies the following areas as relevant yardsticks for rating non-native speakers as pragmatically fluent:

1. use of routinized pragmatic phenomena focused on in the instructional treatment, namely gambits, discourse strategies, and speech acts
2. ability to initiate topics and topic changes using appropriate routines
3. ability to "carry weight" in a conversation manifest in substantive comments
4. ability to show appropriate uptaking, as well as replying and responding behaviour (i.e. appropriate alignment in Goffman's sense), anticipation of end-of-turns as evident in latching, overlapping, and the use of appropriate "second pair parts" in routinized reciprocation
5. appropriate rate of speech, types of filled and unfilled pauses, and frequency and function of repairs

In this work, we can also see how a combination of factors is considered in a definition of fluency, i.e. temporal (rate of speech, pausing), discursive (i.e. topic management) and interactive (i.e. turn-taking behaviour) as well as having command over pragmatically functional formulaic sequences. Thus, it can be seen as counter-evidence to Kormos and Denes' (2004, 146) criticism of fluency research that fails to investigate a combination of relevant variables. In her 1996 paper, House still measured the appropriacy of the (non-native) speaker's pragmatic fluency behaviour against a yardstick of native-speaker behaviour. In her later work, however, as we shall see, House (2002) takes the role of ELF prominently into account, but focuses less explicitly on fluency and more on general pragmatic competence.

With regard to a re-conceptualisation of fluency as a dialogic concept, and thus possibly as a descriptor of interactions rather than of individual language practice, the following points can be seen as crucially relevant. Firstly, psycholinguistic studies focusing on fluency in a sense of automatic language processing assume implicitly that all L1 speakers are perfectly fluent, but these studies generally fall short in not taking systematic account of target language data obtained from L1 speakers and so do not acknowledge that diverse L1 speakers may be considered differently fluent individually and/or across specific contexts. Thus, the implied yardstick used for measuring L2 fluency remains elusive. Secondly, and most importantly, the perception of fluency is influenced quite clearly by the language behaviour of the interlocutor (cf. e.g. Brown 2005). Thus, a person can be judged as more or less fluent, depending on whom he or she is talking to. Such variability suggests that speakers have a range of fluency levels at their disposal, to which they can resort depending on their interlocutors and the entire speech setting. But even more than just influencing fluency, I would argue that fluency is indeed best construed as a collaborative construct, not as one related to individuals. In this sense, then, it is not only the person who speaks quickly and without pausing, who might be regarded as fluent, but the speaker who can adapt to his/her interlocutors by taking up on previous utterances, creating unity and taking responsibility for keeping the conversation running smoothly and in such a way knowing how to act on their language knowledge and ability in a contextually sensitive way. Viewed like this, a fluent speaker might be more like a skilled jazz musician in a jam session than a solo virtuoso performer.

3. Fluency in ELF

In the framework of this publication, there is certainly no need to go into detail regarding the socio-political importance of ELF (for overviews, cf. e.g. Brutt-Griffler 2002, Graddol 2006, Gnutzmann & Intemann 2005, Jenkins 2003 and 2007), suffice it to say here that many of those speakers required to be fluent English speakers in their professional contexts will, in fact, be using ELF, which then is best considered "natural language use" in Brumfit's (1984) terminology. I shall here be following Seidlhofer's (2001, 146) definition of ELF as

> in the strict sense of the word [...] an additionally acquired language system that serves as a means of communication between speakers of different first languages or a language by means of which the members of different speech communities can communicate with each other but which is not the native language of either.

In the light of taking ELF seriously, several issues that have come up in previous discussions of fluency need to be re-evaluated. The first issue that becomes quite apparent when considering the previous research on fluency is that it is impossible to judge what is normatively 'correct' fluency in ELF, and thus the issue of appropriacy has to be developed in a bottom-up way by the interactants or from within the interactions. Using a native speaker yardstick for interactions without native speakers would arguably miss out on vital clues as to what encourages the perception of fluency by participants or observers.

Given their interactivity, naturalistic ELF data are markedly different from both language tests and experimentally elicited (learner) data, notably with reference to the stakes attributed to the interactions and to the relevance placed on linguistic accuracy. Previous research on ELF (e.g. Cogo & Dewey 2006) does, however, suggest that speakers are highly collaborative in creating successful interactions, which might be seen as further indication of the value of adapting the definition of fluency to be a feature of interactions rather than individual speakers. In this sense, the collaborative nature of ELF underlines the notion of fluency as having a strategic component, i.e. being the "maximally effective operation of the language system" (Brumfit 1984 [2000], 69).

Much work in ELF research has addressed the pragmatics of ELF interactions, and clearly, with a dialogic view of fluency, many of these findings are highly relevant. Especially Cogo and Dewey (2006, 68ff.) show how efficiency in ELF is achieved through interactional work, such as overlaps of the co-operative type (including utterance completion), the use of backchannels and of latching, i.e. turns following without pauses, as well as using repetition in order to signal accommodation. Cogo and Dewey (2006, 69) summarise that "ELF speakers make use of interactional features to show support and alignment"; a finding relevant to an investigation of dialogic fluency, which is hard to imagine occurring without the interlocutors each individually contributing to the creation of smooth interaction. A further point that is frequently made with regard to the way in which participants manage to make a success of ELF interactions is to "let-it-pass" and to "make it normal" (cf. Firth 1990; 1996), i.e. not to challenge contributions until or unless the conversation shows that complete understanding would be needed. In that case, the principle of clarity (Ahvenainen 2005) comes into play. House (2002, 568-569) found a strong demonstration of solidarity and consensus-orientation in her data, often in the form of co-constructed utterances. Similarly, she found evidence of *Represents*, also known as echoes, which serve to provide textual coherence, to signal uptake, to request information and to indicate that the floor is still with the previous speaker. These findings from investigations into ELF pragmatics are of relevance in a conceptualization of fluency as dialogic, drawing on Riggenbach (1991; 1998).

Fluency has already received some explicit attention in ELF literature, i.e. in Prodromou (2008). In his book-length study, Prodromou relates fluency to idiomaticity, which he considers "the key issue in the 'real English' versus ELF debate" (2008, 7). Although a clear definition of idiomaticity is not given, the explicit links made refer to patterns of collocation, colligation, and semantic prosody. Later in the work, specific reference is made to idiomaticity in the sense of using particular proverbs, idioms (e.g. *a stroke of good luck*), discourse markers and conversational gambits. Thus, he relates fluency quite clearly to the use of prefabricated language or formulaic sequences (cf. Wray 2002).

As has been outlined under section 2.1., the reason for assuming a link between the use of prefabricated language or idiomaticity and fluency is essentially a psycholinguistic one. Using chunks of language rather than assembling phrases bit by bit speeds up speech production and reduces hesitations and pauses; additionally, the use of prefabricated chunks can aid the listener in directing his or her attention towards particular items in a discourse. Even though Prodromou (2008, 38ff.) does address other features of fluency, including dialogic and cultural issues, his study nevertheless focuses on the use of prefabricated language by ELF speakers, including the variations that can be found in collocations, proverbs and other types of idiomatic language use. An arguable difficulty with this focus is that it relates patterns in ELF use to native English patterns, and fails to address what it might be that actively supports the perception of fluency other than the use of idiomatic language. Additionally, the question remains whether any process of idiomaticity can be linked so directly to the use of specific idiomatic forms.

Fluency, I would argue, encompasses more than just idiomatic language use and at the same time apparently idiomatic language use can occur in interactions that are perceived as not fluent, notably when an idiomatic phrase is used by one speaker, which is not fully understood by the interlocutors, leading in turn to repair sequences (cf. Seidlhofer & Widdowson 2007, 369). There is one conundrum that comes up in the context of linking idiomaticity to fluency in a non-native language, which is that while the overarching psycholinguistic effect of using idiomatic or formulaic phrases to speed up speech processing might well be considered to be working equally in native and non-native varieties of any language, it is empirically extremely difficult to test whether a particular phrase is prefabricated or not for any individual speaker (*pace* Sinclair & Mauranen 2006, who manage to show linear units also in ELF data).

In sum, I would argue that ELF offers a rich field for investigating fluency as it forces us to focus on what creates the perception of fluency rather than applying (real or imagined) yardsticks *a priori*. The highly cooperative nature of ELF encourages a focus on processes and on the ways in which speakers act on their language knowledge and abilities, and is itself support for viewing a fairly psycholinguistic view of single speaker fluency as falling short of capturing the entire range of factors accountable for the creation of a perception of fluency.

As regards previous research into fluency in ELF, this falls into two categories; firstly, research that directly addresses fluency in ELF, such as Prodromou (2008), and research that took place within a larger pragmatic field, but found use being made of devices that in interactive fluency research were considered as (potential) measures of fluency. Both areas clearly need to be taken into account in my attempts to develop a clearer conceptualisation of ELF fluency. As I have argued above, I feel that Prodromou's focus on idiomatic forms in connection with fluency does not give a full picture of this phenomenon and risks staying too closely embedded in a psycholinguistic, 'narrow' view of fluency. With regard to those, especially pragmatic, features that have been observed in e.g. Cogo and Dewey (2006), it will be a vital part of this on-going research project to establish which of these can be considered to constitute features of ELF fluency.

The research agenda I have presented here is one of conceptualising fluency in ELF. My critical reading of the literature on fluency and on relevant aspects of ELF suggests that there are good reasons for assuming that ELF fluency is a contextually sensitive enactment of various aspects of speakers' language knowledge and abilities, most importantly, concerning the abilities to create 'smooth unity' or at least the impression of it. A possible research agenda to investigate fluency in ELF would need to take account of the perceptions of fluency of the speakers involved in an interaction and of observers of the same interactions. In such a way, one might hope to gain insights into what makes an interaction appear fluent. Given the status of fluency as a label accessible to and used by lay persons, such a systematic integration of lay perceptions with linguistic analysis is vital. The conceptualisation of ELF fluency then is to be a bottom-up process of finding out which features are present in interactions viewed as fluent and which are absent, and also a process of finding out what is focused on overtly by lay raters in their evaluations of fluency. Given the changes in the conceptualisation of fluency proposed here, the development of a suitable research methodology is a rather complex process, especially given the nature of ELF data, which does not lend itself easily to comparative evaluations. As this research is ongoing, in the following I cannot yet present results of a fully-fledged study, but will present two examples that serve to illustrate and support some of the points I have raised in the previous discussion.

4. Illustrative Examples

The two examples discussed below were taken from two larger data sets, namely informal, mainly touristic interactions in an Asian setting, and semi-formal interactions on education in a European setting. The examples were considered typical of the larger data sets they represent, and have the advantage of dealing with rather general topics that are easily accessible to observers. The interactants of these conversations could not be contacted for their introspective evaluations of the fluency levels of the interactions or the speakers involved, so I could only access observer or 3rd person data.

The extracts analyzed below were played out to two raters, who were then interviewed regarding their perceptions of fluency of the two extracts, of the speakers involved in the interactions and their overt reasons for such evaluations. No further information regarding what is meant by fluency was given to the raters, as it was precisely their un-reflected lay perception of the construct in relation to ELF that I wished to obtain. The only synonym used for *fluent* was *smooth*. Both raters were female, professional users of English, but not language teachers or testers. Although the raters were presented with a basic 6-point Likert scale to indicate where on a scale of fluency they would position the interaction and/or the speakers, both raters preferred to verbalise their evaluations. It was a conscious decision on my part to use an interview rather than a questionnaire format for obtaining information from the raters on their views on fluency and reasons for such views. It will be one of the major tasks of this on-going research project to develop a questionnaire format to be used with larger groups of raters and on considerably larger databases.

In the discussion below I will connect the features brought up by the raters to observable phenomena in the extracts and link them to points raised earlier regarding a possible conceptualization of fluency in ELF.

4.1. Tourism in Vietnam[4]

This conversation took place in Vietnam and is an informal interaction in a largely touristic environment, having taken place during a boat trip. The stakes of the interactions are thus not too high in the sense that the speakers are mostly involved in getting to know each other and exchanging some information about their own cultures, and do not have to achieve tangible goals within the interaction, as might be the case, for instance, in business transactions. Kordon (2005) has shown using this database how phatic communion does happen in ELF. Example 1 involves two Austrian and one Vietnamese speaker, all female, marked as A1, A2 and V1 respectively. (See Appendix for transcription conventions.)

Example 1

A1: d-do you smoke
V1: I don't smoking @@@@ I don't smo- you know you
smoke
A1: yeah I smoke
V1: you smoke
A2: I don- no I don't I don't [I I*=
A1: [she is*
V1: [ah very good (.) very bad*
A2: =I stopped smoking @ (.) @
V1: oh yes (.) many ehm girl Vietnam no smoking (.) no
smoke
A1: eh:m people [don't smo-*
V1: [the girl Vietnam* (.) [the girl*
A1: [ah the GIRLS*
V1: yeah
A1: ah really
V1: yeah girl
A2: girls don't smoke
V1: yeah many girl no smoking (.) many girl Vietnamese
(.) very little ehm girl Vietnam ehm smoking @
A1: it's good [it's good*
V1: [yeah yeah*
A2: @@@@
A1: =it's much better
A2. much better for [for your your*
A1: [@@@@@@*
V1: no (.) very expensive when people smoking
A1: yeah

Rater A evaluated this example as clearly more fluent than the second example and both raters concurred in evaluating this as in some sense 'smooth'. One rater viewed it as "quite highly fluent", although rater B viewed it as less fluent than Example 2. As adding to the perception of fluency, both raters mentioned that all speakers were involved in the interaction, and actively tried to make it work. Rater A explained her perception of a high level of fluency as due to the absence of noticeable pauses and explicitly focused on the presence of laughter in furthering the perceived degree of fluency. As she said, the "speakers feel good" in this interaction, and therefore the interaction is smooth. For rater B it was also noticeably "one conversation", i.e. a clear coherence and cohesion was referred to in a positive sense related to fluency. Rater A felt it was not possible to evaluate individual speakers' fluency levels and could only evaluate the entire interaction as regards fluency levels. Rater B, however, did distinguish individual fluency levels, and marked speaker V1 as least fluent. As reasons for this perception rater B quoted the lack of grammatical accuracy, especially in lines 10-11 and 19-20, and the need for A2 to ask for clarification in line 18.

In sum, we can note that although the raters do not fully overlap in their evaluation, one important feature towards viewing an interaction as fluent is its being noticeably co-constructed, i.e. showing an active involvement of all participants. Interestingly, while the grammatically non-standard realizations in lines 10-11 and 19-20 are not mentioned by rater A, they are clearly an important feature for downgrading the fluency level of the speaker for rater B. This indicates that the status of lexico-grammatical accuracy for an evaluation of fluency varies and, for ELF interactions, this is clearly a major issue in that it indicates the points of reference used by diverse observers or raters in this respect also vary. With regard to previous investigations of ELF we find that the "let-it-pass" principle (Firth 1996) does not seem to apply here, as the utterance of V1 in lines 9 and 10 is taken up by the other speakers until it is fully clarified. However, there is some support for the principle of joint forces (Smit 2008).

Interestingly, neither of the raters commented upon the speed of the interaction as furthering or lowering the perception of fluency. The average rate of speech for this interaction is 3.3 syllables per second, where in overlapping sections the longest stretch was taken into account. This might indicate that although psycholinguistic, as well as some teaching-related studies on fluency found a relevance of rate and pace of speech, this might not be the case in ELF. Additionally, we can note that there are a number of pauses, both short, unfilled pauses, indicated by (.), and longer filled pauses, i.e. *ehm*, which are not at all taken into account by rater A, although rater B takes these in combination with the hesitations and false starts (lines 1, 2, 6, 27) into account when arguing for her evaluation as V1 being somewhat less fluent than A1 and A2. This effect of pauses has been attested in other studies on fluency, and would be a factor to consider in a large scale study of the ratings of fluency in ELF.

The arguably most interesting observations of the raters as furthering the impression of fluency are the involvement of all speakers, the perception of it being 'one conversation', and the impression of the speakers 'having a good time'. These are, I believe, importantly features *not* related to psycholinguistic measures, and therefore deserve special attention. As to the issue of the speakers all being involved in the discussion, we can note that there are several clearly interactive features that can be taken into consideration here.

4.2. Talking about Teachers

The following extract is taken from a longer discussion on the educational practices and in a tertiary environment, where the medium of instruction is English. The sequence chosen for analysis discusses a particular teacher and the changes in her behavior over a period of time, from quite strict in the beginning to much more relaxed and encouraging of interactivity in class at the time of the interview. The setting is semi-formal, in that the participants are aware of the institutional framework, but the actual event taken into consideration here is not part of the formal instructional setting. The speakers A1 and A2 are Austrian, G1 and C1 are Greek/Austrian, and Chinese respectively.

Example 2

1	A2:	Interesting she didn't allow you to laugh or smile
2	A1:	I think this was to get a respect from the class (.) [so
3		that was
4	G1:	[It
5		was the first two times maybe
6	A1:	but now she is completely different=
7	G1:	=now she is completely different
8	A1:	it's like
9	G1:	so much different (.) very easy going (.) [so much
10		easy going
11	A2:	[and you
12		also (.) too easy going @@@
13	G1:	@@
14	C1:	no (.) I mean if she teaches something (.) I mean her
15		personality (.) her attitude changed very easy (.)
16		because she was so kind of strict or so
17	A1:	because in the first class if you asked her something
18		she said (.) I just did that I just covered that you
19		didn't listen [but now she'd explain [it (.) again (.)
20		that's completely different
21	G1:	[yeah

C1: [yeah

Rater A evaluated this example as less fluent than Example 1, and both raters felt that in this stretch the individual speakers could be evaluated diversely with respect to their levels of fluency. For both raters, A1 was the most fluent speaker in the interaction, although rater B also noted that he was the dominant speaker, which seemed to her to indicate a decrease in fluency for the overall interaction, adding to the impression that this was, unlike Example 1, not an interaction where all speakers participated. For rater A, G1 was the least fluent speaker, for rater B, both G1 and C1 were seen as less fluent than A1 and A2.

Similarly to the first example, neither of the raters makes explicit reference to speed as a factor accounting for fluency, which with 4.4 syllables per second is slightly faster in this example than in Example 1. It is, however, worth noting that in a previous discussion involving some of the same interactants, reference is made to A1 speaking 'too fast' at the beginning of the course, and so being hard to understand for the other participants. The relevant extract is given below:

Example 3

A2: and can you when you talk to them or when they talk
in class, can you understand all of them or
C1: no I don't think so. Maybe someone speaks so quick,
I cannot catch it, but (xxx) in case they speak slowly,
then I can understand
A2: which ones are difficult (.) you can also say I mean I
know the people you can give me the names or the
groups (.) which ones are difficult for you
C1: maybe [A1] (.) he talks so quickly I think

The features that might contribute to a perception of fluency of Example 2 are the echo that is latched on to the previous utterance in line 7, which can be seen as a *Represent* (cf. House 2002), as well as backchannels in lines 21 and 22. There is laughter also in this interaction, but it does seem to function slightly different from the laughter in Example 1 by being related directly to a statement of the teacher having changed from being too strict to arguably being "too easy-going". Although there is certainly an element of group-cohesion in this example as well, the laughter does not appear to be creating such cohesion or phatic communion, but to be an exemplification of it.

To summarise, we can find that various factors were mentioned with regard to being supportive of a higher level of fluency. Some comments related to cohesion and coherence in the widest senses, i.e. interlocutors being perceived as conducting one conversation, but arguably most attention was given to interactive features, i.e. the collaborative nature of especially Example 1, which includes also the use of laughter to create a sense of unity. While the small database makes generalizations at this point impossible, these comments, and particularly the comment by one rater that individual fluency levels could not be perceived in Example 1, support the point raised on the potential of fluency as a descriptor of interactions. Interestingly, speed was not picked up on as a decisive feature for fluency by either of the raters and the one comment by the interlocutors themselves on Example 2 show that there might be views for considering speed as a much more complex measure in an ELF setting, with a potentially 'right' speed, which might not be the fastest possible speed of any individual speaker. The use or lack of specific idiomatic phrases was not commented on by either of the raters. Some issues, especially lexico-grammatical accuracy, received different treatment by the two raters, showing that this is certainly an area to take up on in greater detail in the large-scale study on fluency in ELF envisaged.

5. Conclusion and Outlook

This paper has argued for a view of fluency as a dialogic phenomenon that is enacted by speakers while taking contextual issues into account. ELF provides us with a rich field for investigating such a dialogic nature of fluency and the examples shown have illustrated how ELF fluency is characterized by interactivity, including notably the use of *Represents*, laughter and repetitions, to create a perception of fluency. The comments of the raters on the examples, which indicate that an involvement of all interactants to develop a coherent dialogue contributes to the perception of fluency, are seen as strong encouragement to follow this line of investigation of dialogic ELF fluency. This view of fluency as a dialogic phenomenon is also supported by critical readings of the literature on fluency, which suggests the decisive influence of interlocutors on the perceptions of fluency, the difficulties in using L1 norms in assessing or evaluating L2 fluency, and the observations that the same speakers are differently fluent depending on the interactions in which they find themselves.

Clearly, while this paper has been able to propose a re-conceptualisation of fluency in the light of ELF, much research is still required to substantiate such a re-conceptualisation. Importantly, the encouraging first results of using lay raters systematically need to be developed further, including using a much larger database of ELF interactions. Also, larger groups of raters with diverse levels of experience as users of ELF need to be involved as well as the interlocutors of the actual interactions under scrutiny. Only by gathering as much information as possible, from both an insiders' and outsiders' perspective, can we hope to find out what truly constitutes fluency in ELF.

One final major issue that will need to be taken into account systematically are cultural differences of the interlocutors and the raters, especially with regard to turn-taking patterns in order to establish to what extent these influence perceptions of fluency.

Appendix

Transcription conventions used in this paper are as follows:

@	laughter
[	beginning of overlapping speech
*	end of overlapping speech
=	latched (i.e. one utterance following onto the previous one without a pause)
(.)	short pause
wor-	(i.e. hyphen within words): self-interruption / false start
(xxx)	unintelligible passage (one x per syllable)

Bibliography

Ahvenainen, T. 2005. "Problem-Solving Mechanisms in Information Exchange Dialogues with English as a Lingua Franca." M.A. thesis, University of Jyväskylä, Finland. http://thesis.jyu.fi/05/URN_NBN_fi_jyu-2005219.pdf. (accessed December 20, 2008)

Bolander, M. 1989. "Prefabs, Patterns and Rules in Interaction? Formulaic Speech in Adult Learners' L2 Swedish." In *Bilingualism Across the Lifespan: Aspects of Acquisition, Maturity and Loss*, ed. K. Hyltenstam. & L. K. Obler, 73-86. Cambridge: Cambridge University Press.

Bowe, H. and K. Martin 2007. *Communication Across Cultures: Mutual Understanding in a Global World.* Cambridge: Cambridge University Press.

Brown, A. 2005. *Interviewer Variability in Oral Proficiency Interviews.* Frankfurt am Main: Peter Lang.

Brumfit, C. 1984 [2000]. "Accuracy and Fluency: The Basic Polarity." In *Perspectives on Fluency*, ed. H. Riggenbach, 61-73. Ann Arbor: University of Michigan Press.

Brutt-Griffler, J. 2002. *World English. A Study of Its Development.* Clevedon: Multilingual Matters.

Chambers, F. 1997. "What do We Mean by Fluency?" *System* 25 (4), 535-44.

Cogo, A. and M. Dewey 2006. "Efficiency in ELF Communication: From Pragmatic Motives to Lexico-Grammatical Innovation." *Nordic Journal of English Studies* 5 (2), 59-93.

Ejzenberg, R. 2000. "The Juggling Act of Oral Fluency: A Psycho-Sociolinguistic Metaphor." In *Perspectives on Fluency*, ed. H. Riggenbach, 287-314. Ann Arbor: University of Michigan Press.

Ellis, N. 2003. "Constructions, Chunking and Connectionism: The Emergence of Second Language Structure." In *Handbook of Second Language Acquisition*, ed. J. C. Doughty & M. H. Long, 63-103. Malden, MA: Blackwell.

—. 2001. "Memory for Language." In *Cognition and Second Language Instruction*, ed. P. Robinson, 33-68. Cambridge: Cambridge University Press.

Fillmore, C. J. 1979 [2000]. "On Fluency." In *Perspectives on Fluency*, ed. H. Riggenbach, 43-60. Ann Arbor: University of Michigan Press.

Firth, A. 1996. "The Discursive Accomplishment of Normality: On 'Lingua Franca' English and Conversation Analysis." *Journal of Pragmatics* 26 (2), 237-59.

—. 1990. "'Lingua Franca' Negotiations: Towards an Interactional Approach." *World Englishes* 9 (3), 269-80.

Freed, B. F. 2000. "Is Fluency—Like Beauty—in the Eyes (and Ears) of the Beholder?" In *Perspectives on Fluency*, ed. H. Riggenbach, 243-65. Ann Arbor: The University of Michigan Press.

—. 1995. "What Makes Us Think Students Who Study Abroad Become Fluent?" In *Second Language Acquisition in a Study Abroad Context*, ed. B. F. Freed, 123-48. Amsterdam: John Benjamins.

Gnutzmann, C. and F. Intemann 2005. *The Globalisation of English and the English Language Classroom*. Tübingen: Narr.

Graddol, D. 2006. *English Next: Why Global English May Mean the End of 'English as a Foreign Language'*. British Council.

Guillot, M. 1999. *Fluency and Its Teaching*. Clevedon, UK: Multilingual Matters.

House, J. 2002. "Developing Pragmatic Competence in English as a Lingua Franca." In *Lingua Franca Communication*, ed. K. Knapp & C. Meierkord, 245-68. Frankfurt am Main: Peter Lang.

—. 1996. "Developing Pragmatic Fluency in English as a Foreign Language. Routines and Metapragmatic Awareness." *Studies in Second Language Acquisition* 18 (2), 225-52.

Hüttner, J. (2009 *in press*). "Dialogic Fluency: On the Development of Co-Fluency in English as a Lingua Franca (ELF) Interactions." In *Coherence and Cohesion in Spoken and Written Discourse*, ed. O. Dontcheva-Navratilova & R. Povolna. Cambridge: Cambridge Scholars Publishing.

Hüttner, J. I. 2007. *Academic Writing in a Foreign Language: An Extended Genre Analysis of Student Texts*. Frankfurt am Main: Peter Lang.

Jenkins, J. 2007. *English as a Lingua Franca: Attitude and Identity*. Oxford: Oxford University Press.

—. 2003. *World Englishes. A Resource Book for Students*. London: Routledge.

Kordon, K. 2005. "'You are very good'—Establishing Rapport in English as a Lingua Franca: The Case of Agreement Tokens." *VIEWS* 15 (2), 58-82.

Kormos, J. 2006. *Speech Production and Second Language Acquisition*. London: Lawrence Erlbaum.

Kormos, J. and M. Denes 2004. "Exploring Measures and Perceptions of Fluency in the Speech of Second Language Learners." *System* 32 (2), 145-64.

Lennon, P. 2000. "The Lexical Element in Spoken Second Language Fluency." In *Perspectives on Fluency*, ed. H. Riggenbach, 25-42. Ann Arbor: The University of Michigan Press.

—. 1990. "Investigating Fluency in EFL: A Quantitative Approach." *Language Learning* 40 (3), 387-417.

Linnakylä, P. 1980. "Hi Superman: What is the Most Functional English for a Finnish Five-Year-Old." *Journal of Pragmatics* 4 (4), 367-92.

Lorenzo-Dus, N. and P. Meara 2005. "Examiner Support Strategies and Test-Taker Vocabulary." *International Review of Applied Linguistics in Language Teaching* 43 (3), 239-58.

Myles, F., R. Mitchell and J. Hooper 1999. "Interrogative Chunks in French L2: A Basis for Creative Construction?" *Studies in Second Language Acquisition* 21 (1), 49-80.

Nattinger, J. R. and J. DeCarrico 1992. *Lexical Phrases and Language Teaching*. Oxford: Oxford University Press.

Pawley, A. and F. H. Syder 1983. "Two Puzzles for Linguistic Theory: Nativelike Selection and Nativelike Fluency." In *Language and Communication*, ed. J. C. Richards & R. W. Schmidt, 191-226. London: Longman.

Prodromou, L. 2008. *English as a Lingua Franca. A Corpus-Based Analysis*. London: Continuum.

Rehbein, J. 1987a. "On Fluency in Second Language Speech." In *Psycholinguistic Models of Production*, ed. H. W. Dechert & M. Raupach, 97-105. Norwood, NJ: Ablex.

—. 1987b. "Multiple Formulae: Aspects of Turkish Migrant Workers' German in Intercultural Communication." In *Second Language*

Production, ed. H. W. Dechert, D Möhle & M. Raupach, 114-37. Tübingen: Gunter Narr.

Riggenbach, H. 1998. "Evaluating Learner Interactional Skills: Conversation at the Micro Level." In *Talking and Testing: Discourse Approaches to the Assessment of Oral Proficiency*, ed. R. Young & A. He, 53-67. Amsterdam: John Benjamins.

—. 1991. "Toward an Understanding of Fluency: A Microanalysis of Nonnative Speaker Conversations." *Discourse Processes* 14 (4), 423-41.

Sajavaara, K. 1987. "Second Language Speech Production: Factors Affecting Fluency." In *Psycholinguistic Models of Production*, ed. H. W. Dechert & M. Raupach, 45-65. Norwood, NJ: Ablex.

Schmidt, R. W. 1983. "Interaction, Acculturation, and the Acquisition of Communicative Competence: A Case Study of an Adult." In *Sociolinguistics and Language Acquisition*, ed. N. Wolfson & E. Judd, 137-74. Rowley, MA: Newbury House.

Seidlhofer, B. 2004. "Research Perspectives on Teaching English as a Lingua Franca." *Annual Review of Applied Linguistics* 24, 209-39.

—. 2001. "Closing a Conceptual Gap: The Case for a Description of English as a Lingua Franca." *International Journal of Applied Linguistics* 11 (2), 133-58.

Seidlhofer, B., A. Breiteneder and M.-L. Pitzl 2006. "English as a Lingua Franca in Europe: Challenges for Applied Lingusitics." *Annual Review of Applied Linguistics* 26, 3-34.

Seidlhofer, B. and H. G. Widdowson 2007. "Idiomatic Variation and Change in English. The Idiom Principle and Its Realizations." In *Tracing English through Time. Explorations in Language Variation*, ed. U. Smit, S. Dollinger, J. Hüttner, G. Kaltenböck & U. Lutzky, 359-74. Vienna: Braumüller.

Sinclair, J. M. and A. Mauranen 2006. *Linear Unit Grammar: Integrating Speech and Writing*. Amsterdam: John Benjamins.

Smit, U. 2008. "Classroom Interaction in English as a Lingua Franca: A Discourse Pragmatic Ethnography in International Higher Education." Habilitation thesis, University of Vienna.

Towell, R., R. Hawkins and N. Bazergui 1996. "The Development of Fluency in Advanced Learners of French." *Applied Linguistics* 17 (1), 84-119.

Wennerstrom, A. 2000. "The Role of Intonation in Second Language Fluency." In *Perspectives on Fluency*, ed. H. Riggenbach, 102-27. Ann Arbor: The University of Michigan Press.

Wong Fillmore, L. 1979. "Individual Differences in Second Language Acquisition." In *Individual Differences in Language Ability and Language Behavior*, ed. C. Fillmore, D. Kempler & W. S. Y. Wang, 203-28. New York: Academic Press.

Wray, A. 2002. *Formulaic Language and the Lexicon*. Cambridge: Cambridge University Press.

Yorio, C. 1989. "Idiomaticity as an Indicator of Second Language Proficiency." In *Bilingualism Across the Lifespan. Aspects of Acquisition, Maturity and Loss*, ed. K. Hyltenstam & L. K. Obler, 55-72. Cambridge: Cambridge University Press

Notes

[1] This paper is a substantially extended version of Hüttner (2009 *in press*).

[2] Although distinguishing between broad and narrow fluency acknowledges the existence of various definitions of fluency, it remains slightly unhelpful in suggesting a direct link between the overall oral language proficiency (or 'broad' fluency, comparable largely to lay perceptions of fluency) and the psycholinguistic measures of speed and hesitation markers employed in studies focusing on 'narrow' fluency.

[3] cf. also Wernicke's aphasia.

[4] My gratitude goes to Kathrin Kordon and to Ute Smit for granting me access to their ELF data.

"WE SHOULD NOT WAKE UP ANY DOGS": IDIOM AND METAPHOR IN ELF

MARIE-LUISE PITZL

1. Introduction

ELF is a vibrant field of research. The past three to five years have not only seen an increasing amount of empirical research on ELF in journal articles[1], monographs[2] and special journal issues[3], but have also witnessed an increasing interest in the theoretical debate about and around ELF: what it is, what it is not, how it could develop, and how it relates to other areas of linguistics[4]. Building on this current ELF research, this paper addresses a question which has recently attracted ELF researchers' attention, namely what the role of (so-called) idioms is in ELF. The recurrent patterns of language that are revealed in the corpus analysis of naturally-occurring native speaker English show how idioms and idiomaticity contribute to effective communication in these native speaker contexts (cf. Sinclair 1991). Since ELF is also naturally-occurring and communicatively effective (as shown e.g. in Breiteneder 2005, Cogo 2007, Cogo & Dewey 2006, Dewey 2007a, Hülmbauer 2007, Lichtkoppler 2007, Pitzl 2005), one might therefore expect it also to be idiomatic, i.e. to make use of the conventionalized preconstructed phrases that are conducive to understanding in L1 contexts (cf. Seidlhofer & Widdowson 2007, 361). But although idiomatic expressions occur in ELF, these expressions often display considerable non-conformity in reference to native speaker (NS) norms. Thus, it appears that the concept of idiomaticity as applied to NS usage cannot simply be mapped onto ELF.

The present paper addresses this question by looking at idioms and idiomaticity in ELF from a different angle, that is, by focusing on their metaphorical function. Section 2 explores the decreased importance of territoriality in ELF interactions and examines how this might influence the motivation for using idioms in ELF contexts. Section 3 then investigates the relationship between idiom and metaphor, thereby indicating the difficulty of defining and delimiting both concepts, and it outlines how the metaphorical origins of idiomatic expressions might resurface in ELF. Finally, section 4 explores the theoretical issues raised in an analysis of examples of naturally-occurring ELF discourse taken from the Vienna-Oxford International Corpus of English (VOICE).

2. Idioms in ELF—A Territorial Question?

Idioms and idiomaticity have come to be regarded as central building blocks of ENL speech. Corpus linguists, first and foremost John Sinclair, have shown how naturally-occurring talk of English native speakers operates through the idiom principle to a large degree. In its broadest definition, the "principle of idiom" refers to the fact that "a language user has available to him or her a large number of semi-preconstructed phrases that constitute single choices" (Sinclair 1991, 110). Thus, in employing the "principle of idiom", language users do not construct phrases and expressions bottom-up or 'from scratch', but utilize an already existent repertoire of semi-fixed chunks. Since the corpus data which Sinclair's observations are based on reflect the English produced by native speakers, the "language user" referred to in Sinclair's quote is a native speaker of English. Sinclair's broad definition of which items are covered by the idiom principle includes fixed two-word phrases (e.g. *of course*) and strong collocations (e.g. *hard facts*) as well as idioms, proverbs and the like (Sinclair 1991, 110-112). This definition already indicates the terminological ambiguity that we are facing with regard to the topic of idioms and idiomaticity: Sinclair lists idioms as one category within the principle of idiom, which is bound to make terminology ambiguous, an issue which will be explored in more detail in section 3.

Considering the centrality of the idiom principle that has been suggested for ENL, it is not surprising that ELF researchers have recently also turned their interest towards the question of idioms and idiomaticity in ELF. Seidlhofer and Widdowson (2007) look at the idiom principle and its realizations in ELF. While they suggest that ELF users probably exhibit a greater reliance on the open-choice principle and "construct what they have to say more atomistically, in a bottom-up fashion" (Seidlhofer & Widdowson 2007, 365), they also give examples of how the idiom principle might be at work in ELF via the online construction of new idioms which are then available for a fixed group of speakers at a certain time and in a certain context. Idiom building has to be considered a necessary precondition of the operation of the idiom principle in ENL, so it is not surprising that we should be able to observe a similar process to be operating in ELF. It is important to note, however, that idioms which are newly constructed in ELF do not necessarily conform to the particular wordings of ENL speakers (Seidlhofer & Widdowson 2007, 373). The realization of the idiom principle therefore does not depend on the realization of particular ENL-idiomatic expressions. As a process, the idiom principle may operate outside of native speaker (NS) 'idiomatic' usage. Idiomaticity therefore cannot simply be equated with ENL idioms.

Another important aspect that Seidlhofer and Widdowson (2007) raise, which is central to the argument in this paper, is that communication in ELF generally lacks what they call a "territorial imperative" (p. 368). The territorial imperative can be paraphrased as the need to establish and protect one's own social space as a member of a particular speech community. And one way of performing this territorial imperative is the use of idioms. In ENL contexts, idioms are heavily 'culturally loaded' for the members of a speech community. They serve as "territorial markers of social identity and group membership" (Seidlhofer & Widdowson 2007, 362). When it comes to ELF, there is no culturally fixed speech community in the traditional sense and a re-definition and re-consideration of established terminology is needed (cf. Seidlhofer 2009a).[5] As Seidlhofer & Widdowson (2007, 368) put it, global ELF users "are not using the language to qualify for membership of a pre-defined community". Hence we can assume that they do not feel the same pressures of the territorial imperative that is at work for first language speakers of English or of any other language for that matter.[6]

The territorial imperative and the territorial function of idioms, however, are certainly relevant when English is used as first language among members of one particular speech community. Yet, if we accept that in ELF there is no fixed, culturally defined speech community that ELF speakers can—or would want to—claim membership to, one of the prime functions of idioms among first language speakers, namely their territorial function, is presumably absent in ELF. If idioms are used in ELF, we can thus presuppose that this happens for other communicative purposes than marking one's cultural territory.

Yet, idioms and their territorial function are intricately linked in ENL. As a consequence, there (still) seems to be a strong temptation for some researchers to apply such a territorial perspective also to an analysis of idioms in ELF. What I mean by applying a territorial perspective in analysis is that the use of idioms in ELF is primarily regarded and analyzed from the point of view of ENL speakers, that is, as part of the ENL territory. Prodromou (2007, 20) mentions examples of ELF speakers being penalized, notably by native speakers of English, when they use idioms 'creatively'. He also shows how a varied collocation is much more likely to be rated 'acceptable' by teachers of English if it is produced by a NS than if it is produced by a NNS (Prodromou 2007, 22). The conclusion he draws from these and other observations is the following:

> Of course, the task of acquiring idiomaticity is only a problem if one sets up L1 forms as the norm for English as a Lingua Franca. The question is whether L1-like idiomaticity is a valid strand in the tapestry of ELF. L1-users deploy their mother tongue from a position of deep commonality and, as a rule, L2-users of that language don't. This means that, as far as idiomaticity is concerned, *L1-users* are 'playing at home', with *rules they can bend according to need. L2-users* are 'playing away', and, *if they break the rules, they are penalized.* [...] After all, several of the SUEs [successful users of English] in my corpus display undoubted skill in the manipulation of idiom, if not in the free-wheeling creativity that is the very stuff of common talk in L1 informal conversation. And they seem to have an intuition for where their limits are, *as far as idiomaticity is concerned: they keep away from minefields.* (Prodromou 2007, 23-24; my emphasis)

While I roughly concur with Prodromou's first sentence, his ensuing statements are increasingly problematic and ambiguous for different reasons.

Posing the question whether "L1-like idiomaticity is a valid strand in the tapestry of ELF" I take to be a comment based on the evidence in Prodromou's own data (cf. e.g. Prodromou 2007, 20) that native speakers of English 'penalize' non-native speakers for incorrect, or even simply unexpected, idiomaticity. Firstly, this observation is in stark contrast to the findings of most ELF research, where English native speakers, if present, generally are not seen to judge non-native speakers' linguistic output or to penalize them for it[7]. Secondly, while I do not want to question Prodromou's evidence that such 'penalization' occurs, as indeed it might, I am not certain that questioning whether L1-like idiomaticity may be "valid" for ELF is the only conclusion to draw from this kind of evidence. In order to be 'penalized' for it, a speaker has had to use an idiom in the first place. And the fact that the speakers in Prodromou's examples use idioms only serves to show that it is not possible to say that idioms are not relevant or "valid" for ELF speakers.

Of course, one might object that Prodromou in his second sentence is not talking about idiomaticity in general, but referring to "L1-like idiomaticity". But the problem is that throughout the next sentences in his two concluding paragraphs, "L1-like idiomaticity" becomes simply "idiomaticity" without any reference to first language use. The two terms are, it seems, increasingly conflated and equated. Idiomaticity then implicitly always means L1-idiomaticity, which in turn makes it difficult to see how idiomaticity could possibly exist in or be relevant for ELF at all. Thus, according to Prodromou (2007, 23) "L1-users" can "bend" the rules "according to need", whereas "L2-users" are forced to "break" them. At least this is what the results of Prodromou's teacher survey suggest—it is unclear whether Prodromou himself shares this view or not. Yet, because the speakers are penalized for creative use and variation of idioms in Prodromou's examples, the dejected conclusion they themselves draw, as does Prodromou (2007, 24) is to "keep away from minefields", which means idiomaticity. It is as if they are standing in front of a sign which reads: *Idiomaticity. Native speaker-territory. No trespassing!*

Staying out of harm's way by keeping away from the minefield of idiomaticity is a suggestion which is quite openly territorial. And indeed if we remember that a central function of idioms in ENL is to serve as territorial markers of group membership, then the tendency to adopt this territorial approach is quite understandable. Nevertheless, when dealing with ELF, we need to be willing to shift our perspective and to adopt a new approach. The territorial imperative does not apply to ELF speakers in the same way as it applies to the members of any L1 speech community. We are therefore facing the challenge of having to leave behind the traditional territorial notion of why speakers use idioms and take into account the possibility that ELF speakers may use idioms for various other communicative purposes. The remainder of this paper takes up this challenge by proposing that, in ELF, we need to focus on idiom in relationship with metaphor. By giving prominence to what is metaphoric about the use of idioms in ELF, we are uncoupling the question of idioms and idiomaticity from its association with territoriality in ENL usage—and it seems, as will be exemplified in the data analysis, that this is also what ELF speakers themselves do.

3. The Chicken or the Egg?—On the Relationship between Idiom and Metaphor

The suggestion that there is a close relationship between idioms as conventionalized semi-fixed phrases and metaphors as (dynamic) expressions linking two different concepts is not new but has been pointed out by many researchers with regard to ENL (e.g. Cameron 1999, Gibbs 1999, Grant & Bauer 2004, Hanks 2006, Langlotz 2006). What is common to many observations is that the distinction between what is seen as an idiom and what as a metaphor is, in many ways, a diachronic one in first language use, relating to the effects of language change over time. This is evident in statements which, for example, refer to best-example idioms as "frozen phrases that were originally metaphors" (Hanks 2006, 26). Thus, it is essentially the extensive use of certain metaphors within one speech community which brings about their conventionalization, institutionalization and codification in the course of time and which, in short, turns the metaphor into an idiom.

In this respect, it is common with regard to L1 use to refer to some idiomatic expressions as 'dead' metaphors which have become so conventionalized and frequent that they have lost their metaphoricity in the course of time (cf. e.g. Carter 2004, 122). Whether a specific metaphor within a certain idiom is actually really 'dead' is, however, a question for empirical research in cognitive studies and psycholinguistics. Thus, Gibbs (1999, 146), for example, mentions that some idioms retain metaphoricity in that the corresponding conceptual metaphors are still activated during idiom processing. Goatly (1997, 32) mentions different degrees of conventionality in this respect and distinguishes between 'tired', 'sleeping', 'dead' and 'buried' metaphors.

Goatly's concept of sleeping metaphors is also mentioned by Langlotz, who looks at idiomatic creativity. Working within a cognitive linguistic paradigm, Langlotz (2006, 11) also states that idioms "were originally created as non-conventional metaphors or metonymies". Idioms are regarded as complex linguistic constructions which are intrinsically creative because "their internal structure incorporates the systematic and creative extension of semantic structures" (ibid.). This definition fits the common view according to which the creation, evolution and institutionalization of idioms emerge from and depend on metaphors. But since Langlotz is interested in investigating idiomatic creativity, that is, how certain idioms can be and are varied by (first language) speakers, he importantly goes on to remark that

> the degree to which an idiom can be systematically and creatively manipulated in discourse is dependent on the degree to which the *idiom's intrinsic creativity* remains *accessible to the language user or can be re-established by him or her.* (Langlotz 2006, 11; my emphasis)

With "intrinsic creativity", Langlotz simply refers to the metaphorical origin of the idiom. So in other words, how much an idiom can be formally varied, changed and adapted depends on how active or (re-) accessible its inherent metaphor is to a language user. A metaphor that is 'sleeping' within an idiom, so to speak, might thus be re-awakened in order to re-enliven and structurally vary, adapt, and change the idiom. One could say that an idiom which is varied in this way is 're-metaphorized': it is deconstructed and reassembled in order to create a new or different meaning which relies on the semantic properties of the individual linguistic components and is thus compositional, although not literal.

Some researchers draw an absolute distinction between idioms and metaphors in the sense that they insist on the fixed and non-compositional meaning of idioms which "does not depend on resonance between primary and secondary subjects" (Hanks 2006, 27), resonance being characteristic of a metaphor. So although, as was mentioned above, Hanks acknowledges the relationship between idiom and metaphor, this relationship for him is a purely diachronic one. A particular expression such as *all at sea*, for Hanks, is an idiom—and not a conventional metaphor—because the resonance within the expression is purely historical and no longer active. If the resonance were still active, it would have to be classified as a metaphor (ibid.). So what we are witnessing in positions like this is an either-or distinction: either an expression is an idiom, or it is a metaphor. Since Hanks bases his analysis on the British National Corpus (BNC), he is referring to ENL and does not theorize about idioms and metaphors in non-native speakers' speech or English as a lingua franca.

The general tendency to characterize idioms as being non-compositional is also expressed in reference works such as the *Longman Grammar of Spoken and Written English*, which refers to idiomatic phrases as "expressions with a meaning *not entirely* derivable from the meaning of their parts" (Biber et al. 1999, 1024; my emphasis). So according to this definition an idiom is more than the sum of the meanings of its individual components. It is, at least to some extent, non-compositional. The formulation "not entirely", however, also suggests that the meanings of the component parts of an idiomatic expression may still play some role in interpreting the meaning of the idiom. The extent to which this may be the case is left unspecified however.

Grant and Bauer (2004) address the question of (the degree of) the compositionality of idioms and multi-word units from the point of view of lexicography. They distinguish 'figures of speech' like metaphors from idioms on the basis that "figures of speech can be interpreted according to general cognitive principles, while idioms have to be learnt" (Grant & Bauer 2004, 49). Yet, they point out that "many figurative expressions are referred to as being idiomatic" (Grant & Bauer 2004, 51). Based on this distinction, they devise an idiom test which they apply to a random sample of nineteen entries for idioms taken from two different idiom dictionaries.

In devising the idiom test, they propose a distinction between "figuratives" and what they call "core idioms" which is based on the assumptions that

> * figurative language is recognized as compositionally involving an untruth which can be reinterpreted pragmatically to understand the intended truth [...] but idioms cannot.
> * figurative language can be undone or 'unpicked' to work out the meaning [...] but idioms cannot [...] (or at least cannot without non-linguistic, historical knowledge, cf. *red herring*). (Grant & Bauer 2004, 51)

What Grant and Bauer stress is that figuratives can be made sense of, while "core idioms", which we might dub 'real idioms' or 'pure idioms', cannot be "unpicked" or decoded, or in other words decomposed semantically. Alluding again to the diachronic dimension mentioned above, this is true also for idioms which have arisen "by the freezing of figures of speech" (Grant & Bauer 2004, 52) and are thus figurative in origin, but have lost their figurativeness over time. From the perspective of lexicography, "core idioms" must then be regarded as institutionalized and lexicalized (cf. Lipka 2002, 111ff.) single units whose meaning cannot be guessed if it is not known by a listener.

What is remarkable about Grant and Bauer's re-analysis of their sample of entries in idiom dictionaries is that they find that, in fact, according to their idiom test, none of the tested idioms qualify as "core idioms". Most of the tested idioms are reclassified either as figuratives or as "ONCEs", which are expressions in which only a single word is non-literal or non-compositional, such as *a devil of a job*, with *devil* being the only non-literal element (Grant & Bauer 2004, 54ff.).

What Grant and Bauer's findings thus seem to reflect is the general difficulty of defining what is actually meant by the term 'idiom'. In many contexts, the term 'idiom' is used with a very broad meaning and can cover a wide spectrum of expressions, from highly frequent fixed two-word items like *of course* to much quoted but rarely produced prototypical 'colorful phrases' like *kick the bucket.* This is the broad spectrum of expressions which is addressed by Sinclair's idiom principle. Grant and Bauer suggest a much more narrow definition of the term 'idiom'. This, in turn, suggests that much of what we could subsume under a broad general idiom category might also be something else, i.e. a "figurative" in Grant and Bauer's terminology, by which they mean an expression which is compositionally recognized as involving an untruth—which is in turn a standard definition for metaphor.

I would argue that, if one does not adopt a particularly narrow definition like the 'core idiom' proposed by Grant and Bauer, then one needs to allow for the fact that an idiom (in ENL, but also in ELF) may not only be a non-compositional institutionalized lexical unit. Many expressions which we can refer to as idioms may in fact be decomposable (cf. Abel

2003) and may thus be interpretable according to general cognitive principles. Seen in this light, idioms in ELF, particularly if they are varied and different from their ENL canonical forms, might function as metaphors and can thus be analyzed accordingly. In other words, the relationship of idiom and metaphor is not necessarily an either-or question. Allowing for such a dual perspective opens up an alternative level of analysis which is considerably removed from the territorial perspective on idioms outlined in the previous section. Getting the exact 'idiomatic', i.e. NS-like, wording 'right' becomes less central if we allow for the possibility that the expression functions as a metaphor. This has of course also strong implications for how 'idiom-metaphors' are assessed as far as correctness and appropriateness are concerned.

What we might find in ELF is that the possibly dormant 'sleeping' metaphors 'contained' in idioms are actually quite active and thus allow for a considerable degree of flexibility in the formal use of an idiom, while still maintaining intelligibility through the (re-)activated metaphor. In other words, idioms might undergo a process of what I will call 're-metaphorization' in ELF, where metaphoricity is reintroduced into otherwise conventionalized idiomatic expressions. In many ways, it thus makes sense to reverse the hierarchy of idiom and metaphor in an analysis of ELF data. Instead of regarding an idiom as a frozen or dead metaphor, one might look at some of the deliberate uses of metaphors in ELF as formally resembling already existing English (or also other language) idioms. To put it more simply: while the tendency in ENL is to say that an idiom contains a 'frozen' metaphor, i.e. the metaphor came first and evolved into an idiom, in ELF we could say that a certain metaphor contains an idiom, i.e. the idiom came first (e.g. it was taught in an EFL context as a conventional expression) and undergoes a process of re-metaphorization in ELF use. So while an expression in ELF may resemble an English or other language idiom at the textual surface level, it may first and foremost function as a metaphor in interaction, since the capability of metaphor processing is common to speakers of all languages and is thus shared by all ELF speakers. The subsequent section will present an in-depth analysis of some examples of ELF discourse in order to explore this hypothesis and show how this process of re-metaphorization might be operating in ELF.

4. Re-Metaphorization of Idioms in ELF— A Qualitative Discussion of Forms and Functions

In the following, I will present a qualitative analysis of data extracts from the professional domain of the Vienna-Oxford International Corpus of English (VOICE). VOICE is the first general corpus of spoken ELF and comprises one million words in its first release (VOICE version 1.0 online), which equals slightly over 110 hours of recorded conversations. All speech events in VOICE have been conscientiously transcribed following unified transcription conventions developed to capture the particulars of ELF speech and were subsequently checked and proofread.

The examples of ELF data will be analyzed on two levels: linguistic form and communicative function. The interrelatedness of these levels has repeatedly been stressed with regard to ELF (e.g. Cogo & Dewey 2006, Pitzl, Breiteneder & Klimpfinger 2008, Seidlhofer 2008) and it also appears to be particularly significant for the relationship of metaphor and idiom. On the one hand, the analysis will therefore examine the formal characteristics of the examples of metaphors in VOICE and explore any existing resemblances to codified ENL, and in some cases also other language, idioms. On the other hand, the specific professional context of interaction will be considered in order to identify the communicative functions which the metaphor fulfills in each instance. It will be shown that, while the metaphors may differ from existing idioms in form, they nevertheless successfully fulfill a striking range of communicative functions in different contexts.

The first example (which provides the title of the paper) happens in the course of a business meeting. Two Koreans (S1 and S2) who are employees of a Korean distribution company have come to Austria to visit their Austrian business partners S3, S4 and S5. The context preceding this example in the interaction is that the Korean company has produced a display with a picture of a cartoon character for which they would normally have had to get the approval of the company who owns this cartoon character. But as they were not aware of the copyright issue involved, they failed to seek for such an approval beforehand, produced the display and distributed it in Korean stores without asking permission from the company first. In this context, S4 produces the following expression in utterance 2023 below.

Example 1 (PBmtg3)[8]

2020	S4:	you have it in the stores since WHEN? since a couple of MONTHS (.)
2021	S1:	only <1> e:r </1> one and a half month.
2022	S2:	<1><un> x </un> months </1>
2023	S4:	yeah then (1) i think in THAT case **we should not wake up any (.) any DOGS** by going now
2024	SX-m:	<un> xx <1> x </1></un>
2025	S4:	<1> NOW </1> since it's in <2> the </2>
2026	S1:	<2> o</2>kay
2027	S4:	in the trade
2028	SX-3:	yeah (.)
2029	S4:	NOW <fast> to the <pvc> licenser </pvc> and ask for permission because if they say no you have to remove everything </fast>
2030	S2:	m<3>hm </3>
2031	S4:	<3> i </3> think that's (.) for three hundred displays not (.) not relevant.

From a purely formal perspective which looks at the surface of the text, S4's expression is reminiscent of an English idiom: *Let sleeping dogs lie.* However, S4's variant is considerably different from the conventional ENL form, which can be found for example in the *Oxford Advanced Learner's Dictionary* (OALD). So from an ENL perspective, one might simply conclude that it is the existing English idiom 'gone wrong' and concur with Prodromou in saying that ELF speakers would fare better if they stayed away from the minefield of idioms/idiomaticity as they might 'get them wrong' and thus impinge on NS territory. However, taking the emic perspective of this ELF interaction, it seems unjustified to draw this conclusion and to end the story here. The expression appears to be created and employed successfully in the context. S4's expression is acknowledged and, as far as it is possible to say from the analyst's point of view, understood. It does not seem to cause confusion on the part of the Korean interlocutors and it does not result in an indication of non-understanding (cf. Pitzl 2005) or prompt a repair.

Still on the formal level of analysis, the more specialized *Oxford Dictionary of Idioms* (Speake 1999) also lists the idiom *let SLEEPING dogs lie*, notably under the headword SLEEPING which does not even occur in S4's variant. In S4's expression, the idea of the dogs being asleep is expressed only indirectly: since the dogs should not be woken up, it is implied that they are asleep. The Oxford idiom dictionary also mentions a similar idiom in French: *n'esveillez pas lou chien qui dort* (literally: Do not wake the dog which sleeps). And there is also a similar idiom in German: *schlafende Hunde soll man nicht wecken* (literally: sleeping dogs should one not wake). Thus, underlying the canonical English idiom *let sleeping dogs lie*, there might be a more common and widespread metaphorical image which is not unique to English-speaking cultures. While this observation is presumably irrelevant when the idiom is used among ENL speakers belonging to the same speech community, it is potentially relevant with regard to ELF, which per definition happens in a multilingual and multicultural environment.[9]

As S4's first language is German, it does not seem far-fetched to suggest that both English and German idioms influence S4's new expression *we should not wake up any dogs*. But what is even more important is that the same metaphorical image is inherent to the codified English, German and French idiom as well as to S4's newly created expression. While this metaphor may be sleeping or dead for an L1 speaker when uttering the institutionalized form of the idiom, it seems to be reactivated in ELF. And it is this metaphoricity, I would argue, which allows for the formal variation and adaptation of the expression but at the same time makes it decodable and intelligible.

Turning from the purely formal to the pragmatic-functional level, we can observe that although there is a difference in form, the meaning of S4's expression is the same as the one given in the *Oxford Dictionary of Idioms*, i.e. to "avoid interfering in a situation that is currently causing no problems, but may well do so as a consequence of such interference" (Speake 1999, 325). As has been outlined above, the context of the utterance in the interaction refers to a situation which is somewhat embarrassing for the Korean visitors: they have made a mistake in producing the display without seeking approval first. And in addition to this, their error might have legal consequences and cause liability claims. The safest and proper procedure in the situation would be to notify the licenser, ask for permission and possibly in the meantime remove the displays from the stores. But this is not what S4 suggests.

What S4 suggests with the expression *we should not wake up any DOGS* is that they leave the situation as it is, for which he also gives several reasons: the displays are currently in the trade (utterances 2025 and 2027), if the licenser does not give permission they have to be removed (utterance 2029), and there are only three hundred displays (utterance 2031). The metaphor thus functions effectively to make a suggestion which is somewhat tricky and sensitive. By using the metaphor, S4 hedges his own proposition, i.e. to refrain from asking the licenser, and conveys the propositional content in an indirect way, thereby creating an implicature.

Thus, S4 never directly says that they should not ask the licenser but conveys this via the metaphorical expression. He only states directly what might happen if they asked for permission at this time (*if they say no you have to remove everything*). The metaphoric expression (like all metaphors) intentionally violates the Gricean maxim of quality and hence it creates an effect. In this situation, the effect seems to be to hedge the speaker's own proposition and to allow the interlocutors, S1 and S2, to save face. The use of a clearly non-literal and metaphoric expression ('not waking up dogs') in this otherwise very straightforward business context lightens the mood in a potentially tense and face-threatening situation.

If one regarded this expression solely from the ENL perspective, i.e. as an English idiom 'gone wrong', one might say that it does not mean anything, that it is 'unidiomatic' because its wording is varied in a way which for ENL speakers might be considered unacceptable. Yet, as a metaphor utilized in ELF it means and communicates, though indirectly, a great deal and it does so effectively. In cases like these it seems that metaphors inherent in many idioms are much more active in ELF than they are in ENL speech. And this is why they can be formally varied and are not as fixed as in ENL contexts and still convey the same meaning. Or alternatively, as is the case in the next example, metaphors related to ENL idioms can also successfully convey new meanings.

The next statement is made in a task force meeting of professionals involved in developing the European higher education area. The interactants are discussing a draft document when S1, who is Danish, says they do not need to adapt this *head and tails*.

Example 2 (POmtg539)

234 S1: but (1) as (.) i've already said to some of you when (.) i suddenly (1) decided to gi- give it a look over i (1) i was struck by the extent to which this: (1) in MY opinion at least meets a lot of (.) OUR needs in terms of (undeveloped) specification i mean we do NOT need to aDApt this: sort of (1) **head and tails** but i think there's there's a lot of good thinking in the way in which it is set up (.) there's a (1) and thank god (1) the mutual recognition project already at that time was (1) forward enough to recognize the value of (.)
<1> integrating </1> the: THEN [org2] criteria =

235 SX-2: <1><soft> mhm </soft></1>

236 SX-2: = <soft> hm </soft>

While S1's expression *head and tails* may have a formal resemblance to the ENL expression *heads or tails*, the ENL expression and its meaning referring to the tossing of a coin do not relate to this discourse context. The *Oxford Dictionary of Idioms* also lists the idiom *make head or tail of*, meaning to "understand at all" (Speake 1999, 172). An additional comment states that this idiom is "[u]sually [used] with negative expressed (*make neither head nor tail of*) or implied" (ibid.). And indeed a negative is also expressed in S1's utterance, although the newly coined expression *head and tails* is different from the ENL form and its meaning is not covered by what the *Oxford Dictionary of Idioms* paraphrases.

As already mentioned above, the speakers in this speech event are talking about a draft document. When we decode S1's expression as a metaphor employing terms of embodiment with *head* referring to the beginning of the document and *tails* referring to the end, we can easily understand what he means and gloss his expression *head and tails* with something like 'as a whole' or 'entirely'. The function the metaphor fulfills in the context of this ELF working group meeting is to give emphasis to S1's statement. So even though, at first glance, the expression resembles existing ENL idioms, it is actually not an ENL idiom 'gone wrong' but a newly created metaphor using terms of embodiment (*head* and *tails*). In this sense, the expression is communicatively purposeful and contributes to effective communication in the ELF interaction.

The observation that terms of embodiment such as *head* might be used more frequently and also with regard to idioms in ELF has also been put forward by Seidlhofer (2009b, 205). Similarly, in the next two examples, taken from a business meeting among speakers of Dutch and German, we find metaphorical expressions using terms of embodiment, which, however, do not seem to be related to existing ENL idioms.

Example 3 (PBmtg300)

1030	S2:	we ALWAYS (.) and i tell you this honestly ALWAYS DO (.) the same rate. ALWAYS . (.) why? because we want to avoid (.) <2> this </2> kind of conflict. (.)
1031	S1:	<2> mhm </2>
1032	S1:	absolutely.
1033	S2:	and this this is (.) really we'd erm (.) **put my HANDS** {S1 bangs his hands on the table} **into the fire for it** (1) this is the the scenario we only work. (.) becau:se we want to make (.) no conflicts (.) and believe me <@> this is the thing </@> [org2] ALWAYS does. (1) and we try to avoid (.) ALWAYS this kind of <3> things.</3>

Although the expression *put my HANDS into the fire for it* does not relate to an existing English idiom, it is possible that the expression relates to another language idiom. In German, there is the expression *Dafür lege ich meine Hand ins Feuer* which almost literally translates into S2's *put my HANDS into the fire for it* and means to guarantee something or to vouch for something. S2 is not a native-speaker of German, but a native-speaker of Dutch from the Netherlands, a language rather closely related to German. Although I am not familiar with the Dutch language myself, I am grateful to a professional translator of German and Dutch for the information that a very similar idiom does indeed exist in Dutch: *de hand voor iemand in het vuur steken*. But regardless of whether S2's English expression relates to a German or Dutch idiom or not, what is again important from an ELF perspective is that the expression is decodable as a metaphor. Functionally, the metaphor is again produced for reasons of emphasis and instead of simply saying 'I guarantee' or 'I promise this is not the case', S2 produces the metaphorical image of 'putting one's hand into the fire' to underline the sincerity of his proposition.

A similar type of metaphor occurs in the next example in which the same speaker in the same business meeting again uses terms of embodiment in order to make a humorous and emphatic remark which is metaphorical: it is quite obvious that S2's *big toe*, literally understood, has nothing to do with how much of a *cargo guy* he is.

Example 4 (PBmtg300)

1229	S2:	but again you know (.) and this this is a good scenario for us because (.) i'm (1) **up to my** (.) hh <@> **big toe** </@> **i'm a cargo guy** =
1230	S1:	= @@ <2> @@ </2>
1231	S2:	<2> @ </2> @ hhh and er (1) <3> i </3> (.)
1232	S1:	<3><clears throat></3>
1233	S2:	i want EVERYTHING in cargo to be successful whatever. (.) [...]

S2's metaphorical remark functions to provide emphasis to his statement that S2 considers himself to be a *cargo guy* who wants *EVERYTHING in cargo to be successful*. Yet additionally, the metaphorical insertion *up to my big toe* also clearly has a humorous effect. S2 says *big toe* laughingly (represented with the <@> </@> tag in the transcript) and the remark also prompts laughter (represented via the @-symbols) on the part of S1.

In addition to the purposes already exemplified, metaphors in ELF can also fulfill important communicative functions when it comes to talking about abstract concepts. In a panel discussion about the role of women in the Islamic world, S5, who is a speaker of Arabic, talks about questions of Islamic family law and modernity when she makes the following statement using the two metaphorical/idiomatic expressions indicated in bold print.

Example 5 (PRpan1)

22 S5: […] as if there is this barrier between (.) er the state of being a traditional person **how to draw the limits** (.) between YOU as a traditional and you as as a: MODERN (.) person or state. (.) WE as woman we thought that let's START by: by the question of family law. islamic family law UNIFICATION and MODERNIZATION of family law. and having BETTER rights (.) the way we can using our (1) engagement (.) with the national struggle. using our (.) e:r the **fruit of of our engagement.** (.) in the national struggle. […]

Although both expressions are related to codified ENL idioms, I would again suggest that they both function effectively since they are used and understood as metaphors in the ELF context.

The first expression *how to draw the limits* constitutes a formal variation of the more common ENL-idiomatic expression *to draw the line*. The obvious compositionality of the newly coined expression *draw the limits* supports the suggestion that ELF speakers seem to construct what they say more atomistically "drawing on what is semantically encoded in the grammar and lexis of the language—in other words, by recourse to what Sinclair calls the 'open-choice' principle" (Seidlhofer 2009b, 202). Rather than being stored, processed and uttered as a single lexical unit, i.e. via the idiom principle, the expression *how to draw the limit* seems to be created via the open-choice principle. The semantic properties of the individual words are foregrounded and exploited, which is evident in the word *limit* being substituted for *line*, both words denoting similar semantic concepts. Such a formal variation of an otherwise conventional idiomatic expression reactivates metaphorical resonance.

The second expression *fruit of our engagement* makes use of the conventional expression *fruit of*, which is less fixed and per se open to adaptation to various contexts. While the expression *fruit of* is listed as an idiom in the OALD for example, it would be classified as a ONCE in Grant and Bauer's terminology, as only one word, namely *fruit*, is non-literal within this expression. But regardless of whether one conceives of the expression *fruit of* as an idiom or not, it can be processed and understood as a metaphor, since there is an active resonance between the topic being talked about, i.e. the national struggle in an Islamic state, and the semantic concept denoted by the word *fruit*.

Communicatively, the functions of both expressions relate to talking about abstract concepts. In both expressions, ontological concepts, i.e. 'drawing', 'limit', and 'fruit' are employed to elaborate a point when talking about a situation and ideas which are rather abstract and elusive. This ontological pattern can also be seen in the word *barrier* which precedes the expression *how to draw the limits*. Both metaphorical expressions thus seem to be used in order to increase explicitness and clarity with regard to the abstract ideas being talked about. Additionally, the second expression, i.e. *fruit of*, again also functions to provide emphasis as it is used in a repetition of *the engagement in the national struggle*.

The final example is taken from same business meeting as Examples 3 and 4 and exemplifies how other language idioms and sayings may be explicitly introduced into ELF. The topic of conversation at this point in the meeting is the participants' perceptions of different cultures. The speakers talk about cultural peculiarities, characteristics and stereotypes as regards their own cultures and also the nationalities of companies they work for.

Example 6 (PBmtg300)

2410	S2:	[...] but again they are like the DUTCH we are very KEEN on MONEY?
2411	SX-m:	@@
2412	S2:	and the chinese <5> @@ </5><@> the chinese are even MORE keen on moneys </@> (1) they er <6> want to </6>
2413	SS:	<5> @@ </5>
2414	S1:	<6> as you know </6><@> we have a lot of DUTCH in the company </@> and we work <7> a lot </7> with chinese so NO worries er <1> hhh for understanding you.</1>
2415	S2:	<7> o:h </7>
2416	S2:	<1> i say i say i'm dutch </1><@> myself.</@><2> so er </2> i can say it as a <@> dutch guy </@> (1)
2417	S1:	<2> @@@ </2>
2418	S2:	dutch <pvc> particully {particularly} </pvc> we are famous about moneys i believe
2419	S1:	we er i forgot one point.
2420	S2:	huh?=
2421	S1:	=we are a swiss company.
2422	S2:	mhm=

2423	S1:	=er so for <@> money no no need to <3> discuss with us @@ </3></@>
2424	S2:	<3> @@@@@ </3> no but i say it's a sort of HABIT you know the (.)
2425	S1:	yeah (.)
2426	S2:	they say that's it's a saying in holland that er (.) we don't have savings but under the bed we have a lot of er (.) **money in the sock**. but <4> i </4><8> **checked my sock lately** </8> but (.)
2427	S1:	<4> yeah </4>
2428	SX-8:	<8> @@@ </8>
2429	S8:	@@@ <9> @ </9>
2430	SS:	<9><soft> @@ </soft></9>
2431	S2:	@ <@> **no moneys** </@> (.) <10><soft> @@ </soft></10>
2432	SS:	<10><soft> @@ </soft></10>
2433	S1:	<soft> @@ <11> @@ </11></soft>

Nationalities are very prominent in this extract, as can be seen in the repeated and dense occurrence of the words *dutch* and also *chinese*. S2 is a Dutch person from the Netherlands and works for a Chinese company. The cultural 'stereotype' being talked about in this extract by S2 is that certain cultures and peoples, like the Dutch and the Chinese, are similar in that they are keen on making money. S1 contributes to the topic of cultural affinities to money in utterances 2421 and 2423 by saying that they work for a Swiss company and therefore: *for money no need to discuss with us*, implying that the interest in making money is also part of Swiss culture. In this signaling of sameness, S1 creates an atmosphere of solidarity and strengthens the perception that they are all sitting in the same boat, so to speak.

It is at this point when the atmosphere is very relaxed and communal that S2 puts forward an expression, *a saying* they have *in holland*, namely that the Dutch *don't have savings under the bed* but that they *have a lot of money in the sock*. Thus, S2 explicitly signals that he is transplanting and translating a Dutch idiom into English. This again underlines the fact that the question of idioms in ELF is not only a question of English idioms. ELF is per definition a multilingual and multicultural situation and this fact is bound to affect the interaction and also the use of potential idioms.

How 'correctly' S2 translates the Dutch idiom into English is impossible to say for someone who is not familiar with the Dutch language. But again what I would stress as being important is that the degree of 'correctness' of the translation is largely irrelevant, because the expression is effective in creating a metaphorical image. S2 also goes on to elaborate on the image he is likely to have created in his co-participants' minds and says that he *checked his sock lately* but found *no moneys*.

Besides the communicative function of bringing your own culture into the discourse, the metaphor is expanded and played with in a very openly humorous way. This triggers laughter on the part of the other speakers and thus clearly serves the communicative function of bringing humor into the interaction.

5. Metaphors and Idioms in ELF— Some Suggestions and Possible Implications

The argument and analysis presented in this paper suggest that there is a close and complex relationship between so-called idioms and metaphors in ELF. The concept of a culturally defined L1 speech community does not have the same relevance for ELF as it has for L1 interactions, as speakers in ELF interactions by definition do not all share the same cultural background. The territorial imperative as a social force driving communication and thus motivating the use of idioms is hence presumably absent in ELF (cf. Seidlhofer & Widdowson 2007). Idioms in ELF are not used as territorial markers of group membership. But this is not to say that idioms are per se not relevant for ELF.

There is a myriad of definitions with regard to what we mean by idioms and idiomaticity. Some researchers operate with a very broad idiom concept (e.g. Sinclair 1991), whereas others attempt a narrow definition of ‘core idioms’ (e.g. Grant & Bauer 2004). The majority of researchers will probably position themselves between these two extremes. What seems to be relevant with regard to ELF is that the non-compositionality of idioms is not as much of a sine qua non as is often proposed. Many researchers comment on the relationship of metaphors and idioms. Some (e.g. Hanks 2006) view this relationship as a diachronic either-or question, where a certain expression is either a metaphor if resonance is still active or an idiom if resonance is only historical. Others (e.g. Langlotz 2006) suggest that ‘sleeping’ metaphors inherent in idioms may remain accessible to language users and may be reactivated. In this view, the question of idiom and metaphor ceases to be an either-or question. Metaphoricity may be re-introduced into idiomatic expressions via a process which I have termed re-metaphorization.

It has been shown that this process of re-metaphorization is indeed observable in ELF as it is represented in VOICE. While idioms may be formally varied in ways possibly considered unacceptable by native speakers, such formal variation of idioms does not inhibit their functionality in ELF. The chances of (sleeping) metaphors inherent in idioms being re-activated are presumably much higher in ELF than in

ENL, where the conventionalization and institutionalization of idiomatic expressions can be seen to hamper the possibility for re-metaphorization and make the occurrence of this process (though not impossible) less likely.

At the formal textual level, deliberate metaphors in ELF arise from three different sources: they may be entirely novel with a metaphorical image being created ad hoc by a speaker; secondly, metaphors may be formally related to existing English idioms, re-introducing metaphoricity often via formal variation of the expression; and thirdly, metaphors may be created with other language idioms being transplanted into English.

While it has been suggested that idiomaticity is a 'minefield' in which formal variation and/or creative use of idiomatic expressions might lead to penalization of non-native speakers (cf. Prodromou 2007), the examples from VOICE discussed in this paper suggest otherwise. Although it is true that L1-like idiomaticity, understood as something like the formal accuracy of conventionalized ENL forms, is essentially not relevant in ELF, the same cannot be said of idioms and idiomaticity in abstraction from ENL contexts. The description of ELF requires the researcher to abandon the focus on formal deviations as errors. It rather prompts us to explore which effects these so-called deviations have within an interaction, how they affect meanings and possibly the linguistic system of ELF in general.

Research on ELF has shown that several general processes seem to motivate linguistic innovations in ELF, among these being enhancing prominence (e.g. Dewey 2007b, 339ff.), increasing clarity (e.g. Pitzl, Breiteneder & Klimpfinger 2008, 40-41; Ranta 2006, 112ff.; Seidlhofer 2005) and increasing semantic transparency (e.g. Seidlhofer 2009b). These general motivations are also borne out by the analysis of metaphorical expressions in this paper. The metaphors originating from English and other language idioms presented in the examples fulfill a striking variety of communicative functions, such as providing emphasis, increasing explicitness, elaborating a point, talking about abstract concepts. We have seen too how metaphors can be used to further interpersonal rapport in dealing with a tricky situation, making a sensitive proposition, bringing in your own culture, and adding humor to the interaction. All these different functions are fulfilled via idioms 'gone wrong', or in other words, via the re-metaphorization of idioms. To deprive speakers of this creative linguistic potential by devaluating these expressions simply as errors best avoided would seem to be counter-productive—it would seem (metaphorically speaking) to be 'pouring the child out with the bathwater'.

Bibliography

Abel, B. 2003. *Sprecherurteile zur Dekomponierbarkeit englischer Idiome*. Tübingen: Niemeyer.

Biber, D., E. Finegan, S. Johansson, S. Conrad and G. Leech 1999. *Longman Grammar of Spoken and Written English*. Harlow: Longman.

Björkman, B. 2008. "'So where we are?' Spoken Lingua Franca English at a Technical University in Sweden." *English Today* 24 (2), 35-41.

Breiteneder, A. 2005. "The Naturalness of English as a European Lingua Franca: The Case of the 'Third Person –s'." *VIenna English Working PaperS* 14 (2), 3-26. http://www.univie.ac.at/Anglistik/Views0502 ALL.pdf (accessed December 4, 2008).

Breiteneder, A., M.-L. Pitzl, S. Majewski and T. Klimpfinger 2006. "VOICE Recording—Methodological Challenges in the Compilation of a Corpus of Spoken ELF." *Nordic Journal of English Studies* 5 (2), 161-88.

Cameron, L. 1999. "Identifying and Describing Metaphor in Spoken Discourse." In *Researching and Applying Metaphor*, ed. L. Cameron & G. D. Low, 105-32. Cambridge: Cambridge University Press.

Carter, R. 2004. *Language and Creativity. The Art of Common Talk.* Milton Park: Routledge.

Cogo, A. 2008. "English as a Lingua Franca: Form Follows Function." *English Today* 24 (3), 58-61.

—. 2007. "Intercultural Communication in English as a Lingua Franca: A Case Study." PhD diss., King's College London.

Cogo, A. and M. Dewey 2006. "Efficiency in ELF Communication: From Pragmatic Motives to Lexico-Grammatical Innovation." *Nordic Journal of English Studies* 5 (2), 59-93.

Dewey, M. 2007a. "English as a Lingua Franca: An Empirical Study of Innovation in Lexis and Grammar." PhD diss., King's College London.

—. 2007b. "English as a Lingua Franca and Globalization: An Interconnected Perspective." *International Journal of Applied Linguistics* 17 (3), 332-54.

Ehrenreich, S. this volume. "English as a Lingua Franca in Multinational Corporations—Exploring Business Communities of Practice."

—. 2008. "English as a Business Lingua Franca in Multinational Corporations—Contexts of Use and Attitudes." Paper presented at the *15th World Congress of Applied Linguistics (AILA 2008)—Multilingualism: Challenges and Opportunities*, Essen, August 24-29, 2008.

Gibbs, R. W. 1999. "Taking Metaphor out of Our Heads and Putting it into the Cultural World." In *Metaphor in Cognitive Linguistics. Selected Papers from the Fifth International Cognitive Linguistics Conference. Amsterdam, July 1997*, ed. R. W. Gibbs & G. J. Steen, 145-66. Amsterdam: Benjamins.

Goatly, A. 1997. *The Language of Metaphors*. London: Routledge.

Grant, L. and L. Bauer 2004. "Criteria for Re-Defining Idioms: Are We Barking up the Wrong Tree?" *Applied Linguistics* 25 (1), 38-61.

Hanks, P. 2006. "Metaphoricity is Gradable." In *Corpus-Based Approaches to Metaphor and Metonymy*, ed. A. Stefanowitsch & S. T. Gries, 17-35. Berlin: Mouton de Gruyter.

Hornby, A. S., ed. 2005. *Oxford Advanced Learner's Dictionary of Current English*, 7th ed. Oxford: Oxford University Press.

Hülmbauer, C. 2007. "'You moved, aren't?'—The Relationship between Lexicogrammatical Correctness and Communicative Effectiveness in English as a Lingua Franca." *VIenna English Working PaperS* 16 (2), 3-35. http://www.univie.ac.at/Anglistik/Views_0702.pdf (accessed November 25, 2008).

Jenkins, J. 2007. *English as a Lingua Franca: Attitude and Identity*. Oxford: Oxford University Press.

Klimpfinger, T. 2007. "'Mind you, sometimes you have to mix'—The Role of Code-Switching in English as a Lingua Franca." *VIenna English Working PaperS* 16 (2), 36-61. http://www.univie.ac.at /Anglistik/Views_0702.pdf (accessed November 25, 2008).

Kirkpatrick, A. 2008. "English as the Official Working Language of the Association of Southeast Asian Nations (ASEAN): Features and Strategies." *English Today* 24 (2), 27-34.

Kordon, K. 2006. "'You are very good'—Establishing Rapport in English as a Lingua Franca: The Case of Agreement Tokens." *VIenna English Working PaperS* 15 (2), 58-82. http://www.univie.ac.at/Anglistik/ views06_2.pdf (accessed December 4, 2008).

Langlotz, A. 2006. *Idiomatic Creativity. A Cognitive-Linguistic Model of Idiom-Representation and Idiom-Variation in English*. Amsterdam: Benjamins.

Lichtkoppler, J. 2007. "'Male. Male.'—'Male?'—'The sex is male.' The Role of Repetition in English as a Lingua Franca Conversations." *VIenna English Working PaperS* 16 (1), 39-65. http://www.univie.ac.at /Anglistik/views_0701.pdf (accessed December 4, 2008).

Lipka, L. 2002. *English Lexicology. Lexical Structure, Word Semantics and Word-Formation*. Tübingen: Gunter Narr.

Mauranen, A. 2006. "Signaling and Preventing Misunderstanding in English as Lingua Franca Communication." *International Journal of the Sociology of Language* 177, 123-50.

Mauranen, A. and M. Metsä-Ketelä, eds. 2006. Special issue on English as a lingua franca. *Nordic Journal of English Studies* 5 (2).

Meierkord, C. 2002. "'Language Stripped Bare' or 'Linguistic Masala'? Culture in Lingua Franca Conversation." In *Lingua Franca Communication*, ed. K. Knapp & C. Meierkord, 109-33. Frankfurt am Main: Peter Lang.

Pitzl, M.-L. 2005. "Non-Understanding in English as a Lingua Franca: Examples from a Business Context." *VIenna English Working PaperS* 14 (2), 50-71. http://www.univie.ac.at/Anglistik/Views0502mlp.pdf (accessed December 4, 2008).

Pitzl, M.-L., A. Breiteneder and T. Klimpfinger 2008. "A World of Words: Processes of Lexical Innovation in VOICE." *VIenna English Working PaperS* 17 (2), 21-46. http://www.univie.ac.at/Anglistik/Views0802.pdf (accessed April 15, 2009).

Prodromou, L. 2007. "Bumping into Creative Idiomaticity." *English Today* 23 (1), 14-25.

Ranta, E. 2006. "The 'Attractive' Progressive—Why Use the *–ing* Form in English as a Lingua Franca?" *Nordic Journal of English Studies* 5 (2), 97-116.

Saraceni, M. 2008. "English as a Lingua Franca: Between Form and Function." *English Today* 24 (2), 20-26.

Seidlhofer, B. 2009a. "Common Ground and Different Realities: World Englishes and English as a Lingua Franca." *World Englishes* 28 (2), 236-45.

—. 2009b. "Accommodation and the Idiom Principle in English as a Lingua Franca." *Intercultural Pragmatics* 6 (2), 195-215.

—. 2008. "ELF Findings: Form and Function." Plenary presented at the *1st ELF Forum*, March 6-8, University of Helsinki.

—. 2006. "English as a Lingua Franca in the Expanding Circle: What it isn't." In *English in the World: Global Rules, Global Roles*, ed. R. Rubdy & M. Saraceni, 40-50. London: Continuum.

—. 2005. "English as a Lingua Franca." In *Oxford Advanced Learner's Dictionary of Current English*, 7th ed., R 92. Oxford: Oxford University Press.

Seidlhofer, B., A. Breiteneder and M.-L. Pitzl 2006. "English as a Lingua Franca in Europe." *Annual Review of Applied Linguistics* 26, 1-34.

Seidlhofer, B. and H. G. Widdowson 2007. "Idiomatic Variation and Change in English. The Idiom Principle and Its Realizations." In

Tracing English through Time: Explorations in Language Variation, ed. U. Smit, S. Dollinger, J. Hüttner, G. Kaltenböck & U. Lutzky, 359-74. Wien: Braumüller.
Sinclair, J. 1991. *Corpus, Concordance, Collocation.* Oxford: Oxford University Press.
Speake, J. ed. 1999. *The Oxford Dictionary of Idioms.* Oxford: Oxford University Press.
VOICE. 2009. *The Vienna-Oxford International Corpus of English* (version 1.0 online). http://voice.univie.ac.at/ (accessed May 22, 2009). Director: Barbara Seidlhofer; Researchers: Angelika Breiteneder, Theresa Klimpfinger, Stefan Majewski, Marie-Luise Pitzl.
Wenger, E. 1998. *Communities of Practice. Learning, Meaning, and Identity.* Cambridge: Cambridge University Press

Notes

[1] Some individual journal articles focusing on different topics of empirical ELF research are for example Björkman (2008), Breiteneder (2005), Dewey (2007b), Hülmbauer (2007), Kirkpatrick (2008), Klimpfinger (2007), Kordon (2006), Lichtkoppler (2007), Mauranen (2006), Pitzl (2005), and Seidlhofer, Breiteneder & Pitzl (2006).
[2] For example, Cogo (2007), Dewey (2007a), and Jenkins (2007).
[3] See the contributions to the special issue on English as a lingua franca of the *Nordic Journal of English Studies* 5 (2) (Mauranen & Metsä-Ketelä 2006). A special issue of *Intercultural Pragmatics* 6 (2) on the pragmatics of ELF and a special issue of *World Englishes* 28 (2) focusing on 'Perspectives on lingua franca' have recently come out.
[4] See for example Cogo (2008), Saraceni (2008), and Seidlhofer (2006).
[5] The term communities of practice, coined by Wenger (1998), has been repeatedly suggested as a more appropriate concept for ELF. Though there is, of course, also debate as to how exactly the concept of 'communities of practice' can be made relevant and applied with regard to ELF and in different ELF contexts (e.g. Ehrenreich 2008, and this volume).
[6] This is not to say that ELF is completely non-territorial or 'culture-free'. Studies have shown how ELF speakers tend to build an inter-culture (Meierkord 2002) in the process of interaction and also signal their own culture in various ways, for example via code-switching (Klimpfinger 2007). But the majority of ELF speakers are certainly not 'possessive' of a particular English-speaking cultural territory.
[7] See most of the studies mentioned in the first paragraph of the introduction. Having extensive personal experience in recording, transcribing and proofreading naturally-occurring ELF conversations during the compilation of the Vienna-Oxford International Corpus of English (VOICE), I similarly cannot think of an instance of 'penalization' of a non-native speaker by a native-speaker like the ones mentioned by Prodromou.

[8] See www.univie.ac.at/voice/voice.php?page=transcription_general_information for the VOICE Transcription Conventions which specify the details of the mark-up used in VOICE transcripts and see Breiteneder, Pitzl, Majewski & Klimpfinger (2006) for rationale behind some of the decisions taken in the VOICE Transcription Conventions. The only adaptations made in the examples concern the use of bold print to indicate the metaphorical expressions, and the use of [...] to indicate that an utterance is not provided in its entirety. Numbered tags (e.g. <1> </1>) indicate overlapping speech, @-symbols indicate laughter, (.) and (1) indicate pauses, capital letters indicate emphasis.

[9] See Hülmbauer (2007, 26ff.) for a consideration of how multilingual influence and cross-linguistic transfer may have positive and enhancing effects in ELF when speakers share similar concepts and/or expressions in their first languages.

"WE DON'T TAKE THE RIGHT WAY. WE JUST TAKE THE WAY THAT WE THINK YOU WILL UNDERSTAND"— THE SHIFTING RELATIONSHIP BETWEEN CORRECTNESS AND EFFECTIVENESS IN ELF

CORNELIA HÜLMBAUER

1. Introduction

The concept of English as a lingua franca (ELF) gives rise to a great deal of controversy. Despite the consensus that seems to prevail about its usefulness as a means of intercultural communication, there is still the feeling that it has something unacceptable about it. In addition to phonological issues (as described by Jenkins 2007), this often concerns unconventional, seemingly 'incorrect' lexico-grammatical features which are stigmatized as deficiencies.

Negative attitudes represent only one side of the coin, however. It seems symptomatic that, for example, a native speaker of Dutch in one of the interactions analysed for the present paper claims ELF to be "flat English", but at the same time values its communicative potential as a means of non-native/non-native speaker interaction. He even postulates that his interlocutor understands him "better than a proper Englishman" (cf. Hülmbauer 2007, 4 for a more extensive reproduction of this interaction). The paper at hand takes as a starting point the "linguistic schizophrenia" (Jenkins 2007, 231) revealed by this kind of concurrence of two opposing, if not contradictory, judgements of ELF. There seems to be an inherent friction in lingua franca English: It allows for *effective* intercultural communication, but it frequently departs from what has traditionally been regarded as *correct*. The relationship between *lexico-grammatical correctness* and *communicative effectiveness* is the overarching theme of the present paper.

Before this relationship is investigated, however, another ambivalence implied in ELF needs to be tackled: variability and stability. For the purposes of the paper at hand, the discussion of these two concepts of ELF on the one hand focuses on the *situationality factor* which determines every lingua franca interaction anew and on its own. On the other hand, it deals with the fact that ELF speakers do have something in common, namely their status as non-native and intercultural users of English and the communicative resources they can draw upon through this situation.

Considering the distinctive nature of ELF, i.e. bearing commonalities but at the same time being inherently variable, generalisation is difficult. An evaluation can, thus, only take place with reference to individual interactions. Central issues to be addressed in an investigation of naturally-occurring ELF are: On which criteria is the evaluation of its linguistic forms based? Does *correctness*, i.e. compliance with native speaker norms, or *effectiveness*, i.e. mutual intelligibility in intercultural communication, serve as the main consideration? How do the two relate to each other, and is it justified to assume the former to be a precondition of the latter?

In an attempt to confront the conflicting views towards ELF with regard to lexico-grammar, a second look is taken at 'incorrect' constructions in this paper by investigating not only the forms themselves but how they function in communicative contexts. Five examples of unconventional language use in ELF are discussed in order to illustrate that not only can the 'incorrect' be effective, it can reveal alternative and creative ways of making meaning in intercultural communication. Our Dutch speaker explains it like this: "We don't take, you know, the right way. We just take the way that we think that you will understand". Based on this, the present paper sets out to question what has traditionally been called 'right' and 'wrong' or 'correct' and 'incorrect' and the applicability of these concepts with regard to ELF communication.

2. Distinctive Characteristics of ELF

Opinions about ELF are ambivalent. But there is also a kind of duality about ELF itself. On the one hand, it is not determined by a stable set of features and cannot be located anywhere. Sometimes it departs radically from established norms, sometimes it converges closely to them (cf. Jenkins 2006, 141). On the other hand, it represents an established resource in many people's communicative routine and serves as a reliable means of intercultural exchange in which miscommunication is the exception rather than the rule. Thus ELF involves two opposing forces in constant tension: variable vs. stable aspects (cf. e.g. Seidlhofer 2007, 312).

Communicators from different lingua-cultural backgrounds face the challenge of establishing mutual intelligibility through a language which is not their mother tongue. Usage, therefore, naturally varies alongside with the speakers' first and other languages (L1s and LNs) as well as their individual degrees of norm-adherence. Varied though it may be, what represents a stable component in ELF is the fact that the majority of its users are typically non-native speakers[1], i.e. L2 users of English.[2] This tends to bring about co-operative behaviour and a certain degree of flexibility in language use. Both variability and non-nativeness are equally characteristic of ELF and thus discussed in the following.

2.1. Variability and Situationality

Since typical ELF gatherings are characterised by different lingua-cultural influences, the traditional notion of a stable "speech community" uniting the speakers of a particular language variety cannot apply to lingua franca contexts. Focusing on the shared communicative activity rather than external factors, it is the concept of "communities of practice" (cf. Wenger 1998) which seems to represent the developments most appropriately (cf. Seidlhofer 2007, 313-315; Dewey 2007, 59-61; Ehrenreich, this volume). Through the act of talking to each other, ELF users become members of *situational speaking communities*: They enter into temporary relationships, with speaker constellations frequently being tied and untied anew for each emerging interaction. "Mutual engagement" and a "joint enterprise" (Wenger 1998, 73) are preconditions for ELF talk to be pursued in the first place. The third dimension in Wenger's definition of communities of practice, however, is of particular interest from the perspective of variability: its members make use of a "shared repertoire" (ibid., 82) which is jointly developed on the basis of their specific competencies and designed to suit the particular purposes of their common endeavour. In other words, ELF speakers with their individual backgrounds and resources contribute to a *situational resource pool* which changes as speaker constellations change. Thus, hardly anything can be taken for granted; meaning needs to be negotiated. Variability, i.e. the particularity of constellations as well as their fleetingness, can be regarded as an inherent feature of ELF communication. The speakers need to come to terms with this situation and make use of the means at their disposal in the best possible way.

Therefore, when we attempt to investigate language usage in ELF talk, it has to be taken into account that the varied characteristics of speakers and the linguistic resources they contribute will crucially influence the overall linguistic behaviour and communicative processes. We need to take into consideration what the participants bring to the interaction through their backgrounds as well as potential divergences and parallels between these resources. In practice, however, this is a challenging issue if one has available hardly more than recorded ELF interactions as an empirical basis. Factors such as the speakers' general norm-orientedness or attitudes towards norms are not only difficult to find out about, but also hard to measure. An element which can usually be elicited more easily and which is a feature of every ELF user, i.e. L2 speaker, is his or her first (and sometimes other) language(s).

Cross-linguistic influence from the L1 has already been treated as an important aspect in non-native speaker use in interlanguage studies (cf. e.g. Corder 1982, 95ff.) and can thus be assumed to play an important role in ELF as well. As Cook (2002, 5) explains, "[t]he L2 user stands between two languages, even when apparently using only one, having the resources of both languages on tap whenever needed". Similarly, Grosjean (2001, 7) argues that in the "bilingual's language modes" the language which is not overtly used is not deactivated completely in the mind. What distinguishes lingua franca from interlanguage research, however, is that the former by implication is based on interactive language use, i.e. concerning at least two speakers involved in intercultural communication, whereas the latter tends to focus on linguistic development on the individual level. In contrast to investigations dealing with learners, lingua franca research does not primarily concentrate on speech production of individuals with a relatively stable set of L1 and LNs, but on reciprocal communication processes between speakers with different L1s and LNs. Based on this, we have to take into account two crucial aspects: First, in ELF, language production is inextricably linked with comprehension; and second, the speakers' different lingua-cultural backgrounds are in interplay and likely to exert influence on each other as well as subsequently on ELF. It can thus be regarded as a site of language contact in itself.

Coming back to the larger picture of our globalised world, ELF has become an essential component of the multilingual contexts in Europe in general and of Europeans' plurilingual repertoires in particular. It can be considered a "partner language" complementing and interacting with other European tongues (cf. Hülmbauer, Böhringer & Seidlhofer 2009). The need for investigation in this field is also acknowledged and supported by the European Union. As part of the project DYLAN (see http://dylan.univie.ac.at/), funded under the EU's sixth framework programme, it is the research task of the Vienna-based team to "investigate the linguistic and communicative changes that affect English as a lingua franca under increasing interaction with other languages in multilingual practices" (cf. Böhringer & Hülmbauer 2008). Apart from code-switching as an overt way of incorporating L1s and LNs into ELF (cf. Klimpfinger 2007, also this volume), this also concerns transfer phenomena influencing lingua franca English more covertly. What has to be borne in mind is that it might not only be relevant how the speakers' L1s and LNs relate to English, but also how they relate to each other and thus influence the communication process. Issues such as the linguistic distance or relatedness of all the languages involved and the resulting degrees of transferability (cf. Kellerman 1983, 114) and inferability of forms are likely to play a role in establishing mutual understanding between the communicators.

Due to the variability of speaker constellations in ELF, knowledge of culturally encoded meanings of language forms cannot be taken for granted. This, above all, concerns idiomatic constructions originally developed in and for ENL use. The problematic nature of this phenomenon is highlighted by Seidlhofer (e.g. 2004, 220) who refers to it as "unilateral idiomaticity". Nevertheless, being a member of an ELF community of practice also means being in the position of co-developing, knowing and using one's own situational linguistic in-group resources—as these resources are created and negotiated by the interactants themselves on-line. As Firth (1996, 247) describes it, "participants can learn and use known (and also nonstandard) resources as they become known-in-common during the talk itself". Again, these resources tend to be only valid for the particular situation from which they emerge and cannot be separated from their communicative context. The intelligibility of ELF forms is thus based on a strong interconnection with what could be called a *situationality factor*.

Moreover, contextual elements of different kinds influence an ongoing conversation. Spoken interaction does not take place in a vacuum; as soon as contextual elements are available they are likely to be drawn on as additional resources. Just as grammar can "free [...] us from a dependency on context" (Widdowson 1990, 86), context can to some extent free ELF users from a dependency on grammar. This does not only concern the most obvious case where the shared situation and real-life elements reduce the need to be linguistically explicit. It can also mean the wider context of shared non-nativeness in ELF which makes speakers less dependent on adherence to native speaker rules.

2.2. Shared Non-Nativeness

As mentioned before, certain things cannot be taken for granted in ELF as the speakers do not share a common lingua-cultural background. What prototypical lingua franca users do share, however, is their non-native speaker status. They are L2 users of English and at the same time plurilinguals.[3] First and foremost, it is their learner history and the fact that speaking ELF means using "a language of secondary socialisation" (Seidlhofer 2007, 314) which unites them. Non-native speakers tend to approach and use an L2 in similar, often strategic, ways. Various communicative strategies involving simplification, regularisation and enhanced explicitness have been shown to be commonly and successfully employed in ELF talk (cf. Dewey 2007, 136ff.).

It is not by accident that lingua franca speakers are frequently regarded as language *learners* despite their actual *user* position—the language forms produced tend to be the same in both types of second language use. The difference between EFL and ELF rather lies in the nature of speakers' goals: EFL is considered successful when it converges to a target model, ELF when it is mutually intelligible. This is what brings about a difference in evaluation of the linguistic forms involved. With many grammatical aspects functioning as "a sort of shibboleth" (Widdowson 1994, 381), i.e. as social markers established by native speakers of a language, it seems reasonable for ELF users to do away with redundant features and complexity whenever irrelevant to their communicative purposes. Thanks to the shared non-native perspective, they can be assumed to understand a great number of linguistic constructions even if or even because they deviate from native speaker norms. They often seem to have the ability to infer the production process of such unconventional constructions. Put differently, lingua franca users can "rely upon the nonnative status as a resource for sense-making" (Firth & Wagner 1997, 290).

With regard to phonology, Bent and Bradlow (2003, 1607) argue that non-native speaker-listener groupings tend to have a comprehension advantage over native/non-native constellations—a phenomenon which they call "interlanguage speech benefit". According to them, non-native speakers tend to apply similar schemes in language production and non-native listeners tend to pay attention to similar features of this output. Based on these findings, joint non-nativeness can definitely be considered an asset. It would be interesting to investigate whether this tendency is also true for the lexico-grammatical area. Generally, what Corder (1982) postulates for learner language is applicable in part also to ELF contexts: He argues that particular deviances from a native speaker norm "are not unique to an individual but shared by others having similar cultural background, aims or linguistic history" (ibid., 19). The ELF speakers' cultural backgrounds might diverge, but intercultural communication as a common "aim" and learner biographies as a common general "linguistic history" definitely contribute to mutual understanding in lingua franca contexts.

In addition, having learned more than one language also makes you "multi-competent" in Cook's terms. Cook argues that the minds of L2 speakers differ considerably from those of monolingual speakers, and that these speakers therefore develop special cognitive competences such as more flexible thinking and a heightened degree of meta- and cross-linguistic awareness (Cook 2002, 7; cf. also Jessner 2006, 32ff.). Particularly in ELF communication as a site of intercultural language contact, the ability to approach languages in a more holistic, integrated way and to establish meta-linguistic links between them clearly appears to be an asset.

As far as the evaluation of non-standard forms among lingua franca speakers themselves is concerned, intelligibility is regarded as a main factor. In a questionnaire survey among European academics conducted by Mollin (2006), almost 60 % of the respondents agreed with the following statement and around 15 % had a neutral attitude towards it: "I am not bothered about mistakes that other learners of English make as long as I understand what they want to say" (ibid., 178). We have to be aware here that the ELF users participating in the survey can be assumed to have undergone L2 learning in an institutional environment and are thus used to stigmatising mistakes. On top of that, Mollin's formulation of the statement even adds to this deficit approach by presupposing that her respondents regard themselves as "learners" rather than users of the language. In spite of these two aspects, the fact that only around a quarter of the respondents seem to have negative feelings about deviances from the ENL norm only reinforces the priority given to mutual intelligibility in ELF.

The special nature of ELF communication, i.e. its variable character and common non-nativeness, makes it quite obvious that native speaker standards of language do not apply to it. With ENL norms as a point of reference, the definition of an error would be

> [a] linguistic form or combination of forms which, in the same context and under similar conditions of production, would, in all likelihood, not be produced by the speakers' native speaker counterparts (Lennon 1991, 182).

Since in ELF we are dealing with intercultural settings and multi-competent L2 speakers, we can neither assume "the same context" nor "similar conditions of production". A definition like this, therefore, does not seem to be of much use for the evaluation of ELF forms. Moreover, when judging second language communication, we also need to take into account "the mind of the L2 user in all its richness and complexity" (Cook 2005). An attempt to do justice to all these variables in the evaluation of ELF forms makes it hard to generalise about their potential degrees of correctness and effectiveness. Rather than imposing preconceived notions upon these constructions, it is necessary to judge them on the basis of the particular situations from which they emerge.

3. *Not the right way?*—Looking for Empirical Evidence

It has become obvious that the evaluation of ELF forms is not possible in isolation or by mere consideration of external factors. It can only be carried out by taking into account its *situationality features* and the processes for making meaning developed by the participants within individual interactions. The crucial question to ask is whether the speakers themselves can be assumed to experience their communicative processes as 'right' or as 'wrong', i.e. as appropriate or inappropriate for making meaning in a given situational context. In the following, five selected extracts of ELF talk involving 'incorrect' or unconventional forms are analysed with regard to their effects in communication, addressing the following question: Does 'not taking the right way', i.e. the conventional way, of formal production automatically mean not pursuing an effective path towards mutual intelligibility?

3.1. Data and Methodology

The transcribed extracts of naturally-occurring ELF talk[4] selected for the following analysis are taken from a dataset consisting of 16 separate interactions involving 44 different speakers with 13 different L1s. In total, this amounts to approximately four hours of recorded data. All of the speakers are international students who are encountering each other in ERASMUS contexts—which makes them a relatively homogenous group. One half of the recordings is made up by casual talk among the students in informal settings mainly in Vienna. For the other half, advisory service talk taking place during the welcome weeks at Vienna University was recorded. In contrast to the first type of conversations, the second is more goal-oriented with information exchange as a clearly defined aim. There are thus some differences as regards the degree of interactionality versus transactionality of the data. Still, due to the common student status, hierarchy and power issues are not prominent. The Austrian students involved take the role of 'knowledge providers', but seem to regard themselves as student helpers rather than professionals. This is reinforced by the generally relaxed and friendly atmosphere.[5]

The analytical focus of this paper is on seemingly 'incorrect' forms as they occur in successful ELF interaction, i.e. on items that do not conform to ENL norms but which are nevertheless involved in effective communication. The frequently assumed straightforward relationship between correctness and effectiveness, i.e. the former bringing about the latter, is challenged by these instances of communication. Focussing on such instances does not mean to imply, however, that 'incorrect' language use is always effective. It is rather an attempt to raise awareness of the communicative potential that can underlie 'erroneous' and thus seemingly deficient constructions. For this purpose, a comparison to ENL norms and forms will be made at times—an approach which, probably due to its methodological closeness to interlanguage analyses based on a deficit view, is often condemned (cf. e.g. Dewey 2007, 72). Nevertheless, especially when arguing against a native speaker bias in ELF, the very norms to be reconsidered or even dismissed first need to serve as a point of reference. As Mauranen (2005, 275) argues,

> [d]ifferences from L1 speakers are not important for judging the success, let alone correctness of ELF performance—a backdrop needs to be provided in order to discern variation and innovation in ELF.

A similar situation arises with regard to a theoretical point of reference. ELF is a relatively young and unprecedented phenomenon. However, non-native language use in other contexts and for other purposes has been investigated for decades. It thus seems appropriate to take into account the massive body of research into second language acquisition and interlanguage. Rather than holding on to traditional paradigms, however, findings about learners' linguistic behaviour need to be reconsidered in the light of non-native speaker language use in ELF. It can serve as a starting point in developing new concepts for new contexts. Indeed, matching the spirit of this paper even though interlanguage-based, Corder (1982, 19) declares:

> My principal reason for objecting to the term *error*, *deviant*, or *ill-formed* is that they all, to a greater or lesser degree, prejudge the explanation of the idiosyncrasy.

In order to counteract this pre-judgement in ELF, it is necessary to investigate communicative processes and contexts rather than isolated forms. Such an approach makes it possible to take into consideration how meaning is negotiated by particular speakers in particular situations and constellations. It must be clear, however, that qualitative analyses with the researcher as an outsider always involve a certain degree of subjective interpretation. Interviews and tests could be conducted at a later stage to complement this kind of ELF research. For the time being we are in need of descriptive work to find out about potential tendencies in ELF usage in the first place. Due to the variability and flexibility involved in ELF communication, the frequency of a feature cannot be regarded as the only valid indicator of whether this feature might be a valuable resource for ELF communication and whether it is worth our attention. A qualitative study based on a small-scale dataset like the present one can look into specific forms brought about by specific processes. Its aim, however, is not and cannot be to provide representative findings backing general claims. It rather seeks to make a contribution towards unravelling and pointing to the communicative potential still hidden beneath prejudice against ELF. Some steps in this direction are taken through the following analysis.

3.2. 'Incorrect' Forms and Their Effects in ELF

3.2.1. Accommodative Dovetailing

Since ELF users differ from each other with regard to both their lingua-cultural backgrounds and the related norms, it seems they need to co-operate and converge through their linguistic behaviour in an ongoing interaction. Processes of accommodation, more precisely of convergence (cf. Giles & Coupland 1991, 60-67) have been shown to be a common and valuable phenomenon in ELF talk (cf. Cogo, this volume; Jenkins 2000, 167-180; Seidlhofer 2009). Extract 1 illustrates a case of two speakers adapting their language to each other. S1 is explaining the bad reputation of the Spanish people's English pronunciation by saying *it's supposed to be the bad*. While he is still hesitating and probably searching for what, in his opinion, would be a more appropriate construction, S2 interrupts him by repeating his words.

Extract 1
(S1: L1=Spanish; S2: L1=German)

S1: yeah (.) but er (1) i mean e::r i know i come from a: roman country
and e:r our english pr- pronunciation it's supposed to be the bad e::r=
S2: =the bad <1> in europe </1>
S1: <1> the bad </1> in europe
S2: yes?
S1: hm:

Taking up S2's 'incorrect' expression and reproducing it, S1 does not only signal understanding of an intended meaning like 'the worst' or 'the bad one' but also that she considers *the bad* effective enough to use it herself. When S1 then adds *in Europe*, S2 for his part accommodates in repeating the construction in its entirety. Repetition, in this case, can be argued to fulfil the functions of "ensuring accuracy of understanding", thereby confirming each other's constructions, and "showing listenership" as described for ELF contexts by Lichtkoppler (2007, 56-57). The double convergence established by the speakers in this extract illustrates the enhanced reciprocity of ELF talk—willingness to negotiate and mutual support are recognised as essential for successful communication. As Cogo and Dewey (2006, 70) explain,

> repetition is used as an accommodation strategy in order to achieve efficiency and, at the same time, to show cooperation among speakers. [...] Reusing the interlocutor's expression is also a way of aligning to them and showing support and approval.

It is important to note that accommodation is taking place irrespective of 'correctness' criteria related to ENL norms. Form, nevertheless, does play a role in this process. From this angle, the general claim that ELF communication is more about meaning than form needs to be put into perspective. It is true that ELF speakers tend to use language more flexibly and show a tolerant attitude towards a broad range of forms as long as the intended meaning can be successfully conveyed. When accommodation comes into play, however, the focus is not only on meaning but also on form—not in the sense of adherence to externally established norms, but of reinforcing meaning through adherence to formal criteria established by the interlocutor. The crucial point is to confirm the effectiveness of a construction and to encourage the interlocutor by formal means. This way, accommodation can also be a tool for the development of new shared resources, which can be seen in the next example.

3.2.2. Making the Innovative Common

In Extract 2, S1 mentions an uncle of hers to whom she is obviously only distantly related. She explains that *this uncle is the brother of* [her] *grandfather*, i.e. that he is her great uncle. Instead of only taking up the information passively, her interlocutor, S2, re-works it into a novel construction.

Extract 2
(S1: L1=Italian; S2: L1=German)

S1: and so thi- (.) this uncle is the brother of my (1) grandfather
S2: o:h (.) okay @@
S1: so @@ er
S2: far away uncle @@=
S1: =yes (.) far away uncle and er but er (1) she er he is very friendly and er (.) he writes us a lot

The creation of the term *far away uncle* can be regarded as an attempt at creatively summarising the explanation provided by S1. S2, therefore, does not only signal understanding, she also actively participates in the process of making meaning by creating a potential additional resource. Uttering the construction *far away uncle*, she offers this resource to S1 who repeats it and even explicitly confirms it with *yes*. As the new term is preceded by S1's definition, its meaning is known to both interactants. Through creative language use in combination with the cooperative act of accommodation, the expression has become 'known-in-common' and is incorporated into the pool of shared resources.

The fact that *far away uncle* might seem unconventional or 'incorrect' in comparison to 'great uncle' cannot be regarded as reducing the communicative value of the expression. It is negotiated and designed according to the interactants' needs in this particular conversation. Seidlhofer and Widdowson (2007, 371) describe "the production of idiomatic coinages on-line in response to communicative requirement" as a crucial phenomenon in ELF. Idiomatic and creative language use in lingua franca English (cf. also Pitzl, this volume) is, again, closely tied to the *situationality factor* discussed above. The constructions emerging from ELF creativity, thus, often seem to represent in-group resources not supposed to make sense to outsiders. The original linguistic behaviour to be found in Extract 2 gives a clear indication that ELF can go well beyond using language as a transactional tool and that it can be far more than "the denuded tree" (Rinvolucri 2008, 17) it is frequently claimed to be.

3.2.3. Benefiting from Shared Non-Nativeness

The asset of shared non-nativeness among most ELF speakers does not only manifest itself in cooperative behaviour and flexibility, but also more concretely in common patterns of exploiting the in-built potential of the language for their purposes (for an initial compilation of such patterns cf. Seidlhofer 2005, R92). Strategies range from doing away with redundancy and complexity to augmenting explicitness. Indeed, the recorded ELF talk exhibits extensive use of a wide range of these strategies. One example to illustrate this is the use of non-concord tags, as in Extract 3. In this extract, S1 enquires about the relatedness of the Spanish and the French lexicon, assuming that Spanish and French have words in common. Requesting a confirmation of her supposition, she employs the tag-question *no?*.

Extract 3
(S1: L1=German; S2: L1=Spanish)

S1: okay (.) okay but (.) there are similar words in in spanish and french no?=
S2: =YEAH (.) that's why we can (prove) our french in just e:r a few weeks

The emphatic *yeah* uttered by S2 as an immediate reaction leaves hardly any doubt about the clarity of S1's message and the effectiveness of the tag. This is reinforced by the fact that he feels the need to elaborate on the issue brought up by his interlocutor, adding an argument in support of her assumption. He confirms it, more indirectly, a second time.

In total, *no?* is used as a tag in 6 cases [6 occurrences/produced by 4 different speakers = 6/4] in the recorded 4 hours. In this, it is outnumbered by *or?*, which comes up 17 times (for an example involving *or?* cf. Hülmbauer 2007, 21-22). As regards the general use of question-tags in the students' interactions, 25 occurrences produced by 13 different speakers would be 'incorrect' (*no?* [6/4] *or*? [17/7], *yes?* [1/1], *aren't?* [1/1]) as opposed to 3 'correct' ones (*isn't it?* [2/2], *aren't there?* [1/1]) if the standard concord use of tag questions were to be taken as a point of reference. But if one considers the distribution between non-conforming and conforming usage such a point of reference does not appear to be of particular relevance to the ELF users. The much higher number of the non-conforming items could be an indication of non-concord, all-purpose tags emerging as a general pattern in ELF communication.[6]

A look at English around the world provides evidence that such a development would not be extraordinary, but in line with a more widespread simplification process taking place in other repertoires as well. The phenomenon is not restricted to non-native speaker language use. On the contrary, apart from being a feature of various New Englishes (cf. Kortmann & Schneider 2006), invariable *isn't it?* or *innit?* has also been reported to emerge in different ENL repertoires (cf. Krug 1998, 171). Krug even considers it plausible for Standard English to develop a less complex tag system (ibid., 147-148). Moreover, Canadian English knows all-purpose *eh?* (cf. Fee & McAlpine 1997, 177) which is not unlike the *no?* and *or?* in terms of formal divergence from the concord variants. Considering the scope of it, 'incorrectness' does not seem to be an appropriate term for this phenomenon. The fact that non-concord tags are also present in ELF communication can rather be taken as an additional indicator of its potential for flexibly realising linguistic trends—in this case towards reducing complexity—at an early stage. Since innovative usage is, at least in the present dataset, much more prominent than the traditional one, the process can even be considered accelerated as compared to other language repertoires (cf. also Dewey 2007, 206ff.).

Efficiency is generally taken as a main reason for a development like the one just outlined. In ELF, it interconnects with effectiveness as a main priority in language usage (cf. Cogo & Dewey 2006, 73).[7] With an inherent negation as well as interrogation element, the tag *no?* as in Extract 3 can be argued to convey the intended meaning in a simpler and probably even more explicit, immediate form. On top of that, Williams (1989, 131) argues that all-purpose tags are "easier to process than variable ones" and Vulanovic (1991, 203) explains that generally "grammar is more efficient [...] when it is able to give more information [...] with less conveyors". Prompting the desired reaction and fulfilling its pragmatic function, *no?* represents both *efficient* and *effective* communication.

Moreover, it can be inferred from the empirical evidence that there seems to be a general tendency among the recorded speakers to create and use less complex tags, like *or?* and *no?*, rather than *isn't it?*.[8] Whether this tendency is an idiosyncrasy emerging in and through the particular recording context or whether it has more general validity, needs to be investigated in future corpus analyses. One underlying criterion for favouring the less complex forms could be that, by being simple and explicit, they meet both the "principle of clarity" and the "principle of economy" at the same time. As Poulisse (1997, 51) explains,

> [t]o comply with both principles simultaneously, speakers must strike a balance between the intelligibility of their messages and the processing effort they and their listeners put into the production and reception of these messages.

In the case of the ELF form *no?*, it seems that neither of the principles needs to be neglected. The processes at work in lingua franca communication, such as exploiting redundancy or enhancing explicitness, can be complex and intertwined and need not be mutually exclusive (cf. Dewey 2007, 137ff.).

In addition to "intralingual" factors, another driving force towards the preference of forms like *no?* and *or?* could be "interlingual" influences (cf. Ellis 2005, 65). Zobl describes the interconnnection of the two types of factors for non-conforming elements in learner language:

> Errors which seem to show influence from the L1 presumably begin as L2-developmental errors which are subsequently reinforced by an L1 structure compatible with the developmental error (Zobl 1980, 470 quoted in Winer 1989, 169).

As its intercultural users make ELF a multilingual context, the conventions of language usage encoded in their L1s and LNs are likely to feed into the situational resource pool, exerting additional influence on their linguistic behaviour. The fact that many European languages contain invariable rather than concord tags does not only represent favourable conditions for the formation but also for the interpretability of the non-concord variants. In other words, particular speaker constellations could foster the invariable usage of tags as a commonality concerning the production as well as the comprehension side. With the possibility of cross-linguistic influence in mind, the production of *no?* in Extract 3 might be supported by S1's L1 German containing the tag *nicht?*, whereas its comprehension could be facilitated by *¿no?* being a common tag in S2's L1 Spanish. Expressing it with deficit terminology, one could even go as far making the following claim: If a feature is shared by the communicators, two 'wrongs' can make a 'right' in ELF. It would be interesting to investigate the behaviour of speakers whose L1s do know concord tags. As illustrated by Extract 3, interlingual and intralingual influences often cannot be clearly separated (cf. Kellerman 1983, 112-113). A situation in which plurlingual resources come into play more prominently can be seen in the next example.

3.2.4. Exploiting Plurilinguality

Transfer phenomena have been recognised as fundamental in non-native language production, although their influence is often far from welcome. The sheer notion of "negative transfer" (e.g. Odlin 1989, 36-38) in interlanguage production unambiguously implies that both L2 learners as well as teachers should regard it as a nuisance and find ways of doing away with it. As already indicated in the preceding section, this does not necessarily have to be the case in ELF.

In Extract 4, S1 reports on her experiences in France and about the celebrations at a particular occasion. As part of her account of the events there, she produces the construction *all busses were overfulled* which is not specifically commented on by S2, nor is it pointed to as not understandable.[9]

Extract 4
(S1: L1=German; S2: L1=Norwegian)

S1: but (.) but really (1) crazy (.) all (.) all busses were <pvc> overfulled </pvc> (1) all of the french one jump around and <imitating> yeah </imitating> and sing their songs and (.)
S2: <@> i see </@>
S1: yeah (.) it was really crazy
S2: yeah

As far as the production part of *overfulled* is concerned, it seems quite obvious that S1, as a native speaker of German, creates the expression with the German word *überfüllt* in mind. She performs almost a literary translation of an L1 item which is in contrast to ENL terms such as *crowded*. Apart from conforming to its equivalent in S1's L1, *overfulled* also seems to work as a lexical item which conveys meaning in a more straightforward way than *crowded*, at least from a non-native speaker perspective. Indeed, "compositionality and semantic transparency" (Seidlhofer 2009), which have been shown to play a crucial role in the on-line creation of idiomaticity in ELF (cf. also Seidlhofer & Widdowson 2007) also seem to support S1's decision for transferring the item. As Arabski explains,

> [t]he most important and universal feature of negative transfer is its simplifying character. It is used in order to simplify target language structures under the influence of L1 (Arabski 2006, 14).

Enhanced transparency, i.e. enhanced simplicity, is likely to make the processing of an utterance easier. The less complex nature of the formal representation *overfulled* referring to the semantic concept 'crowded' could potentially be an asset also on the listener's part. The less normative way of using language in this case does at least not impair understanding. But approaching the communicative situation from a multilingual perspective, there is another aspect which might influence comprehension fundamentally. Interestingly enough, S2's L1 Norwegian contains a term which is very similar to the one created by S1, namely *overfylt*. Thus, the transfer process carried out by S1 is likely to be completely plausible from her interlocutor's viewpoint as well. The items *überfüllt* and *overfylt* both back *overfulled* as an effective expression for the particular speakers involved. Drawing on the other languages available in this communicative context, i.e. their individual L1s, speakers are able to enlarge their shared situational resource pool. Summing up, both non-nativeness in general and L1s in particular can be regarded as valuable components for making meaning in ELF. The common and the variable speaker features complement each other. Ten Thije argues that

> [z]u oft wird [interkulturelle] Kommunikation analytisch nur wie ein Zusammenstoß, eine Mischung oder eine Konfrontation von Kultursystemen behandelt. Die Alternative [...] ist eine Analyse, die die interaktive Konstitution der kommunikativen Basis durch die Aktanten selbst als Mittelpunkt hat
> [too often intercultural communication is treated like a crash, a mixture or a confrontation of cultural systems. The alternative is an analysis which centres on the interactive constitution of the communicative base by the actors themselves] (Ten Thije 2002, 92; my translation).

In Extract 4, we have been concerned with a cross-linguistic phenomenon which triggered the creation of a new expression. The underlying production process can be inferred easily, the intended meaning is quite obvious. However, as soon as the influence from an L1 does not affect the formal properties of a word but its semantics, i.e. when an existing word is used to convey a different meaning, cross-linguistic influence is generally assumed to become problematic. Taking into consideration the situational character of ELF speaker constellations, again, might put this assumption into perspective—which is illustrated by the next example.

3.2.5. Making Friends with Cognates

In Extract 5, the interactants jointly try to locate a particular place on a map. When S3 believes to have found it, she utters *here on my card*, pointing at the map. She obviously wants to express the concept 'map' through the term *card*. Thus, in a communicative situation like this, the literal meaning of a word "may prove rather useless when a speaker's intended meaning of the same utterance differs widely from [it]" (Purpura 2004, 63).

Extract 5
(S1: L1=German; S2: L1=Italian; S3: L1=Greek)

S1: so it's somewhere here (1) you have to look at the streets
S2: quite far from here?
S1: no (.) it's not THAT far (2) e:rm=
S3: =here on my card (1) sixteenth
S1: sixth (1) er district
S2: sixth?
S1: mhm

Considering the fact that in S3's L1 Greek the item *chartis* is used to refer to the concept of 'map', her linguistic behaviour can be assumed to be influenced by cross-linguistic factors. In interlanguage terminology, the English word *card* as a cognate that is formally related to *chartis*, but that semantically diverges from it would be regarded as its "false friend" (cf. Odlin 1989, 77-79). At the same time, the wider context surrounding the communicative situation, i.e. Vienna University, is actually a German one. S3 could be observed to have considerable competence in this language as well, using it for communication with other students before the service encounter. German is thus also a component of S3's plurilingual repertoire. It seems plausible that the German word *Karte*, which also carries the meaning 'map' and resembles both the Greek term *chartis* and the English item *card*, reinforces S3's usage of *card* in her utterance. Näf and Pfander (2001, 10) describe the phenomenon as "inferencing from a double sequence", e.g. Greek-German, to a triple sequence, e.g. Greek-German-English, referring to it as "translingual over-generalisation" triggered by "doubly supported interference". Thus, plurilingual forces are at play already at the production part of this utterance.

As far as comprehension is concerned, the physical presence of the actual map is a fundamental factor in establishing mutual understanding among the interactants. Potential support towards this understanding is revealed as soon as the situational speaker constellation, i.e. the L1s involved, is considered. Not only is S3 likely to be affected by L1/LN terms when producing *card*. S2, as a native speaker of Italian, has *carta* as an equivalent expression in her repertoire, and S1 could, again, activate the German *Karte* for comprehension. Both, S2 and S1 are likely to be familiar with linking mother tongue cognates of *card* to the concept 'map'. All the participants are, thus, potentially able to relate to the utterance *here on my card* through their plurilingual resources. Coming back to Näf and Pfander's "translingual over-generalisation" (2001, 10), one could argue that in the case of these ELF users, we are concerned not only with double, but with multiple support for this process as it is based not only on one, but on several speakers' interlingual perspectives. In this view, then, *map* could even seem to be the 'odd one out'. This is in line with the concept of "continental features" established by Ferguson (1982, x), which he defines as being "at variance with the English of England but shared by other speakers". Ringbom (2007, 5) describes semantic similarity and difference as two positions located on different ends of a continuum. For ELF situations like in Extract 5, it seems, we could open up and extend this two-dimensional scheme. A third dimension could contain a particular ELF form (e.g. card) having both similarity relations (e.g. L1/LN elements like *chartis*, *Karte*, *carta*) and contrast relations (e.g. ENL elements like *map*). It then naturally depends on various kinds of other linguistic and non-linguistic factors—and is therefore difficult to judge—if and how this situation influences the communication process.

Summing up, the evaluation of transfer in ELF is subject to situational speaker constellations and plurilingual resource pools. By recourse to the ELF users' multi-competence, a shift in the categorisation of transfer seems likely. The traditional definition of "positive transfer" as

> facilitating effects [...] due to the influence of cross-linguistic similarities [... and] convergence of behaviors of native and non-native speakers (Odlin 1989, 168)

could be extended in the light of ELF towards

> facilitating effects due to the influence of cross-linguistic *similarities between the ELF speakers' different L1s and LNs* and convergence of behaviors of *non-native speakers and fellow non-native speakers.*

This would, in turn, mean that false friends have the potential to become 'true friends' in ELF, given that there is an overlap between the speakers' plurilingual mental lexicons.[10] Where literal meaning is neglected in favour of intended meaning, "perceived" similarity (cf. Kellerman 1977, 95-96; Ringbom 2007, 7-8) can become more important for effective communication than actual similarity. It is important to note, however, that this line of argumentation is founded explicitly on the particular speaker constellations characterising the selected extracts. Descriptive efforts of a larger scale would be needed to gain evidence for more far-reaching claims. It seems paramount to pursue investigations in the prominent multilingual potential underlying ELF and in ways of exploiting it in accordance with other situational as well as shared elements.

4. Conclusion

Summing up, what all the extracts analysed have in common is that they contain supposedly 'incorrect' items which do not only turn out to serve the purposes of ELF communication, but are also based on processes equally relevant to production and comprehension in the interactions. The effectiveness of these items reveals that their use does not mean making mistakes but, on the contrary, making sense for the speakers involved. Their formal properties seem more than justified in these cases.

ELF communication processes can manifest themselves in traditional non-native speaker strategies as well as in innovative linguistic behaviour. This variability does not have to be a disadvantage. Rather than lamenting that—due to the lack of a stable set of formal criteria—ELF does not seem to qualify as a language variety in the traditional sense (cf. e.g. Mollin 2006), we should ask ourselves whether this would be desirable in the first place. If this meant establishing new norms and thereby positioning ELF speakers as 'error-committers' once again, it would probably not be. If it meant sacrificing valuable features such as linguistic flexibility, expanded resources and the exploitation of strategic competence, it would not be either. What tends to serve as common ground despite the hardly predictable nature of ELF forms are phenomena like communicative cooperation, mutual accommodation as well as meta- and cross-linguistic sensitivity, all feeding into successful ELF talk (cf. Hülmbauer, Böhringer & Seidlhofer 2009).

ELF is the kind of English which is a reality for an ever-increasing number of communicators around the globe (cf. also Widdowson 1994, 386). Rather than artificially aiming at convergence with native norms, i.e. correctness in the original sense, its users should be encouraged to embrace ELF for its specific communicative potential and to exploit their own resources, i.e. their ways of 'right' communication, in the best possible way. Indeed, reporting on interviews carried out with international students about English norms, Adolphs (2005) claims that native-like competence tends to diminish in value as soon as communication via English is put to a real-life test. As she explains,

> [t]he reason for this process of fragmentation of the 'native speaker' concept seems to lie in an increased awareness of what is really important in any international context and that is the ability to understand and be understood (ibid., 130).

The lesson to learn should be clear: What suits the users' purposes and helps establish effective communication has the potential for being 'just right' in ELF—regardless of traditional correctness criteria. It is hoped that the paradigm change currently under way will eventually enable speakers to arrive at a point where they can embrace this potential without perceiving themselves as second-rate language users.

Bibliography

Adolphs, S. 2005. "'I don't think I should learn all this'—A Longitudinal View of Attitudes towards 'Native Speaker' English." In *The Globalisation of English and the English Language Classroom*, ed. C. Gnutzmann & F. Intemann, 115-27. Tübingen: Gunter Narr.

Arabski, J. 2006. "Language Transfer in Language Learning and Language Contact." In *Cross-Linguistic Influences in the Second Language Lexicon*, ed. J. Arabski, 12-21. Clevedon: Multilingual Matters.

Bent, T. and A. R. Bradlow 2003. "The Interlanguage Speech Intelligibility Benefit." *Journal of the Acoustic Society of America* 114 (3), 1600-10. http://www.ling.northwestern.edu/~abradlow/bent&bradlow03.pdf (accessed August 23, 2007)

Böhringer, H. and C. Hülmbauer 2008. "DYLAN's Transversal Research Task (RT) 4.2: 'Emergent Varieties'." In *Conference Report of the International UNESCO Conference on 'Everyday Multilingualism'*, Eisenstadt, 13-15 June 2008, 208-10. http://www.bmukk.gv.at/medienpool/17399/gesamtberichtderkonferenz_co.pdf (accessed December 12, 2008)

Cogo, A. this volume. "Accommodating Difference in ELF Conversations: A Study of Pragmatic Strategies."

Cogo, A. and M. Dewey 2006. "Efficiency in ELF Communication: From Pragmatic Motives to Lexico-Grammatical Innovation." *Nordic Journal of English Studies* 5 (2), 59-93. http://hdl.handle.net/2077/3148. (accessed October 20, 2006).

Cook, V. 2005. "Multi-Competence: Black Hole or Wormhole?" http://homepage.ntlworld.com/vivian.c/writings/papers/slrf.htm. (accessed October 10, 2008)

—. 2002. "Background to the L2 User." In *Portraits of the L2 User*, ed. V. Cook, 1-31. Clevedon: Multilingual Matters.

Corder, S. P. 1982. *Error Analysis and Interlanguage*. Oxford: Oxford University Press.

Dewey, M. 2007. "English as a Lingua Franca: An Empirical Study of Innovation in Lexis and Grammar." PhD diss., King's College London.

DYLAN—Language Dynamics and Management of Diversity, Research Task 4.2. http://dylan.univie.ac.at/index.php?id=33735 (accessed February 12, 2009).
Ehrenreich, S. this volume. "English as a Lingua Franca in Multinational Corporations—Exploring Buisness Communities of Practice."
Ellis, R. 2005. *Analysing Learner Language*. Oxford: Oxford University Press.
Fee, M. and J. McAlpine 1997. *Guide to Canadian English Usage*. Toronto: Oxford University Press.
Ferguson, C. A. 1982. "Foreword." In *The Other Tongue*, ed. B. B. Kachru, vii-xi. Urbana: University of Illinois Press.
Firth, A. 1996. "The Discursive Accomplishment of Normality. On 'Lingua Franca' English and Conversation Analysis." *Journal of Pragmatics* 26 (2), 237-59.
Firth, A. and J. Wagner 1997. "On Discourse, Communication, and (Some) Fundamental Concepts in SLA Research." *Modern Language Journal* 81 (3), 285-300.
Giles H. and N. Coupland 1991. *Language: Contexts and Consequences*. Buckingham: Open University Press.
Grosjean, F. 2001. "The Bilingual's Language Modes." In *One Mind, Two Languages. Bilingual Language Processing*, ed. J. L. Nicol, 1-22. Malden: Blackwell.
Hülmbauer, C. 2007. "'You moved, aren't?'—The Relationship between Lexicogrammatical Correctness and Communicative Effectiveness in English as a Lingua Franca." *VIenna English Working PaperS* 16 (2), 3-35. http://www.univie.ac.at/Anglistik/Views_0702.pdf. (accessed October 20, 2008)
Hülmbauer, C., H. Böhringer and B. Seidlhofer 2009. "Introducing English as a Lingua Franca (ELF): Precursor and Partner in Intercultural Communication." In *Enseigner—Apprendre—Utiliser le Francais Langue Internationale en Europe Aujourd'hui: Pour une Perspective Comparatiste. Synergies Europe* 3/08, ed. C. Cali, M. Stegu & E. Vetter, 25-36. http://ressources-cla.univ-fcomte.fr/gerflint/Europe3/hulmbauer.pdf. (accessed April 2, 2009)
Jenkins, J. 2007. *English as a Lingua Franca: Attitude and Identity*. Oxford: Oxford University Press.
—. 2006. "Points of View and Blind Spots: ELF and SLA." *International Journal of Applied Linguistics* 16 (2), 136-62.
—. 2000. *The Phonology of English as an International Language*. Oxford: Oxford University Press.

Jessner, U. 2006. *Linguistic Awareness in Multilinguals: English as a Third Language*. Edinburgh: Edinburgh University Press.

Kellerman, E. 1983. "Now You See It, Now You Don't." In *Language Transfer in Language Learning*, ed. S. Gass & L. Selinker, 112-34. Rowley, MA: Newbury House.

—. 1977. "Towards a Characterisation of the Strategy of Transfer in Second Language Learning." *Interlanguage Studies Bulletin* 2, 58-145.

Klimpfinger, T. 2007. "'Mind you sometimes you have to mix'—The Role of Code-Switching in English as a Lingua Franca." *VIenna English Working PaperS* 16 (2), 36-61. http://www.univie.ac.at/Anglistik/Views_0702.pdf. (accessed May 3, 2008)

Kordon, K. 2003. "Phatic Communion in English as a Lingua Franca." M.A. diss., Vienna University.

Kortmann, B. and E. W. Schneider, eds. 2006. *Varieties of English. A Multimedia Reference Tool*. Berlin: Mouton de Gruyter. http://www.varieties.mouton-content.com. (accessed September 14, 2007).

Krug, M. 1998. "British English is Developing a New Discourse Marker, Innit? A Study in Lexicalisation Based on Social, Regional and Stylistic Variation." *Arbeiten aus Anglistik und Amerikanistik* 23 (2), 145-97.

Lennon, P. 1991. "Error: Some Problems of Definition and Identification." *Applied Linguistics* 12 (2), 180-95.

Lichtkoppler, J. 2007."'Male. Male.'—'Male?'—'The sex is male.' The Role of Repetition in English as a Lingua Franca Conversations." *VIenna English Working PaperS* 16 (1), 39-65. http://www.univie.ac.at/Anglistik/views_0701.PDF. (accessed April 23, 2008)

Mauranen, A. 2005. "English as Lingua Franca: An Unknown Language?" In *Identity, Community, Discourse. English in Intercultural Settings*, ed. G. Cortese & A. Duszak, 269-93. Bern: Peter Lang.

Mollin, S. 2006. *Euro-English. Assessing Variety Status*. Tübingen: Gunter Narr.

Näf, A. and D. Pfander 2001. "<Springing of> a <bruck> with an elastic <sail>. Deutsches im Englisch von französischsprachigen Schülern." *Zeitschrift für Angewandte Linguistik* 35, 5-39.

Odlin, T. 1989. *Language Transfer. Cross-Linguistic Influence in Language Learning*. Cambridge: Cambridge University Press.

Pitzl, M.-L. this volume. "'We Should Not Wake Up Any Dogs': Idiom and Metaphor in ELF."

Pitzl, M.-L., A. Breiteneder and T. Klimpfinger 2008. "A World of Words: Lexical Innovations in ELF." *VIenna English Working PaperS* 17 (4),

21-46. http://www.univie.ac.at/Anglistik/Views_0802.pdf. (accessed January 5, 2009).

Poulisse, N. 1997. "Compensatory Strategies and the Principles of Clarity and Economy." In *Communication Strategies: Psycholinguistic and Sociolinguistic Perspectives*, ed. G. Kasper & E. Kellerman, 49-64. London: Longman.

Purpura, J. E. 2004. *Assessing Grammar*. Cambridge: Cambridge University Press.

Ringbom, H. 2007. *Cross-Linguistic Similarity in Foreign Language Learning*. Clevedon: Multilingual Matters.

Rinvolucri, M. 2008. "What Sort of Standard Does English as a Lingua Franca (ELF) Need to Reach? A Response to Jenkins." *Modern English Teacher* 17 (2), 16-17.

Seidlhofer, B. 2009. "Accommodation and the Idiom Principle in English as a Lingua Franca". *Journal of Intercultural Pragmatics* 6 (2), 195-215.

—. 2007. "English as a Lingua Franca and Communities of Practice." In *Anglistentag 2006 Halle Proceedings*, ed. S. Volk-Birke & J. Lippert, 307-18. Trier: Wissenschaftlicher Verlag Trier.

—. 2005. "English as a Lingua Franca." In *Oxford Advanced Learner's Dictionary of Current English*, 7th ed., ed. A. S. Hornby, R92. Oxford: Oxford University Press.

—. 2004. "Research Perspectives on Teaching English as a Lingua Franca." *Annual Review of Applied Linguistics* 24, 209-39.

Seidlhofer, B. and H. G. Widdowson 2007. "Idiomatic Variation and Change in English. The Idiom Principle and Its Realizations." In *Tracing English through Time. Explorations in Language Variation*, ed. U. Smit, S. Dollinger, J. Hüttner, G. Kaltenböck & U. Lutzky, 359-74. Wien: Braumüller.

Ten Thije, J. D. 2002. "Stufen des Verstehens in der Analyse interkultureller Kommunikation." In *Kultur(en) im Gespräch. Studien zur Fremdheit und Interaktion*, ed. H. Kotthoff, 57-97. Tübingen: Gunter Narr.

Vulanovic, R. 1991. "On Measuring Grammar Efficiency and Redundancy." *Linguistic Analysis* 21, 201-11.

Wenger, E. 1998. *Communities of Practice: Learning, Meaning, and Identity*. Cambridge: Cambridge University Press.

Williams, J. 1989. "Variation and Convergence in Nonnative Institutionalized Englishes." In *The Dynamic Interlanguage. Empirical Studies in Second Language Variation*, ed. M. R. Eisenstein, 117-36. New York: Plenum Press.

Widdowson, H. G. 1994. "The Ownership of English." *TESOL Quarterly* 28 (2), 377-89.
—. 1990. *Aspects of Language Teaching*. Oxford: Oxford University Press.
Winer, L. 1989. "Variation and Transfer in English Creole-Standard English Language Learning." In *The Dynamic Interlanguage. Empirical Studies in Second Language Variation*, ed. M. R. Eisenstein, 155-73. New York: Plenum Press.
Zobl, H. 1980. "Developmental and Transfer Errors: Their Common Bases and (Possibly) Differential Effects on Subsequent Learning." *TESOL Quarterly* 14 (4), 469-82.

Notes

[1] This refers to prototypical ELF interactions and does not mean that native speakers are excluded entirely from ELF contexts (cf. Seidlhofer 2004, 211).
[2] The terms *L2 user*, *bilingual* and *plurilingual* are used in line with Cook (2005): "The term 'L2 user' was originally intended to counteract the implication that people with a second language are learners for life [...]. This is not to say that the same person cannot be both an L2 learner in a classroom and an L2 user in the street outside. Nor [is ...] 'L2 user' related to a level of success in the second language, certainly not reserved either for 'balanced bilinguals' or for 'native passers'."
[3] The term 'plurilingual' is used in a broad sense in this paper, referring to people knowing at least two languages.
[4] All the extracts provided are transcribed according to the VOICE transcription conventions [2.0]. http://www.univie.ac.at/voice.
[5] Selected interactions from the dataset now also form part of the VOICE corpus. For more details on the collected data see Hülmbauer 2007, 12-3.
[6] Initial observations by the VOICE team (personal communication) could point to a tendency in ELF also towards *huh?* as an all-purpose tag.
[7] This is not meant to imply that ELF merely serves as a transactional tool. The phatic function of language, for instance, has been shown to be developed in ELF as well (cf. Kordon 2003).
[8] Although it doesn't occur in my data to a great extent, *isn't it* is mentioned among other potential invariable tags used by ELF speakers according to initial observations by Seidlhofer (2005, R92).
[9] For a more detailed discussion of lexical innovations like this in ELF, also with reference to the <pvc> tag established to capture them in the transcription process, see Pitzl, Breiteneder & Klimpfinger (2008).
[10] Note that Cook (2002, 18) argues that language systems in the minds of plurilinguals cannot be separated but constitute an "integration continuum". In line with this assumption, the notion of transfer would, thus, need to be reconsidered as a whole.

"SHE'S MIXING THE TWO LANGUAGES TOGETHER"— FORMS AND FUNCTIONS OF CODE-SWITCHING IN ENGLISH AS A LINGUA FRANCA

THERESA KLIMPFINGER

1. Introduction

Considering the fact that much has been written about the mixing and switching of languages in different fields of research and from different viewpoints, it seems somewhat ironic that code-switching in English as a lingua franca (ELF) has not received more attention up to this point, as ELF, *per definition*, involves typically three languages: the speakers' first languages and English. The fact that ELF speakers sometimes mix these languages is exactly what one of these speakers refers to with the utterance *she's mixing the two languages together*.

In the past few years, research into ELF has grown considerably (see, e.g., Seidlhofer 2004, 218-220 and Seidlhofer, Breiteneder & Pitzl 2006, 8-13 for overviews of recent empirical work), and by now two international conferences specifically dedicated to ELF (in Helsinki 2008, and in Southampton 2009) bear witness to the ever-increasing importance of the role of ELF. So far, however, little has been said about the use and role of other languages in ELF. Exceptions in this respect are Meierkord (2002), who discusses verbal manifestations of culture in ELF interactions, as well as Pölzl (2003; 2005), who explores the use of other languages as a means of expressing cultural membership. More recently, Pölzl and Seidlhofer (2006) have shown how ELF users integrate their first language communicative norms into ELF conversations, and Hülmbauer (this volume) calls for a re-evaluation of cross-linguistic influence (affecting lexicogrammar) in the light of ELF communication. More explicitly, Cogo (2007) reports on code-switching as a pragmatic strategy in ELF interactions, "used by the participants to make the communication work, to ensure understanding and efficiency in conversation" (Cogo 2007, 181; see also this volume).

Seidlhofer, Breiteneder and Pitzl (2006, 21) stress that

> [a]t this stage [...] there is an urgent need for significantly more qualitative studies to be conducted, the data from which can then be incorporated into emerging larger corpora of ELF.

It is thus the aim of this paper to contribute to the description of ELF by shedding light on the use of other languages in naturally-occurring ELF talk. After a brief overview of different approaches to code-switching in section 2, section 3 starts out with a quantitative approach to present some initial findings on the use of other languages in VOICE, the Vienna-Oxford International Corpus of English. These numbers serve as a starting point for the subsequent qualitative analysis in section 4. The qualitative analysis is based on a dataset of eight workshop and working group discussions of speakers from a variety of European language backgrounds, all of whom use English successfully as their only common means of communication. The forms code-switching takes in ELF interactions will be examined and their communicative functions evaluated.

2. Code-Switching in ELF: The Theoretical Background

Most of the research concerning code-switching refers to bilingual speech communities with two or more languages in more or less regular contact (e.g. Hoffmann 1991; Myers-Scotton 1993, 45-51; Romaine 2001, 23-77; and Schendl 2002 and 2004 for code-switching in the history of the English language). ELF interactions, however, do not frequently take place in such stable communities but involve *ad hoc* groupings of speakers of different first language backgrounds who then establish a "shared set of norms and rules for the use of language" (Romaine 2000, 23). The levels of proficiency of ELF speakers may vary, but since equal competence in both languages is not a prerequisite for bilingualism[1], ELF speakers are considered to be bi- and/or multilingual, or rather "multi-competent" (Cook 2002a, 10) users of English as well as their respective first language (L1), and other languages (LN). Grosjean (2008, 14) illustrates this holistic concept of the bilingual speaker by using an analogy to sports:

> The high hurdler blends two types of competencies, that of high jumping and that of sprinting. When compared individually with either the sprinter or the high jumper, the hurdler meets neither level of competence, and yet when taken as a whole the hurdler is an athlete in his or her own right. [...]

> In many ways, the bilingual is like the high hurdler: an integrated whole, a unique and specific speaker-hearer, and not just the sum of two complete or incomplete monolinguals.

In ELF contact situations, by definition, more than two languages are present (each speaker's L1 and English), which makes code-switching into all of them possible. The phenomenon of code-switching has undergone a conceptual shift from being stigmatised as a sign of deficiency (e.g. Haugen 1956 and Weinreich 1970 [1953]) to today's perception of the creative manifestation of bilingual speech behaviour similar to shifts in styles and varieties among monolinguals (Romaine 2001, 121). Within the framework of bilingual research, a distinction is made between 'code-switching', 'code-mixing', and 'borrowing', the three terms denoting the alternate use of two or more languages within one sentence, utterance, or interaction. As this analysis, however, does not focus on the conceptual differences between the three, the term 'code-switching' will be used to cover all such instances of other-language use in the ELF context.[2]

Code-switching may involve single words, phrases or whole sentences (Grosjean 2008, 160) and is generally categorised according to the syntactic arrangement of the switches (Poplack 1980, Romaine 2001). Thus, a distinction can be made between tag-switches (i.e. the insertion of an exclamation, a tag, or a parenthetical), inter-sentential switches (switches at clause or sentence boundaries), and intra-sentential switches (switches within word, clause and sentence boundaries including single lexical items). In contrast to that, however, Romaine (2001, 124) argues for an approach that constitutes code-switching as "a continuum ranging from whole sentences, clauses and other chunks of discourse to single words, which could be inserted into a grammatical structure". As this approach allows for a more flexible consideration of types of code-switching, it serves as a good starting point for the analysis of the instances of code-switching in my ELF data, which includes word-fragments, single words, and clauses up to whole passages.

By looking at the forms code-switching takes in ELF, the question of why people switch codes still remains. Romaine (2000, 57) notes that

> there is increasing evidence to indicate that this mixed mode of speaking serves important functions in the communities where it is used and that it is not random.

Gumperz (1982, 75-81) stresses the strategic use of code-switching in discourse in order to mark quotations, specify an addressee, highlight interjections, reiterate something, qualify the message, and mark personalisation vs. objectivisation. Appel and Muysken (1995) suggest a referential, a directive/integrative, an expressive, a phatic, a metalinguistic, and a poetic function as explanations for code-switching.[3] For the purpose of the present analysis, some of these partly related and overlapping functions were considered useful: the 'directive/integrative function' (Appel & Muysken 1995), which is similar to 'addressee specification' (Gumperz 1982, 75ff.), and the 'referential function' (Appel & Muysken 1995). These functions do not only account for the majority of the switches I identified, but also place ELF contact situations within the framework of bilingual research. As will be illustrated with examples from the data, ELF speakers use code-switching to direct their speech to a specific addressee to integrate her/him in the conversation, in short for specifying an addressee. They also resort to code-switching for introducing another idea, by which they seem to imply that the language switched into is more appropriate to discuss this particular subject (cf. the referential function, Appel & Muysken 1995).

A different perspective on code-switching is offered by the field of research concerned with communication strategies. Although communication strategies —the "mutual attempt of two interlocutors to agree on a meaning in situations where requisite meaning structures do not seem to be shared" (Tarone 1984, 65)[4]—have traditionally been linked to L2 learning contexts exclusively, more recent research also involves native speakers and extends its investigation beyond L2 usage (e.g. Bialystok 1990). The idea that a communication strategy enhances the effectiveness of communication "in the absence of problematicity" (Bialystok 1990, 4) has come to the fore. This approach seems applicable to the ELF context and leads Hübner (2003, 25ff.) to propose that some ELF speakers consider the use of a communication strategy "not as a solution to a *problem*" (my emphasis), but rather as an effective "way to reach a certain communicative goal and thus successfully convey one's thought". One such strategy is the 'appeal to authority', which may implicitly be indicated by, for example, rising intonation. An appeal may also be uttered explicitly by asking for the missing term or phrase, by repeating a non-understood phrase, and/or by metalinguistic comments (Færch & Kasper 1983). "[B]eing able to draw on their multifaceted linguistic repertoire" (Cogo 2007, 166), ELF speakers always have the possibility to switch into another language when appealing for assistance, which will be illustrated with examples from my data.

Yet another function for code-switching in ELF relates to culture and identity: Language constitutes an integral part of culture and, consequently, one's identity, which deserves attention when analysing code-switching in

ELF. In the context of ELF research it has been recognised that "its users are not required to adopt the culture(s) associated with English as a native language" (Pölzl & Seidlhofer 2006, 153), but "have to know the code [...] to manage successful and effective communication across cultures" (ibid). This implies that ELF speakers use English as a language of communication and display expertise in a code that is not their L1, whereas their primary language of identification, the language they are bound to by birth, is predominantly another one, usually their L1 (cf. Hüllen 1992). In ELF talk, a variety of linguistic and cultural backgrounds along with their different communicative norms are involved and speakers are usually not always familiar with their interlocutors' L1s. Speakers are engaged, at least at the subconscious level, in a process of negotiation of norms and signs and may have to deal with unexpected situations. Hence, Pölzl (2005) argues for a third space, which is established by participants who come from diverse linguacultural backgrounds and use ELF as their common language. The Third Space

> is an imagined space of negotiation and at the same time 'encountered hybridity' through which new intercultural meaning, practices and identifications are created. (Pölzl 2005, 112)

The third space is co-constructed together with the other ELF speakers in every ELF situation anew and parallel to each one's individual primary culture. This implies a dynamic concept and always allows speakers, consciously or unconsciously, to blend in their L1 or another LN to emphasise their membership of different groups.[5] As examples from my data suggest, 'signalling culture' in ELF may be performed in two ways: Speakers may switch to another language for exclamations, pause fillers, or function words to implicitly give a linguistic emblem of this culture, i.e. by emblematic switches. They may also code-switch in order to explicitly refer to concepts associated with a specific culture, such as a name of a city or a greeting.

I have presented different types of code-switching and a number of explanations for code-switching based on different theoretical and methodological perspectives. The four functions, i.e. *specifying an addressee*, *introducing another idea*, *appealing for assistance*, and *signalling culture*, have emerged as the most suitable for the purpose of my analysis. Before going into detail with the analysis, however, a quantitative overview of instances of code-switching in VOICE will be given to illustrate the wide scope of code-switching in ELF.

3. Code-Switching in VOICE

VOICE, the Vienna-Oxford International Corpus of English, is the first general corpus of spoken ELF and, at the moment, comprises 151 fully transcribed speech events equalling about a million words. The elements uttered in another language than English are marked by tags, differentiating between a speaker's first language (L1), a language that is neither English nor the speaker's first language (LN), and a language where it is unknown whether this is the speaker's first language or another one s/he knows (LQ) (VOICE Transcription Conventions [2.1], VOICE Project 2007, 9). This way it is relatively easy to search for foreign language elements in the corpus.

Conducting my research of code-switching in ELF, I used VOICE as a starting point and resorted to those 90 speech events of the corpus that had been checked and converted into XML (equalling about 700,000 words).[6] By using Xaira[7], an XML-based analysing software tool, 2,184 instances of code-switching could be identified. Of these 2,184 code-switches, 1,179 are into speakers' first languages, 965 into speakers' other languages, and 40 into languages which cannot clearly be identified as the speaker's first or other language. The results are illustrated in Table 1.

Table 1. Instances of code-switching in VOICE.

Language switched into	Number of instances
L1	1179
LN	965
LQ	40
Total	2184

These large numbers clearly show that code-switching forms an essential part of ELF interactions. The following table (see Table 2) breaks down these numbers and gives the languages being switched into. This table nicely illustrates the great variety of languages ELF speakers in VOICE switch into: a spectrum of 28, mainly European, languages is represented.

Table 2. Instances of code-switching in VOICE according to languages switched into.

Language switched into	Number of instances	Language switched into	Number of instances
German	1366	Czech	6
Maltese	281	Danish	5
French	160	Romanian	5
Italian	71	Portuguese	4
Spanish	69	Polish	3
Korean	61	Japanese	3
Arabic	37	Latin	2
Unidentified	22	Finnish	2
Dutch	20	Latvian	1
Serbian	14	Slovenian	1
Slovak	12	Hungarian	1
Lithuanian	11	Turkish	1
Norwegian	9	Chinese	1
Moldavian	8	Russian	1
Bulgarian	7		

With the caveat that working with a corpus must always include a careful evaluation of the output one is presented with, one cannot simply take the numbers and ignore certain factors. As can be seen in the table, a clear majority of switches in VOICE is into German. This, however, does not mean that German is the language ELF speakers prefer to switch into. Given the fact that VOICE has been compiled in Vienna, Austria, it seems only natural that German speakers make up a high percentage of the speakers represented in the corpus. Similarly, it is sometimes impossible to determine the language a speaker switches into with certainty, which here results in 22 switches into one or more unidentified languages. In order to be able to infer any generalisations from the numbers presented in the table, it would therefore be necessary to involve also other factors in the analysis, such as the distribution of speakers' first languages and types of speech events in VOICE. At the same time, the preliminary results point to the potential and need for further research into this area.

4. Data and Methodology

The data this qualitative study is based on consists of 12 hours of naturally-occurring, spoken conversations—six workshop discussions and two working group discussions which were recorded at a conference in Vienna in July 2004. Of these eight speech events, the two working group discussions were later incorporated into VOICE, whereas the six workshop discussions were not, as they turned out not to sufficiently fulfil the criteria for inclusion into the corpus.[8] The 50 speakers are academics and represent different European universities, which are members of a network of universities in Europe concerned with issues of higher education and the development of joint study programmes. The two-day conference constituted the first meeting of this kind with the aim of exchanging ideas, taking stock of experiences, and developing a working programme for the future. In this sense, the participants followed a clear agenda and primarily exchanged information, which makes the data goal-oriented and transactional in nature. The number of participants varied, but a main group of about 30 people was present all the time. The primary cultures and first languages represented in this data are Croatian, Czech, Danish, Dutch (B), Estonian, Finnish, French (B, CH, F), German (A, D), Greek, Italian, Latvian, Norwegian, Polish, Portuguese, Slovenian, Slovak, Spanish, and Swedish. As can be seen, the participants came from diverse linguacultural backgrounds and, as members of an international committee, used English on a regular basis for communication with their international colleagues, and thus "[carry] out their ordinary lives through several languages" (Cook 2002b, 332).[9]

The process of transcription is a challenging task that is also affected by the subjective perception of the person doing the transcription (Breiteneder et al. 2006). This also holds true when identifying code-switches in ELF data. The VOICE Transcription Conventions [2.1] (VOICE Project 2007), according to which the data were transcribed, state that "[u]tterances in a participant's first language (L1) are put between tags indicating the speaker's L1" and that "[u]tterances in languages which are neither English nor the speaker's first language are marked LN with the language indicated". This sounds fairly straightforward, but nonetheless involves tricky instances where it is not clear whether a word uttered by an ELF speaker constitutes a switch or not. I experienced this dilemma especially with terms denoting special cultural concepts or names of persons and places, but also with certain expressions, such as *bon voyage* in the following extract[10]:

Extract 1
(S1: L1=Swedish)

S1: and <LNfr> **bon voyage** {have a nice trip} </LNfr> er: (6)
{S6 leaves the room}

The phrase *bon voyage* constitutes a borrowing from French into English (Romaine 2001, 55). This status is confirmed with an entry in the *Oxford Advanced Learner's Dictionary* (7th edition), according to which it is an exclamation "(from French) said to sb who is leaving on a journey, to wish them a good journey". In the case of Extract 1, the decision to represent it as a code-switch was governed mainly by the 'French pronunciation' of S1 and the fact that the whole utterance is directed to S6, a French speaker. Although the transcriber is sometimes forced to make such decisions which lead to a certain idealisation, such classifications are important for the statistical purposes of corpus analysis (McEnery & Wilson 1997, 63).

5. Code-Switching in Current Data

Participants in ELF conversations come from a variety of language backgrounds and speakers use English as their only common means of communication. They do not, by definition, share equal knowledge of each others' first languages. According to Cook (2002b, 332), however, "code-switching proper is possible only when both participants are aware that they share the same two languages." This might make it seem unlikely that code-switching takes place in ELF interactions and, indeed, its occurrence has so far not been reported as frequent.[11] However, a considerable number of instances of code-switching, both into speakers' L1s but also LNs, can be found in the current data.

The present analysis constitutes a qualitative analysis and considers the phenomenon of code-switching in ELF in eight speech events—two of which form part of VOICE—in greater detail. The total number of code-switches in these eight speech events is 104, of which 50 are into speakers' L1s and 54 into speakers' LNs. Table 3 breaks down these numbers and gives the languages switched into according to speakers' L1s and LNs.

Table 3. Instances of code-switching according to speakers' L1s and LNs and languages switched into (Total 104).

language switched into: L1s	**number of instances: 50**	**language switched into: LNs**	**number of instances: 54**
French	34	French	32
Czech	6	German	17
German	5	Dutch	3
Italian	4	Polish	1
Spanish	1	Spanish	1

The following analysis of forms and functions of code-switching in ELF is based on a larger study, but due to limits of space, only a selective portion will be presented with the aim of showing the diverse nature of code-switching in ELF and its rich potential for further research.[12]

5.1. Forms

As has been indicated, code-switching may involve single words, phrases, and whole sentences. Following Romaine's (2001, 124) approach of the code-switching continuum, the instances of code-switching in the present data can be grouped accordingly and they range from single words, to short, more or less fixed phrases, to whole clauses and sentences. The different types of code-switches in the data are represented in Table 4:

Table 4. Types of code-switching. The respective languages are given in parentheses (according to ISO 639-1 codes).

Single words	Short phrases	Longer chunks
alors (fr) also (de) bei (de) carré (fr) consécutifs (fr) cotutelle (fr) die (de) diplom (cs) divertissement (fr) donc (fr) economia (it) empfehlungen (de) englisch (de) fachhochschule (de) genug (de) habilitation (fr) habsburg (de) mitteleuropa (de) [name] (de) oui (fr) papyrologie (de) paris (fr) punkt (de) reich (de) roma (it) saal (de) seite (de) sí (es) sondage (fr) steuerungsgruppe (de) umweltschutz (de) vereine (de) visitatiecommissie (du) warszawa (pl) xx (fr)	aus [place] (de) bon voyage (fr) c'est vrai (fr) comme un grand carré (fr) commission de coordination (fr) cotutelle d'accord (fr) die seite (de) e [place] (it) grand merci (fr) je prend la parole (fr) l'électron libre (fr) le troisième cycle (fr) master complementaire (fr) oui un grand carré (fr) [place] et et (fr) point b e (fr) tour de table (fr) tres discrete (fr) vous etes et (fr)	xx comité xx grand effet xxx (fr) c'est très difficile pour moi [...] parler anglais je vais diré en français (fr) on peut essayer d'arriver une solution commune et originale (fr) université libre de bruxelles ou bien er monsieur le recteur ou bien [S32] (fr)

The clear majority of the switches in the data involves single words, viz. filler and functions words, nouns and adjectives, but also place names and terms for special cultural concepts. The second group consists of short, more or less fixed phrases, and the last group of switches involves longer chunks, clauses, and sentences. In contrast to Poplack's (1980) findings that full sentences are the most frequently switched elements, these types of switches are rather scarce in my data. As English is the only common means of communication for the speakers, each switch also includes a certain risk of misunderstanding and/or possibly excludes other speakers, even more so when the switch is a longer passage. Within intra-sentential switches, Poplack (1980) finds nouns to take the largest proportion of switches, which also holds true for my data. One reason why nouns are so frequently code-switched is that they are relatively free of syntactic restrictions.

5.2. Functions

As was discussed in detail earlier, code-switching serves a number of functions in ELF. The four functions of *specifying an addressee*, *signalling culture*, *appealing for assistance*, and *introducing another idea* have turned out to be useful for the purpose of my analysis, but are not meant to be exhaustive. As has already been indicated, they interact and partly overlap. While some instances of code-switching can be assigned to one of the four categories relatively easily, others seem to fit more than one scheme.

5.2.1. Specifying an Addressee

Code-switching in ELF serves, among other things, the function of *specifying an addressee*. It is performed to direct one's speech to one specific addressee in contrast to the whole group, as can be seen in Extract 2.

Extract 2
(S2: L1=French [B], S3: L1=French [CH])

S2: if you are interested er i let it <un> xx </un> and er via email send er er to you and=
S3: =<to S2> also the french version. </to S2>=
S2: =<to S3> <L1fr> **oui oui oui oui oui** {yes} </L1fr> </to S3> <1> @@@@ <@> of course <@> @@ @@@@ </1>
SS: <1> @@@@@@@@@@@@ </1>

S2, a French L1 speaker, has just finished her presentation on joint master programmes and suggests sending the paper via e-mail to those who are interested, when S3, also a French speaker, requests that also the French version of the paper should be made available. Recognising S3 as a fellow native speaker of French, S2 switches into their shared L1 to turn to S3 and immediately answer the request with a repeated *oui* 'yes'. S2's switch seems to be encouraged by S3 actually mentioning the term *french.* Following the switch, S2 starts to laugh, which is joined in by her fellow participants. S2's laughter may indicate an apology for having initiated a short dialogue with S3 in French, whereas the laughter of the others seems to express their acceptance of the switch. This indicates that a switch into the addressee's L1, in this case combined with laughter, may also serve the purpose of evoking social approval and decreasing social distance (Myers-Scotton 1993, 147), even more so when a speaker uses the addressee's first name and/or title (cf. examples of switches in Table 4). By switching, S2 blends in her L1, which also allows for an interpretation in terms of signalling culture.

5.2.2. Signalling Culture

When switching into a language other than English, usually into their language of identification, speakers blend in their cultural background and communicate their bi-/multilingual identity by *signalling culture*. One way of doing so is by what has been introduced as emblematic switches: A tag, an exclamation, or a parenthetical in one language is inserted into an utterance of another language. Since there is no need for syntactic adjustment to the rest of the utterance, they are usually fitted in easily. In most cases these seem to happen unintentionally and pass almost unnoticed as they do not carry much significance with regard to message content (see Extract 3).

Extract 3
(S4: L1=Italian, S3: L1=French [CH])

S4: er s- may i say (.) er is a little thing my dean says {whispered parallel conversation starts} that the best way to learn a language is to have a boy g- er er friend or <4><un> xx </un> @ </4> @@@
S3: <4> er <L1fr> **oui oui** {yes yes} </L1fr></4>
SS: <4> @@@@ </4>
SS: @@@@ <5> @@@ </5> <6> @@@@@ </6> @@@
S3: <5> yes of course </5>
S4: <6><un> xxxxx </un> @@@ </6>

S3 switches into her L1, but in contrast to Extract 2, the switch happens apparently without any obvious reason and without addressing anyone directly or in specific. S3 is the only French speaker participating in this workshop. The switch as such does not carry much content, is easily fitted in and seems to pass unnoticed. However inconspicuous it appears and however little attention it gets, the switch nevertheless serves the central function of expressing S3's multilingual identity. Irrespective of the affirmative function S3's *oui* fulfils, it is here the language switched into that serves as an emblem of her cultural identity and not so much the content of what is being said.

Another way of signalling culture via code-switching involves references to homelands, backgrounds, or special expressions associated with a specific culture, by which a speaker creates an even stronger cultural association for the interlocutors, which is illustrated in Extract 4.

Extract 4
(S4: L1=Italian, S1: L1=Norwegian)

S4: and e:r (.) even if the program is not (.) similar (.) <ono> brrrrrr </ono> it it it is nor<5>mal (.) in </5> in <L1it> **roma** {rome} </L1it> we have three (.)
S1: <5> hm hm </5>
S4: different public universities (.) and the program are not the same (.) <6> in </6> the same city. <7> so </7> i can ex- expect that (.)
S1: <6> hm </6>
S1: <7> hm </7>
S4: <@> you're (.) teaching (.) something (.) equal to me (.)

The Italian speaker S4 elaborates on the similarities and differences between the educational profiles of different universities and, as an example, presents the situation at her home university in Italy. By switching into Italian for *roma* she signals her Italian background in two ways: by her language choice as well as the reference to her hometown. Compared to the preceding example, the switched term carries more information as regards content. Due to the universal character of this city name, however, it does not raise difficulties and a translation seems dispensable.

Switches may be performed into the speakers' L1 or into any other language available to them. A switch into speakers' L1 signals the speakers' linguacultural background and may express the wish to affirm their unique status in the ELF group. Signalling a speaker's multilingual identity by switching into one's LN, on the other hand, may indicate a special bond to another language or culture. Pölzl and Seidlhofer (2006,

172) argue that "the role culture plays depends partly on where the interaction takes place", which also seems to be the case in Extract 5.

Extract 5
(S1: L1=Norwegian, S4: L1=Italian, S5: L1=German [AUT], S6: L1=Latvian, S7: L1=Portuguese, S14: L1=Finnish)

S1: [...] but could we just (1) take your (.) first name and (.) and (.) your (.) university (.) just very quickly around the table <1> just </1> to see who is here (1)
S14: <1> okay </1>
[...]
S4: [S4] from [place12] (.)
S5: [S5] from [place13] (.)
S6: [S6] from [place14] (.)
S7: [S7] (.) <LNde> **aus [place7]** {from [place7]} </LNde>
S1: <soft> hm </soft> (.)

S1, the chair of the working group discussion, welcomes the participants and, as not everybody is familiar with each other, asks for a quick round of introduction. This request prompts each speaker to state their first name and the city where they come from, or rather where the university they represent is located. When it is S7's turn to introduce himself, he switches into German. S7's L1 is Portuguese, but he knows German—he even has a doctorate from a German university—and demonstrates this knowledge a number of times in the course of the conference by code-switching (see Klimpfinger 2005). The fact that the conference takes place in Vienna and a lot of German can be heard around might have triggered strong associations with the German language and culture for S7. By switching, S7 brings this culture into his own performance and at the same time shows his acknowledgement of the hosts' cultural background, which illustrates once again that "ELF is a global phenomenon, but locally realized" (Pölzl & Seidlhofer 2006, 172).

5.2.3. Appealing for Assistance

Using code-switching for *appealing for assistance* can be risky in ELF interactions, as there is no guarantee that speakers of the same L1 or LN are present to assist. The present data contains two such instances, one into the speaker's L1 and one into the speaker's LN. Extract 6 features S2, a French speaker, who turns to her Dutch-speaking colleague for assistance.

Extract 6
(S2: L1=French [B], S7: L1=Dutch)

S2: er it start with er er e:rm (2) definition of what is er a joint er program. (2) er it could be (.) one (1) er study program (.) in com- er delivered in COmmon in the different er (.) institution or one program (.) conceived together and located in one's side. or or two programs interconnected (2) or (.) er <to S7> <L1fr> **consecutifs**? {consecutive} </L1fr> </to S7>
S7: <un> xx </un> consecutive
S2: and consecutive. er (.) or one program with (.) a system of module (.) taken in another university.

S2 elaborates on the definition of a joint programme and seems to lack the right word, an assumption based on the pauses and hesitation shortly before her switch. It appears that to ask for the word is the fastest and in this situation also the most effective way to achieve her intended communicative goal. It might thus be argued that in ELF communication a switched appeal is sometimes employed strategically in order to enhance faster understanding (Hübner 2003, 25ff.). S2 therefore turns to S7, a fellow Belgian—even though a native speaker of Dutch—of whom S2 knows that she speaks French and who sits next to her, which also allows for the interpretation in terms of specifying an addressee. By rising intonation she indirectly performs the request, which is answered by S7. Knowing that a number of French native speakers are present, S2 can switch into French without risking misunderstanding. Hence, the switch ensures understanding beyond cultural differences and, more importantly, brings about efficiency—two issues Cogo (2007, 182) found to be underlying motivations for code-switching in ELF.

Minimal queries in the form of appeals but also metalinguistic comments serve to identify and clarify a problematic sequence. Explicitly stated comments on a problem allow for a short and precise clearance; they neither disrupt the flow of the conversation nor give rise to uncooperative behaviour (Vasseur, Broeder & Roberts 1996, 88). Explicit appeals are expected to occur with greater frequency in goal-oriented talk where speakers need to clarify problems efficiently in order to follow the conversation and arrive at conclusions. This can be supported by findings from VOICE: The four instances where speakers switch into German for direct appeals starting with *was heisst* 'what does xx mean' occur in the professional domain exclusively and involve panel discussions and service encounters, speech event types which are very goal-oriented in nature.

5.2.4 Introducing Another Idea

Code-switching in order to *introduce another idea* implies that another language than English would be more appropriate to express the topic. English is used as the speakers' language of communication in this situation but the speakers are used to discussing these topics in another language, in most cases in their L1. Thus, a strong correlation between the respective subject under discussion and this language (referred to as 'topic language' in the following) prevails, which may lead to code-switching. Since the speakers in my data act as representatives of institutions or universities, they frequently refer to their background with pronouns (e.g. *I, we, us*) or proper nouns (e.g. *Netherlands*). These expressions stress the role of the speaker as a representative and reinforce the link between topic and topic language, which in turn influences or even seems to trigger the switch. In contrast to the instances of code-switching we have looked at so far, the following ones involve a translation, a paraphrase, or an attempt to do so.

Extract 7
(S1: L1=German [AUT], S3: L1=Dutch [B])

S3: that's what we expect (1) to have. (2) erm for the quality ass- assurance no we have a ready systems of quality assurance. with each university we have (.) er evaluation <un> xx </un> academic er er (2) er (call) er we have a er (.) <un> xx </un> of er the academic (file) a to be er to have the evaluation. er to have also a system together with the netherlands we have a <L1nl> **visitatiecommissie** {visiting commission} </L1nl>
S1: mhm
S3: <u>it's called</u> for certain programs. and so they visit they come and visit the university and stay at the university and they then there is a overall assessment er.

In Extract 7, S3, a Dutch speaker from Belgium, tells the other participants about the system of quality assurance of Belgian universities: An organisation was newly founded together with the Netherlands in order to assess courses at colleges and universities and guarantee the continuing quality of (joint) study programmes. When she mentions the special concept of a visiting commission, she switches into her L1 Dutch. S3 stresses her position as a representative of one such Belgian university by frequently using the pronoun *we*, but also by directly mentioning the Netherlands, which refers to the academic world rather than the country as such. This might function as an even stronger trigger for the subsequent switch into her L1, which at the same time is the topic language. Hence, it also allows for a classification of the switch as a signal of S3's culture. It does not seem as if S3 switches due to linguistic needs: There are neither any hesitation signs nor any filler words preceding the switch. Additionally, the switch is immediately followed by a paraphrase that involves the most important words for the concept of the switched term: *visit* and *assessment*. It seems that the speaker wants to stress the character of the switch as a momentary borrowing in contrast to mere linguistic needs. This is intensified by the phrase following the switch, *it's called* (underlined), which is what Cogo and Dewey (2006, 68ff.) call a "key clue" that "provides a frame" for the listeners to pay attention to what follows, interpret it appropriately, and "place it into context". The concept of the key clue is similar to what Romaine (2001, 153) calls "flagging", a strategy of speakers to introduce or mark their switches with pauses, fillers, hesitation signs, and/or metalinguistic comments. In contrast to flagging, however, a key clue does not only highlight the switch as such but rather its idiomaticity. Furthermore, it refers to a particular group of people who would normally use the term in its original language (cf. Cogo 2007, 180), i.e. in the case of the example mentioned those people involved in quality assurance at S3's home university.

For very similar reasons, S3 performs a number of switches into both her L1 French and her LNs Dutch and German in Extract 8.

Extract 8
(S3: L1=French [CH])

S3: and then we decided they decide to have a coordinating body (.) er i- er among the rectors' conference to prepare the role (1) regarding bologna. (.) and the (ROLE) was (adapted) in december two thousand three. (1) okay. then they say we have done our job. (.) but beside that (.) they have put their (.) working on <LNde> **empfehlungen** {recommendations} </LNde> recommendations for the university how to implement (.) bologna. h and also erm in this er framework we have a steering group for <spel> e c t s </spel> and then we have a <LNde> **steuerungsgruppe** {steering group} </LNde> er <spel> e c t s </spel> <LNde> **steuerungsgruppe** {steering group} </LNde> i'm the president of this then i know what we have done. and i think we have written <un> x </un> recommendations for the universities and the <LNde> **fachhochschule** {college of higher education} </LNde> <pvc> overschool </pvc> how to implement <spel> e c t s </spel> in the er frame of <un> xxx </un>. THAT's the theory. [...]

In line with the preceding example, we find the pronoun *we*, stressing S3's position as representative of a Swiss university. What is interesting in this case, however, is the fact that S3, a French speaker, switches into German, which indicates that a topic language does not necessarily have to be the speaker's L1. Working in the field of joint study programmes in a multilingual country such as Switzerland implies collaboration with universities from other parts of the country and probably also involves the use of the other official languages of Switzerland. Similarly to Extract 7, it is this strong connection between the topic and the language she usually uses to discuss it that seems to trigger her switches into German. For all her switches, S3 provides translations or paraphrases, which once again emphasises the switched terms as borrowings rather than gaps due to linguistic needs: *recommendations* for *empfehlungen*, *steering group* for *steuerungsgruppe*, and the coinage *overschool* for *fachhochschule*. In the latter case it seems to be the concept of 'a higher school' that prompts the formation of the coinage and thus makes it feasible in this context.[13]

6. Conclusion and Outlook

The analysis of forms and functions of code-switching in ELF clearly illustrates that it is a common and effective feature of ELF conversations to *mix the two languages together*, as one ELF speaker in the VOICE corpus remarks. As my analysis has shown, this mixing takes different shapes and is performed for different reasons. It thus calls for recognition "as a legitimate mode of communication in its own right" (Romaine 2000, 57).

When analysing the forms of code-switching in the present data, one finds the instances to range from single words and short, more or less fixed phrases to longer chunks and passages. The vast majority involves single words or short idiomatic phrases, including nouns, adjectives, and filler and function words, which are relatively free of syntactic restrictions and are easily inserted at different points in the interaction. In most cases the switches are self-explanatory and can be assumed to be understood by the other participants at least from context. Since function words and similar linguistic forms do not carry much significance as regards message content, they pass almost unnoticed. Forms that are similar in different languages, such as city names, have a certain universal character as they are often used in their 'original' form. In the other cases, translations or paraphrases are provided by the speakers themselves or "a person may call upon the knowledge of a number of languages to make sense of a text" (Council of Europe 2001, 4).

Code-switching in ELF interactions serves a number of different functions. The examples from my data show that it is employed for specifying an addressee, signalling culture, appealing for assistance, and introducing another idea. ELF speakers switch to another language to direct what they say to one or more specific addressees, but also to communicate their bi-/multilingual identity and show group membership. Furthermore, they switch to get assistance from another speaker or because it seems that another language is more appropriate to express a certain idea. In most cases a code-switch does not serve only one of the four functions introduced, but allows for a flexible interplay of more than one explanation.

The present analysis of forms and functions of code-switching in ELF conversations shows that when speakers are code-switching, they are "bringing the whole of their linguistic equipment into play" (Council of Europe 2001, 4) and exploit their multilingual competence. According to the Council of Europe, these kinds of speakers can:

> [i]n different situations, [...] call flexibly upon different parts of this competence to achieve effective communication with a particular interlocutor. (Council of Europe 2001, 4)

Thus, code-switching forms an "extra tool in communication that is at the disposal of multilinguals and allows for meaning making and greater nuances of expression" (Cogo 2007, 182; see also Cook 2002b, 338; and Romaine 2001, 143). Although ELF speakers cannot expect their interlocutors to share the same language knowledge, they self-confidently and strategically make use of code-switching, actively show their skills, and successfully contribute to achieve shared understanding.

Given its frequent and systematic use, it has become clear that code-switching is an intrinsic element of ELF interactions, which supports the claim of "making [ELF] a feasible, acceptable and respected alternative to ENL in appropriate contexts of use" (Seidlhofer 2001, 150). As examples from my data illustrate, ELF speakers resort to more than two languages in a most creative way to fulfil different discourse functions, to apply certain communication strategies, and to communicate their multilingual identity, which calls for a view that constitutes code-switching an integral part of the discourse practices of ELF conversations.

Bibliography

Appel, R. and P. Muysken 1995. *Language Contact and Bilingualism.* London: Arnold.

Bialystok, E. 1990. *Communication Strategies: A Psychological Analysis of Second-Language Use*. Oxford: Blackwell.

Breiteneder, A., M.-L. Pitzl, S. Majewski and T. Klimpfinger 2006. "VOICE Recording—Methodological Challenges in the Compilation of a Corpus of Spoken ELF." *Nordic Journal of English Studies* 5 (2), 161-87. https://gupea.ub.gu.se/dspace/handle/2077/3153. (accessed October 9, 2008).

Cook, V. 2002a. "Background to the L2 User." In *Portraits of the L2 User*, ed. V. Cook, 1-31. Clevedon: Multilingual Matters.

—. 2002b. "Language Teaching Methodology and the L2 User Perspective." In *Portraits of the L2 User*, ed. V. Cook, 327-43. Clevedon: Multilingual Matters.

Cogo, A. this volume. "Accommodating Difference in ELF Conversations: A Study of Pragmatic Strategies."

—. 2007. *Intercultural Communication in English as a Lingua Franca: A Case Study*. PhD diss., King's College London.

Cogo, A. and M. Dewey 2006. "Efficiency in ELF Communication: From Pragmatic Motives to Lexico-Grammatical Innovation." *Nordic Journal of English Studies* 5 (2), 59-93 https://gupea.ub.gu.se/dspace/-handle/2077/3148. (accessed October 9, 2008).

Council of Europe 2001. *Common European Framework of Reference for Languages: Learning, Teaching, Assessment.* Cambridge: Cambridge University Press.

Færch, C. and G. Kasper 1983. "Plans and Strategies in Foreign Language Communication." In *Strategies in Interlanguage Communication*, ed. C. Færch & G. Kasper, 20-60. London: Longman.

Gumperz, J. 1982. *Discourse Strategies.* Cambridge: Cambridge University Press.

Grosjean, F. 2008. *Studying Bilinguals*. Oxford: Oxford University Press.

Haugen, E. 1956. *Bilingualism in the Americas.* University: American Dialect Society.

Hoffmann, C. 1991. *An Introduction to Bilingualism.* London: Longman.

Hornby, A. S., ed. 2005. *Oxford Advanced Learner's Dictionary of Current English*, 7th ed. Oxford: Oxford University Press.

Hübner, A. 2003. *Communication Strategies Versus Learning Strategies—A Critical Analysis Illustrated by Examples from Conversations in English as a Lingua Franca*. MA thesis, University of Vienna.

Hüllen, W. 1992. "Identifikationssprachen und Kommunikationssprachen." *Zeitschrift für Germanistische Linguistik* 20 (3), 298-317.
Hülmbauer, C. this volume. "'We don't take the right way. We just take the way that we think you will understand'—The Shifting Relationship between Correctness and Effectiveness in ELF."
Jacobson, R. 1960. "Closing Statement: Linguistics and Poetics." In *Style in Language*, ed. T. A. Sebeok. Cambridge: Massachusetts.
Jenkins, J. 2007. *English as a Lingua Franca: Attitudes and Identity*. Oxford: Oxford University Press.
Klimpfinger, T. 2007. "'Mind you sometimes you have to mix'—The Role of Code-Switching in English as a Lingua Franca." *VIenna English Working PaperS* 16 (2), 36-61. http://www.univie.ac.at/Anglistik//Views_0702.pdf. (accessed October 9, 2008).
—. 2005. *The Role of Speakers' First and Other Languages in English as a Lingua Franca Talk*. MA thesis, University of Vienna.
Mackey, W. 1968. "The Description of Bilingualism." In *Readings in the Sociology of Language*, ed. J. Fishman, 554-84. The Hague: Mouton.
McEnery, T. and A. Wilson 1997. *Corpus Linguistics*. Edinburgh: Edinburgh University Press.
Meierkord, C. 2002. "'Language Stripped Bare' or 'Linguistic Masala'? Culture in Lingua Franca Conversation." In *Lingua Franca Communication*, ed. K. Knapp & C. Meierkord, 109-33. Frankfurt/Main: Language.
Myers-Scotton, C. 1993. *Social Motivations for Code-Switching: Evidence from Africa*. Oxford: Oxford University Press.
Pitzl, M.-L., A. Breiteneder and T. Klimpfinger 2008. "A World of Words: Processes of Lexical Innovation in VOICE." *VIenna English Working PaperS* 17 (2), 21-46. http://www.univie.ac.at/Anglistik/Views_0802.pdf. (accessed October 9, 2008).
Pölzl, U. 2005. *Exploring the Third Space: Negotiating Culture in English as a Lingua Franca*. PhD diss., University of Vienna.
—. 2003. "Signalling Cultural Identity: The Use of L1/Ln in ELF." *VIenna English Working PaperS* 12 (2), 3-23. http://www.univie.ac.at/Anglistik/ang_new/online_papers/views/03_2/POEL_SGL.pdf. (accessed October 9, 2008).
Pölzl, U. and B. Seidlhofer 2006. "In and on Their Own Terms: The 'Habitat Factor' in English as a Lingua Franca Interactions." *International Journal of the Sociology of Language* 177, 151-76.

Poplack, S. 1980. "Sometimes I'll start a sentence in Spanish y termino en español: Toward a Typology of Code-Switching." *Linguistics* 18 (7-8), 581-618.

Romaine, S. 2001. *Bilingualism*. Oxford: Blackwell.

—. 2000. *Language in Society. An Introduction to Sociolinguistics*. Oxford: Oxford University Press.

Schendl, H. 2004. "English Historical Code-Switching in a European Perspective." In *Language and Language Practices*, ed. C. Dabelsteen & J. N. Jørgensen, 194-208. Copenhagen: University of Copenhagen.

—. 2002. "Mixed-Language Texts as Data and Evidence in English Historical Linguistics." In *Studies in the History of the English Language. A Millennial Perspective*, ed. D. Minkova & R. Stockwell, 51-78. Berlin: Mouton de Gruyter.

Seidlhofer, B. 2004. "Research Perspectives on Teaching English as a Lingua Franca." *Annual Review of Applied Linguistics* 24, 209-39.

—. 2001. "Closing a Conceptual Gap: The Case for a Description of English as a Lingua Franca." *International Journal of Applied Linguistics* 11 (2), 133-58.

Seidlhofer, B., A. Breiteneder and M.-L. Pitzl 2006. "English as a Lingua Franca in Europe." *Annual Review of Applied Linguistics* 26, 1-34.

Tarone, E. 1984 [1981]. "Some Thoughts on the Notion of 'Communication Strategy'." In *Strategies in Interlanguage Communication*, ed. C. Færch & G. Kasper, 61-74. London: Longman.

Vasseur, M.-T., P. Broeder and C. Roberts 1996. "Managing Understanding from a Minority Perspective." In *Achieving Understanding. Discourse in Intercultural Encounters*, ed. K. Bremer, C. Roberts, M.-T. Vasseur, M. Simonot & P. Broeder, 65-108. London: Longman.

VOICE Project 2007. *Transcription Conventions [2.1]*. http://www.univie.ac.at/voice/voice.php?page=transcription_general_information. (accessed October 9, 2008).

VOICE. *The Vienna-Oxford International Corpus of English*. (version 1.0 online) http://www.univie.ac.at/voice corpus (accessed November 13, 2008).

Weinreich, U. 1970 [1953]. *Languages in Contact. Findings and Problems*, 7th ed. The Hague: Mouton.

XAIRA, XML Aware Indexing and Retrieval Architecture. http://www.oucs.ox.ac.uk/rts/xaira/ (accessed October 9, 2008).

Notes

[1] Concerning the definition of bilingualism, recent views have moved away from the notion 'two monolinguals in one' towards a broad definition of bilingualism along a continuum governed by the concept 'more than one' (Mackey 1968). For a discussion of different levels of proficiency see also Hoffmann (1991) and Romaine (2001).

[2] For more information on the differences of code-switching, code-mixing, and borrowing, as well as other related phenomena see e.g. Appel and Muysken (1995), Grosjean (2008), Gumperz (1982), Hoffmann (1991), and Romaine (2001).

[3] Appel and Muysken's (1995) functions are based on Jacobson's (1960) six functions of language, i.e. the referential, emotive, conative, phatic, metalingual, and poetic one.

[4] For a detailed discussion of the definition of communication strategies see the first part of Færch and Kasper (1983).

[5] For a detailed description of the role of attitudes and identity in ELF see Jenkins (2007).

[6] Note that this was the status quo in February 2007 when this study was conducted.

[7] XAIRA (XML Aware Indexing and Retrieval Architecture) is a tool for searching large XML corpora and is best used with TEI-conformant documents (http://www.oucs.ox.ac.uk/rts/xaira/). It was originally developed at the Oxford University Computing Services in 1994 and was intended to be used with the British National Corpus.

[8] For more details on the criteria for including data in the corpus see Breiteneder et al. (2006, 162-167).

[9] For more details on the collected data see Klimpfinger (2005).

[10] All extracts of my data are transcribed according to the VOICE Transcription Conventions [2.1] (VOICE Project 2007). The instances of code-switching are written in bold letters for better identification.

[11] Meierkord (2002) explicitly mentions that she does not find her data to contain code-switches, with the exception of certain tags. On the other hand, Pölzl (2003, 2005), Pölzl and Seidlhofer (2006), Hübner (2003), and Cogo (2007), who investigate casual conversations, identify a number of code-switches in their data.

[12] For more examples of code-switching see Klimpfinger (2005; 2007).

[13] For similar cases and a more detailed discussion of lexical innovations like this in ELF see Pitzl, Breiteneder and Klimpfinger (2008).

CONTRIBUTORS

Beyza Björkman is Lecturer in English at the Royal Institute of Technology in Stockholm, where she teaches Technical English. She has taught EAP/ESP since 1995. She is currently working on her doctoral thesis at Stockholm University, Department of English, on the effectiveness of spoken ELF in engineering. Her publications on her doctoral work include "English as a Lingua Franca at a Swedish Technical University: An Effective Medium?" (2009), "English as the Lingua Franca of Engineering: The Morphosyntax of Academic Speech Events" (2008) and "'So where we are': Spoken Lingua Franca English at a Swedish Technical University" (2008). Her main research interests lie within applied aspects of academic English.

Tim Caudery is Director of Studies at the Department of English, University of Aarhus, Denmark. His primary general area of research is second language acquisition and second language teaching; the first half of his career was in English Language Teaching in Sweden and Cyprus. He moved into university work in 1988, but retained his interest in language teaching, language testing, and teacher training. He is particularly interested in second language writing skills and vocabulary acquisition.

Alessia Cogo is Lecturer in Applied Linguistics at the Department of English, University of Surrey, UK. She is also working on the LINEE project aimed at investigating linguistic diversity in Europe, especially the role of English in the European multilingual landscape. She did her PhD at King's College, London, where she researched ELF pragmatic strategies in intercultural communication. She has published papers in the area of ELF and is currently working on a monograph with Martin Dewey, due to come out in 2010 (Continuum Publishers). Her research interests include bi-multilingualism, World Englishes, intercultural communication, language learning and teaching.

Martin Dewey is Lecturer in Applied Linguistics at King's College London, where he teaches courses in Sociolinguistics, World Englishes and Teacher Education on undergraduate and postgraduate programmes, and supervises PhD students working in areas related to the globalization of English and English language teaching. His primary research interests focus on the use of English as a lingua franca (ELF), especially with regard to the implications of ELF research for curriculum change in language pedagogy, including, in particular, reconsiderations of contemporary practice in language teacher education and current conceptualizations of teacher knowledge.

Susanne Ehrenreich is Senior Lecturer in Applied Linguistics at Ludwig-Maximilian-University Munich, Germany. From 2006 to 2007 she was Acting Professor of ELT and Applied Linguistics at the University of Eichstaett-Ingolstadt. Her main research interests are English as a lingua franca, language and culture learning in the context of study abroad as well as teacher education and ELT. She has published books and articles in these and related fields, e.g. *Auslandsaufenthalte in Schule und Studium* / Stays Abroad in Secondary and Tertiary Education (Waxmann 2008). She is currently researching the use of and the attitudes towards English as a lingua franca in German multinational corporations.

Cornelia Hülmbauer studied English and Art History at the University of Vienna. She currently holds a position as a research assistant at the Department of English Studies of the University of Vienna. Since 2007, she has been involved in the European FP6 project DYLAN, Language Dynamics and Management of Diversity. She was also a member of the transcription team for VOICE, the Vienna-Oxford International Corpus of English. In her research, she has mainly dealt with lexico-grammatical processes and plurilingual phenomena in ELF, on which she has published several articles.

Julia Hüttner is Senior Lecturer at the Department of English Studies, University of Vienna. Her research interests lie in the area of genre and discourse analysis and her current research project investigates oral language use and proficiency. She is the author of the monograph *Academic Writing in a Foreign Language: An Extended Genre Analysis of Student Texts* (Peter Lang 2007) and has published numerous articles, for instance, in *International Journal of Applied Linguistics* and *System*.

Jennifer Jenkins is Professor of English Language at the University of Southampton, where she teaches and researches English as a Lingua Franca and World Englishes. She has published numerous articles on these subjects as well as two books, *The Phonology of English as an International Language* (OUP 2000) and *English as a Lingua Franca:*

Attitude and Identity (OUP 2007), as well as a university course book, *World Englishes* (Routledge 2009, 2nd ed.). She was also co-editor (with Constant Leung) of *Reconfiguring Europe: The Contribution of Applied Linguistics* (Equinox 2006) and (with Kumiko Murata) *Global Englishes in Asian Contexts* (Palgrave 2009).

Jagdish Kaur obtained her doctorate in Linguistics from Lancaster University in the United Kingdom, where she produced a thesis titled "The Co-Construction of Understanding in English as a Lingua Franca". She is currently Senior Lecturer at the Faculty of Languages and Linguistics, University of Malaya in Kuala Lumpur. Her research interest lies mainly in the microanalysis of ELF interactions, using conversation analytic procedures, to gain insights into how speakers of ELF communicate and achieve success in communication.

Theresa Klimpfinger is a full-time researcher on the VOICE (Vienna-Oxford International Corpus of English) project at the University of Vienna. She has published on code-switching in ELF ("'Mind you sometimes you have to mix'—The Role of Code-Switching in English as a Lingua Franca" 2007) and lexical innovations in ELF ("A World of Words: Processes of Lexical Innovation in VOICE" 2008, together with Angelika Breiteneder and Marie-Luise Pitzl). Her research interests include ELF, corpus linguistics, and multilingualism, more specifically the use of first and other languages in VOICE.

Anna Mauranen is Professor of English at the University of Helsinki. Her current major research interests are English as a lingua franca, corpus linguistics, and modelling spoken language. Her publications focus on spoken language, corpus linguistics, contrastive rhetoric, translation, and academic discourses. She is director of the ELFA project, which has compiled a 1-million word corpus of academic ELF. Publications include: *Linear Unit Grammar* with Sinclair (John Benjamins 2006), *Translation Universals – Do They Exist?* with Kujamäki (John Benjamins 2004), *Academic Writing. Intercultural and Textual Issues* with Ventola (John Benjamins 1996) and *Cultural Differences in Academic Rhetoric* (Peter Lang 1993).

Margrethe Petersen is Associate Professor with the Department of Language and Business Communication at the Aarhus School of Business (ASB), Aarhus University, Denmark. She is also Head of the English Section of the Department and a member of the ASB Research Unit for

Knowledge Communication. Her current research interests include the sociolinguistic aspects of the 'internationalised' university and of knowledge communication in academia.

Marie-Luise Pitzl is a full-time researcher for the Vienna-Oxford International Corpus of English (VOICE) at the University of Vienna. Her recent publications include: "Non-Understanding in English as a Lingua Franca: Examples from a Business Context" (2005), "English as a Lingua Franca in Europe" with Barbara Seidlhofer and Angelika Breiteneder (2006), "A World of Words: Processes of Lexical Innovation in VOICE" with Angelika Breiteneder and Theresa Klimpfinger (2008). She is currently working on her PhD thesis which explores the forms and functions of creativity in spoken ELF.

Patricia Pullin Stark is currently Head of English at the University of Zurich/ETH Language Centre in Switzerland. She has a BA (Hons) in English Language and Literature and an MA in Education (TESOL) from the University of London. She did her PhD in Applied Linguistics at the University of Birmingham. Her main research interests are workplace discourse and English as a lingua franca in academic and professional settings. Her current research concerns lecturing in English in non-English speaking universities. She has also published on English for Specific Purposes in multilingual settings and task-based learning and teaching.

Elina Ranta is a researcher in the ELFA (English as a Lingua Franca in Academic Settings) project at the University of Tampere. Her main research interests include English as a lingua franca, language variation and change, and English language teaching. Her current research focuses on syntactic features in spoken ELF, on which she has published the article "The 'Attractive Progressive—Why Use the –ing Form in English as a Lingua Franca" (2006). She has also published on teachers' and students' perceptions of English in secondary education in "English in the Real World vs. English at School—Finnish English Teachers' and Students' Views" (2009).

Barbara Seidlhofer is Professor of English and Applied Linguistics at the University of Vienna. Her teaching and research focus on sociolinguistics, corpus linguistics, discourse analysis and pragmatics, in particular in their application to language teacher education. Her publications include the books *Pronunciation* with Christiane Dalton (OUP 1994), *Approaches to Summarization: Discourse Analysis and Language Education* (Narr 1995),

Principle and Practice in Applied Linguistics, co-edited with Guy Cook (OUP 1995), *Language Policy and Language Education in Emerging Nations*, co-edited with Robert de Beaugrande and Meta Grosman (Ablex 1998) and *Controversies in Applied Linguistics* (OUP 2003). She was also for several years editor of the *International Journal of Applied Linguistics* (Blackwell). Barbara Seidlhofer is the founding director of the Vienna-Oxford International Corpus of English (VOICE), which aims to provide a basis for the linguistic description of English as a Lingua Franca.

Philip Shaw has taught English and linguistics at universities in Thailand, Germany, England, and Denmark, and is currently a professor in the Department of English at Stockholm University. He is co-author of *World Englishes: An Introduction* (Arnold 2003) and co-editor of *The Map and the Landscape: Norms and Practices in Genre* (Peter Lang 2006). His most recent publication (with Irena Vassileva) is an article in *Journal of Pragmatics* 2009 on the development of the academic economics article across cultures. He is interested in uses of English, mainly in business and academic settings, from both a genre-analytic and reception-process standpoint.

Ute Smit is Associate Professor in English language studies at the University of Vienna, Austria. Her research interests fall into the intersection of applied and sociolinguistics and focus presently on English as a lingua franca as classroom language. Previous publications include *Empirical Perspectives on CLIL Classroom Discourse* with Christiane Dalton-Puffer (2007) and numerous papers published in, for instance, *System* and the *International Review of Applied Linguistics*.

AUTHOR INDEX

SUBJECT INDEX